'I urge you to read Adam LeBor's excellent new biography of Slobodan Milosevic. I fancied that I already knew a great deal of the story but LeBor has combined journalistic flair with a historian's grasp of detail to bring us a haunting portrait of the man the West said it 'could do business with' . . . For those who witnessed the destruction of the former Yugoslavia this will be a sad book. For those who stood by and did nothing it is a book that should make them wince. I recommend it to both but also to a wider public who should know about the policies pursued in their name' Fergal Keane, *Mail on Sunday*

'It charts a cogent path through the interminable complexities of Balkan politics, and the sense of victimhood on which Milosevic's rise to power was based' *Evening Standard*

'An engaging account of the Milosevic years and the misjudgements that caused ethnic cleansing, official corruption and a collapse into war and penury' *Financial Times*

'The most engrossing biography so far of a man as complex and shifting as the regions he tore apart. This vigorous book takes Milosevic himself as its focal point: LeBor is able to point to a remarkable black hole at the centre of modern Balkan history – Milosevic's complete lack of moral scruple which infected almost all those closest to him' *The Times*

'LeBor charts with dexterity and black humour the rise, and eventual fall, of this provincial Communist functionary . . . LeBor is right to link Milosevic's politics with his domestic life, and peek behind the closely-guarded doors leading into Slobo and Mira's kitchen. For it is there, it appears, that the destinies of millions were decided' *Independent*

Milosevic

A Biography

Adam LeBor

BLOOMSBURY

First published in Great Britain 2002
This paperback edition published 2003

Bloomsbury Publishing plc, 38 Soho Square, London WID 3HB

A CIP catalogue record for this book
is available from the British Library

ISBN 0 7475 6181 8

10 9 8 7 6 5 4 3 2 1

Typeset by Palimpsest Book Production Limited,
Polmont, Stirlingshire
Printed in Great Britain by Clays Limited, St Ives plc

In Loving Memory
Maurice LeBor
1924–2001

A miracle alone can save the Balkans from war, and I firmly avow the belief that the days of miracles are over, even at the risk of proving myself a false prophet. The Near East is nothing but a vast field of conjectures, and so it is difficult to know where to begin.

Reginald Wyon, British foreign correspondent
The Balkans from Within (1904)

Acknowledgements

My thanks, firstly, go to those who granted me interviews, especially individuals from the former Yugoslavia. They gave their time generously, often at some emotional cost, relating the details of their lives and their involvement with Slobodan Milosevic and his regime, whether chosen or not. Such encounters have deepened my understanding of the complexities of his rise and fall, and of the destruction of Yugoslavia. Bleak subject matter aside, I have also been fortunate to experience many stimulating and enjoyable discussions in the cafés of Belgrade, Zagreb and Sarajevo.

I have benefited greatly from the guidance and advice of my editors at Bloomsbury: Bill Swainson, a steady hand at the tiller through sometimes dark and choppy waters, and Pascal Cariss, whose eagle-eye has helped hone a manuscript into a book, Katharina Bielenberg for her meticulous proof-reading and Douglas Matthews for his excellent index. Thanks also to Ruth Logan and Katherine Greenwood for keeping the wheels rolling. As ever, I am very grateful to my agent Laura Longrigg, always a source of encouragement and inspiration. Many thanks must go to my present and former colleagues at the Budapest International Press Centre, who have freely shared with me their knowledge and experience of reporting on the former Yugoslavia: Neil Barnett, Christopher Condon, Simon Evans, Jim Lowney, Mark Milstein, John Nadler, Erwin Tuil and Robert Wright. Their advice, input, good humour and steady supply of coffee – and occasionally stronger Balkan libations – is much appreciated. I am also grateful to Celia Hawkesworth of the School of Slavonic and East European Studies in London for her advice and expert knowledge, and to the Society of Authors for a generous grant.

The genesis of this book was my experience as a reporter for the *Independent* and *The Times* during the early 1990s, covering the Yugoslav wars. As a young and then inexperienced foreign correspondent I was fortunate to meet a fine group of colleagues. In places such as Sarajevo and Split, Vitez and Travnik, Zagreb and Belgrade, their comradeship eased the passage of sometimes unnerving days and nights. They know who they are.

It would be near impossible to write a book of this kind without considerable local assistance. Many have been generous with their expertise, contacts and good offices. In Belgrade: the staff of the Belgrade Media Center, Charles Crawford, Mihailo Crnobrnja, Braca Grubacic, Tahir Hasanovic, Ljubica Markovic, Nebojsa Radic, Aleksandar Nenadovic, Seska Stanojlovic, Milos Vasic, Buca Zimjonic and especially, Mark Tomlinson. Thanks to Dragan Milanovic for an illuminating walk around Pozarevac. Thanks also to three fine journalists who have helped in many ways: Vesna Peric-Zimjonic, Daniel Sunter and Vlastimira Stankovic. In Zagreb: David Austin, Sanja Markusic, and especially Laura Irena Lui. In Ljubljana: Natasha Gorse. In Budapest: Agnes Csonka for virtuoso French translations, Hugh Martin for politesse at its best; Vesna Kojic for many hours of interpreting, Janet Garvey, Pablo Gorondi, Lutz Kleveman, David Landsmann, Dr Robert Ligeti, Dr Jancis Long, Djordje Radic, Rob Scott, Julius Strauss, Vladimir Vlaskalic, and also Dusan Mitevic for granting me a series of lengthy interviews.

Thanks to Tony Lang at Bestsellers bookshop for his support over the years, the same holds true for Roger Boyes in Berlin and Justin Leighton. In London: Sir John Birch, Adrian Brown, Yigal Chazan, Leonard Doyle for a steady supply of accreditation letters, Tim English at the BBC press office, Tim Judah, Dessa Trevisan and Francis Wheen. I am especially grateful to Norma Percy, Paul Mitchell, Angus Macqueen and the staff of Brook Lapping Associates for their generous provision of video tapes and transcripts of the six-part series *The Death of Yugoslavia*, an invaluable resource for any student of this period. In the United States my thanks go to Charles Lane and Peter Maass, and in Moscow, Matthew Chance and Ian Traynor. Several others in various cities have also helped with their knowledge and expertise, but have asked not to be named. *De a legnagyobb köszönettel életem fénysugáranak, Ligeti Katalinnak tartozom.*

CONTENTS

List of Illustrations

Maps

AUSTRIA

Ljubljana
●**Ljubljana**

Zagreb

SLOVENIA

CROATIA

Trieste●
●Koper

Pakrac

Glina● Jasenovac

Brioni

Plitvice
National
Park

*Goli
Otok*

Gospic

Keraterm *Sava*

Bihac Omarska■
Banja Luka

BOSNIA -
HERZEGOVINA

Travnik●
●Zadar

Knin

Zenic

Kiselj

Trogir
●Split

Mostar
Dretelj

Neretva

ADRIATIC SEA

ITALY

Dubrovi

| 0 | 50 | 100 | 150 | 200 Miles |
| 0 | 50 | 100 | 150 | 200 | 250 | 300 Kilometres | ⋯⋯*Highway of Brotherhood and Unity* |

TITO'S YUGOSLAVIA (1945–91)

Budapest 135 miles
217 kilometers
North of Karadjordjevo

HUNGARY

Danube

Szeged●

Tisza

●Karadjordjevo

k Erdut
ovo
lo
ʻukovar
●Sid

VOIVODINA

Novi Sad ●

ROMANIA

*Batajnica
Military Base*

ko
Bijeljina●
●Tuzla
vornik●

Belgrade ●

Danube

●Pozarevac

●Mali Zvornik

Morava

Srebrenica
rajevo Zepa
Pale
●Visegrad
Gorazde

*Sumadija
Region*

Drina

●Cacak

SERBIA

●Nis

MONTENEGRO

Kosovska
Mitrovica

Kosovo Polje *Gazimestan*
Pec● ● ●**Pristina**
Donji ●Racak
Prekaz

Podgorica ●

KOSOVO

Skopje

*Drin
Gulf*

MACEDONIA

BULGARIA

ALBANIA

SERB-OCCUPIED CROATIA AND BOSNIA (1992)

Dramatis Personae

Antic, Dragan Hadzi	Former chief of *Politika* newspaper, associate of Milosevic family
Arkan	Paramilitary leader, indicted for war crimes
Austin, David	British diplomat, negotiated with Slobodan Milosevic in mid-1990s
Avramovic, Dragoslav	Former governor of Yugoslav national bank. Stabilised economy in 1994
Babic, Milan	Political leader of Krajina Serbs during early 1990s
Bassiouni, Professor Cherif	UN Special Rapporteur on Bosnia. Author of standard work on ethnic cleansing in Bosnia
Berisavljevic, Zivan	Former Yugoslav ambassador to London
Bildt, Carl	European diplomat representing the EU in negotiations with Milosevic. Worked with David Austin
Boban, Mate	Leader of Bosnian Croats in early 1990s
Bogdanovic, Radmilo	Serbian interior minister under Milosevic
Bulatovic, Momir	President of Montenegro 1990–8
Carrington, Lord	Host of the 1991 peace conference at The Hague, under EU auspices
Christopher, Warren	US Secretary of State under Clinton
Clarke, General Wesley	NATO Supreme Commander during 1999 bombing of Serbia
Cosic, Dobrica	Serbian nationalist writer, seen as nation's intellectual god-father
Covic, Nebojsa	Former mayor of Belgrade in mid-1990s, Serbian deputy prime minister in post-Milosevic government
Crnobrnja, Mihailo	Former economic adviser to Milosevic, until 1989
Curuvija, Slavko	Murdered opposition journalist
Dedakovic, Milan	Leader of defence of Vukovar
Djilas, Milovan	Yugoslavia's most famous dissident in the Tito era
Dizdarevic, Raif	Former president of Federal Yugoslavia
Djindjic, Zoran	President of Serbia after Milosevic era. Assassinated in March 2003
Djokic, Ljubislav	Bulldozer driver during 5 October 2000
Djukic, Slavoljub	Serbian biographer of Milosevic
Doko, Jerko	Former Bosnian defence minister
Draskovic, Danica	Wife of below
Draskovic, Vuk	Opposition leader in Milosevic era
Eagleburger, Lawrence	Former US ambassador to Belgrade
Gajic, Milica	Wife of Marko Milosevic
Gajic-Glisic, Dobrila	Former secretary of Serb defence minister General Tomislav Simovic
Galic, Stanislav	Bosnian Serb General, commander of soldiers shelling Sarajevo. On trial at ICTY for war crimes

Ganic, Ejup	Muslim Bosnian politician
Garasanin, Ilija	Nineteenth-century Serb nationalist theoretician
Gotovina, Ante	General in Croatian army, commander of Operation Storm in summer 1995 when Serbs fled from Krajina
Grubacic, Braca	Belgrade publisher of *VIP* newsletter
Gracanin, Petar	President of Serbia 1988-9
Grizelj, Jug	Former leader of Yugoslav journalists' association
Hadzic, Goran	Serb leader in Vukovar area in 1991
Hasanovic, Tahir	Vice president of the New Democracy Party, former boyfriend of Marija Milosevic
Holbrooke, Richard	US Special envoy to the Balkans. Regarded as author of Dayton peace agreement
Hurd, Lord	Former British foreign secretary
Ilic, Vladimir	Mayor of southern Serbian city of Cacak. A leader of the 5 October uprising
Izetbegovic, Alija	Former president of Bosnia during war of independence
Jansa, Janez	Minister of defence in Slovene independence war in summer 1991
Jezda, Gazda	Full name Jezdimir Vasiljevic. Head of Jugoskandik pyramid scheme
Jashari, Adem	KLA leader killed by Serb forces in March 1998
Jovic, Borisav	Former high-ranking Serb politician and close associate of Milosevic
Kadijevic, Veljko	Federal minister of defence 1988-92
Kapetanovic, Muhamed	Bosnian youth, injured by shelling in Sarajevo
Karadjordjevic, Prince Aleksandar	Yugoslav ruler before WWII
Karadzic, Radovan	Bosnian Serb leader, indicted for war crimes
Karic, Boguljub	Banker, businessman and former minister in Milosevic government
Kertes, Mihalj	Head of customs under Milosevic
Kontic, Radoje	Yugoslav prime minister in mid-1990s under Milosevic
Kostunica, Vojislav	President of Yugoslavia
Kovacevic, Vlada	Aka 'Tref'. Belgrade businessman, partner of Marko Milosevic
Kovacevic, Zivorad	Former mayor of Belgrade and Yugoslav ambassador to the United States
Krajisnik, Momcilo	Bosnian Serb leader. In custody at ICTY, charged with war crimes and genocide
Krunic, Bosko	Communist Party official in Novi Sad in 1988
Kucan, Milan	President of Slovenia
Lilic, Zoran	Former president of Yugoslavia in mid 1990s
Lukovic, Milorad (Legija)	Former commander of Special Operations Unit. Wanted at time of writing (April 2003) by Serbian authorities in connection with murder of Zoran Djindjic
Mandic, Klara	Head of Serbian-Jewish Friendship Society
Markovic, Ante	Yugoslav prime minister in early 1990s
Markovic, Draza	Former partisan and politician. Uncle of Mira Markovic
Markovic, Ljubica	Daughter of Momcilo Markovic (i.e. half-sister of Mira)
Markovic, Mira (Mirjana)	Wife of Slobodan Milosevic
Markovic, Momcilo (Moma)	Father of Mira. Serbian politican, brother of Draza
Markovic, Rade	Head of Serbian intelligence service late 1998 to end 2000

Arrested by new regime in January 2001

Markovic, Mihailo — Serbian nationalist ideologue, later joined the Socialist Party

Matic, Slavoljub — Mayor of Pozarevac after fall of Milosevic

Milan, Martic — Leader of Krajina rebel Serbs. Surrendered to ICTY in spring 2002

Mesic, Stipe — President of Croatia

Milanovic, Dafina — Former head of Dafiment pyramid scheme

Milanovic, Zoran — Former bartender at 'Madona' disco, owned by Marko Milosevic (son of Slobodan)

Miletic, Vera — Mother of Mira Markovic

Milosevic, Borislav — Brother of Slobodan

Milosevic, Darinka — Sister of Svetozar Milosevic, father of Milosevic

Milosevic, Marija — Daughter of Slobodan

Milosevic, Marko — Son of Slobodan

Milosevic, Simeun — Grandfather of Slobodan

Milosevic, Stanislava — Mother of Slobodan Milosevic

Milosevic, Svetozar — Father of Slobodan Milosevic

Minovic, Zivorad — Former editor of *Politika* newspaper

Milutinovic, Milan — Former president of Serbia. Surrendered to ICTY in January 2003

Mitevic, Dusan — Former head of Belgrade Television

Mladic, Ratko — Former head of Bosnian Serb army. Indicted for war crimes

Montgomery, William — US diplomat in Belgrade in 1970s. Ran the Office for Yugoslav Affairs in Budapest in summer 2000

Nagy, Imre — Leader of Hungarian revolution in 1956

Naumann, General Klaus — NATO General who negotiated with Milosevic in October 1998 and early 1999

Nenadovic, Aleksandar — Former editor of *Politika* newspaper

Neville-Jones, Pauline — Former senior British diplomat, worked with Douglas Hurd for NatWest Markets

Ojdanic, Dragoljub — Former Yugoslav army chief of staff. Surrendered to the ICTY in 2002

Oric, Naser — Former bodyguard of Milosevic. Leader of Srebrenica Muslim fighters

Owen, Lord — European Union envoy to former Yugoslavia

Plavsic, Biljana — Former Bosnian Serb president. Sentenced at the ICTY in February 2003 to eleven years in prison for crimes against humanity

Panic, Milan — Serb-American businessman. Briefly Yugoslav prime minister in 1992

Pavkovic, General Nebojsa — Army chief of staff under Milosevic, sacked in June 2002

Pavlovic, Dragisa — Serb politician, opponent of Milosevic in late 1980s

Perisic, General Momcilo — Former army chief of staff, opponent of Milosevic in late 1990s

Predojevic, Vaso — Former officer in Yugoslav army

Popov, Nebojsa — University colleague of Milosevic, later opposition leader

Racan, Ivica — Croatian prime minister

Radovic, Aleksandar — President of the Commission for Investigating Economic and Financial Abuses of the Milosevic Regime

Rankovic, Aleksandar — Head of Tito-era secret police

Reihl-Kir, Josip — Croatian police chief in eastern Slavonia in 1991

Ristic, Ljubisa	Theatre director, president of Jugoslav United Left party, ally of Mira Markovic
Rose, General Sir Michael	British General in charge of UN troops in Bosnia in 1994
Smith, General Sir Rupert	Successor to General Sir Michael Rose
Rugova, Ibrahim	President of Kosovo (albeit unrecognised)
Sainovic, Nikola	Former minister in Serbia. In detention at the ICTY. Co-indicted with Milosevic for war crimes in Kosovo
Sarinic, Hrvoje	Tudjman's secret envoy to Milosevic
Seselj, Vojislav	Leader of ultra-nationalist Serbian Radical Party and former Milosevic ally. Surrendered to ICTY in February 2003
Silajdzic, Haris	Bosnian Muslim politician
Simatovic, Franko (a.k.a. Frenki)	Former commander of the Special Operations Unit (JSO). Arrested by Serbian authorities in March 2003
Simovic, Tomislav	Former Serb defence minister
Singer, Aca	Head of Yugoslav Jewish community
Sogorov, Milan	Communist party leader in Voivodina in 1988
Solevic, Miroslav	Former Serb nationalist leader in Kosovo
Spegelj, General Martin	Former Croatian defence minister
Stambolic, Bojana	Daughter of Ivan Stambolic
Stambolic, Ivan	Former friend and mentor of Slobodan Milosevic. Murdered in the summer of 2000
Stambolic, Katja	Wife of Ivan Stambolic
Stambolic, Petar	Uncle of Ivan Stambolic
Stanisic, Jovica	Head of Serbian State Security under Milosevic. Arrested by Serbian authorities in March 2003
Stanojlovic, Seska	Schoolmate of Milosevic, journalist at *Vreme* magazine
Stojicic, Radovan 'Badza'	Police chief under Milosevic
Stojilkovic, Vlajko	Interior minister under Milosevic
Stoltenberg, Thorvald	UN envoy to former Yugoslavia
Susak, Gojko	Former Croatian defence minister
Tijanic, Aleksandar	Journalist and former minister for information under Milosevic
Thaci, Hashim	KLA leader
Todorovic, Zoran 'Kundak'	Key ally of Mira Markovic
Trevisan, Dessa	Former *Times* corrrespondent for Balkans
Trgovcevic, Ljubinka	Historian, opponent of Milosevic
Tudjman, Franjo	Former Croatian president
Tuporkovski, Vasil	Macedonian politician
Varady, Tibor	Briefly minister for justice in pro-reform Yugoslav government of Milan Panic
Vance, Cyrus	American UN mediator to Yugoslavia in 1991
Vasic, Milos	Belgrade journalist
Vasiljevic, Jezdimir	Former head of Jugoskandik pyramid scheme in 1992
Vitezovic, Milovan	Serbian writer
Vllasi, Azem	Kosovo Albanian leader
Vucic, Borka	Milosevic's shadow finance minister, oversaw the regime's offshore financial empire
Vucelic, Milorad	Former head of Belgrade Television
Vuksic, Dragan	Former Yugoslav army officer
Walker, William	US diplomat working for the OSCE in Kosovo, former ambassador to El Salvador
Zimmerman, Warren	US ambassador to Milosevic regime in early 1990s

Preface

Any reader of a biography is entitled to know the relationship between author and subject. This is not an authorised work; I have neither sought, nor received Slobodan Milosevic's consent. Nor has he seen the manuscript before publication. However, I thought it right that he know about my project. The former Serbian leader is forbidden from speaking to journalists and writers but he authorised his wife Mira Markovic to grant me a lengthy interview in Belgrade, for which I am grateful. So to some extent, Milosevic's voice, or at least his opinions, may be heard throughout the book in his wife's words.

The Milosevic era was a time of great destruction; many lives were lost and others damaged for ever. The fate of the former Yugoslavia, understandably, can arouse furious passions. I offer here some ground rules for readers. The reference to any named person, or the inclusion of their words, does not imply their agreement with the book's overall contents. (Neither, of course, does it exclude that possibility.) Regarding spellings and terminology: I have used anglicised versions of place names, such as Belgrade rather than Beograd. I have also used terms commonly accepted in the West to describe disputed places and regions. There is no political sub-text here of approval for one or another nation's competing claims. To write of *Krajina* for example, is not to belittle Croatian sovereignty, just as using the word *Kosovo*, rather than the Albanian term *Kosova,* brings with it no judgement. Referring to Bosnia, rather than Bosnia-Herzegovina, is merely a convenience.

I have also adopted a political shorthand, reducing such titles as 'Chairman of the Presidium of the Central Committee of the League of Communists of Serbia' to 'head of the Serbian Communist Party'. I refer to the Serbian or Yugoslav 'Communist Party', rather than its actual title of the 'League of Communists'. My only aim is to ease the comprehension of the reader, many of whom will not be Balkan experts.

On a different note, I was fortunate to find in the library of my great friend Erwin Tuil an enthralling book called *The Balkans from Within,* written at the turn of the century by Reginald Wyon, a British foreign correspondent. Like all of us who reported on that captivating and infuriating region, he was dazzled by its physical beauty, rich cultural heritage and boundless hospitality of its peoples. Puzzled too, at the concurrent ease with which they could set about each other with weapons. Reading *The Balkans from Within*, it sometimes seemed only dates and names change. (Which is not to support the weary claim that the Yugoslav wars of the 1990s were the inevitable result of 'ancient ethnic hatreds'. They were not, as this book attempts to make clear.)

Wyon gives several accounts of meetings with a man called Hilmi Pacha. Pacha was a sly and wily Ottoman functionary in today's Macedonia, charged with implementing reforms, a task he carried out with only enough enthusiasm to maintain his own grip on power. As I researched the life of Slobodan Milosevic, Hilmi Pacha became an ever more familiar figure. Wyon's timeless observations on Balkan power play, I hope, add an extra layer.

In a sense this is a work in progress. The Milosevic trial continues as this book goes to press, and could do so until some time in 2004. As events at The Hague unfold, and more witnesses appear, many episodes here are likely to be further clarified and illuminated. I hope in future editions to make use of such material. The life and times of Slobodan Milosevic make a lengthy and complicated story. I have striven for accuracy, but any mistakes are mine.

I

CHILDHOOD

Growing up in Brotherhood and Unity
1941–58

From the beginning we were all equal. We each had one coat, one shirt and one dress. Everybody looked almost identical, we shared the same ideological views and we believed in Socialism and Communism.

Seska Stanojlovic, schoolmate of Slobodan Milosevic.[1]

Slobodan Milosevic arrived in Serbia just over four months after the Wehrmacht, on 20 August 1941. He was born in the eastern town of Pozarevac, about an hour's drive from the capital Belgrade, not far from the Romanian border. Slobodan was a ruddy-faced child, and in later years relatives nicknamed him 'rumenko', meaning red-cheeked. His parents were teachers from the southern province of Montenegro. Svetozar was six foot tall with blue eyes, brown hair and a luxurious moustache. A spiritual man, he was talented at intoning the Serbian orthodox liturgy. He sang beautifully and loved to play the *gusle*, a traditional one-stringed bowed instrument. If he did not have his *gusle* in his hand, he carried a book of philosophy, or perhaps some of his own poems. Stanislava was a classical Montenegrin beauty, slim and stately, with flashing black-brown eyes and high Slavic cheekbones above a strong chin.

Svetozar and Stanislava had married in 1935 and their first son, Borislav, had been born a year later. Svetozar had studied Russian and theology at Belgrade University, while his wife was a primary school teacher. Svetozar had not wanted to leave Montenegro, but as an employee of the Yugoslav education ministry, he had no choice. Stanislava made the best of it, but Svetozar hated Pozarevac. It was a drab provincial city of one main street, surrounded by farmland. Its main claim to fame was a nearby large prison where many revolutionaries had been locked away, and for giving its name to a treaty signed in 1718 between the Ottomans and the Habsburgs, confirming Habsburg conquests of former Ottoman lands south from Austria-Hungary to Belgrade.

Their homeland of Montenegro, in contrast, was part of the Mediterranean, a place of wine and sunshine, passion and vendettas, somewhere where life was more colourful and intense. It was a land of mountains and magic, with a proud and stubborn population, ready to spill blood for loyalty or vengeance. Montenegrins were divided into clans, and life was governed by a complicated set of rules defining codes of loyalty, and the punishment meted out to those who broke them.

The Milosevic family, many of whom still live in Montenegro, was well respected as educated and cultured. Svetozar's father, Simeun Milosevic, had been a farmer, he had died before the Nazis invaded. Stanislava's father, Djuro Koljensic, had been an officer in the Montenegrin army, and was killed in 1913 in the Balkan Wars. History, tradition, due respect, these were the building blocks of Montenegrin society. It was also deeply conservative. Although she was born in 1911, Stanislava's papers registered her birthdate as 1914, so that her brother Milislav would be the eldest of the family.

When the German tanks rolled across the borders, Svetozar, Borislav and Stanislava, who was now five months pregnant, had quickly headed south to Montenegro. Svetozar wanted to see his mother, Jokna, and sister Darinka. In the baking heat of a Balkan summer, travel was hazardous, and there was little food. Roads were cut by battles between German and Italian troops, the partisans, and Albanian guerrillas loyal only to themselves. Eventually, the family reached Kosovska Mitrovica, in the province of Kosovo, where intense fighting prevented Stanislava and Borislav going any further. Svetozar pressed on through the mountains on foot, promising to return soon.

Borislav Milosevic now lives in Moscow, where he served as Yugoslav ambassador for his brother's regime. He remembers a childhood of extreme privation. 'My father eventually found his mother and his sister and, three months later, we all returned to Pozarevac and German occupation. Slobodan was born in August, and we spent the war and all our childhood in Pozarevac. They were very miserable times. We were always hungry. It was very hard to find something to eat, and my mother had to sell everything to survive. She sold all her shoes, her dresses and finally even her wedding ring.'[2]

*   *   *

For a country that prided itself on its warrior tradition, Serbia's collapse was swift and ignominious. At the end of March 1941, under increasing pressure from Hitler, and lacking any real promise of aid from the Western Allies, Yugoslavia's ministers had reluctantly signed up to the Axis. But Yugoslavia's membership lasted less than two days. With the assistance of British secret agents, on the night of March 26, pro-Allied Yugoslav generals had launched a military coup, triggering nationwide celebrations. In Belgrade tens of thousands of demonstrators poured on to the streets, '*Bolje rat nego pakt, bolje grob nego rob,*' (Better war than pact, better graves than slaves) the demonstrators roared.

In Berlin an enraged Hitler ordered that the onslaught on Yugoslavia 'be carried out with inexorable severity and that the military destruction be carried out in a lightning-like operation.' On 6 April hordes of Nazi bombers levelled much of Belgrade. The stubborn chants of the demonstrators were no longer expressions of defiance, but a ghastly prediction. *Bolje rat nego pakt, bolje grob nego rob*. War came to all, and graves or slave labour awaited many.

The Kingdom of Serbs, Croats and Slovenes – as Yugoslavia was first known – was a weak and uncertain construct, established only in 1918. Yugoslavia roughly translates as 'country of the south Slavic peoples'. But the south Slavs had never before lived together in one state. Yugoslavia had been divided between the Ottoman and Habsburg empires. Istanbul's territories included most of present day Serbia, Bosnia-Herzegovina and Macedonia. Vienna ruled Croatia, Slovenia and the northern Serbian province of Voivodina.

Although Yugoslavs spoke the same language – Serbo-Croat, as it was known – they were divided by culture, religion and ethnic identity. Istanbul's Balkan possessions were known – and viewed in the west – as Turkey-in-Europe. For much of the nineteenth century the Serbian capital Belgrade was the northernmost point of Turkey-in-Europe. The main division was between the eastern and western Christian churches dating from the schism of 1054, when the eastern (Orthodox) church was based in Byzantium and the western (Catholic) church in Rome. This division, which cut across the Yugoslav lands, was broadly reflected in the frontier between the Ottoman Empire in the east and the Habsburg Empire in the west. From the sixteenth century until 1878, the western frontier of the Ottoman Empire was roughly the present border between Croatia and Bosnia-Herzegovina.

Yugoslavia was a constitutional monarchy, but not a very solid one.

In an attempt to forge a centralised state in 1929 King Aleksandar Karadjordjevic abolished parliament and seized power. The Kingdom of Serbs, Croats and Slovenes was renamed the Kingdom of Yugoslavia (also known as Royal Yugoslavia). It was not enough to guarantee the state's or his survival. Five years later King Aleksandar was assassinated in Marseilles by a Macedonian linked to an extreme Croat nationalist party, known as the Ustasha.

After its collapse in 1941 Yugoslavia's irredentist neighbours greedily helped themselves to its territories. Hungary immediately annexed Voivodina. Bulgaria took Macedonia and parts of southern Serbia. Slovenia was divided between Italy and Germany. Italy also took much of the Croatian coast and its islands in the Adriatic. The Nazis placed Serbia under direct military rule, implemented with customary brutality. The German High Command ordered Wehrmacht units to execute one hundred prisoners for every soldier killed, and fifty for each one wounded. With Italian and German help the Ustasha set up their Independent State of Croatia (NDH) under the leadership of Ante Pavelic, with the support of the Catholic church. The NDH encompassed Croatia and Bosnia-Herzegovina. The NDH's strategy for dealing with over two million Serbs on its territory was simple: 'Kill a third, expel a third and convert a third.'

Not surprisingly, many Serb villages demanded to be converted to Catholicism. Catholic priests presided over these mass conversions. But Croat promises of baptism were often a trap. In the village of Glina, in 1941, hundreds of Serbs were locked into a church and burnt alive. Fifty years later, when Croatia again declared independence, Glina was one of the first places to come under attack from Serb paramilitaries. Many of the Yugoslav army generals whose forces attacked Croatia, and later Bosnia, were from families whose members had been killed by the Ustasha. The father of General Ratko Mladic, the military leader of the Bosnian Serbs, was killed in 1945 while leading a partisan attack on Ante Pavelic's home village.

For many Serbs, the NDH's brutality was summed up in a scene from the Italian journalist Curzio Malaparte's account of his wartime experiences, *Kaputt*. Malaparte interviews Pavelic, and is joined by the Italian ambassador Raffaele Casertano:

While he spoke, I gazed at a wicker basket on the Poglavnik's [Leader's] desk. The lid was raised and the basket seemed to be filled with mussels, or shelled oysters – as they are occasionally displayed in the windows of Fortnum and Mason in Piccadilly in London. Casertano looked at me and winked,

'Would you like a nice oyster stew?'

'Are they Dalmatian oysters?' I asked the Poglavnik.

Ante Pavelic removed the lid from the basket and revealed the mussels, that slimy and jelly-like mass, and he said smiling, with that tired good-natured smile of his, 'It is a present from my loyal Ustashas. Forty pounds of human eyes.'[3]

There is some debate as to whether this actually happened. It may be an exaggerated version of something not quite as grisly, or indeed a product of Malaparte's imagination. However, the guards at the NDH's network of concentration camps certainly took sadistic pleasure in killing the inmates by hand. Their victims were Serbs, Jews, Roma (Gypsies) and anti-Fascist Croats. The most notorious NDH concentration camp was at Jasenovac. The numbers of those killed there is disputed. Official Yugoslav statistics estimate 600,000 deaths. Franjo Tudjman, the first president of independent Croatia, put the figure at between 30,000 and 40,000. Some Serbs claimed that one million died at Jasenovac. The respected Croatian historian Ivo Banac calculated that 120,000 people were killed in all the NDH camps. In the Balkans, the grim arithmetic of genocide can be a badge of macabre pride, and victimhood is seen as legitimising national aspirations.

Serbia itself was ruled by a quisling, a former general called Milan Nedic. As in the NDH, Nedic's regime quickly set up a network of concentration camps for Jews, Gypsies and anti-Nazis. Thousands of Serbian Jewish women and children were gassed in vans which lumbered back and forth over the Danube. The savagery and brutality of the German occupation proved to be the best recruiting agent for the two main resistance movements. Royalist Serbs joined the Chetniks, who took their name from the *ceta*, or bands of armed Serb guerrillas that had attacked and harassed the Turks when Serbia was part of the Ottoman empire. They draped themselves in religious symbols of the Serbian Orthodox Church.

By contrast the partisans, led by Tito, stood for a Marxist, classless society. They were proudly multi-national. Any pretence at a common front between the two movements against the Nazis soon collapsed. Instead, both sides fought each other in a murderous civil war. In many areas the Chetniks reached accommodation with both the Nazis and the Italians. In London, Churchill decided to abandon the Chetniks and give wholehearted support to Tito.

Tito and the partisans found many recruits in Pozarevac and its surrounds. This area of Serbia, known as Sumadija, had long been a heartland of Serb resistance, stretching back through centuries of Ottoman occupation. In medieval times bandits and outlaws known as *hajduks* had found sanctuary in the dense forests that covered the region. The Serbs of Sumadija did not like outsiders giving them orders. As a child Borislav noticed strange comings and goings at odd hours at home. 'During the war my mother carried out underground work. I was young then, but I remember that she hid people in our house. She was not in the forest with the partisans, but she worked as a courier, carrying secret messages. My father knew about it, more or less, but he did not get involved because he had to work as a teacher of religion so we could get some money.'

Tito, born Josip Broz, was himself half-Croat, half-Slovene. Captured by the Russians during the First World War, he became a Communist, and stayed in Russia until 1920, when he returned to Croatia and joined the Yugoslav Communist Party. He rose quickly up the party ranks. In August 1928 bombs were found in his flat in Zagreb, and he was arrested. In court Tito was proud and defiant. He announced that he did not recognise the legality of the proceedings, setting a tradition among Yugoslav leaders on trial that continues to this day. He insulted the court and said he would only recognise a Communist judiciary. He was sentenced to five years.

According to one version, Tito's name came from his habit of giving brief orders: you – *Ti* – do that – *to*. As partisan leader Tito's masterstroke was a political strategy that focused not just on some distant millenarian dream of a classless society, but also on a 'national liberation struggle'. First the Germans had to be killed or expelled, and the Yugoslav nations freed from the Nazi terror. Once this was achieved, the partisans would set up a 'liberation committee' to run their new territories.

Momcilo (Moma) Markovic, future father-in-law of Slobodan, joined the partisans with his brothers Draza and Brana. (Brana was killed in 1942, but Moma and Draza later became senior politicians in Tito's Yugoslavia.) Now in his eighties, Draza Markovic lives in Belgrade and vividly recalls his wartime years. 'My duties as political commissar included moral and political education, explaining the movement and the war itself. We were fighting against the enemy occupiers and also struggling for a new society. But the fight against the enemy came first. That's why we had wide support, especially from the peasants who faced inconceivable violence and terror.'[4]

Caught between the Chetniks, the partisans and the Ustasha were Bosnia's Muslims. Bosnia was part of the NDH, and its leadership courted Bosnia's Muslims, declaring them to be 'the flower of the Croatian nation'. This apparent contradiction was resolved by the Ustasha claim that Bosnian Muslims were not really Muslims, but rather were Croats who had converted to Islam under the rule of the Ottoman empire. As such they should be welcomed back into the national fold. (They were also claimed by Serb nationalists.)

Through all these complications one simple truth is evident. Wartime Yugoslavia was a charnel house. Over one million Yugoslavs were killed in the years between 1941 and 1945, but many died at the hands of their compatriots in the civil war. About half of those killed were Serbs.[5] Almost a third of all casualties, 328,000, were killed in Bosnia.

In October 1944, when Slobodan was three years old, Tito and the partisans liberated the capital, Belgrade, and then Pozarevac too. The swastika was replaced by the red flag. Across Yugoslavia a new, Communist regime was established. Although Svetozar was not a party member, as a teacher, and a respected pillar of the local community, he was appointed vice president of the regional Popular Front. Like many, Svetozar was duped. The Popular Front was a deception, widely used in eastern Europe as the Communists took over. The idea was to have a political structure controlled by Communists behind the scenes, but with non-Communist figureheads, to disguise its true orientation.

Stanislava had welcomed Tito's victory. This was the Marxist dream in which she believed. Svetozar had increasing doubts. In Yugoslavia, and across eastern Europe, the educated, the middle class, those who owned property, were seen as the class enemy, and ground down. Bourgeois manners such as Svetozar exhibited – an educated way of speaking, soft hands – were now a sign of shame. Even his beloved Orthodox liturgy was considered suspect. The works of Marx and Lenin were the compulsory new gospel, to be 'discussed' at political meetings, discussion being a euphemism for parroting the party line. Conversations with friends and acquaintances were guarded, short, for who could be trusted? Evenings were spent at home, listening to the radio, or reading more party texts.

Yet many accepted all this as the price for building the new Jerusalem. As a loyal party member Stanislava did not question the decisions of the country's male leaders. Milica Kovac, a widow in her sixties, was a member of the same local Communist Party branch in Pozarevac. 'Stanislava was as straight as an arrow, and always held her chin high. She was a woman of great energy, with a strong voice that told you about her strength of character. She was a true believer in the idea of communism, and of equality.'⁶ She was a woman of upright bearing, boundless energy and social conscience, a fine role model for her pupils at the Petar Petrovics-Njegos primary school where she taught, remembers Kovac. 'She believed that the party had set the right course. That was beyond question. She was a hard-liner. But she did not elaborate about these things. Her energy was dedicated to humanitarian work.'

In 1947, perhaps inevitably, Svetozar Milosevic returned to his beloved Montenegro. A deeply spiritual man, he could not settle in Pozarevac. 'My father was not unhappy because of political differences with my mother,' says Borislav. 'It was much more the ambience in Pozarevac. He could not live in such an atmosphere. It was very provincial, it was a small city, and he was a man of the mountains.' But Svetozar kept in touch with his family. He wrote and, when he could, he sent money.

Stanislava covered up her sadness at the break-up of her marriage by throwing herself into her work as a teacher and dedicated party member. Certainly everyone knew there was no point trying to hide a single dinar when Comrade Milosevic organised collections for the disadvantaged. Scrupulously honest, she ensured every coin was accounted for. Milica Kovac remembers her as 'a real party activist, full of enthusiasm for humanitarian and volunteer work. She always insisted on collecting and distributing aid to poor families, especially the Gypsies. She was extremely strict about that. But she liked her word to be the last one. If she put forward an idea, she insisted it was accepted, and followed.'

In Pozarevac the town gossips clucked disapprovingly at Svetozar's departure. The small town was still a deeply conservative society. Yet nobody could fault Stanislava's dedication to her sons, or to the cause of Communism. Even nowadays, in a western European welfare state, it is difficult enough for a single parent to bring up children alone. In provincial Serbia during the 1950s this was a feat of Stakhanovite dimensions. The country was still recovering from the ravages of the war. Stanislava's modest salary was enough to feed and clothe herself and her sons, but only just. The three of them lived in two rooms and a kitchen in a pre-war one-storey house, just off the main street. 'She dressed modestly, because those were modest times,' says Milica Kovac. 'Nobody had money to be elegant or eccentric, especially not provincial teachers. She wore flat shoes, because of her height, and clothes in the usual colours of middle-aged women in those times, brown, black and grey.'

Beneath the modernist veneer of Communism, the country where Slobodan Milosevic grew up was profoundly traumatised. Tito's Yugoslavia[7] was made up of six republics: Serbia, Croatia, Bosnia-Herzegovina, Slovenia, Macedonia and Montenegro. But whether in 1920, 1950 or 1990, Yugoslavia suffered from the same two fundamental weaknesses. The first can be described as philosophical. 'Yugoslavism', the doctrine of uniting the diverse south Slav peoples in one land, was an idea. For Yugoslavia's educated, urban population it had great appeal, but high up in the mountains and down in the rural heartlands Yugoslavism took shallow roots. The call of the nation was far more powerful. Especially when in living memory former family friends had slaughtered each other because they had a different nationality.

The second weakness was constitutional. Serbia was the biggest and most powerful of the Yugoslav nations, as they were defined under the constitution. Serbs saw Yugoslavia as a means of ensuring that all Serbs lived in one country, including the Serbian minorities in Croatia and Bosnia, even if that country was called Yugoslavia rather than Serbia. So either Yugoslavia would be dominated by Serbia, or it would have to be constructed in such a way that Serbia would be constitutionally constrained. A Yugoslavia dominated by Serbia – dubbed 'Serboslavia' – would fuel the nationalist aspirations of the other republics. But a Yugoslavia with a weakened Serbia would increase Serbian resentment and fuel Serbian nationalism.

The Slovenian president Milan Kucan, like Milosevic, was born in 1941. He argues that the first Yugoslavia collapsed because nobody believed in it. 'Yugoslavia fell apart in seven days in 1941. Nobody defended it because nobody felt it was their homeland. That was the consequence of a dictatorship established under Yugoslavia as Serboslavia. It was not understood as a homeland by Croatians, Slovenes or Macedonians. The raison d'être for the country ceased to exist. In the second Yugoslavia Serbs also often believed that Yugoslavia should also predominantly serve Serbian interests.'[8]

Even so, after the war, for the young and the believers, these were days of hope. In many ways, Tito's Yugoslavia was a remarkable creation. It was a multi-national federation, whose borders stretched from Austria, Italy and Hungary in the north to Romania, Bulgaria and Greece in the south. The rich ethnic mosaic also included substantial minorities such as Albanians, Italians, Hungarians, Turks, Romanians, Bulgarians, Czechs, Slovaks, along with Gypsies and the remnants of the country's Jewish community, each with their own language.

Yugoslavia's diverse cultures spanned European history, boasting a complex heritage of long-vanished empires. Here were the coastal towns of the Roman and Venetian empires, seaside cities such as Trogir and Split, and Dubrovnik, the medieval walled city that was the jewel of the Adriatic. Roman legions had marched through here; as had their successors the janissaries of Suleyman the Magnificent, and Napoleon's rowdy armies. The Romans had built Diocletian's palace at Split, the Ottomans the beautiful mosques of Sarajevo and Travnik with their needle-sharp minarets pointing skyward to Allah.

The French soldiers had bequeathed a love of wine and liberty. Like many foreign visitors they, too, were entranced by the fiery temperaments and almost oriental cheekbones of the country's women, whom they christened 'petit-chat', now shortened to the slang word *picka*, an altogether less gallant term. Rome, Istanbul, and Paris all left their legacy, and Vienna too, which once ruled Croatia, Slovenia and Bosnia. The Habsburg spirit of civic pride lived on in the spacious squares and ornate apartment buildings of cities such as Zagreb and Novi Sad, in the former Habsburg territory of Voivodina, and stolid municipal buildings painted the characteristic Habsburg ochre stood as far south as Bosnia.

Tito had created eastern Europe's own mini-Soviet Union, a diverse ethnic mix held together under the Marxist mantra of 'Brotherhood and Unity'. The idea behind Brotherhood and Unity was admirable, if optimistic. The memories of the ghastly atrocities committed by the Chetniks, Ustasha and partisans were to be buried, and a new Yugoslav identity formed. Tito believed, probably correctly, that any genuine examination of wartime activity would pull his nascent country apart in bloody recriminations. But fifty years later, the price of his failure to come to terms with Yugoslavia's past would be high indeed. Wartime memories, and victims, of massacre and murder did not fade away. Instead, like ice-age mammoths, they were perfectly preserved under Communism's permafrost, ready to be dug up – sometimes literally –

and displayed as proud symbols of victimhood when Yugoslavia began to collapse.

Tito's six federal republics enjoyed considerable autonomy, and were run by their own Communist parties. But this autonomy existed only within the overarching state framework of the Federal Republic, which was responsible for national matters such as defence and national economic and foreign policy, conducted – in theory at least – in the spirit of brotherhood and unity. This was a delicate balancing act. Unlike France or Germany, Yugoslavia was not a nation-state. It was a state of six nations. The existence of, for example, the Serbian Communist Party, in the Serbian republic, allowed nationalist-minded comrades to assert some control over the destiny of their homeland. But at the same time, the fact that nation-based political structures existed at all gave nationalists a framework in which to operate.

Alone among eastern European Communist leaders Tito had broken with Stalin and survived. After the war Stalin had determined to Sovietise the country and install a pro-Moscow regime. Alex Bebler, later Yugoslav ambassador at the United Nations, recalled: 'Russian [army] officers started behaving as if they were the masters and wanted to command our unit. Our officers did not like it and began to protest. Our officers were all partisans who fought in the war, and naturally objected to being deprived of their commands.'⁹

Stalin soon discovered that when he pushed in Belgrade, unlike in Warsaw or Budapest, the local Communists pushed back. Angry at resistance to his plans, he expelled Yugoslavia from the Cominform (the international Communist organisation) in March 1948. At first, many Yugoslav Communists simply could not comprehend what had happened. There was fear, confusion, even suicides. Others proved more ideologically nimble. Draza Markovic observed: 'We had looked to Moscow absolutely. Without any question, Moscow was the centre. But the Russians told so many lies about us, that we were revisionists, traitors, agents of the West and liars, so eventually it was not so hard to take that step.' Fearful of Soviet armed intervention – for which preparations were indeed made – Tito launched a terror campaign. An Orwellian shift in propaganda announced the new party line, that yesterday's black was now today's white, and Moscow was no longer the benevolent uncle but a deadly enemy. Those Yugoslavs who were already suspect, or who switched allegiance from Moscow to Belgrade too slowly, were sent to a concentration camp on Goli Otok, an island in the Adriatic.

Aca Singer, later head of Yugoslavia's Jewish community, and a prominent Belgrade banker in the 1970s and 1980s, was a prisoner at Goli Otok, sent there in 1951. Singer was no Stalinist, but his criticism of the government and his Jewish origins made him suspect. On Goli Otok the camp bosses demanded ever more fervent pledges of allegiance to Tito. This was a macabre new twist for Singer, a survivor of several Nazi camps including Auschwitz. 'On Goli Otok you had to prove that you were pro-Tito, not pro-Soviet. The Germans did not ask me in Auschwitz to say Heil Hitler, but there I had to praise Tito, and shout "Long live Tito".'[10]

In the West, Tito's break with Stalin was greeted with euphoria. A Communist country that had leapt free of Moscow was a dream come true for Cold War policymakers. Material, military, and most of all, lavish economic aid poured into the renegade Marxist state. Washington supported the start of the series of loans from the IMF and World Bank that would prop up the Yugoslav economy for the next three decades. Yugoslavia's geographical position in the heart of Europe, between Vienna and Istanbul, and its long Adriatic coastline gave it vital strategic importance for the United States and western Europe. Western tax-payers' dollars for many years paid Yugoslav wages, viewed by European and American policymakers as a price well worth paying.

The break with Stalin signalled not only a massive influx of western aid, but also the start of a liberalisation unmatched in the rest of the Communist world. As Tito positioned himself as a buffer between the capitalist and Communist blocs, and billions of dollars poured in, the repression eased. Pozarevac transformed from a sleepy provincial settlement into a bustling regional centre. Pavements were laid, roads were asphalted and buildings went up. More shops opened, and eventually, a department store.

The town's cinemas reflected Yugoslavia's position perched between east and west. Cinema-goers could watch *Dial M for Murder*, westerns with Doris Day or admire Marilyn Monroe, as well the best of the 1950s Soviet film industry. 'From the early 1950s we felt that we were back in Europe. We listened to Radio Luxembourg, especially at night. We knew about the latest new films, American, British and French new wave. We talked about films and music like young people in the west,' remembers Seska Stanojlovic, a childhood friend of Slobodan Milosevic, and now a journalist with the Belgrade liberal news weekly *Vreme*. The two first met at the age of five, on a school holiday to the eastern Serbian mountains. Like all Yugoslav children they played not cowboys and Indians but partisans and Germans. Plenty of women had fought with the partisans, but Stanojlovic, like every girl, was forced to play a nurse. Slobodan was almost certainly a partisan.

In many ways Titoist Yugoslavia in the 1950s resembled austere post-war Britain. The state always provided just about enough, but luxuries were rare and there was little choice. Clothes and shops were drab. As Stanojlovic noted, everyone had but one of everything. But nobody froze or starved, even if supper was often bread covered with dripping or home-made jam. There was no television or central heating. Boilers were fired up with wood and coal, to warm enough water for a bath. Yet there was a feeling of optimism in the air, that fundamentally Tito was steering a good course, and life was getting better.

Although Stanojlovic's family were members of the haute bourgeoisie, who had once owned considerable property, as a schoolgirl she was a loyal Communist. 'My mother and my grandmother were quite rich. We had a big house and some land, but it was nationalised. My grandmother was angry, but I was a small child, and I just accepted that we were growing up in this kind of society. We accepted this idea of a new society, that we were all equal, as something normal, that this is how we have to grow up.'

Slobodan's doting mother attempted to fill the vacuum left at home by the departure of her husband. Stanislava Milosevic became the centre of her son's childhood universe. Stanislava was an ambitious woman for her children as well as herself. Other mothers made do with whatever clothes were to hand when they dressed their children for school. But Stanislava took care every day to send Slobodan out in a fresh white shirt, like a junior version of the Communist official she hoped he would be. The serious young boy made few friends at school and avoided sports. 'Stanislava was a protective and dominant mother. Slobodan did not even go to the gym in case he sweated and caught a cold,' says Milica Kovac. Milosevic gained the nickname 'silky'. He never got into a fight, or raided the orchards in the lush farmland around Pozarevac. Friendless and fatherless, mocked for his weediness and unwillingness to join the rough and tumble of the playground, the young schoolboy instead took refuge in his studies. Milosevic spent his

spare time writing for the school magazine and working for the pupils'
Communist youth organisation. And still, there was something different
about the young Slobodan. Not exactly a star quality, but an aura of, at
the very least, unusual determination. 'Slobodan was his own person,'
said Seska Stanojlovic. 'He was an excellent student. Even at that time
it was clear to me that he was absolutely devoted to his personal
ambitions.'

In this more cynical age it might seem hard to believe, but Yugoslavia's
first post-war generation really believed it was constructing a new society.
For a few years at least, the rosy faces of the Young Communists and
Young Pioneers that shone from Communist-era posters were modelled
on real life. Communist states expended much energy on their young
generation, regarding them as untainted by capitalist society. Pressed
into the correct Marxist mould, they would be the building blocks of
the new classless Yugoslavia.

Even now, many adults in eastern Europe recall their Communist
childhoods with nostalgia. As recently as the late 1990s, one of the
best-selling CDs in neighbouring Hungary was *The Best of Communism*,
featuring youthful choirs singing homages to Lenin, Stalin and various
Marxist worthies. 'After the war, when I was a young man, our
generation was full of hope, even though the country was ruined,'
said Hungarian film director Peter Bacso. 'We believed in a new world
based on justice. I was so enthusiastic that when I was a young poet, I
even wrote lyrics for the songs we sang in the summer camps.'[11] Bacso
later found fame exposing the absurdity of the one party system in his
film *The Witness*, in which Communist Party officials claim that a lemon
is the first Hungarian orange.

At that time, in the 1950s and 1960s, Yugoslav young people were
frequently drafted into labour brigades to build roads or railways.
The working holidays were arduous, but enjoyable, bringing together
idealistic youth of the different Yugoslav republics and foreign volunteers
as well. Like the founders of the first kibbutzim, the young Communists
believed that physical prowess was part of the process of building the
new, socialist, man and woman. Roads and railways were more than a
means of efficient transport, they bound the diverse nations of Yugoslavia
together, linking republic capitals such as Belgrade in Serbia and Zagreb
in Croatia, Ljubljana in Slovenia, and Skopje in Macedonia. The road
linking Belgrade and Zagreb was even known as the 'Highway of
Brotherhood and Unity'. Under Tito such projects were also a symbol

of modernity. Even now Yugoslavia's network of motorways is far more efficient than those in Poland or Hungary.

So it was perfectly natural that the school students of Pozarevac would also be called to do their socialist duty. Together with her schoolmates, Seska Stanojlovic went to Slovenia to help build a motorway there. Slobodan helped organise the trip. But while the workers' state of course had to be constructed that did not mean he personally had to wield a pickaxe, and he stayed at home. 'Slobodan did not participate. He did not like to work, only to be a leader,' she said. Years later Stanojlovic asked a local photographer if he had a picture of Slobodan in the youth work brigade at home in Pozarevac. He had such a picture, he informed her. It showed all the young people working, and Milosevic standing at the side.

2

MEETING MIRA

Teenage Sweethearts
1958–62

He is an extremely handsome man, a superior man with fine human qualities. He has strong feelings for other people, for their problems and needs. He is a good speaker, and he has a strong and natural inner stability.

Mira Markovic, on her husband.[1]

Slobodan Milosevic was a loner, but his schoolmate Mira Markovic certainly liked the way he looked. She noticed that he always wore neat and clean clothes. He behaved properly and had good manners. He was well regarded by the school teachers, who even trusted him enough to fetch the disabled weapons used in military training classes.

And Milosevic certainly knew all about Mira Markovic, a young woman with a powerful name. With her thick dark hair and luminous black eyes, she had a certain appeal, although she was not the most beautiful girl in school. She was a daughter of the most famous revolutionary family in Pozarevac. She lived in one of the grandest houses in the city, a fine mansion once owned by a Serbian duke, whose walls included Roman ruins. Both her parents, Vera Miletic and Moma Markovic, had been partisans, and Moma was now a government minister, one of the most important politicians in Yugoslavia. So when Slobo bumped into Mira outside the library, and saw that she was upset after getting a bad grade, he was happy to offer comfort.

Mira recalled: 'We went to a mixed school and we used to see each other at break time. The first time that we really talked was mid-term, and we got our marks. I had a C in history, and I was desperate. I had all As, and a C in history. I was totally desperate. My wish was not only to be an excellent student, but to be the best student.'

When Mira became desperate, she turned to her favourite book for comfort. *Antigone*, by Sophocles, is the story of Oedipus's daughter – by his union with his own mother. It is a Greek tragedy of suicide and death and certainly a morbid choice for a school girl of sixteen. Antigone defies the command of Creon, king of Thebes, that the body of her brother should remain unburied. Creon sentences her to death, but eventually relents. By then it is too late. Antigone has killed herself in her prison cell. Her great love, Haemon, son of Creon, then commits suicide in sympathy. That in turn prompts Creon's wife to kill herself. The play ends with Creon alone and desolate. With hindsight it is easy to see its grim themes as a harbinger of the destruction of Yugoslavia itself.

But Mira could not get into the school library to read *Antigone*, because her library card had run out. 'I didn't have the money to renew my card. I met Slobodan in the street and I asked him if he had the small change I needed. I told him that I only got a C in history and I was desperate. He comforted me because of that C. Then I told him why I wanted to read *Antigone* for the zillionth time. I saw that he did not quite understand why.' All grade As and one grade C did not seem too terrible to Milosevic, but none the less, he saw his chance to make a connection. He sensed too a driving ambition in the young woman with such powerful family connections.

Sympathy was offered and the conversation soon flowed naturally. 'Somehow he tried to establish a connection between the C in history and the destiny of *Antigone*. He put an effort into that.' He succeeded. In fact, it seems that Slobo swept Mira off her feet. 'It is even more romantic than I am able to tell you. Everything was romantic, but I am restrained from telling you how romantic it was.'

Slobodan and Mira became inseparable. They blotted out the rest of the world, finding in each other the emotional support missing in the rest of their lives. At school they were known as 'Romeo and Juliet II'. Their fractured family backgrounds had much in common. Slobodan had been abandoned by his father. Mira's father was a partisan hero but he barely acknowledged his daughter's existence. Although Mira said that she had 'normal' relations with her father, virtually the only time she saw him was on summer holidays with the Yugoslav elite at Tito's favourite holiday home on the island of Brioni. Moma had married and started another family, with whom he lived in Belgrade. He did not take much interest in either Mira or his son Ivan, by a different, third, woman.

Mira was brought up by her maternal grandparents. It was a childhood full of love, according to her. 'It was very romantic. I grew up in an old house dating back to the nineteenth century, with a big garden, with a lot of flowers and trees. My mother was killed in the war, and my grandparents kept me with them. They would not give me away to my father and my stepmother, which I think was correct. There was a gentle atmosphere, and I had a lot of attention as a child. Everybody in the family, every cousin that my mother had, they all took care of me because I was a child living with my grandparents and they loved me a lot.'

In Mira's repeated assertions of how much she was loved, there is perhaps the small voice of a young girl who never knew her mother, and whose father was indifferent to her. Ljubica Markovic, who is Mira's half-sister, did live with Moma. A former journalist for the Yugoslav state news agency Tanjug, she is now director of the independent Beta news agency in Belgrade. As a child she idolised her older sister, but as Milosevic rose to power they fell out and have hardly spoken for twenty years. 'I asked my mother why Mira did not live with us, as well as my father's other son Ivan. My mother said she had asked, but Mira's grandparents said they could not give her away, that she has all the love she needs. My mother did not push, she thought she had fulfilled her obligations, but I don't think it was enough. I would have pressed and taken the child. Mira only stayed with us at holiday time. I think it must have been very painful for her, as a young girl, that you have a family and then it is taken away. There must be a strong motivation in her life of family deprivation and compensation for what she didn't have.'[2]

The two sisters first met when Ljubica was six or seven, and Mira was six years older. 'I well remember the first time I saw her. She came suddenly from nowhere, and we were told "this is your sister". It was a shock, we were completely unprepared, and I reproached my father because he did not bring her up properly. She should have been living with us, it is normal that children are together. But I accepted her immediately, as I did my brother Ivan. Within a short time Baca, as I called her, became a big sister for me, and I wanted to copy her, the way she dressed and the way she talked, but I was too young.'

Mira compensated for her absent father by idolising her mother, Vera Miletic. After the Nazis invaded Yugoslavia Miletic had joined the partisans and begun an affair with Momir Markovic. Mira recalled what she knew about her mother: 'Before the Second World War she was a student at the faculty of philosophy at Belgrade University. She was a Communist Party activist, and she became a partisan when the war started. Two years after the war started, she was transferred to the Belgrade party organisation. She was the chief of the Belgrade party organisation. She was one of the organisers of the student demonstrations, of the 14 December 1939 demonstration.' On 10 July 1942, Miletic gave birth to her and Markovic's daughter Mirjana. 'I was born in the woods, which is a partisan expression. I was born where my parents were with the partisans, near the banks of the Morava river.'

Soon afterwards the party leadership sent Vera Miletic to work underground in Belgrade. At the most crucial time of any child's emotional development, when physical contact with parents is of prime importance, the baby girl was handed down a chain of partisan bases and safehouses, or sometimes stayed with her maternal grandparents. Mira Markovic's first and most formative years were spent on the run. 'During the war I was moved frequently, from one spot to another, from one family to another so as not to get my mother caught. Even as a baby, I had a Gestapo arrest warrant out for me. They thought if they had me, they could somehow find my mother, because she was one of the organisers of the partisan movement in eastern Serbia. So when Gestapo learnt that she was pregnant, that she had a baby and the baby was with the grandparents, they were looking for the baby to try to get at the mother.'

In Belgrade Vera Miletic's cover did not last. Mira said: 'She was arrested. Of course we think that someone betrayed her, because she was found precisely where she was hiding. The Gestapo took her at that exact spot.'

There is still controversy over the precise circumstances of Vera Miletic's death. Many believe that she gave away details of the underground party networks to the Nazis. 'It is considered that she was weak in front of the police, because she named the whole party organisation to them,' said Draza Markovic. 'I don't know how many people that was. The biggest loss was a spy in the secret police, Janko Jankovic. But it is impossible to tell whether she made her confession under torture or not.'[3] According to Mira Markovic, her mother was held by the Gestapo for six months, and was then transferred to the Bajnica prison camp in Belgrade. 'She was shot by a firing squad in September 1944, and one month later Belgrade was liberated. She was twenty-four and I was two. She had never seen me.'

Others claimed that Miletic was one of many to be executed by the partisans themselves once they liberated Belgrade. In post-war Yugoslavia, which lionised its partisan heroes, Vera Miletic was condemned as a traitor. For the young and idealistic Mira Markovic, already neglected by her father, the news that her mother was considered a traitor was traumatic. 'Supposedly, the first time Mira heard about her mother was when she was ten or so years old. During a history lesson the teacher said that her mother was a traitor. That was shocking for her because she was convinced her mother was a courageous partisan, and since then she has done everything she can to rehabilitate her,' said Draza Markovic.

In later years Mira Markovic published a book about her mother, praising her wartime feats in the resistance. Mira's rehabilitation campaign also included wearing a rose in her hair, as Vera Miletic had done, until it became an object of mockery. She carefully preserved a red star her mother had made in prison in Belgrade. Even calling herself Mira – a shortened version of Mirjana – was part of this drive, as Mira had been her mother's partisan nom-de-guerre.

What is clear is that Vera Miletic was brave and courageous to have ever joined the partisans in the first place. Nobody was expected to resist forever. 'Traitor was the word used about her at the time, but I remember that one of my friends told me he could hold out for two days, and we could be sure for that time. But after that we should disperse, because he would talk,' said Draza Markovic. The true facts will probably never be known, as files relating to the case disappeared once Milosevic came to power. Many in Belgrade believe that Mira ordered the records to be removed.

But Mira had her adored Sloba, as she calls him. Even now she keeps their youthful love letters, bound in ribbon. After they met, Mira joyfully announced to Ljubica Markovic that Sloba was the only one. 'Before Slobodan she always had to be in love with someone. She was sixteen when she fell in love with him. She told me that there was a big event happening, all the others were behind her. That was a big event for her.'[4] Milosevic's former schoolmate, Seska Stanojlovic says, 'When I think about our teenage years, I cannot see him without Mira. They were always together. I remember him in his beige raincoat, and her in a blue winter coat.' Teachers too looked fondly on the young couple, recalled the Belgrade writer Filip David, whose mother-in-law taught at Pozarevac high school. 'Everyone knew about their love. From the early days they were dependent on each other. My wife's mother said she always had good memories about a boy and girl who loved each other very much and who were always together.'

As well as love, there was also mutual interest. For Milosevic, Mira's partisan pedigree offered an entrée to Yugoslavia's elite. The young Slobodan was better looking than his girlfriend, said Seska Stanojlovic. He could have chosen someone else. 'He was a handsome boy, and Mira was never pretty, as you can see. But she was the only person in Pozarevac with such a prominent revolutionary background. That was my impression from the beginning, although I don't deny they developed a special relationship. He relied on his mother and Mira, and I think she is the only person he trusts.' Even as teenagers Slobodan and Mira courted those with power. In Pozarevac, as in other Balkan and Mediterranean towns, the main evening entertainment was the *corso,* or the nightly promenade. This was a chance to socialise, catch up on the gossip, see and be seen. The *corso* had its own rules, but Slobodan and Mira broke them. While their classmates walked together on the road, the young couple took care to stroll on the pavement, in the company of their teachers, and the older students.

Milosevic's diligence at school, and loyal espousal of the party line had been well noticed by the party grandees in Pozarevac. The Markovic connection certainly helped. In post-war Yugoslavia the partisan generation were both kings and king-makers. Milosevic became a full Communist Party member in January 1959, at the comparatively early age of seventeen. This was unusual and an honour, granted only to the most promising school students. This was the party's method of perpetuating itself, by picking future leaders at an early age who would then be encouraged to follow a political career. Acceptance demanded a high level of self-belief and confidence.

There was no shame in not being a full party member. Some students of Milosevic's age felt that they were not ready for party membership, as they were not yet sufficiently versed in the principles of Marxism, or ideologically pure enough for such an honour. The young Milosevic had no such doubts about joining the party. Nor did Mira. Although she has always been hugely ambitious, possessed of a nervous, febrile personality, Mira has never liked public appearances or glad-handing. She understood that she would never be a successful politician in Communist Yugoslavia, which was also a highly sexist society. But in the friendless, highly ambitious schoolboy, cosseted by his over-protective mother and abandoned by his father, she saw the raw material that she could shape into a future leader. Mira's literary leitmotif was less Greek tragedy than Pygmalion.

'The relationship between Slobodan and Mira is very strong and quite pathological. Milosevic was intelligent enough, but Mira gave him the love for power, and the ambition. She made him what he is,' said Dusan Mitevic. An ebullient Serb from Kosovo, and one-time head of Belgrade Television, Mitevic was one of Milosevic's key behind-the-scenes political advisers, and a friend of both Milosevic and Mira, until the two men broke in the early 1990s. 'But to understand their relationship you must understand its start. She was from one of the most Communist families in Serbia. His father was religious. These are Serbia's two ideological opposites. When they came together she poured all her left-wing ideology into him, and he accepted it.'[5]

After graduating from high school at Pozarevac, Milosevic went to Belgrade University to study law. There he took a room in a student hostel among the concrete wastelands of New Belgrade, built to cope with the post-war housing shortage in the capital. Most students shared three or four to a room. As a full party member, Milosevic used his connections to obtain a single room. This was a considerable privilege. The first stirrings of a generational change were taking place in Yugoslavia when Milosevic arrived at university during the early 1960s. Those born in the war years enjoyed a full education, unbroken by wars or invasions. There were 65,000 students enrolled at Belgrade University. Milosevic was one of many ambitious young party members to arrive in the big city and consider possible future career paths in politics, or running a state-owned enterprise.

The Communist grandees had clearly laid out the path to career success for Milosevic and his fellow students. The party issued instructions which were to be followed, not questioned. When economic reforms were introduced during the 1960s, party activists explained them to their fellow members. Loyalty to the decisions of the party leader, and patience, were the most useful assets for a young apparatchik. The rewards could be considerable: a new flat, a good job running a hospital or a factory, even an ambassadorship abroad for those who followed the party line. This was all very cosy, but many of the early 1960s generation, often better educated and more sophisticated than their partisan elders, planned to jump the queue.

Slobodan's brother Borislav provided an easy entrée to the university's political elite. One of Borislav's best friends was Dusan Mitevic, then the president of the students' union. 'Slobodan always looked a bit nerdy, with his plummy face. He wore a white and shiny nylon shirt, the kind you can wash, and leave overnight, and a tie. He was always with Mira. I think that Mira was a kind of wall between him and other people. He never really had friends.' Borislav, in contrast, was hugely popular. He had grown into a tall and handsome young man, with dark hair and Slavic good looks. With his guitar and repertoire of songs, he was a must at every party. Borislav – Bora – had always been the one tipped for success, while Slobodan, most people assumed, would become a successful mid-level official.

Apart from Mira, perhaps the only true friend Slobodan Milosevic ever had was his fellow law student Ivan Stambolic. Stambolic was five years older, but like Milosevic he was from a provincial background and bright. Stambolic had worked in a factory in the southern city of Cacak and had come late to higher education. Unlike Milosevic he was not afraid of physical work. Although he was intelligent, Stambolic had studied at a technical school, rather than the usual secondary school. He was insecure about the gaps in his education and was not confident about his handwriting. While Milosevic wanted top marks in every subject, Stambolic was happy just to pass. Their personalities were quite different: Milosevic was somewhat distant, and always seemed to be calculating how best to exploit events for himself. Stambolic was much more popular, a warm and genuine person with a wide circle of friends. Yet somehow the two students struck up an alliance among the sometimes snobbish circles of Belgrade's political elite.

There was more. Stambolic's uncle Petar, a former President of Serbia, was, like Moma Markovic, one of the most powerful men in the country. Both men had perfect credentials as wartime Communist leaders. Milosevic well understood the value of these names.

In spring 1961, Milosevic took his first step up the ladder of party power that would, thirty years later, bring him to the very summit of Yugoslav politics. One day one of Milosevic's fellow law students, Nebojsa Popov, was walking through Tasmajden Park, just behind Belgrade Law School, with a colleague when he bumped into his friend Ivan Stambolic. During the 1990s Popov became a leading figure in the opposition, and a respected academic. But in the 1960s he was a young idealist who like many of his generation believed that Titoist Communism was humanity's great hope. Popov recalled: 'I had just been elected secretary of the Communist Party at the law faculty. I need someone to be my right hand, my organisational secretary as it was called. I was walking with Ivan and he told me that Slobodan would be the ideal candidate. Without knowing him, I accepted, because I had complete trust in Ivan.' Milosevic was soon offered the post. He accepted 'with delight', said Popov.[6]

Popov and Milosevic soon divided up the work. The relationship between the two men was broadly like that of a regional company president and his chief executive officer. As party secretary Popov was responsible for implementing the instructions issued by the Communist hierarchy, and keeping things on the right political track. Milosevic's job was to sort out the day-to-day business of organising the administration. Although Popov was theoretically his superior, Milosevic controlled the minutiae of organisation. He kept records of who attended party meetings, processed applications for membership and controlled the flow of endless paperwork that Communist bureaucracy generates. Used correctly, the job of organisational secretary could be turned into an immensely powerful position. Encouraged by Mira, Milosevic set about doing just that.

By the early 1960s, the repression had eased off. Tito's country was still a one-party state, to be sure, complete with secret police and a stultified bureaucracy, but compared to East Germany or Czechoslovakia there was considerable room for manoeuvre for those who wished to push the boundaries of freedom. Popov did. Milosevic did not. Popov and his colleagues organised controversial debates and theatre performances that tested the limits of Titoist tolerance. Amphitheatre number five of the Belgrade law faculty was soon a centre of Belgrade agit-prop. 'Like many party activists at that time, I thought the party could be somewhere to do something about bringing culture to the wider public,' said Popov. We were naïve, but we believed the party could help promote culture and intellectual values. We thought our basic job was to widen the education of both party members and ordinary students. We organised debates and theatre performances, and they were packed. Students came from all over Belgrade, not just from our university.'

These were exciting times, with something of the air of post-1917 revolutionary Moscow, when Vladimir Mayakovsky had draped Moscow in red banners and brought theatre to the workers. 'We staged performances in amphitheatre five, and then we asked the actors to stay. Then the audience, the actors and the directors all discussed the play and the performance. We concentrated on ethical and political problems. For some of us, this was the most important thing we could do as party activists.'

Not for Milosevic. The last thing the dutiful, pedantic junior apparatchik was interested in was radical theatre that inspired creativity and innovation. Instead of challenging evenings at amphitheatre five, he attended seminars on party organisation and the structure of the hierarchy. He soon became known as a 'cyclist', a term then current for a typical party functionary who bowed his head under authority, but pushed down hard on the pedals – those underneath them in the party hierarchy.

Zivan Berisavljevic was another university friend of Borislav Milosevic. Berisavljevic, from the northern city of Novi Sad, later became Yugoslav ambassador to London. 'When Slobodan was mentioned it was as Bora's little brother. I knew him superficially then and hardly remember him from those days, he was too pale and marginal. But there is an African proverb, the higher the monkey climbs, the redder his arse gets. It means the more you climb up, the more you are observed and analysed.'[7]

In later years Milosevic would be more observed and analysed than any other figure in Yugoslav history, apart perhaps from Tito. In some ways the young Milosevic resembled Stalin, a man initially – and how wrongly – categorised by his rivals as so unremarkable, he was dubbed the 'grey blur'. Like Stalin, Milosevic initially preferred to operate behind the scenes. Both men spent much time studying and mastering the mechanism of the apparat – as the party structure was known – its cell structure, the party hierarchy, and the way the party 'line' was developed, as a prelude to eventually taking power.

On a personal level, Milosevic and Stalin also share a history of paternal deprivation, together with a whole range of twentieth-century political leaders, including Bill Clinton and Saddam Hussein. Psychologists argue that an absentee father is likely to produce feelings of low self-esteem in a young boy. A child will question why his father has left, or does not want to be with him. The lack of a suitable domestic male role model also means the child is deprived of guidance in forming relationships in the wider world. In later life this can create a powerful drive to overcompensate. Some will seek to validate their self-worth through sexual promiscuity. Others enter politics.

Like Mira Markovic, Milosevic certainly had little contact with his father, who left Pozarevac for good in 1947. Perhaps a provincial background and dysfunctional paternal relationship is a requirement for a career as a political leader. Stalin, born Josef Dugashvili, passed a miserable childhood in the Georgian city of Gori, where he was beaten by his drunken cobbler father and brought up by his mother. Bill Clinton never knew his father, a travelling salesman who was killed in a car crash before he was born. Bill Clinton's stepfather, Roger Clinton, was an alcoholic and a gambler who beat his wife. Saddam Hussein, born in the village of Tikrit in northern Iraq was abused by his stepfather, who prevented him from going to school, made him herd sheep and called him a son of a dog. Names too, seem to play a role. Saddam translates as 'one who confronts'. Dugashvili later chose the name Stalin, meaning 'man of steel', even though he was short, with a withered arm. Perhaps it was mordant Balkan wit then, that gave Slobodan Milosevic a first name that translates as 'freedom'.

In 1962, tragedy struck the Milosevic family. Isolated and alone in Montenegro, Svetozar slid into depression and shot himself in the head with a pistol. Svetozar was a deeply religious man, who took comfort in the spirituality of Serbian orthodoxy. One of the key tenets of Orthodoxy is a sense of continuity and affirmation. The sonorous chants, contemplative tradition, even the wafts of incense that characterise an Orthodox mass are all threads in a spiritual cord of faith, stretching through the centuries, from the time of Jesus right to the present day.

In Communist Yugoslavia, across the Balkans, that link was severed. For believers, Marxism was no substitute. Svetozar left a suicide note, which his sister Darinka found, explaining his decision. Like so many of his generation. Svetozar Milosevic had seen his life torn apart by the war, and he had never been able to make his peace with the new order, said his older son Borislav. 'The death of my father was a surprise. It was not a straightforward event. For him, the war was the central event of his life. After that the old world was broken, and there was a new one that he did not understand. His ambitions and intentions were different, and he was not satisfied, because his life lacked enough activity and meaning. There were many people in the same situation, but most did not do what my father did.'[8]

Borislav was closer to his father than Slobodan was, and greatly missed him when he returned to Montenegro. In 1954, after graduating from secondary school, Borislav had spent a memorable summer with his father, walking and talking in the hills. Stanislava had encouraged Borislav to join the Communist youth movement, but he was still his father's son. He wondered about theology and spiritual matters. Svetozar told him about the philosopher Immanuel Kant, but said that some mysteries could never be fully understood, quoting Emil du-Bois Raymond's epigram, 'Ignoramus et ignorabimus', 'we are and shall be ignorant'. Borislav recalled: 'I asked him about God. He told me that the church says something different, but I should know that Jesus of Nazareth was not born as the son of God. He was born as a normal man. He became a perfect man, he was Christ, the Messiah, but he was a genuine man, a man like me, who then became Christ the Messiah.' In Svetozar's own theology there is perhaps an echo of the universal, humanist ideals that drew many to Communism in those days.

So restless and unhappy was Svetozar Milosevic that he tried to make a new life in the West. He wrote to Belgrade, requesting a passport. The request was refused. Svetozar then left Yugoslavia illegally. He travelled to France, but was quickly arrested and expelled. 'Because he was a man over fifty years old, without a passport he was not allowed to stay,' said Borislav. 'The police extradited him back to Yugoslavia. He spent several months in prison, for crossing the border illegally.'

Slobodan only went to see his father once in Montenegro, after graduating from secondary school, according to Mira. 'His mother thought it would not be a good idea to keep too much in contact with his father. Their relations were pretty loose, but that was mostly his mother's decision.' Slobodan, away on a study trip, did not attend Svetozar's funeral. Nor has he made any effort to keep a relationship with the many relatives who share his name in his father's home village. Suicide was stigmatised in conservative Montenegro. Outside the immediate family neither Slobodan nor Borislav discussed the death of their father by his own hand. Their friends, such as Dusan Mitevic, did not mention the subject, and it would have been bad manners to do so. 'I did not find out from Bora that their father had committed suicide, because it was seen as something shameful. Someone else told me.'

The names of both of Svetozar's sons are inscribed on his tombstone: 'To a brother and father. With broken hearts and pain in our souls we build this as a symbol of our eternal remembrance. Your sister Darinka and sons Borislav and Slobodan.'

3

BUILDING IN

First Steps up the Party Ladder
1962–77

Milosevic would have long telephone conversations with Mira at the Communist Party office in the law school. Or rather, she would speak most of the time. He would say 'yes' or 'no'.

Nebojsa Popov, fellow law student at Belgrade university in the early 1960s.[1]

Milosevic's first real political success was the affair of Tito's Secret Letter. This may sound like a 1930s thriller by Eric Ambler, but would make a fine title for the kind of Communist comic opera staged nowhere better than the Balkans. In March 1962 the Yugoslav leader had written a closed letter, for party members' eyes only, about a mini-crisis that had erupted in the complicated power structure of the Yugoslav state. This was an event of high drama. Special couriers were despatched to pick up a copy of the document which could not fall into the hands of non-party members. Telephones shrilled from Slovenia to Macedonia, as time-serving functionaries struggled to work out the implications for their careers once the letter landed on their desks.

The party then organised meetings to discuss the crisis. These meetings were open to the general public, but only party members could know about Tito's secret letter and its contents. Any party member who inadvertently mentioned its existence to a non-party member would be expelled from the party in disgrace. How the government crisis could be discussed by the general public when only party members had been informed of what was happening – or what their leaders said was happening – was just one of the many opaque mysteries of life in a Communist state. Either way, all this gave vast scope for intrigue, double-dealing and denunciations. The party Organisational

Secretary lived up to his title. Milosevic thrived in this conspiratorial atmosphere, according to Nebojsa Popov. All the necessary arrangements for distributing the letter and setting up the meetings to discuss its contents were faultlessly planned and implemented. Popov said: 'He enjoyed every minute of it.'

Milosevic was also happy to carry out the less popular duties of an organisational secretary, of implementing party discipline, said Popov. Unruly members could be suspended, or expelled from the party, which could have serious implications for their future career. 'Milosevic did not have a problem with this. On the contrary, he liked pronouncing strict disciplinary measures,' said Popov.

Buoyed by his success, Milosevic decided it was time to position himself in public. He chose the occasion of a nationwide debate organised in 1963 by the Communist Party on renaming the country, then known as the Federal People's Republic of Yugoslavia. The word 'People's', felt some comrades, was not sufficiently ideologically zealous. It had echoes of the post-war era of the 'Popular Front'. Every country in the world had its own people, and most were in any case republics. Party officials suggested a new name: the Federal Socialist Republic of Yugoslavia. A directive went out from Belgrade across the country: comrades are expected to organise and attend meetings to discuss the proposal. Young cadre members such as Milosevic were particularly encouraged to take part, though only within the boundaries of Marxist orthodoxy, of course. Any proposal, for example, to rename the country the Kingdom of Serbs, Croats and Slovenes, as it had been known until 1929, would not have been well received.

The meeting at Belgrade law faculty followed the standard pattern. The party grandees lined up on the podium outlined the reasons for the name-change proposal to the rows of students in front of them. Most of the audience nodded sagely. But Milosevic had a better idea. Would it not be better, he asked, to put the word 'Socialist' first, to stress the country's political orientation? Let Yugoslavia be called the Socialist Federal Republic of Yugoslavia, he proclaimed. This brings to mind the scene in Monty Python's *Life of Brian* when one revolutionary becomes confused as to whether he is a member of the Judean People's Front or the hated 'splitters', the People's Front of Judea. Not to mention the Judean Popular People's Front. But that satire is funny precisely because it draws on the Marxist obsession with tiny delineations of *nomenklatura* that demonstrate the 'correct' ideological rigour. The twenty-two-year-old

Milosevic was not known for his sense of humour, but his political antennae were well tuned. His proposal was duly forwarded to the constitutional commission dealing with the matter and then ratified by parliament. Milosevic's fellow students looked anew at the man in the white nylon shirt and polyester tie.

Just as noticeable was Milosevic's close bond at university with Mira Markovic. They were infatuated with each other. Former friends and associates of Milosevic point knowingly to the fact that Mira is the only girlfriend he ever had. This is considered highly unusual in the still deeply macho society of the Balkans where women are expected to adopt a traditional role of home-maker while men are not necessarily expected to stay faithful. Even now it is common in Yugoslav homes for women to serve food to the menfolk, retire to another room and eat later among themselves, as in the Middle East.

In Pozarevac Stanislava Milosevic began to feel neglected. Her son visited less, preferring to spend his weekend in the capital with his girlfriend. The two women did not get on. Mira guarded her time with Milosevic jealously. She had a curious hold on him.

The other students joked about his devotion, said Tibor Varady, a contemporary of Milosevic at Belgrade University. If a Communist Party meeting ran over time Milosevic would rush to the telephone to tell Mira that he would be late. 'We are a macho society, so this was observed with some cynicism,' observed Varady, who was briefly Yugoslav minister for justice in 1992, before becoming a professor at the Central European University in Budapest. 'His attachment to her was unusual. In Belgrade, in the 1960s, even if you were absolutely infatuated you would not show such an obvious sign of "weakness". The Communist Party then was pretty much a male party, and he was politically aware of these implications, but the bond between them was very strong.'[2]

While still at university, Milosevic and Mira celebrated New Year with Ivan Stambolic and his girlfriend. Stambolic described Mira as 'an unusual girl', Nebojsa Popov said. She refused to drink a small glass of home-distilled brandy. Such a refusal is usually considered a serious snub across eastern and central Europe, where great pride is taken in turning the harvest of plums, pears or apricots into fruit brandy. 'She said, "I don't drink plebeian drinks".' Popov recalled. 'This was a kind of quasi-aristocratic behaviour, ridiculous at those times. Maybe she was used to better things on Tito's island of Brioni.' And surprising, perhaps, for such a self-proclaimed leftist.

At university Mira sometimes seemed to live in a kind of regal parallel universe, a trait that would greatly increase over the next decades. Inconvenient or unwelcome aspects of reality would simply be blotted out. Popov remembered he first met Mira when he went to visit Milosevic when he was ill and stuck in his room in the student hostel. Mira had arrived empty handed, which was considered poor manners. 'Slobodan complained he was hungry, so I asked Mira why she did not bring anything with her, as she knew he was ill. She calmly said everything was closed in Belgrade because it was Sunday. I said there were kiosks selling food in front of the residences. She said she had not seen them.'

After graduating from Belgrade University in 1964, Milosevic completed his year of national service, as every Yugoslav male was required to do. He was sent to the seaside town of Zadar, on the Croatian coast. Recruits at the college for junior army officers were given six months' officer training before emerging as lieutenants. Milosevic did not greatly enjoy his time in the army. At university he got a nine or ten in most subjects but in military skills he only scored seven. Considering the later course of events in Yugoslavia this was quite ironic. As Dusan Mitevic noted: 'The student who got his worst marks for pre-military training ended up as the commander-in-chief.'

Slobodan and Mira Markovic married in March 1965, while she was in her third year at university. (A daughter, Marija, was born later that year.) At the wedding, Ivan Stambolic was Milosevic's *kum*, which is the equivalent of best man, but *kum* has a deeper, Balkan, intensity. It means something like blood brother, that the two men are bonded for life. Photos of them together show Milosevic looking uncharacteristically happy, embracing his friend. Mira was more troubled about Milosevic's friendship with Ivan Stambolic. She wanted all of Slobodan for herself. She was jealous of Milosevic's ties with Stambolic, said Popov. 'That got on her nerves. It was her ambition to be a Pygmalion. If someone was to make something out of that little boy, it would be her, not Ivan.'

Mira made the trek from Belgrade to Zadar as often as she could. An incident on one visit has now entered Yugoslav folklore. Walking across the main square of Zadar, together with a cousin, Mira saw a picture of Tito in a shop window. 'That's where my Slobodan's picture will be one day,' she reportedly said. Her cousin was startled. At this time, barely twenty years after the end of the war, Tito was considered unassailable, a leader whose place was assured for years to come. Mira herself described it as 'an ordinary fiction' and denied it took place. 'It is like if I one day said I would have blonde hair. Everything you read like this is not true.'[3]

At this time Yugoslav politics were turned upside down. In 1966 Tito sacked his former partisan comrade, Aleksandar Rankovic, the Serb head of the UDB (the domestic secret police) for twenty years. Rankovic, like every intelligence chief in a Communist country, was an extremely powerful figure. A former tailor with little education, Rankovic approved neither of Yugoslavs travelling abroad nor of western tourists – who surely included spies – being allowed into Yugoslavia.

Tito was introducing economic reforms. These liberalised the Yugoslav economy, based on the principle of workers' self-management. Instead of rule by western capitalists or Soviet-type bureaucrats, the factories would belong directly to the workers. But such idealism was hard to implement when there were no clear principles defining the system, and it did not observe basic economic laws of supply and demand. Tito's reforms aimed to loosen state control, and allow some firms to keep more of their hard currency profits. It was a kind of 'market socialism', and a logical step in the country's liberalisation.

Many believed that Rankovic was obstructing Tito's plans. The Yugoslav military counter-intelligence service, known as KOS, had put Rankovic under surveillance. The evidence they presented to Tito was enough to convince him to sack Rankovic. This was KOS's revenge for Rankovic's purge of 1948 when he had removed supposed Stalinists from the military. Rankovic was even accused of bugging Tito's bedroom.

More significantly, the fall of Rankovic, and the subsequent political easing, released much deeper stresses in the Yugoslav state. In the Croatian capital Zagreb restless nationalists saw the sacking of Rankovic as a signal. They declared that Croatian was a separate language from Serbian. Yugoslavia's official language at that time was Serbo-Croat, unified and codified by Joint Agreement signed by Serbs and Croats in 1850. The language was written in Latin in the Catholic Croatian lands, while in Orthodox Serbia and Montenegro the Cyrillic script predominated. In the late 1960s, Croatian nationalists sought to maximise the slight differences in Serbian and Croatian usage. But the fact remains that the language is linguistically one, with different 'variants' evolved in different historical circumstances. In the Balkans, as throughout the world where language helps define national identity, these are political, not linguistic questions. By 1971 a wave of popular patriotism had swept through Croatia, a period known as the 'Croatian Spring'. Just as medieval theologians had discussed how many angels can dance on the head of a pin, Croat intellectuals agonised in nit-picking semantics over the wording of the definition of the Croatian nation, meaning basically whether or not the Serbs who lived in Croatian territories could be considered Croats. In Belgrade there were increasing fears of civil unrest, and worse. The Croatian Communist Party was purged, the nationalist leaders, among them future president Franjo Tudjman, were imprisoned.

In the Albanian-majority province of Kosovo, Rankovic had been hated for running a pure police state, with much harsher repression than in the rest of Yugoslavia. Kosovo Albanians made up about three-quarters of Kosovo's population, but unlike Serbs or Croats, they did not have their own republic. Kosovo was merely a region of southern Serbia, ruled from Belgrade. It was one of the poorest regions in Yugoslavia, left behind in the waves of modernisation further north. Most government officials, and almost all of the police, were Serbs. The Serbs were fearful that the Kosovo Albanians were plotting either to unite with the neighbouring ultra-Stalinist regime of Enver Hoxha, in Albania, or to secede from Yugoslavia by force.

With Rankovic out of the way, repression eased. Kosovo Albanian nationalist prisoners were released and rehabilitated. An Albanian language university opened in the capital Pristina, and contacts began with Albania itself. Kosovo Albanians were appointed to the police and government positions. Massive state subsidies poured in from Belgrade. Emboldened by their success. Kosovo Albanian nationalists drew up long-term plans for secession and eventual independence.

In Belgrade, the opening to the West and the financial aid that flowed in had inevitably brought in its wake other contributions. The theoretical journal *Praxis* began to challenge Marxist orthodoxy. In 1968, as in Paris, London and Berlin, student riots erupted on the streets of the capital. They condemned the war in Vietnam and demanded that Yugoslav universities be turned into revolutionary Marxist institutions. Such scenes in a Communist country, even liberal Yugoslavia, were unimaginable. The situation was slipping out of control. There were dangerous precedents. In Hungary students had been in the vanguard of the 1956 revolution that had eventually triggered a Soviet invasion.

The Serbian political leader Petar Stambolic, uncle of Ivan, demanded that Belgrade University be closed down and the troops sent in. Tito, the grandmaster of Balkan politics, appeared on television. He declared to an incredulous nation that not only did *he* support the students, but if their demands were not met, he would resign. The joyous students went home. It was a move of deft duplicity. A fortnight later Tito demanded that the professors around *Praxis* magazine be sacked, for 'corrupting' Yugoslavia's youth. The attack on *Praxis* heralded a massive purge of reformist Communists, known as the Serbian liberals. Like Mikhail Gorbachev more than a decade later, they wanted a greater role for the nascent market forces in the economy, more freedom of speech. 'Tito was afraid. He thought this was the result of bad foreign influences, that intellectuals and technocrats were challenging the power of the party and leaning towards western democracy,'4 said Aleksandar Nenadovic, a former editor of the daily newspaper *Politika*.

The liberals lost. They had progressive, modern ideas, but the hardliners had the army, parliament and the police. With hindsight it is clear that the defeat of the Serbian liberals was a key moment, both in the history of Yugoslavia and in the subsequent rise of Milosevic. Had Tito allowed further liberalisation, no matter how cautious, he would have strengthened those who wanted to further modernise and westernise Yugoslavia. Instead he reverted to Communist authoritarianism.

With his military service out of the way, Milosevic had began working for the Belgrade municipal government. Meanwhile Mira gained a doctorate in sociology at the University of Nis in southern Serbia, which later landed her a post as professor of sociology at Belgrade University. The family moved to a small one-room flat in New Belgrade, among the concrete tower blocks that had been built to ease the capital's chronic housing shortage after the Second World War.

Tito's Yugoslavia in these years, the early 1970s, was a very different place from that of the early post-war era. The cult of Tito was unchallengeable, but even after the defeat of the Serbian liberals, his dictatorship was a soft one compared with orthodox Communist countries. Life was very different from East Germany under Erich Honecker, where mines and sharpshooters guarded the Berlin Wall, or Ceausescu's Romania where flats were unheated for months on end, women were required to have five children, and abortion and contraception were banned.

To some extent, Tito's relatively lax dictatorship was shaped by national temperament. Such terms are hard to quantify, but Yugoslavia was essentially a Mediterranean country. Across the Balkans, as in Spain or southern Italy, life was lived at a slower, more relaxed pace. Great value was placed on human relationships. This was especially true in the more southern and eastern Yugoslav republics such as Serbia, Bosnia and Macedonia, with their Ottoman heritage. It was even true of Slovenia and Croatia, too, if to a lesser extent, though they were also prone to occasional outbursts of Germanic rigour. If anything, the Communist system of state planning accentuated Yugoslavia's *mañana* syndrome: the state would provide, things would sort themselves out, and there was always time for another coffee, cigarette, and a chat. In short, there was simply little or no national appetite in Yugoslavia for a Soviet-type intrusive regime.

For many Yugoslavs these were the golden years. Although inflation ate away at people's earnings, families began to acquire the requisites of modern urban life: washing machines, fridges and televisions came to even remote villages. Access to hard currency made them the envy of their Communist neighbours. Tito may even have won free elections, had he risked holding them, said Tibor Varady. 'Most university students believed in the philosophy of the non-aligned movement, and life was improving in those times. Real wages were climbing year after year, and whether it was because of good economic policies, international loans or other assistance, we were far ahead of any other eastern European country.'

Out of the political arena, in everyday matters, Yugoslavs enjoyed an atmosphere of comparative laissez-faire. There was an unspoken accord between the state and its subjects: as long as the monopoly of the Communist Party was not challenged, and the correct protocol of obeisance was observed, things would be as comfortable as possible. The key difference between Yugoslavia and other communist states was that Yugoslavia had open borders. A country with open borders can no longer be described as a dictatorship as its citizens are free to leave. The question is whether they will come back.

During the 1970s hundreds of thousands of Yugoslavs left for the car factories of Germany and Austria, and the construction sites of the Middle East and Asia. As guestworkers they usually lived in dormitories, several to a room to save as much of their wages as possible and send funds back to their families. But when their contracts ended, they did come home, often bringing enough money to build a house. Across the country, stacks of bricks and lumber soon piled up by churning cement mixers.

Concrete skeletons sprouted across fields and verges. Once ramshackle villages boasted streets of modern multi-roomed villas, all paid for with wages from BMW and Mercedes, and the Gulf oil states.

Mira recalled those halcyon days: 'The country in which I lived when I was a high school student, a university student, where my children were born, was a wonderful country. First of all because it was one of the rare societies that was aware of the perspective lying ahead. We had a very good life and it was for example then, but we were sure that it was going to be an even better life tomorrow, that was our vision.'

The traffic at Yugoslavia's borders was two way. Under pressure from Croatia and Slovenia, the two most westward-looking republics, the country opened up to mass western tourism. Visitors from all over Europe poured in to enjoy Croatia's beautiful beaches and archipelago of islands dotted across the Adriatic, Slovenia's lakes and mountains, and Bosnia's tranquil Ottoman architecture. English and German were widely spoken. The exodus of guestworkers, the mass influx every summer of foreign tourists, and the western loans on which the economy increasingly relied, also subtly changed Yugoslavia's political atmosphere. It was no longer credible, or even desirable, to attack the West as imperialists, planning to destroy the workers' paradise.

'We were building a more human, a better form of socialism, because we were squeezed between the East and the West. Our country was described as a salon, or entry-chamber of Communism. That's how the West spoke about us. For a long time I thought that Yugoslavia could serve as a model for the establishment of European union, for connecting the countries within Europe some time in the future,' said Mira. 'I hoped to write a lot, and have beautiful children. Also, I hoped for a lot of friends, and to have an open home that would always be filled with people. And as far as I was concerned, that was the case.'

In Pozarevac, Milosevic's mother Stanislava had few visits from friends or family. She became increasingly depressed until, in 1974, she hanged herself at the family home, at the age of sixty-two. She had been passed over for a promotion at the school where she taught, and it is possible that her fractured marriage, and the departure of Slobodan and Borislav, had counted against her. 'Stanislava was a very ambitious Communist, and she was in line for a promotion. But in the end she did not get it, and one reason was that she had been left alone, with no husband and no sons living with her,' said Dusan Mitevic.[5]

Although Stanislava had long been separated from her husband Svetozar, his suicide ten years earlier had also profoundly affected her. She spent much time reading, but her eyesight began to fade. Milosevic rarely visited. Just as with Ivan Stambolic, Mira was jealous of Milosevic having any other close emotional ties. 'People who know them say that when Stanislava went to visit Slobo in Belgrade, Mira left the apartment the minute Stanislava stepped inside,' said Milica Kovac.[6]

The death of his mother was one of the few occasions when Milosevic is known to have shown emotion. According to Ljubica Markovic, Mira's half-sister, Slobodan blamed himself for her suicide. 'My mother later told me that Slobodan was completely upset, and said he was guilty, that he didn't go to visit her enough, she was lonely, that he should have given her more time.'[7] Apparently Mira's response to the news that Stanislava had committed suicide, and to her husband's grief and self-recrimination, was icier. 'My mother told me that Mira told Slobodan to put it out of his head, that it was nothing to do with him, and that it was his mother's decision,' said Ljubica. Mira herself said she had nothing but praise for her mother-in-law. 'It was terrible for Slobodan when she died, because she was his mother. She had some heart trouble, but she was not very old. She was still active in school. She was a proud and modest woman, who was very diligent and dedicated to her sons. A brave person and a serious one. I had and still have the best opinion of her.'

The following year, Yugoslavia ratified a new constitution, which was to have a major effect on the course of Yugoslav history. The class struggle was fading, and the nationalist one was stirring. At this time, the very notion of what Yugoslavia actually meant was changing. The anger and resentment the 1974 constitution provoked among Serb nationalists later helped fuel Milosevic's rise to power. It also accelerated the decentralisation of Yugoslavia and the subsequent weakening of the federal power structure. It encouraged the competing nationalists in each republic to press for an ever larger slice of the federal cake. Arguably, it heralded the break-up of Yugoslavia itself.

Under the 1974 constitution Yugoslavia remained a federal state composed of six republics – Serbia, Croatia, Bosnia-Herzegovina, Slovenia, Macedonia and Montenegro – and two autonomous provinces within Serbia: Kosovo in the south and Voivodina in the north. But it devolved further power away from the centre, that is the federal capital Belgrade, to the six republics and the two provinces. Each of these had its own Communist Party, national bank, judicial system and so on. Kosovo and Voivodina essentially became republics in all but name. The republics were given the power of veto over any piece of federal – that is, nationwide – legislation of which they did not approve. Yugoslav citizens were even required to choose citizenship of one republic, as well as being a citizen of Yugoslavia itself. The *kljuc*, or key, system was supposed to prevent the domination of any one republic within the federation. It was based on representatives of the different republics filling federal posts on a rotating quota basis. This was similar in principle to the positive discrimination policies of universities in the United States, which favour minority students and set aside a number of places for students of different ethnicities.

But by setting quotas for each republic, and forcing Yugoslavs to define their own national identity, the key system bolstered the very nationalism it was supposed to counter. Each republic increasingly began to consider its own interests rather than those of Yugoslavia as a whole. Here again was the classic contradiction of the Yugoslav ideal, in fact the age-old problem of running an empire of ethnically diverse provinces. A strong centralised state that suppressed the six republics' political power would eventually trigger a resentful nationalist backlash. But a weak, decentralised state that offered the republics greater autonomy would encourage them to press for more, until ultimately they demanded independence.

The answer to this contradiction was the emergence of a strong Yugoslav identity and loyalty that could counter nationalism. To some extent this did begin to happen. Mixed marriages were increasingly common. What could the child of a Serb father and Croat mother be except a Yugoslav? By 1981 over three million people out of the total population of twenty-two million were either in a mixed marriage, or the children of such a union. A distinct Yugoslav culture was also emerging that reflected the complexity and cultural sophistication of the new state. A post-war generation of writers such as the Nobel laureate Ivo Andric, or the Serbian-Jewish author Danilo Kis were widely read from Slovenia to Macedonia. Rock groups such as Sarajevo's Blue Orchestra and Belgrade's Fish Soup toured the whole country to a rapturous reception, sometimes selling half a million copies of their latest release. Daring and avant-garde theatre companies led by directors such as Ljubisa Ristic began to gain an international reputation.

Serbs bought holiday homes on Croatia's Adriatic coast. Slovenes went white-water rafting in Montenegro. But the question of the viability of the Yugoslavia idea will be debated for decades. Certainly its roots were deeper in sophisticated cities such as Belgrade, than in the villages and mountains. But Belgrade was not just the capital of Federal Yugoslavia, it was also the capital of Serbia. Serbian nationalists became increasingly angry at how their republic was being steadily weakened. Tito had constructed post-war Federal Yugoslavia's system of republics to prevent the country being dominated by Serbia, as pre-war Royal Yugoslavia had been. There was particular resentment in Serbia over the quasi-republic status of Kosovo and Voivodina, which were physically part of Serbia but were outside Serbia's political control with their own seats in the Federal presidency. Kosovo and Voivodina had a say in the government of Serbia, but Serbia had no control over them. Not only Federal Yugoslavia, but Serbia itself was being steadily weakened.

Tito's experiment in constitutional decentralisation was certainly brave and innovative. But even a state that was reasonably ethnically homogenous, with its own cohesive national identity, would have had problems governing in such a complex system. Yugoslavia was neither homogenous nor cohesive. Nationalism – once deliberately re-animated – would prove a powerful and more durable ideology than Yugoslavism.

4

THE CAPITALIST YEARS

Slobodan in America

1978–82

Two things impressed me about him: his readiness to listen and his readiness to learn.

Mihailo Crnobrnja, economic advisor to Milosevic, 1974–89.[1]

While Milosevic paper-pushed at the Belgrade city hall, his *kum* Ivan Stambolic was running Tehnogas. Tehnogas produced gases for industry, such as oxygen and argon. Stambolic soon brought Milosevic over to Tehnogas, and by the early 1970s Milosevic held a senior management post. Although working for Tehnogas was not as prestigious as working for the gigantic steel works and car factories in which Communist countries specialised, for Milosevic this was still a promotion. Tehnogas was a Yugoslav-wide company, with branches in Croatia, Bosnia and Macedonia as well as Serbia. It was well regarded internationally, a flagship Yugoslav enterprise.

It was understood that Milosevic was Stambolic's designated successor, and when Ivan left Tehnogas, Milosevic took over as president. Milosevic knew little about economics and even less about producing industrial gases. But he was a fast learner, according to Mihailo Crnobrnja, then an economic consultant at Tehnogas. A US educated professor of economics, Crnobrnja worked as a consultant at Tehnogas. He was one of Milosevic's key economic advisers from 1974 until 1989, when he was appointed Yugoslav ambassador to the European Union. Milosevic was a quick and adept student. 'His learning curve was in most cases very rapid. There were very few things that he needed to have repeated. If he was not dynamic, if he did not listen, I would not have bothered to work with him for so long.'

Milosevic's approach to managing Tehnogas was unusual for those

times. Although it was a liberal dictatorship, Yugoslavia still functioned
on Communist principles of command and control, imposed from the
top down. Yugoslav managers often tended to bark out their instructions
and regard questions or alternatives as insubordination. Milosevic had
adopted this approach at university, where he had a finely developed
sense of his own status, according to Nebojsa Popov. On a visit to a
motorway construction site, Milosevic refused to don the customary
workers' clothes or even loosen his tie, as it would diminish his prestige.
And he did not like his new nickname, 'Boban'. In Serbia, like all Slavic
countries, names are usually reduced to a diminutive, especially by
friends and family. When Popov and his colleagues addressed Milosevic
as 'Boban' he refused to answer, as he thought it lacked gravitas. The
more serious sounding 'Slobo' was more acceptable, he decided.

But there was none of this pomposity at Tehnogas, at least when dealing with senior managers. Milosevic wanted to do well, and was certainly
intelligent enough to realise that he, and Tehnogas, would flourish if
he drew on the expertise of those who had greater knowledge and
experience. Age and family responsibilities also played a role. The callow
university youth had matured. Milosevic's approach was thoughtful and
considered when chairing board meetings, said Crnobrnja. 'Throughout
my working relationship with him, he generally preferred to listen and
conclude at the end. He did not intervene often, and only on very few
occasions did he set the agenda in advance by using the technique of
"this is what I want to hear from you".'

Yet others, less useful to the chairman of the board, saw a different persona. The veteran Belgrade journalist Milos Vasic, then a young reporter
for the news weekly *Nin*, was despatched to interview two Tehnogas
engineers who had developed an innovative recycling process. Milosevic
insisted on sitting in on the interview. He was cold and unwelcoming.
'What I remember most of all was his very limp handshake, like giving
you a cold fish. He would not let them talk to the press alone, but sat
there probably not understanding a word of it. His behaviour was very
arrogant to those men,' Vasic remembered. 'They were technically his
subordinates, but in other aspects were much better men than him.
Milosevic made a very distinct negative first impression.'[2]

Milosevic became a skilled industrialist, but he found his true metier
as a capitalist when he left Tehnogas to become president of Udruzena
Beogradska Banka (UBB) in 1978. A conglomerate of nineteen banks,

UBB was one of the most important financial institutions in Yugoslavia, with extensive links abroad, including an office in New York. Milosevic asked Mihailo Crnobrnja to come with him, and set up a centre for economic research. Milosevic thrived at the bank. He quickly grasped the essential principles of high finance and capitalism and, with Crnobrnja's assistance, soon mastered his brief. He looked set for a successful career in finance, at an exciting time when Yugoslavia was opening its commercial and trade links with the West.

There was then no talk at home of a career in politics for her husband, claimed Mira. Milosevic was happy at UBB. Their paths were set. 'Fundamentally, he has the personality of a bank manager. He never thought much about being involved in politics. The structure of his personality can be described as a manager of a bank, although a modern and up-to-date bank, not an old-fashioned one, like a village bank. I saw myself then as a professor at the university, and a writer in the field of sociology. I saw him as a man in economics and finance, and that is the truth, if you want to believe it, believe it. I really don't know how these things happened to us.'[3]

At that time in Yugoslavia bankers, like all managers, were divided into two castes: the professionals, and the 'party' people. The professionals were trained experts who made their career in banking, who studied and understood the world of finance. The party bankers were loyal Communists, whose appointments were approved by the party. The right party connections such as Milosevic had, together with the support of Ivan Stambolic, could ensure a high position in a bank, a foreign trade company, a state utility like Tehnogas, all without any previous experience whatsoever. Milosevic, though, was well regarded by his peers in other banks. 'Communists always presented themselves as universal kinds of experts, but Milosevic was not like other bankers that appeared from political circles,' said Aca Singer, who was also making a name for himself as a banker, at the rival Ljubljanska Banka. 'I was interested in what kind of a banker he was, so I asked his associates, because subordinates always give the best estimate of their superiors. They told me Milosevic was very organised and he rose very quickly as a banker. He really wanted to learn the world of banking, and how it worked. But it would have been better for him, and better for the people here, if he had stayed as a banker.'[4]

Milosevic's move to UBB was well timed. In 1979 the World Bank and International Monetary Fund held its annual meeting in Belgrade.

Many westerners were keen to meet one of the new generation of Yugoslav bankers, who would drag the country's financial system into the twentieth century. At a meeting hosted by the then US ambassador to Belgrade, Lawrence Eagleburger, Milosevic met a small group of half a dozen top figures, including David Rockefeller of Chase Manhattan Bank. He easily held his own in the world of high-level international finance, said Mihailo Crnobrnja. 'There was a discussion for twenty, or twenty-five minutes. Milosevic spoke in very good English. He was not dogmatic, and I would say that he made a strong impression on David Rockefeller with what he had to say.'

UBB had opened an office in Manhattan, and Milosevic began to travel frequently to New York. There he grew to understand the West, how it works, and the value placed on good faith, and honesty perhaps better than any other Balkan politician. He learnt to schmooze and glad-hand, skills that served him well when western leaders courted his support. Milosevic admired the American 'can-do' ethos, in stark contrast to the torpor that often characterised Balkan communism. Wall Street, Rockefellers, Eagleburgers, all this was heady stuff for the boy from Pozarevac. There was also here a hint of the inferiority complex that even now bedevils the region's politicians. Leaders of small eastern European countries want nothing more than to be accepted as equals by the superpowers. In later years Milosevic always relished getting a telephone call from President Clinton, or a visit from the pugnacious American negotiator Richard Holbrooke, whose 'cut the crap' straightforward approach Milosevic found greatly appealing. In the banking world, he first found the respect he wanted.

At this time Mihailo Crnobrnja was UBB's chief economist. He became Milosevic's guide to the United States. 'He was fascinated by the efficiency, by the technical sophistication that he met every step of the way.' The long hours at university spent dissecting the power structures of the Communist party gave Milosevic an analytical understanding of organisations and hierarchy that was also useful for capitalism. Blessed with a good memory, Milosevic always prepared thoroughly for meetings, and even spoke without notes. 'When we met other bankers, Milosevic was sufficiently eloquent and knowledgeable to have them listen, not just out of courtesy, but with attention. I remember him as a man who did the job of a high-level banker well.'

Milosevic wanted to see more of the United States. He and Crnobrnja hired a car for the weekend. They drove to Boston and also visited

Harvard, which Milosevic compared favourably with his own alma mater, Belgrade University. He joked that 'Now when people ask me about my education, I can legitimately say I spent some time at Harvard!'

Despite her own leftist leanings, Mira was immensely proud of her husband's achievements 'He was a brilliant banker. Although I don't know much about banking, and I know nothing about finance, I saw that he looked like one of the future bankers of the world. He very quickly understood the ideas and skills of banking. He thought that to work in banking and the economic sector was to be at the top of one's career. He communicated with the most important bankers in the world.'

While it seems disingenuous to claim, as Mira does, that Milosevic never thought about a career in politics, there is an interesting ambiguity about Milosevic's capitalist years. Many accounts of Milosevic's career have portrayed him as single-mindedly dedicated to the pursuit of political power throughout his life. Certainly at school and during his university years he was a dogged apparatchik. But Milosevic's workplaces after university are not classic stages on the path to power in a Communist state. In a one-party system the only way up the political ladder is through the party. This was the path taken by Milosevic's contemporary, the Slovenian leader Milan Kucan. By 1978, when Milosevic took over UBB, Kucan was already president of the Slovene parliament. Kucan was steadily progressing on the long march through the institutions.

Milosevic was not. Tehnogas was a prestigious company but it brought no real political base with it. And to move from Tehnogas to a bank – in what was still a Communist country – was a curious choice. 'Where in socialism or communism, does a banker become head of state?' said Mihail Crnobrnja. 'It is unheard of. If you want to become head of the party, or head of state, you become a small political apparatchik, then a bigger and bigger one until you make it to the politburo. Politically speaking, Milosevic sat in relative oblivion for seventeen years, from 1967 to 1984.'

Of course Milosevic was ambitious, and wanted to build his political contacts. But Milosevic's life and career – at least at this time – like that of most people, was defined by luck, choice and opportunity as much as ruthless determination. Ivan Stambolic's influence certainly helped as well. It is notable that Stambolic also left Tehnogas for a position at a government commercial office. A new class was evolving in Yugoslavia, of technocrats, of adept managers with some understanding of how

business and economics really worked, skills that would also be vital
for a future generation of political leaders.

By this time, the Milosevic family had long left the concrete wastelands
of New Belgrade. The family had moved into a comfortable three-room
flat on December 14 Street, in Belgrade's city centre. But while there was
more space, it was still comparatively modest, for a bank president with
a wife and two young children. Marija was at school, and she now had
a brother, Marko, born in 1974. Apart from Milosevic's frequent travel
abroad – and his return was eagerly awaited by his children, not least
for the presents he brought – the Milosevic family life was similar to that
of their friends, said Mira. 'We were surrounded by people of the same
opinion. We did not differ much from the general atmosphere we all
lived in.'

Belgrade then was a buzzing, cosmopolitan city. Its grand avenues
offered a fine selection of contemporary theatre, and both Yugoslav
and foreign cinema. Unlike other eastern European capitals, there was
also a good selection of restaurants offering plentiful local produce. It
was bright and livelier than dismal Bucharest or comparatively sleepy
Budapest. Romanians and Hungarians came to Yugoslavia, amazed at
the range and choice of goods on offer and the variety of foodstuffs.
Milosevic himself was quite a gourmet, according to Dusan Mitevic.
He loved eating seafood, for which Yugoslavia is famous, washed down
with dry white wine, and also liked roast lamb and baby piglet on a spit.
Like Tito, Milosevic enjoyed a glass of whisky. Tito's favourite brand
was Chivas Regal, but Milosevic was less choosy. In many ways he was
a typical Serb, who relished a bountiful spread of food and drink, and
good company with whom he could enjoy it.' Mira was a trickier case,
as Milosevic's friends soon discovered. 'They have very different tastes
and it is difficult to please them when they are together,' said Mitevic.
'It is difficult to give her something to eat, because she is very fussy.'5

Like Gordon Brown, Milosevic spent some of his spare time reading
economics books, to further master his financial brief. His trips to the
United States had also given him a taste for American writers such
as Ernest Hemingway. Mira recalled: 'He prefers American literature,
mostly of the mid- and second half of the twentieth century.' Mira herself
loves Russian literature the most, preferably heavily laden with a good
dose of Slavic angst. Dostoevsky is her favourite author. In *Crime and
Punishment* and *The Brothers Karamazov* can be seen an echo of the

extremes of tragedy, truth and moral fulfilment that resonate through her schoolgirl favourite of *Antigone*. Mira takes a romantic view of the qualities of the Russian classics. 'They have a noblesse, a nobility of the soul, which only Slavs can understand. It's partly irrational, but we are also prone to forgive, without any reason, for we understand everything. An irrational emotional life, and an imbalance between reason and emotions, is a Slavic trait.' She also made the implausible claim, considering the course of recent events in Yugoslavia, that 'Slavic people who live in these areas have shown the least disrespect for other nations and other ethnic communities that they lived with.'

By building his international contacts, Milosevic was also following a wider trend among the Yugoslavian leadership. The 1970s were the golden years of Yugoslavia's diplomatic prestige. Belgrade was a centre of the non-aligned movement, composed of countries from the developing world which had emerged from foreign colonial rule but did not want to join the Soviet bloc. According to Yugoslav history books the movement was born in 1956 at a meeting between Tito, Prime Minister of Egypt, Gamal Abdel Nasser, and Jawaharlal Nehru, Prime Minister of India, on the island of Brioni, where Mira Markovic took her annual holidays with her father Momir. (Others date its inception to a summit in Bandung, Indonesia, the year before.) The movement was part of Tito's diplomatic balancing act, a third way between the Soviet bloc and the West. Tito watched both East and West warily, flitting back and forth like a village girl at a folk dance considering her suitors.

Non-aligned summits brought to Belgrade heads of state and diplomats from across Asia, Africa and the Middle East. Surrounded by gun-toting female bodyguards in tight-fitting combat uniforms, Colonel Gaddafi rode in on a white horse. In the late 1970s the Soviets unsuccessfully tried to hijack the non-aligned movement, through their client state Cuba. But Tito easily outmanoeuvred the clumsy Russian leaders, said Zivorad Kovacevic, who, as mayor of Belgrade between 1974 and 1982, was frequently present at Tito's meetings with foreign leaders. Tito's considerable international prestige allowed him to exhibit a low-key and understated style in his dealings with other foreign leaders, such as Algerian president Houari Boumedienne.

Boumedienne had arrived in Belgrade for a meeting of foreign ministers on the eve of the non-aligned summit in Havana in 1979 but was unwell. Tito did not trouble his guest with excessive protocol and unnecessary pleasantries. 'Boumedienne was very pale, and you could see he was in pain and suffering. There was silence for five, then ten minutes. Tito simply said to Boumedienne that the summit meeting would start the next day. He asked Boumedienne not to let the Cubans make trouble. Boumedienne told him not to worry. That was it,' recalled Kovacevic.[6] 'Boumedienne was a good French student. He knew all the procedures and the rules. Each time the Cuban foreign minister tried to take the floor, Boumedienne said the item was not on the agenda, told them not to make speeches, asked for a motion. It was a total fiasco for the Cubans, and everyone understood what was happening. For me this was symptomatic of Tito's approach. He did not bother his guest, he gave him a simple message, and it was sufficient. Tito was able to be very jovial and pleasant.'

Tito was Yugoslavia's greatest strength. He had built the state, knocking nationalist heads together, breaking with Moscow, turning to the West and opening Yugoslavia's borders. He had implemented the rotating key system, economic self-management and non-alignment, the three foundations of national, economic and foreign policy. His central role, however, was also Yugoslavia's greatest weakness. While Tito took an active role in politics, his prestige and authority was enough to keep his fractious satrapies together. But in the late seventies his involvement in affairs of government and state reduced, as age and infirmity took a growing toll on his health and energy. Seeking comfort not confrontation, he preferred entertaining foreign dignitaries in his string of villas, hunting lodges and mansions to Belgrade's political infighting. There the young lions circled, as the leader of the pride aged, and slowly weakened. Still he was unchallenged, and his word was law.

Sometimes there was no need for Tito to even speak to make his wishes known, as former Belgrade mayor, Zivorad Kovacevic, discovered when Tito asked to see him. So much milk was being sold to Greece at a profit, that there was not enough for the capital's schoolchildren. Embroiled in a political battle over the issue, Kovasevic publicly threatened to resign. The president asked to see him at eleven o'clock the next day. But when he arrived he found that Tito's office was empty. Eventually, Tito's chief of cabinet appeared and said that Tito had gone to his villa at Brioni. This was puzzling, so the official asked why he had been called in if Tito was not there. Tito's chief of cabinet said he had left something for his visitor.

It was a signed picture of the president. Kovacevic was baffled and said that he had not asked for a signed picture. Then he saw that it was personally dedicated, by name, with Tito's best wishes. Kovacevic returned to his office and his political enemies asked how his meeting with the president had gone. When they saw the signed picture, it was understood by all that no more milk would be diverted for sale to Greece. Supplies soon resumed to Belgrade's schoolchildren.

This episode encapsulates the Tito era as he reached the end of his life. Such was the power of his name that a mere photograph, with an absolutely unremarkable dedication, was enough to rescue Belgrade's mayor, and ensure supplies of milk for the city's schoolchildren. There was no need for telephone calls, or meetings. It was subtle, Ottoman in its simplicity, the work of a sultan rather than a Communist dictator. But the sultan was in Brioni, not Belgrade, running his empire by remote control. There was no son, no successor nominated to take over after his death. Tito's closest allies could not provide a new leader for Yugoslavia. Leaders such as Petar Stambolic or Draza Markovic were approaching the end of their political careers. Milosevic, like many, sensed the need for a generational change.

In May 1980, Tito died. During his last few months in hospital in Ljubljana he was kept alive by medical technology and received few visitors other than official delegations. But he was mourned in pomp and circumstance. His remains were sent across the country on a funeral train, draped in red, before being buried in Belgrade. From Macedonia to Slovenia, his citizens wept genuine tears: for themselves, for their country, and perhaps for the future they saw coming. Like all good Yugoslavs, Milosevic left his portrait of Josip Broz in place on the office wall after his death. For the moment there was no suitable replacement. Such a picture had saved Belgrade's mayor, but it would not be enough to save Yugoslavia.

Meanwhile, Milosevic needed to learn more about the technicalities of controlling money flow. Crnobrnja had taught Milosevic about economics, but for the mechanics of loan financing and syndicated credits he needed another mentor, Borka Vucic. Now in her seventies, Vucic is a former teenage partisan turned capitalist. She boasts of knowing hundreds of bankers throughout the world and keeps a silver plate once given to her by Barclays Bank. 'Borka Vucic was a great teacher. She was the best banker in Yugoslavia, and she helped Milosevic because she was already working at Beogradska Banka when Milosevic arrived.

Under her Milosevic learnt a lot, how to think in a western way about the economy,' said Dusan Mitevic.

Vucic was a moderniser who wanted to remodel Yugoslavia's creaking state-owned and subsidised banks into financially viable institutions. But such ambitions were hard to implement when there were no clear principles defining the Yugoslav economy, and it did not observe basic economic laws of supply and demand. The doctrine of workers' self-management eventually degenerated into total confusion over who owned or managed what. So complicated did this system become that the Law of Associated Labour, which governed the system in the 1970s, had 671 articles.

The combination of state funds and no clear chain of responsibility for their disbursement encouraged local financial kingpins to build their own mini-economic empires. The policy of economic decentralisation encouraged the growth of patronage and nepotism. Party bosses would sanction the building of a factory for political reasons, to bring jobs and boost a local economy, even if it might be totally unviable economically. The system soon became mired in endemic corruption, and the situation was not helped by Yugoslavia's six republic governments each arguing for a larger slice of the federal economic cake. The capitalist reality was much clearer: western loans and financial aid kept Yugoslavs in fridges.

Milosevic was known as a loyal official of the Communist system that had created this economic mess. Unlike Crnobrnja, who had worked with Milosevic at Tehnogas, Vucic and other managers at Beogradska Banka were initially frightened of Milosevic. They believed he would immediately sack them, according to William Montgomery, a US ambassador to Belgrade who was the American embassy's banking specialist in the late 1970s. He knew both Borka Vucic and Milosevic well. 'Borka Vucic was our primary contact. I liked her, she and the rest of the bank's management were trying to make the bank more modern. We had good relations with her.'[7]

The fears of Vucic and her colleagues were groundless. Not only Yugoslav bankers such as Aca Singer, but also westerners observed how deftly Milosevic played the system to boost both Beogradska Banka and his own standing. Bolstered by his support in the Communist Party, he boldly dragged Beobank into the harsh world of genuine capitalist economic competition. The old comrades muttered, but with Ivan Stambolic behind him, Milosevic seemed impregnable. 'He took a very active interest. He established relations that enabled Beogradska Banka to make great progress in terms of being a more western bank, and to compete with other banks. His position in the Communist Party gave him freedom of movement to allow Beobank to be more western orientated than other banks,' said Montgomery.

Borka Vucic and Milosevic soon became close. Vucic's son had died at the age of twenty-six, and she poured her maternal instincts into looking after Milosevic. 'There was a strong emotional bond. Milosevic became her substitute son, and he accepted her, although the tie was more on her side than his. He loved her dearly, although not as a mother, though by age she could easily have been his mother,' said Crnobrnja. Milosevic preferred strong-minded women, although Mira would never have countenanced too strong an emotional attachment with another woman. Milosevic, like many Balkan men, knew when it was easiest to submit to female authority.

Together with Mihailo Crnobrnja and Borka Vucic, Milosevic travelled in 1981 to Washington, D.C. for an IMF meeting. The two men were chatting in Milosevic's room when Borka Vucic walked in and noticed that Milosevic's trousers were crumpled. Vucic immediately offered to press them. 'Don't be silly, there is room service here, call them up and they will iron them,' he replied. 'No, no, they don't know how to iron trousers,' she proclaimed. Crnobrnja, who watched the exchange with amusement, recalled: 'She practically forced him to say, OK, OK. With this mother-hen behaviour she wanted to take care of him, from ironing his trousers to who knows what else.'

Still, for many it all looked too good to be true. Was Milosevic really a Balkan version of Armand Hammer, the American millionaire financier who had helped bail out his friend Lenin when the Soviet economy appeared about to crash? What was he really up to? From the outside it was hard to disentangle the conflicting strands. Serbia's political heritage of Balkan double-dealing crossed with Communist half-truths makes its politics even more opaque than they seem. 'Milosevic always had his own agenda. He had a kind of reserve about him, you never knew quite what was on his mind,' said Montgomery.

5

CAPTURING BELGRADE

Using the Network

1982–4

Hilmi Pacha is a great talker and a past master in the art of the keeping the conversation in his own hands. Whenever an awkward subject is broached Hilmi seldom allows the other man to say much after the first question, yet it is done so unostentatiously that the questioner often does not realise that he is not even getting a word in edgeways.

Early twentieth-century British foreign correspondent Reginald Wyon on Hilmi Pacha, Ottoman Inspector General of Reforms in Monastir, Macedonia.[1]

As a rising young politician, Dusan Mitevic had enjoyed the perks and privileges that Yugoslavia granted its favoured youth. He had status, prestige, a car with his own driver. After his term as student president at Belgrade University, Mitevic was spoken of as a future political leader, a man who could see the broader picture. But the fall of Aleksandar Rankovic was for him a sharp lesson in the realities of political power in a Communist state. Stalin had his rivals and those who crossed him taken down into the bowels of the Lubyanka prison and shot. Tito only sacked them, but Mitevic 'saw that if they can do that to Rankovic they can do it to anyone.'[2]

So Mitevic chose influence instead of power. His programmes at Belgrade television such as *Eye to Eye* pushed new boundaries. 'Everyone heard our political leaders, but you could never see them. So I gathered people from political life into the studio, and everyone could call in and talk to them. I asked politicians how much they earned. At that time this was unheard of. Or I brought workers into the studio, interviewed politicians, and the workers would then comment.' In a Communist country putting the leaders before the workers, without multiple barriers of secretaries and party officials between them, was unprecedented, although the questions had to stay within certain limits. It would not have been a good idea to ask, for example, why Yugoslavia remained a one-party state. Nonetheless, these limits were moving.

Away from Belgrade Television, Mitevic kept up his connections with his student-era friends, such as Ivan Stambolic. Mitevic gave Stambolic a job after leaving university, helping organise the construction of Belgrade's House of Youth (state sponsored cultural centre). By 1982 Ivan Stambolic was president of the Belgrade Communist Party and a most useful ally. He was also Mitevic's conduit to Petar Stambolic, a grandee of the partisan generation and a wartime comrade of Mira's father, Moma Markovic. The world of the Belgrade leadership was comparatively small.

Like every political elite, Serbia's leaders sought to perpetuate themselves through the age-old methods of expedient alliances, marriages and dynasty building. Petar Stambolic remained a powerful and influential figure. Mitevic and Ivan Stambolic often strolled together in one or other of Belgrade's many parks. Ivan Stambolic fed Mitevic the latest news from the corridors of power, and Mitevic helped improve his general knowledge. 'We lived near each other and he told me what was going on. He knew from Petar Stambolic, although he would never say that. Ivan was very intelligent but there were lots of things he did not know, because he had this gap in his education. He used to ask me about things.'

Stambolic was wondering about his friend Milosevic. Slobodan was certainly doing well at UBB, making a name for himself as bright young technocrat in Yugoslavia, as well as abroad, just the kind of figure needed to pull the country out of the post-Tito mess. He needed to be put on the political ladder. But as Mihailo Crnobrnja had noted, working in international finance was hardly a classic route to power for a Communist politician. Mitevic recalled: 'Ivan Stambolic asked me, what shall we do with Milosevic, how could we help him make his political career? You could not just take someone from a bank and put him in a political position. You needed some kind of credentials, to be promoted in politics you need a base.'

The two walked some more and considered the matter. Parachuting Milosevic in from a great height, for example, straight onto the Serbian central committee would only backfire. There were too many powerful vested interests who would resent a newcomer without adequate political experience. On the other hand, if Milosevic's starting point was too obscure, he might never emerge into the bright lights of big city and national politics. It could not be a post in the provinces, it had to be something in Belgrade. A position with suitable gravitas, but not too presumptuous. The two men decided that Milosevic would be made the head of Belgrade Stari Grad (Old Town) party committee. Stari Grad was the biggest municipality in the city. Stambolic made the requisite calls, meetings were held, and votes cast. Although this was not a full-time post, and Milosevic kept his day job at UBB, his political career had begun.

These were times of growing political and economic uncertainty. Yugoslavia was more than ever a 'state of nations' rather than a nation-state. Each time a concession was made to the republics, they gained more political power at the expense of the federal government. The weaker the federal government became, the more power the six republics demanded. Yugoslavia was devouring itself.

'Tito created the idea of Brotherhood and Unity. He succeeded in that we forgot many of the scars of the war, which was right in a way because that was not conducive to keeping the country together. But he regarded the autonomous republics as competitors, and he never came to terms with them. He did not understand the new people leading them, and he became gradually isolated,' said former Belgrade mayor Zivorad Kovacevic. Tito's crushing of the Croatian spring and the Serbian liberals showed that he was out of touch, said Kovacevic. 'That was the last chance for change. That was the best proof that he did not understand the situation.'[3] Many felt that Tito had held on to power for too long. There is certainly a powerful argument that had Tito resigned gracefully in the 1970s, groomed a successor, and retired to enjoy his string of lavish villas and hunting lodges the whole course of Yugoslav history would have been different.

In addition, Yugoslavia's increasing reliance on foreign aid and loans was destabilising the economy. The bill for Yugoslavs' material comforts was mounting. By early 1981 the foreign debt had reached $19.2 billion, and inflation was running at over 25 per cent. Market socialism was proving increasingly expensive. Ironically, Tito's opening to the West, and the comparative lack of firm central economic planning made the Yugoslav economy much more vulnerable to global economic trends. The country's strategic importance, as a bridge between East and West, was also declining. Détente was good news for those who feared a nuclear war, but bad for Yugoslavia's creaking economy. As tensions between the superpowers eased, the West's enthusiasm for pouring cash into Belgrade's coffers diminished.

And the Iron Curtain was twitching. In 1981 martial law was imposed in Poland after workers in the Baltic port of Gdansk set up the independent trade union Solidarity. There were tanks on the streets of Warsaw, mass arrests and state-imposed terror of the kind not seen for decades. Yugoslav party hardliners and army chiefs watched events in Poland with alarm. Such chaos, they concluded, showed the consequences of too much tolerance. But Belgrade was not Warsaw. There would be no tanks on the streets there yet. So many articles supportive of Solidarity appeared in the Yugoslav press that the Polish embassy protested. Petitions were circulated across Belgrade condemning martial law, and several hundred intellectuals signed.

Among them was the writer and former partisan Dobrica Cosic. White-haired and bespectacled, Cosic had forsaken Communism to become Serbia's most famous nationalist dissident. He was the author of a highly successful trilogy of novels about Serbian heroism and suffering in the First World War, and had proclaimed in print that Serbs were being exploited by other Yugoslav nationalities, a refrain that once voiced, found an increasing resonance inside Serbia, and triggered similar sentiments across the other republics. Too famous to arrest, he pushed the boundaries of free speech, announcing that Yugoslavia was a 'pragmatic tyranny'.[4]

That same year Kosovo exploded into violent riots. Although Kosovo was an autonomous province of Serbia, it was a republic in all but name, thanks to the powers it received under the 1974 constitution. Since then Kosovo's ethnic Albanian majority had acquired some political control, and progressively 'Albanianised', that is taken over, the local government and administration. All this was paid for with massive federal subsidies, provoking resentment in Croatia and Slovenia, although those republics' political leaderships were happy to ally with Kosovo when necessary to outvote Serbia in federal matters.

Tito's attempt in the 1960s to defuse Kosovo's ethnic tensions by granting greater autonomy had fuelled, not dampened, Albanian national ambitions. But the instruments of physical, and legal, power – the police and army – remained under federal control. Increasing numbers of Albanian activists were arrested and charged with 'separatism', that is, planning to split Kosovo off from Yugoslavia. Endemic poverty, unemployment, a ramshackle infrastructure, ethnic tension between the Albanian majority and Serb minority, highly-charged folk memories handed down from generation to generation, a violent police force, all these made for a volatile mixture. Belgrade deployed special police units and the army to put down the protests. Through brute force they succeeded, but ethnic relations further worsened. The exodus of Kosovo's Serb minority increased.

The riots were symptomatic of an inherent contradiction in Yugoslavia's structure. By 1981 Albanians were Yugoslavia's fifth most populous nationality, 1.73 million strong, and almost as numerous as the 1.75 million Slovenes. But while Slovenia was a full republic, Albanians were still defined as a 'nationality' rather than a 'nation'. While Kosovars had some limited autonomy, Belgrade refused to make Kosovo the seventh Yugoslav republic, because that would remove it from Serb control.

In August 1983, the Kosovo Albanians' old enemy Aleksandar Rankovic was buried in Belgrade. The former head of Tito's secret police had lived in quiet obscurity since his sacking and disgrace in 1966. He had kept order in Kosovo (not least in 1981) and shown the Albanians there who was boss: Belgrade. His funeral was a stark illustration of the enduring strength of Serb patriotism. Tens of thousands of mourners attended, shouting nationalist slogans, such as 'Serbia has arisen'.

While Milosevic and Mira Markovic celebrated his debut on the political stage as chief of the Stari Grad party, at home seven-year-old Marko had a question for his father.

'Dad,' he asked. 'This new firm that you are working for, does it have a representative office in New York?'

'No, Marko,' replied Milosevic.

'So why would you work there, if they don't have an office in New York?'[5]

Marko may have been thinking about the excitement and glamour of a trip to the United States, and the presents his father brought home, but it was a good question.

One answer was political ambition. But whatever Milosevic's plans were at this time, he also needed good contacts within the party. In a Communist one-party state these play a much greater role than in a democracy. When the party runs the country, then the right friends are a necessity. Every ambitious manager, whether in the media, banking or industry understood that economic and career success demanded high-level contacts. These could grant everything from a promotion to a new and bigger apartment.

Milosevic had Ivan Stambolic and Dusan Mitevic, but outside the Belgrade party, Yugoslavia's bankers and some western diplomats, he was an unknown and relatively unremarkable figure. He was a member of the economic, rather than the political, *nomenklatura*, as the Communist elite was known. Nora Beloff's *Tito's Flawed Legacy: Yugoslavia 1939–1984*, for example, makes no mention of Milosevic, although there are several lines about a dissident called Vojislav Kostunica,[6] who in October 2000 succeeded Milosevic as Yugoslav President.

Milosevic considered where to position himself. At this time he was only in his early forties. He had not yet mapped out his future ideological path. Like many successful politicians, he made his decisions based as much on the balance of political forces at a particular time as on any particular beliefs or ideology. Milosevic was, of course, aware of the rise of Serbian nationalism – he had witnessed the chanting crowds at Rankovic's funeral – but that was hardly a sufficient power base for a career as a nationalist. Open nationalism was anyway not an option. Tito had only recently died and the doctrine of Brotherhood and Unity was still considered sacrosanct among the political elites. 'We never thought about who belonged to what nationality in those times, it was not important. We were Yugoslavs,' said Mira Markovic. 'I did not care about being a Serb. In that Yugoslavia, people did not care about nationalism, or what you were, especially among the young and educated.'

With hindsight and our knowledge of Yugoslavia's destruction it is now tempting to see Milosevic's rise through the political battles of the 1980s in simple good/bad terms, lining up those in favour of a free market and multi-party democracy on one side, and authoritarian communists who eventually became nationalists on the other. Such a straightforward paradigm does not really apply to Belgrade in the early and mid-1980s. The truth is more complicated.

Yugoslavia was an extremely complex country, with several competing political forces. As well as the divide between the six republics and the federal state, there was also an intra-republic power struggle between the Communist parties and governments. Serbia fought to protect its interests within Yugoslavia against, for example, Croatia or Slovenia. But within Serbia itself the Communist Party was competing with the Serbian government. The weakening of the federal structure, and the parlous state of the economy only added to the unhealthy state of flux. In this fevered atmosphere different groups merged and split like amoebas.

Milosevic began his political career as he later continued it: he hedged his bets and spoke with two voices. Like St Augustine, who prayed for 'chastity and continence, but not yet', Milosevic wanted economic reform, but not too much. His commercial experience, and knowledge of the United States brought him onto the 1983–4 commission led by the Slovenian Sergei Kreigher, which called for economic reforms to liberalise Yugoslav markets and increase free trade. Milosevic supported these demands, prompting the accusation that he was a 'revisionist', a term of abuse in the Marxist lexicon for an individual who seeks so much reform that he is revising the essential tenets of Communism. (Kucan and other Slovene leaders now present themselves as trailblazers for political and economic liberalisation within Yugoslavia. This was clearly not the case in 1984.) But Milosevic was no revolutionary dismantler of state control. The Kreigher Commission was a creature of its times. It proposed liberalising the market but stopped far short of calling for denationalisation of socially-owned industries and companies, and the introduction of a genuine free economy.

Milosevic would tinker with the economy, but he carefully kept within the limits of Titoist political orthodoxy. He needed to maintain the support of the partisan generation around Petar Stambolic as well as the hard-line generals who had helped Tito crush the Serbian liberals. Milosevic was typical of many Communist officials in eastern Europe and the Soviet Union then, who wanted to square the circle, and somehow combine the dynamism of capitalism with state ownership of property that would keep the levers of economic power in party hands. At this time in the region there was much talk of what was known as the 'South Korean model', which combined an authoritarian political system with foreign investment and limited economic liberalisation.

Attempts to bring about political reform also foundered on the jagged rocks of the republics' vested interests. The Kreigher Commission was followed by another, headed by the Croatian politician Josip Vrhovec. This was even more retrograde, rejecting outright the idea of multi-party elections and criticising the Kreigher Commission proposals as incompatible with the idea of workers' self-management.

In this atmosphere of refusal, rejection and inability to compromise, Lenin's age-old question, 'What is to be done?' was as pertinent as

ever. Those who might have been able to supply some imaginative
and dynamic answers, the Serbian liberals of the 1970s, had long been
purged from the party. But somebody had to free the logjam.

In the spring of 1984, 'cadre rotation' came round once more. Stambolic
moved up the ladder to become president of the Serbian Communist
Party. He then engineered Milosevic's election as president of the
Belgrade Communist Party. Now Milosevic really did have a new
workplace. He left UBB and started his career as a full-time politician.
'This was a quantum leap,' said Mihailo Crnobrnja. 'Ivan Stambolic
pulled him out from practically nothing, from oblivion, in terms of
political power. To make him the head of the Belgrade party could
never have happened without Stambolic.'[7]

Milosevic's great leap forward did not happen without struggle. One
of the flaws of a one-party system is that people who essentially have quite
different views of the world, and thus in a democracy would be political
opponents, find themselves sitting around the same table, as it is the
only one available. The old guard were highly suspicious of Milosevic.
Who was he, this unremarkable forty-three-year-old banker, who had
appeared more or less from nowhere, and had spent years travelling back
and forth to New York? There were whispers that Milosevic was a spy
for the CIA. Draza Markovic led the charge against Milosevic.

He had witnessed Milosevic in action at committee meetings of the
Belgrade party, and he was sceptical.

> That was the first time I could observe his personality, and that was
> sufficient enough to make a negative impression. He was self-serving,
> intolerant and exclusive. Milosevic used to come to meetings, say
> what he had to say, and simply leave. I used to protest about such
> behaviour. However, Ivan Stambolic always tried to defend him. I
> disagreed with his standpoints, ideologically, politically and in every
> other aspect.[8]

But Markovic was outvoted.

Dusan Mitevic and Ivan Stambolic celebrated Milosevic's triumph.
Mitevic, an arch-manipulator, was attempting to play a Machiavellian
game, using Milosevic to topple finally the partisan generation of both
Petar Stambolic and Draza Markovic. Tito was dead, and it was time
for his associates to finally retire and open the door for a new generation

to take power. This was a widespread view at the time, although not everyone saw Milosevic as the man for the job.

Milosevic's first major decision as Belgrade party chief was to launch a campaign against liberals and dissidents in 1984. He certainly relished the language of Communism, according to Milos Vasic.

> When he spoke to the Belgrade party central committee he used the cold war language of the 1950s. He talked about 'people's democracy', 'great steps forward in the service of socialism', no other Communist leaders used this jargon. Living under Communism and seeing all these leaders changing themselves, you develop a keen ear for nuances. He was obviously a Stalinist.[9]

By using such antiquated language in party meetings, Milosevic sent a message, instantly understood by both party hardliners and liberals.

Milosevic's crackdown was not greeted with universal enthusiasm, even by those who might have been expected to support the new hardline, said Milos Vasic. Party hardliners welcomed it, but those in the security services, who had a clearer idea of how the world was changing, were not so keen. 'I used to go hunting with some people who worked for state security. I remember them saying to me that they don't understand Milosevic, what does he want? Even the Soviets did not prosecute dissidents any more. From their point of view Milosevic was out of date and anachronistic.'

The easing of cold war tension had exposed the underlying stresses and contradictions of Yugoslavia and the Soviet Union, two multi-national constructs. In Moscow Mikhail Gorbachev was grappling with the same economic and political conundrums as the Yugoslav leaders: how to reform a moribund Communist economy without sacrificing party control, and how to ease nationalist tensions without then encouraging independence movements.

Although Gorbachev was ten years older than Milosevic, there were some parallels between the two mens' careers. Both had risen from provincial backgrounds up through the party apparat. Like Milosevic, Gorbachev was the protégé of an older, conservative politician who came to understand that a younger, more dynamic generation needed to be groomed for power. For Milosevic that was Stambolic; Gorbachev's mentor was the former KGB chief Yuri Andropov.

In 1978, the year Milosevic joined Beobanka, Gorbachev moved to Moscow, where Andropov began to advance his protégé's career. Two years later, while Milosevic was preparing to join the Serbian party committee, Gorbachev was appointed to the Soviet politburo. By 1985, as Milosevic cemented his control over the Belgrade Communist Party, Gorbachev was general secretary of the Soviet Communist Party and began to introduce the revolutionary concepts of *glasnost* ('openness') and *perestroika* ('restructuring'). Such terms sound unremarkable today, but in the Soviet era such phrases, with their overtones of accountability and efficiency were revolutionary concepts. There was movement too on the Soviet Union's national question. Gorbachev decentralised political power away from Moscow to assemblies in the Soviet Union's member republics, just as had happened in Yugoslavia under the 1974 constitution.

Glasnost and *perestroika* sent shockwaves across eastern Europe, including Yugoslavia. Suddenly the world had turned upside down. Moscow was setting the pace of reform. Yugoslavia was not a member of either the Warsaw Pact or Comecon, the Soviet-bloc trading organisation. But it was still a one-party Communist state, with close political ties to the Soviet Union. Had Milosevic been a politician of vision and statesmanship, or a different kind of man, he could perhaps have developed into a Balkan Gorbachev. After all, he had some reformist credentials. He had experience in the West, and knew something of how the world and capitalist economies worked. He spoke English, he was relatively young, and he had a powerful political mentor in Ivan Stambolic.

Film of Milosevic walking beside Ivan Stambolic before laying a wreath on Tito's grave shows a confident politician, who would look quite at home at a Soviet May-Day line-up. He is wearing the characteristic grey suit of a party functionary. The suit pinches slightly, which combined with Milosevic's wooden gait gives him a somewhat robotic air. His movements are quick and decisive. His expression is one of stony determination, pugnacious confidence in his own ability. His eyes are alert and calculating, his mouth is narrow and his grey hair is swept back over a wide, round forehead.

His political radar never stops sweeping the area as he processes the environment around him. Milosevic appears the archetypal Communist official, who knows how to play the apparat, or system, for his own personal and political benefit, who can follow the switches in party policy.

Although Milosevic – like his wife – does not enjoy public appearances, the demands of Communist pageantry, and the need to build up his image, dictated that he adopt a more visible profile. In Belgrade, the London *Times* correspondent Dessa Trevisan, doyenne of the Balkan press corps, came to know Milosevic quite well over the next few years. 'He had fascinated me since he became head of the Belgrade party in 1984. I started watching him on television. I realised that here was a man who talked quite differently to the usual functionaries. He told me that "one must be short, and clear".'

In his role as the people's tribune, Milosevic projected himself as someone who cuts through the party bureaucracy, and talks directly to the man and woman on the street. This was in stark contrast to most Communist leaders, who loved to deliver long and rambling speeches based on their own insights into Marxist theory. Fidel Castro spoke for hours at a time. Milosevic preferred to talk for a few minutes. His very dullness was somehow remarkable, said Trevisan. 'I watched him, and he appeared to be nothing out of the ordinary, this man with a puddingy face and a turned-up nose. But somehow he was not verbose like Ivan Stambolic. He talked differently from the other apparatchiks, and those left over from the partisan generation. I thought, is this the new generation of party leaders?'[10]

Milosevic did not like long speeches because he did not have much to say. He met the demands of Yugoslavia's political system, paying due homage to Titoism when necessary. Otherwise he shut up. He knew that the Yugoslav public was weary of having to endure long political tirades. Unlike most Communist leaders Milosevic has never felt the need to explain his political philosophy, to be published in rows of eternally unread volumes, or to share his thoughts with the world at large. He has published one book of collected speeches, which tends towards the emptily epigrammatic – statements such as: 'The difficulties are neither unexpected nor insurmountable', or: 'The future will still be beautiful and it is not far away'.[11] He used orthodox Communist language, but was not prolix. Words became empty rhetorical devices, and sentences were full of terms such as 'future', 'triumph' and 'inevitable'.

Milosevic's relationship with Communism is complex. There is a need to distinguish between the utopian ideals of Communism and the more mundane political methodology that was actually used to govern Communist countries. Unlike his partisan predecessors such as Draza Markovic, Milosevic was not an idealistic believer in class struggle, who wanted to build the workers' paradise and destroy capitalism. In this he was hardly alone. By the mid-1980s the Communist system was so atrophied, and riddled with cynicism and corruption, that even the least prescient comrade could see that Marxism's prognosis was poor, not just in Yugoslavia but across the world. The Communist system had degenerated into a system of interest protection. These were primarily the personal interests of those who enriched themselves by corruption and stealing, and the political interests of those who exercised power through the one-party state. The two groups overlapped considerably. More far-sighted officials realised that once Communism collapsed, it would be replaced by the free market.

Yet Milosevic was undoubtedly influenced by some aspects of Marxism, particularly its deterministic philosophy and authoritarian methodology. 'Little Lenin', as Milosevic became known while running the Belgrade party, had grown up under Communism, and was known for his orthodoxy. The works of Marx and Lenin decreed that history moved inexorably according to the laws of class struggle, that the victory of the proletariat was inevitable, and the triumph of Communism was preordained. The Communist system of government worked on a command and control theory. Instructions were issued, and were then carried out. Both found a ready echo in Milosevic's authoritarian psyche. Even at party committee meetings Milosevic stated his points as though they were self-evident, and once he had finished talking, he left. Like Marxism, Milosevicism – the pursuit and maintenance of power – was based on a sense of an inevitable victory, whether of the working class, or a provincial Communist official from Pozarevac. 'Power was his only ideology and he didn't care about anything else. But Milosevic grew up under Communism, and if he had any ideology, it was Communism and socialism, and some of the values we produced in that society,' said Seska Stanojlovic.[12]

Dusan Mitevic saw things clearest. 'At that time in Yugoslavia they said "After Tito, Tito". I told Ivan Stambolic, you have to understand, there is no Tito after Tito. When somebody is dead, they are dead. The one who understands this will win and take power. This was a revolutionary thing to say after Tito died. Ivan Stambolic used this sentence. He did not really understand what it meant. But he told it to Milosevic. He did.'

6

ALL THE PRESIDENT'S MEN

Wooing Two Constituencies

1985–6

When Milosevic was recruiting his own people, he behaved like someone seducing a girl. He had fantastic patience. He would listen to you like you were the only person in the world at that moment.

Braca Grubacic, editor at a Yugoslav publishing house
in the mid-1980s.[1]

Mira was matchmaking. She was worried about her daughter Marija. It was August 1985 and Marija's twentieth birthday was one month away. Marija already had one broken marriage behind her, and their mother-daughter relationship was bumpy. In the last few years Marija had been unhappy in Belgrade, as her parents' increasing devotion to Milosevic's career left her feeling neglected.

Like many children of successful parents Marija and her eleven-year-old brother Marko lived in a trap of privilege. Milosevic's salary as president of Beogradska Banka had ensured they never lacked for material goods. In fact, both were over-indulged, and relatives noticed the lack of firm parental guidance. Ljubica Markovic remonstrated with her half-sister Mira when the family gathered at the birthday party of their father Moma in 1980. 'Marija was still a teenager then, and she was already completely spoilt. She had a lot of make-up on, and gold jewellery. She was impolite and did not even know the names of all the family members.'[1]

But make-up and jewellery were not enough. To her parents' anger, Marija married a Yugoslav diplomat and moved to Tokyo while still a teenager. The escape brought no relief. Left alone all day at home, with no friends, and little interest in Japan, she soon became bored there. The life of a diplomat's wife held no appeal for an unhappy young woman. The marriage had ended and now she was back home.

The man Mira had in mind for her daughter was Tahir Hasanovic, a physics student at Belgrade University. He was one of her favourites, bright, politically committed and a real Yugoslav. His family were not Serbs, but Turks, who had moved to Belgrade in the nineteenth century. Yugoslavia's small Turkish Muslim minority was part of the ethnic mosaic that made the country such a cosmopolitan place. Hasanovic was a dynamic young student politician, tipped for great things once he graduated from university. Mira and Slobodan had already helped him set up a student organisation at university. They decided to make Hasanovic the guest of honour at Marija's party, and he was flattered to accept.

While the guests arrived, Hasanovic made small talk, and looked over the bookshelves. They were lined with rows of Serbo-Croat translations of the German philosophers, and Russian authors such as Dostoevsky whom Mira enjoyed so much. Milosevic himself was not that much of a reader. Mihailo Crnobrnja recalled how when he had recommended that Milosevic read the 1980s business best-seller *In Pursuit of Excellence*, he had asked for a five-page digest of the most important parts.

Most of the guests at the party were politicians, friends and acquaintances of Slobodan and Mira. None of these were of much interest to Marija. But she was quickly attracted to the young man with such exotic, dark, good looks. Hasanovic too liked what he saw in the slim and vulnerable young woman with thick dark hair and large brown eyes. To Mira and Slobodan's satisfaction, the two young people were soon going out together. 'She did not have any friends at the time, because she had just come back from Japan,' said Hasanovic. 'We were together for a year. It was an extraordinary love, especially from Marija, but in the end it was not enough for her,'[3] Hasanovic is now vice president of Serbia's liberal New Democracy Party, but in the mid-1980s, when Milosevic was head of the Belgrade Communist Party, the older man was his political mentor and he became known as 'Milosevic's young lion'. By 1985, he was president of Belgrade Communist Party's youth organisation. Hasanovic had initially been wary of becoming emotionally involved with a member of Milosevic's family, fearing that Milosevic might damage his career if his relationship with Marija went wrong. But Hasanovic was always warmly welcomed at their home, where he saw a side of Milosevic revealed to few outside his immediate family.

In these early years at least, Slobodan and Mira exhibited little appetite for luxury or conspicuous consumption. They spent their weekends quietly in Pozarevac. 'They behaved like completely average people,' said Dusan Mitevic.

> They would go on Friday evening, come back on Sunday afternoon, and have lunch with their friends. They had a completely normal relationship with their neighbours. Their neighbours used to give them a bowl of stuffed peppers. When I first knew them they did not even have guards at the house. They liked to sit in the garden. Later on, when Milosevic became more important, the police built a high wall around it, but he did not like that.[4]

Milosevic's tastes remained modest: a glass or two of whisky or his favourite drink, Viljamovka, the Serbian pear brandy, and a cigarillo. He showed no interest then in fashionable western clothes, luxurious cars or expensive jewellery, and he never has since.

Like Mitevic, Hasanovic recalled an unassuming couple, who although ambitious, still remembered their roots in provincial Serbia. Milosevic later harnessed Serbian nationalism and xenophobia in his drive for power, but there was never a hint of prejudice in his attitude towards Hasanovic. In fact the two men became quite close. 'Slobodan and Mira lived modestly at this time. I was lucky to be with them when they remembered how poor they had been, and how they first fell in love. They never cared that I am from a Turkish background. This was in the first phase of his career, before he became a god.' Hasanovic also heard a surprising side of Milosevic, especially after he had downed a glass or two of Viljamovka 'Slobo sang beautifully, Russian ballads, French chansons and old Serbian songs. There was a warm atmosphere at their home.'

In 1987, Hasanovic was sent to do his military service. His relationship with Marija cooled down. Her letters became infrequent, and eventually her visits stopped altogether and the two ended their relationship. Hasanovic was nervous when he met Milosevic for the first time after the break-up, but his fears that Slobodan might damage his political career were groundless. 'I asked him if he was angry with me, but he was a complete gentleman. He never mentioned it, and he continued to help me with my career at the youth organisation.' The next year, with Milosevic's support, Hasanovic was appointed the foreign secretary of the federal Yugoslav youth organisation, charged with overseeing official relations between young people from Yugoslavia and foreign countries.

Outside the inner circle though, relations between Mira and her relatives were breaking down. Her father Moma Markovic and her brothers and sisters only saw Mira and Slobodan about once every six months or so, usually at Moma's house. Ljubica did not look forward to the bi-annual meetings. Mira often appeared on the verge of hysteria, and she seemed to have developed a hygiene mania. 'She told my father that she hates to shake hands with people because she has to clean her hands with alcohol afterwards.'

The atmosphere was in any case strained, because Mira was devoted to her husband and his career, and could not stand to hear any kind of criticism. 'It was a ritual, and very cold. I didn't like going there, because I didn't feel comfortable. My father and Mira were often quarrelling. Milosevic was making his political career and my father criticised him. Mira could not bear it, she was always on the edge of crying, and hysterical.'

As Milosevic planned his advance through the party apparat, he understood that with Yugoslavia in a state of flux he could simultaneously appeal to two opposing interest groups within the party: the old guard around Petar Stambolic, and the reformers who wanted to topple the elderly Tito-era leaders. This he achieved by the simple device of speaking in different voices to different audiences. Zivorad Kovacevic, former mayor of Belgrade, recalled: 'Some elderly leaders believed that Milosevic had something of Tito's stature. I remember that one said to me that "Sloba is a real pearl of our party". I said what are you talking about? He said, "He has something, he is a real Tito".'[5]

Milosevic's admirer might have revised his opinion had he seen the memento of his Wall Street days on the table by his bed: a photograph of himself with the powerful American banker David Rockefeller. However, Mira, the great leftist, did not seem to mind her husband's capitalist connections.

The people who led the country at the time were mostly politicians who knew nothing about the economy. He was young and educated, he was seen as the ideal person to be involved in politics to bring modern economic development, to reinforce political life and have a certain influence in decision making. The political leaders of Serbia started to pressurise my husband to get involved in politics.[6]

Whatever the degree of pressure was, Milosevic – and Mira – did not object.

Milosevic's wooing of two constituencies was skilful, but he was also aided by the fact that the time had not yet come to demand a clear choice between an authoritarian state and a multi-party system. It was then possible to ride two horses at once. Although Yugoslavia – and the Communist system across the region – was increasingly in political and economic crisis, few then predicted that it would collapse so rapidly and completely. To many it seemed feasible to modify the political system enough to kick-start the economy, but still retain the supremacy of the party. And those who were beginning to understand that, ultimately, a multi-party system was inevitable, also looked to Milosevic.

Young politicians such as Tahir Hasanovic believed that Milosevic would steer Yugoslavia in a modern direction.

I was on the wing of the party which was aware of him as a reformer, and a man who will build capitalism. I strongly believed then that he knew what a market economy was, and he was ready to build it. When Milosevic was in New York, he really became a banker. He knew the value of money, how the market economy worked and what tools to use to improve Yugoslavia, and makē it into a modern society.

Diplomats too, shared this view. Thanks to his years at UBB, and his time in America, Milosevic was able to power-schmooze diplomats into thinking he was a reformer. He understood the language of capitalism, and presented himself as a moderniser when speaking to westerners. The Stalinist language Milosevic spoke at central committee meetings was not heard at US embassy receptions, where he was a popular guest at the 4 July Independence Day party in 1986, with a glass of whisky in hand. Quite the opposite. 'Milosevic was seen as a reform Communist, perhaps even a potential Balkan Gorbachev,' said Janet Garvey, who started work at the US embassy in Belgrade in 1983.[7]

During the mid-1980s there was still considerable international good-will towards the maverick Communist state. Yugoslavia already had one foot in the West, many diplomats believed. With enough help, and encouragement it could evolve into a Balkan success story. Milosevic, many thought, could be the man to turn Yugoslavia into a modern democracy. 'At this time Belgrade was one of the liveliest cities in Europe. As long as you didn't criticise Tito you could do anything. Yugoslavia was seen as being so far ahead of everywhere else in eastern Europe, and they were seen as the good guys in the Communist world. The optimistic scenario was that Yugoslavia could be in the EU by the early 1990s,' said Garvey.

Meanwhile, Mira Markovic was building her network at Belgrade University. In 1984, the same year that Milosevic took over the Belgrade party, Markovic joined the leadership of the university Communist Party. Markovic was not highly regarded among the more forward-looking professors, who were in touch with developments in western intellectual thought. She was viewed as dogmatic and narrow-minded, capable only of parroting received Communist wisdom. Mihailo Crnobrnja, who was also a professor at Belgrade University, recalled: 'She is a figure who has a very high opinion of herself and she is not deserving of that opinion at all. She does not have one likeable characteristic. She is not charming, she is not intellectual and she is not pretty. Her literary achievements are next to nothing. She is a miserable intellectual of poor quality.'[8] Tahir Hasanovic was equally disappointed with her. 'I often tried to start discussions with her, but she was not in touch with modern issues. I asked her about Karl Popper and I tried to learn about political science, but she was never ready to discuss these things.'

Although she was highly strung and prone to crying fits, Mira was not unpopular with students, as she was known as an easy grader. And she had plenty of allies in the corridors of academia. For lazy academics there were few places where it was easier to coast along for years without much work than at a university in a Communist country. The ideological demands of the curriculum, the necessity to conform to Marxist theory, acted as a positive disincentive to think in challenging or radical new ways. Plenty of Mira's colleagues felt threatened by reformist ideas and were ready for the 'return to Marxism' that Milosevic proclaimed at Belgrade party meetings. The steady advance of her husband also strengthened Mira's influence.

In July 1985, Milosevic and Markovic chose the first testing-ground for their power and perspective. The issue was the apparently minor question of classes in compulsory Marxist education at Belgrade University.

Marxist education quickly became a totem for both sides. Liberals – backed by some allies of Ivan Stambolic – wanted the classes ended. Hardliners, led by Milosevic and Markovic, demanded their retention. Milosevic and his wife won. The classes stayed.

The wooing by Milosevic and Mira of Belgrade's political elite did not go unnoticed, especially by those who knew Milosevic from old, such as Seska Stanojlovic. 'By that time, in the mid-1980s, it was clear to me that Slobo and Mira were building their parallel organisation. They really went to work on that. I was getting information about this, and I believed it.'9 Stanojlovic decided not to go to Ivan Stambolic, because she doubted he would listen. Instead she visited Dragisa Pavlovic, a member of Serbia's political leadership who was also a close associate of Ivan Stambolic. 'I was going back to work for my newspaper, so I went to see Pavlovic as it was the end of our time of working together.' Stanojlovic warned Pavlovic that Milosevic was planning something. Pavlovic did not take heed. 'He told me that if he was in the forest with the partisans, Slobo would protect his back. That meant Pavlovic thought he could absolutely trust Slobo, that he was the most reliable person.'

At this point Milosevic was careful not to unleash nationalist passions. He knew that to maintain the support of party conservatives, and the army generals, he must still pay homage to Titoism. So when a publisher in Belgrade planned to publish the works of Slobodan Jovanovic, a writer whom Titoist orthodoxy branded a nationalist renegade, Milosevic denounced him as a 'war criminal'. There would be no new edition of Jovanovic's books, he proclaimed, and anyone who wanted a copy would have to hunt through the second-hand shops. Like a Titoist Torquemada, Milosevic also invited those who had authorised a new edition of Jovanovic's work to justify themselves. Such language and repressive tactics only boosted Milosevic's support among the conservatives.

When Draza Markovic's open opposition to Milosevic failed to prevent his election as Belgrade party chief, Draza's brother Moma went to visit Petar Stambolic to try and warn him about Milosevic. Ljubica Markovic recalled: 'I heard that my father told Petar Stambolic when Milosevic was rising upwards that he should be careful because Milosevic was dangerous. That was when Milosevic was important but not yet number one.' But the family rivalry between Draza Markovic and Petar Stambolic meant that Moma's warning was disregarded, and his efforts rebounded into the family, with unhappy consequences. 'Petar Stambolic immediately went to Ivan Stambolic and told him what Moma had said,' Ljubica reported. 'Ivan Stambolic then immediately told Milosevic.' Relations further soured between Slobodan and Mira and her father.

The endless political battles within the Serbian Communist party, and the growing rancour between the republics, were making life complicated for young managers trying to read the runes, such as Braca Grubacic. Now the publisher of the *VIP* newsletter, a respected insider's guide to Yugoslav politics, Grubacic was then an editor at *Mladost*, the publishing house of the Yugoslav young people's organisation (the word *Mladost* means 'Youth'). *Mladost* was a Yugoslav – federal – organisation, not part of one of the six republics. But the republic's nationalist squabbles were increasingly disrupting Grubacic's work.

> I gave Milosevic a call, as he was party chief. I thought he was not bad, he was younger than the others, and had more energy. You could see that something was going on. We were having a lot of problems, between the Serbs, Croats and Bosnians. It was clear that relations between the republics were not going well. I was having difficulties at the federal level.

Grubacic recalled Milosevic's silky recruitment technique.

> He listened to me for about forty minutes. At this time, when Milosevic was recruiting his own people, he behaved like someone who was seducing a girl. He had fantastic patience. Milosevic told me not to worry, that I was being supported.

Grubacic was heartened by this. Here was a party chief who had time to listen to his work difficulties with the federal authorities, someone who could advise him which way to turn in these troubling times. 'I was thinking that, well, it seems that I am important to this guy, I was flattered in a way.'

All this charm and attention came at a price. Grubacic was thinking of publishing a memoir by one of Tito's former military advisors, General Jaksic. 'At the end of our meeting, Milosevic said to me that he had heard I had General Jaksic's manuscript. I told him that I did, and that it was a very interesting book, and very controversial.' But controversy then was not on Milosevic's agenda. This was still a time of consolidation with the old guard, not confrontation.

Milosevic said something which really struck me. He said that it was not a good idea for the book to come out now, because General Jaksic had written some nasty things about Comrade Tito. This phrase, Comrade Tito, meant Milosevic was very much one of Tito's supporters. One message was, OK, you are supported. Second thing is take care, don't publish it.

This was all that Grubacic needed to hear to understand with whom he was dealing. The reference to 'Comrade Tito' instantly placed Milosevic as a hard-line conservative. Here then was a useful lesson in Serbian power politics. Grubacic understood that the fact he had been granted forty minutes with Milosevic was a sign he could be a potential future ally. But only if he did not publish the memoirs, because it would be politically inconvenient for Milosevic at that time. Grubacic backed down. In a one-party state it was not commercially viable or even possible to publish books against the will of the authorities. 'At that time if you tried to do that, they would stop the book at the printers, so it was no use. You would invest money and then you would get fined. The book was interesting, but not enough to lose your job and bankrupt the company.' Nor did Milosevic gain a new recruit for his network.

Sitting at home in May 1986 the Milosevic family was listening to the news, when the newsreader announced the name of the new head of the Serbian Communist Party. 'Dad's changing jobs again!' exclaimed Marko. Even though this new position did not involve trips to New York, Mira tried to explain to her son that it was still a great promotion.

As a banker Slobo travelled everywhere, to Tokyo, to New York. As president of the party Slobo went to small towns all over Serbia. Marko got wonderful presents when Slobo came back from abroad, but there was not much to bring back from provincial Serbia, and not much to say about what he saw when he was travelling there. Marko could not understand why that was better.

In later years, of course, Marko would understand. He exploited his parents' political connections to build a shady economic empire for himself, with involvement in organised crime and black marketeering. Milosevic's rise had been meteoric. In four years he had progressed from being head of a bank to leader of the biggest and most powerful Communist party in all of Yugoslavia' six republics. He had wooed both the old guard and the liberals, but more than that, he was backed by the leaders of the most conservative section of Yugoslav society, the army. The Yugoslav military, along with Tito and the Communist Party was one of the three key pillars upon which Yugoslavia had been built. The army enjoyed immense prestige and popularity. It was the heir of the partisans, who had expelled the Nazis and destroyed Fascism. Yugoslavia's military was prepared to defend the country against attack by either NATO or the Warsaw Pact. If need be it would fall back to the mountain redoubts of Bosnia, just as Tito and the partisans had done over forty years earlier, and wage guerrilla warfare. In Bosnia there were plenty of weapons stashed in arms dumps, and men willing to use them.

Every Yugoslav male was required to serve in the military. Just as in Israel – another multi-ethnic country born out of the Second World War – military service was a kind of glue, holding together a complicated patchwork. It was in the army that Yugoslavs from all six republics ate, lived and worked together. Here under military canvas, on the firing range, 'Brotherhood and Unity' was a reality, although there came to be resentment, particularly in Slovenia and Croatia, about Serbian dominance. Initially, however, a career in the army was highly sought after by many. Army officers lived a privileged lifestyle, with good pay and pensions, comfortable apartments and access to the best medical treatment. Once retired, ex-army officers could choose to live wherever they wanted in the country, and a place would be provided for them and their families. The military was almost a state within a state. Like every powerful vested interest in a time of flux, it sought a political protector. Milosevic understood this.

The Serbian writer Aleksa Djilas noted Milosevic's adept use of words in wooing the military: 'From the moment he became the head of the Belgrade Communists in 1984, Milosevic had deliberately adopted a political style meant to appeal to the military. He insisted on a combative spirit and a readiness to make sacrifices. Statements appealing to pride and dignity struck a deep chord both among officers and among the militaristic Serbs in the population.'[10] Milosevic courted the army, building links with the military leadership and taking care not to threaten their privileges.

It worked. Milosevic spoke the right language, according to General Nikola Ljubicic. A former minister of defence, Ljubicic had been Tito's most loyal servant, and the man who had led the crackdown on the

Serbian liberals during the late 1960s and early 1970s. It was here, in the military high command, that the real dinosaurs could be found, not among Draza Markovic and his colleagues. General Ljubicic observed: 'Slobodan is committed to our struggle against nationalism and will oppose the liberals in Belgrade. Slobodan is a great foe of counter-revolution, and I wish to see activism such as his carried on with even greater intensity.'[11]

Backed by Ivan and Petar Stambolic, the modernisers and the army, Milosevic was unstoppable. When Stambolic wavered about putting Milosevic's name forward as his sole possible successor as Serbian party leader, Milosevic almost pleaded with his *kum* that this was his only chance to advance. Stambolic's generosity won. Despite the intense, but ultimately futile opposition of Draza Markovic and his supporters, after a two-day meeting in which Stambolic steadily persuaded Milosevic's critics of his protégé's merits, Milosevic was unanimously confirmed as the new Serbian party chief. The next day Milosevic drove to see Ivan's uncle, Petar Stambolic, who was staying at a mountain resort in southern Serbia, to tell him the good news in person.

Draza Markovic later recalled how he had underestimated the depth of the bond between Ivan Stambolic and his protégé. 'I told Stambolic that Milosevic was practically unknown, a man without much experience, so the proposal for him to be president of the Serbian party was not a good idea. I suggested that Milosevic could perhaps be an assistant, or a vice-president.'[12] Some days later Draza Markovic met Milosevic.

Milosevic asked me why I was against him. Then I realised that Stambolic and Milosevic were very close. Stambolic had told Milosevic what I had said about him. I said to Milosevic what I had said to Stambolic, that nobody knew him, that he should take it easy. At that time I didn't know his peculiar personal characteristics. Ivan Stambolic thought it would be for ever, that he would be director and Slobodan Milosevic would be his assistant.

Not everything went Milosevic's way. Although there was an unwritten rule that the party head could decide who his successor would be, Stambolic was not completely beguiled by Milosevic. He saw that Milosevic was a hypocrite. A few days earlier Milosevic had emotionally appealed to Stambolic that he should be the sole candidate for leader of the Serbian party. But when Stambolic put forward his own candidate for Milosevic's old job as Belgrade party chief, Milosevic was not happy and proposed several alternative names. Stambolic's man was his chief of cabinet, Dragisa Pavlovic. Pavlovic was a popular and intelligent figure who was definitely not part of any of the various cliques around Milosevic. He was his own man, a genuine liberal reformer who was not beguiled by Milosevic's Wall Street years and talk of market mechanisms. This battle Milosevic lost, and Pavlovic duly took over the Belgrade party. Lines were being drawn for the coming political conflicts.

In later years Ivan Stambolic himself reflected on his reasons for engineering Milosevic's succession to the post he had held. He said he planned to create what he called a dynamic and homogenous team of the middle generation, of politicians in their forties with enough experience and a sufficiently similar outlook to face the coming challenges. 'Milosevic was well received in Yugoslavia because of the sharp actions that he carried out in Belgrade. He was considered a real communist, even less in doubt than myself.'[13] Yet even at that time Stambolic saw possible problems ahead with Milosevic's authoritarian management style. 'I saw that sometimes he was too abrupt, that he took shortcuts, that he took some steps too quickly, that he made superficial decisions, that he judged too harshly . . . and that he made other mistakes characteristic of a hard-hearted man.' Ironically, his criticisms echoed those made by Draza Markovic. Stambolic also noticed that when he criticised Milosevic for being too hasty he 'took it very hard' and was unable to conceal his reaction.

But ultimately, friendship, loyalty and trust won over Stambolic's doubts. He had made the biggest mistake of his life.

7

EPIPHANY

Unleashing Nationalism
1986–April 1987

No one should dare to beat you.

Slobodan Milosevic, to a crowd of Serb demonstrators
at Kosovo Polje in April 1987.[1]

Milosevic liked giving instructions, but he also knew when to
follow them. One evening he and Mira were enjoying a nightcap
at their home, together with Mihailo Crnobrnja and his wife Goca. The
four of them had just returned from an evening at the theatre, and a
pleasant dinner. Milosevic put on a record that soon had Goca tapping
her feet. 'Darling, can't you see that Goca feels like dancing, why don't
you dance with her,' said Mira. Milosevic, recalled Crnobrnja, 'stood
up like a robot' and asked his wife to dance.[2]

But as Yugoslav politics began to fracture, the question increasingly
being asked across the country was, to which tune? Not far from
Milosevic's office in downtown Belgrade, at the headquarters of the
Serbian Academy of Sciences and Arts (SANU), dissident writers were
preparing a nationalist broadside. Their weapon was known simply as
'The Memorandum'. The mundane label belied its explosive contents.
The first half analysed Yugoslavia's political and economic system. The
country's general malaise is blamed largely on the reforms of the
1970s, such as the 1974 constitution and the inefficiency of the system
of workers' self-management. The Memorandum argued, accurately
enough, that: 'The entire system is constituted upon the principle of
the activity of the summit of the political hierarchy, and the hopeless
passivity of the people.'[3] Such an analysis was true of any Communist
state, but the document then catalogued a list of highly exaggerated
grievances against Serbs and Serbia.

The Memorandum claimed 'The physical, political, legal and cultural genocide of the Serb population of Kosovo and Metohija is a worse historical defeat than any experienced in the liberation wars waged by Serbia from the first Serbian uprising in 1804 to the uprising of 1941.' Such apocalyptic language is often the lingua franca of aggrieved nationalist intellectuals across the region. But it was a black historical irony that the unleashing of Serb nationalism that followed the Memorandum did indeed eventually lead to a chain of events that resulted in the destruction of the centuries-old Serb community of Kosovo.

Of course, any Serb concerned about 'losing' Kosovo was quite free to go and live there, yet SANU's thinkers preferred to pontificate from the comfort of the Belgrade Writers' Club, with its agreeable garden restaurant. The real issue was more likely to be the steady growth in the Albanian population. Serbs in Kosovo, on the very edge of the republic, certainly felt nervous and outnumbered. But instead of admitting that Serbs left Kosovo because there were more jobs and better opportunities further north, The Memorandum proclaimed that a 'genocide' was taking place against them.[4]

Sections were leaked to the Belgrade newspaper *Vecernje Novosti*, where they were published in late September 1986. Appalled at its contents, the editors at the newspaper dubbed the Memorandum 'A Proposal for Hopelessness'. Reactions across Yugoslavia fell into an increasingly predetermined pattern. Political battlelines were being drawn, ever more clearly. In the northern republics of Slovenia and Croatia, the Memorandum was seen as proof of Serbia's desire for hegemony over all Yugoslavia, and fuelled the small but growing independence movements. Certainly the Serb minorities living in Kosovo and Croatia had legitimate grievances. It is true that the political concessions made to Kosovo's Albanian majority over the previous years, and the growth of an educated elite among Albanians, had increased the sense of isolation felt by Kosovo Serbs.

The province remained the poorest and least developed region of Yugoslavia. Unemployment was high, the infrastructure unsound. In Croatia nationalist rumblings had unnerved many Serbs. But neither of these problems was insoluble. Yet instead of proposing solutions based on consensus and compromise, which would have actually aided their beleaguered Serb compatriots, the authors of the Memorandum used wild and emotional language. Forty-five years earlier, in 1941, Serbs in Croatia and Bosnia really had faced systematic destruction. When the nation's intellectual leaders proclaimed that another genocide was taking place, average citizens of Serbia sat up and listened.[5]

The thoughts of SANU's thinkers created such a furore that they suddenly and inevitably framed the terms of political debate. The Memorandum demanded a reaction, and such a response was also a way of defining different views about the future of Yugoslavia. Ivan Stambolic, then President of Serbia, attacked the Memorandum, and demanded that its authors issue a public retraction, which they refused to do. As a leading Yugoslav politician, Stambolic was virtually required to lead an onslaught on this dangerous manifestation of the federation's most volatile nationalism.

The Memorandum also deliberately stirred up dark folk memories of the Ottoman era. A hapless Serb farmer called Djordje Martinovic became a bizarre cause célèbre for Serbian nationalists. Martinovic had somehow suffered an injury to his backside in a Kosovo field. News reports had claimed that Martinovic had been assaulted by two Albanians with a bottle, which had been forced inside his rectum. Martinovic's ordeal was discussed for months, indeed years, afterwards. This bizarre event was 'reminiscent of the darkest days of the Turkish practice of impalement', announced the Memorandum, claiming yet another Serb victim of Albanian terror in Kosovo.

Impaling had entered Serbian folk memory through both historical reality and one memorable scene in a novel by the Nobel laureate Ivo Andric. In Andric's most famous work, *The Bridge on the Drina*, a Serb who attempts to sabotage the construction of the bridge at the Bosnian city of Visegrad is impaled. His ghastly punishment is described in slow and gruesome detail, down to the pools of blood that collect underneath the victim. 'Turks, Turks, Turks on the bridge . . . may you die like dogs . . . like dogs,' the Serb peasant hisses in his last moments. Djordje Martinovic was not impaled, but he was certainly badly hurt somehow and taken to hospital. There his story changed. Local authorities and the Kosovo police blamed Martinovic himself for his injuries, saying the farmer had confessed in hospital.

A police statement said 'it appears that the wounded performed an act of "self-satisfaction" in a field, that he put a beer bottle on a wooden stick and stuck it in the ground . . . then sat on the bottle'. A commission of enquiry was formed to examine the whole case. It was impossible for a Serb to inflict such injuries upon himself, the doctors claimed. The Serb warrior tradition could never countenance such aberrations. Martinovic

said he had been made to sign a false confession. He then switched back
to his original account, that he had hurt himself.

Eventually the investigating judge announced that both versions were
possible. Martinovic's humiliation was finally over, but by then he had
entered modern Serbian folklore as an example of Albanian terror against
Serbs. Years later even sophisticated Belgrade liberals would recount
Martinovic's ordeal with a frisson of delighted horror. Certainly this
episode had a particular resonance in the national psyche. It went hand
in hand with claims that Albanian men were systematically raping Serb
women, although in fact incidents of rape were lower in Kosovo than
elsewhere in Yugoslavia.[6] Perhaps Martinovic's ordeal by bottle was a
metaphor for the deep-seated fear of Serbs, that somehow the Albanians
were violating Kosovo, the spiritual heart of Serbia.

Meanwhile, Slobodan Milosevic, head of the Serbian Communist
Party, watched and waited. He followed the Titoist line, but avoided
making any significant public attacks against the Memorandum. He
began to realise that increasingly, Serbian leaders were stuck in a double
bind over the Memorandum. They could not support it openly, even
though they may have sympathised with some of its demands. But the
more they condemned SANU, the more they delegitimised themselves
among the wider Serbian population, for favouring the wider interests of
Yugoslavia over the immediate ones of Serbia. Serbs began to feel that not
only had Yugoslavia failed them, but even their own political leadership
was neglecting them. Here then, saw Milosevic, was an opportunity.

On 20 April 1987, he took it. Ivan Stambolic despatched Milosevic on a
mission to Kosovo Polje, the hamlet known as the 'Field of Blackbirds',
built on the spot where in 1389 Prince Lazar had been defeated in a
historic battle with the Ottoman army of Sultan Murad I. Stambolic
wanted Milosevic to defuse the nationalist tensions between Serbs
and Albanians that were threatening social peace in the impoverished
province, and indeed the stability of all federal Yugoslavia. Milosevic
gave the assembled Serbs the standard party line of 'Brotherhood and
Unity': 'Exclusive nationalism based on national hatreds can never be
progressive.' In response a Serb demonstrator shouted that, 'We have
waited here since Tito's days. The Communist Party has done nothing
for us. Nothing!' To that Milosevic gave an intriguing reply: 'We
are aware of this in the Central Committee of Serbia. We could
do more.'[7]

Accosted by a local Serb leader, a paunchy nationalist called Miroslav Solevic, Milosevic agreed to return four days later to discuss what that 'more' could be. Milosevic had been taken aback by the depth of feeling in Kosovo and the sheer passion and fury of the local Serbs. Until then he had not been particularly interested in Kosovo, said Dusan Mitevic. 'I am from Kosovo and I was trying to persuade him to go there and see the problems. Milosevic thought that Stambolic should be involved, not him, that it was a government affair, not one for the party president.'[8]

But Milosevic was a Serb, as were his wife and his key advisers. He understood the power of the Kosovo myth for most Serbs. Serbs regard Kosovo as their Jerusalem. Kosovo is seen as the cradle of Serb civilisation, its loss condemning Serbs to centuries of darkness – as they saw it – under Ottoman rule. The question was how to harness it for his own career, without openly slipping into nationalism that could provoke a backlash from other political leaders. Thus began his mastery of what may be called post-Tito ambiguity: the ability to exploit rising nationalism within the framework of Titoist orthodoxy. More simply, to ensure that when he was accused of being a nationalist, Milosevic had what is known in Washington, D.C. as 'plausible deniability.'

Back in Belgrade, Milosevic consulted his closest advisers about how to handle the situation in Kosovo Polje when he returned there. 'He consulted me,' said Mira. 'Should he speak? How far should he go? I said the time had come to back the Kosovo Serbs.' Milosevic himself said: 'The situation in Kosovo was intolerable. Serbs had been deprived of their rights. Who would think our country capable of such discrimination?'[9] Meanwhile, in Kosovo, Miroslav Solevic was preparing a riot. 'We had no time – three days to organise everything. We each took an area to organise. We told our lads to prepare for a real fight. We parked two lorries full of stones. We didn't say they were there for the police. They were there "just in case".'[10] The aim of the coming violence was to pit the Serb demonstrators against the mostly Albanian police, in order to further polarise the growing ethnic division in the province and deligitimise Belgrade's rule, for failing to protect the local Serbs. Even if they were instigating the violence themselves.

Fifteen thousand angry Serbs awaited Milosevic on his return. He arrived with the local Albanian Communist leader, Azem Vllasi, and the two men had to be escorted into the local *Dom Kulture* (House of Culture) by squads of police, holding back the angry Serbs. Vllasi was one of Tito's protégés, a Yugoslav politician who stood for dialogue between the Albanians and Belgrade. He later claimed that Milosevic had earlier sent an agent to Kosovo to prepare the confrontation. Whatever Milosevic's precise relationship with Solevic, and the planning of the demonstration, he was certainly taken aback by the ferocity of the Serb crowd. More used to inner-party intrigue than screaming demonstrators, Milosevic was nervous and almost shaking.

The Serbs outside the hall hurled a barrage of insults and stones, and surged forward in an attempt to get inside. The police repeatedly beat them back. Inside speaker after speaker took the podium to berate the authorities and the Albanians as the rocks rained down on the walls. Some of the speakers inside the House of Culture declared that Serbs did not have a problem with illiterate Albanian peasants, but educated ones could not be tolerated. According to Vllasi, '[they said] the ones that went to school were to blame, that they could no longer put up with Albanian women wearing hats, Albanian women driving cars, etc. I swear they did mention hats.'[11] Miroslav Solevic harangued the audience: 'We must stop this Serb exodus. We have to stem this flood, or there will be no Serbs left. Our dearest wish is to live here . . . but not like this! No and no!'[12] Outside the hall scuffles were breaking out between crowds and the police. The mob was howling.

Vllasi and other educated Albanians were particularly hated. In their twin obsessions with supposed Albanian rapists and Albanian education, the Serbs unconsciously echoed the fears and insecurities of whites in the deep south of the United States, of black sexual prowess and 'uppity niggers' getting ideas above their station. Language played a similar role in Kosovo to the deep south. The reasonably respectful term 'negro' was, by a minuscule phonetic alteration, turned into the insulting 'nigger'. Albanians called themselves *Shqiptars* in their own language. Serbs, by a slip of the tongue, used the term *Shiptar*, the Balkan equivalent of 'nigger'.

In his work *Crowds and Power*, the Bulgarian Nobel laureate Elias Canetti classified crowds according to their prevailing emotion. Every crowd is composed of individuals who have subsumed their individuality to a collective desire, whether to lose themselves in the music at a pop concert or feel the power of Hitler's rhetoric at a Nazi rally. In a one-party state and authoritarian political regime such as Communist Yugoslavia, which had no democratic outlet for political dissent, any unauthorised crowd was a collective decision to defy the authorities. It meant trouble. The angry mob of Serbs and Montenegrins outside

Kosovo Polje's *Dom Kulture* roughly conformed to Canetti's concept of the 'Reversal Crowd'. A Reversal Crowd is a revolutionary phenomenon, dedicated to overturning the established order. The French mob who stormed the Bastille on 14 July 1789, triggering the French Revolution, was an example of a Reversal Crowd.

> People who are habitually ordered about . . . can free themselves in two different ways. They can pass on to others the orders which they have received from above; but, for them to be able to do this, there must be others below them who are ready to accept their orders. Or they can try to pay back to their superiors themselves what they have suffered and stored up for them.[13]

Yugoslavia was not the totalitarian tyranny of Romania, but it was still a one-party state. To some extent every Yugoslav, not just Kosovo Serbs, was 'habitually ordered about'. But the growth of an educated Albanian elite and the end of the old hierarchy – symbolised by Albanian women driving cars and wearing hats – meant that there was no longer an underclass ready to 'accept their orders'. So, just as Canetti predicted, the Serbs demonstrators tried to pay their superiors back for what they had suffered.

Crowds and Power was published more than twenty years before the events in Kosovo, but Canetti predicted Solevic's modus operandi with uncanny precision. Solevic was merely an archetypal foot soldier in a 'Crowd Crystal': 'small, rigid groups of men, strictly delineated and of great constancy, which serve to precipitate crowds . . . Its members are trained in both action and faith.' Solevic and his 'lads' went to work and duly precipitated the crowd. Solevic recalled: 'Our boys outside ran for the stones we had parked there. They turned and pelted the police. Each policeman got a "gift" from the masses. On the head, on the helmet, on the back.'

This was Milosevic's moment of truth. The physical guarantors of the Yugoslav state – in this case the police – were facing defeat by a riotous mob. Somebody had to take control. Solevic went to Milosevic. 'I said the police outside are beating our people. He couldn't pass this hot potato to anyone else. So he walked outside. He was obviously afraid. He knew he was playing for high stakes.'

Film of the event shows Milosevic coming out of the *Dom Kulture* dressed in his usual grey suit, with his characteristic robotic gait, looking around as he tries to process the situation. Milosevic was skilled in the politics of the committee, but was less at home with those of the street. Physical confrontation had never been his style and he was visibly nervous at the potential for further violence. The Serbs were demonstrating not just against the Albanians, but also the Communist state which they believed had betrayed them. And the head of the Serbian Communist Party was just a few feet in front of them. After hesitating a few seconds, Milosevic calls out 'Comrades, comrades!' An old man shouts back, 'The Albanians got in among us. We were beaten up. Please! They're beating us up.'[14]

It is one of the enduring mysteries of history that the decisions of certain individuals at a particular time have the power to turn the world upside down. Such events may be dramatic, or more prosaic. Decaying empires are perhaps the most vulnerable. On 28 June 1914 the Serb student Gavrilo Princip shot dead Archduke Franz Ferdinand as he was driven through Sarajevo. Soon after, the First World War was declared, and the Habsburg empire was among its casualties. Milosevic's delivery of the coup de grace to Tito's Yugoslavia was mundane in comparison, although it too ultimately led to years of war. Fearful of the crowd, but aware he should try and take command of the situation, he declared: 'No one should dare to beat you again!'

These apparently anodyne words changed everything. A delegation was invited in for a meeting that lasted twelve hours. Like all Communist officials Milosevic was hardly used to the idea of being accountable. But he was astute enough to put protocol aside, listen and understand the political value of what he was hearing from the Kosovo Serbs. In itself, to proclaim that no one should be beaten was neither revolutionary nor nationalistic. But he understood the power of that moment. He told his audience:

> This is your land, your fields, your gardens, your memories are here. Surely you will not leave your land because it is difficult here and you are oppressed . . . You should also stay here because of your ancestors and because of your descendants. Otherwise you would disgrace your ancestors, and disappoint your descendants. I do not propose, com- rades, that in staying you should suffer and tolerate a situation in which you are not satisfied. On the contrary you should change it.[15]

Back in Belgrade, the brotherhood and unity between Milosevic and

Stambolic was also beginning to fray. Stambolic, the old-style Yugoslav, was aghast at how Milosevic had openly sided with one ethnic group in Kosovo, and had aligned the Serbian Communist Party with the Serbian national cause, and against the police, symbol of the state itself. But the very turn of events that had horrified Stambolic, the believer in Yugoslavia, was precisely what attracted a growing number of Serbs to Milosevic. Stambolic said: 'I asked him, "if you go on like this, what will become of our country?" I saw we were totally opposed in our methods. We had two different policies on Kosovo. The distance between us began to grow.'[16] Mira Markovic took a different view. According to her, the Kosovo Serbs 'fell in love with Slobodan because he gave them support against the violence they were experiencing'. She explained: 'It is very simple, if I protect you, you begin to love me. You look at me like a saviour and that is what they thought about him. There is nothing mystical in this. He said, nobody can beat you anymore, and they were beaten before. So that is why they were encouraged to have someone in whom they could hope.'[17]

If Milosevic was losing old friends, he soon gained new ones. His speech in Kosovo found an appreciative echo in an unusual constituency. A week after his visit to Kosovo Polje, a poem appeared in the cultural magazine *Knjizevne Novine*.

> But a handsome young speaker arrived
> the setting sun falling on his brushed hair
> I will speak with my people in open spaces, he says,
> in schoolyards and in fields[18]

For liberals such as Zivorad Kovacevic, this sudden outbreak of mutual admiration between nationalists and a Communist official was both curious and significant. 'Milosevic immediately gained the support of the Serbian intellectual and nationalist elite. They thought that after the famous Kosovo episode that Milosevic was their man. The idea of course was that they would use him. But he used them.'[19]

Now began a delicate wooing. During the summer of 1987 Milosevic deployed all his powers of political seduction to his different constituencies. The nationalists were simple, especially after Dusan Mitevic went to work at Belgrade Television. Film of Milosevic proclaiming, 'No one should dare to beat you again' was broadcast repeatedly. It was a well-turned phrase, with some factual basis. More problematic was the way in which Milosevic's promise was exploited. Milan Kucan remembered: 'The fateful words by Milosevic, when he justifiably reacted to the Albanian policemen beating the Serbs in Kosovo, are well known. He said: "No one will beat you again," "you" being Serbs. He did not say, no one will ever beat anyone again in Kosovo. He said the Serbs will never be beaten again.'[20]

But Milosevic faced strengthening opposition among Stambolic and his associates, who still exerted considerable power and influence. It was still too early to move against them openly. Milosevic bought time to prepare his campaign, and in public still spoke the language of Titoism, stressing his commitment to Yugoslavia. He visited the interior minister to assure him that he had not meant to denigrate the police in Kosovo by his rhetoric. 'Milosevic was afraid of the reaction of the Communist apparat when he came back from Kosovo Polje. In one party meeting, he even said that Serb nationalism was dangerous,' said Tahir Hasanovic.[21] In June 1987 Milosevic delivered the following analysis of the Memorandum to a select audience of party officials:

> The appearance of the Memorandum of the Serbian Academy of Arts and Sciences represents nothing else but the darkest nationalism. It means the liquidation of the current socialist system of our country, that is the disintegration after which there is no survival for any nation or nationality . . . Tito's policy of brotherhood and unity . . . is the only basis on which Yugoslavia's survival can be secured.[22]

All this left Stambolic with a serious problem. Attempting to reconcile the demands of both Serbian nationalism and Titoist Communism, he ended up satisfying no one. Although he was essentially a man of good will, a pragmatist ready to negotiate, he was a prisoner of his upbringing in a one-party state. The nationalists believed that, unlike Milosevic, he was not a strong enough defender of Serbian interests in Kosovo. The Communists – especially among the military – believed he was not a strong enough defender of Yugoslavia. The next logical step would be for Stambolic and others in the leadership to move towards liberalisation, as Gorbachev was doing in Moscow.

But Stambolic could not make the political leap of faith, said Milos Vasic.

He was aware of the crisis in Kosovo and the growth and revival of

Serb nationalism. Stambolic tried to negotiate with them. But this was an inevitable shortcoming of the Communist way of thinking, and the Communist apparatus. They could not conceptualise a political alternative to nationalism. They saw that the whole structure of Communism was falling apart world-wide. But by definition they could not support liberal democracy. It was unthinkable for them.[23]

Milosevic had grasped something more than the power of nationalism on his visit to Kosovo. He witnessed at first hand the power of the mob. He had been seduced by the mercurial ferocity of the crowd, its easy menace and hair-trigger potential for violence. Milosevic himself was a somewhat wooden speaker, who lacked the charisma of Tito. But he was an able student of mob dynamics, who could, through simple and repetitive language, voice the grievances of the Serbian masses, and manipulate them for his own ends.

Like Benito Mussolini and Adolf Hitler, Milosevic understood that whoever controls the streets will ultimately control the government. Especially at a time of transition, when control is slipping away from the ancien régime – whether Germany's Weimar Republic or Tito's Yugoslavia – and the old instruments and symbols of authority are losing their power. Still, he had to be careful. Milosevic did not want to make a revolution and smash Tito's Yugoslavia. He wanted to co-opt the existing power structures – of state, party and army – for Serbia. So the power of the mob had to be deployed quite carefully. State power – especially Yugoslav, federal power – had to be steadily transferred to the Serbian Republic. To do that the Yugoslav leadership and its political prestige had to be weakened.

In mid-June 1987 Milosevic set up a meeting of the Yugoslav party leadership to discuss Kosovo. Milosevic and his allies believed that Serbia should be a unified republic, and the autonomy of both Kosovo and Voivodina cancelled. Bosko Krunic was a political leader from Serbia's northern province of Voivodina.

My first impression of Milosevic was of an ambitious, bold man. He was very straightforward about the autonomy of Voivodina. He opposed it. Even when we met informally, from the beginning our relationship was very cold. Both Stambolic and Milosevic wanted to cut down on this autonomy. Stambolic wanted to do it together with the other republics, Milosevic was strictly against any autonomy.[24]

With the aid of Miroslav Solevic, three thousand Serbs made the journey from Kosovo to Belgrade. The angry crowd assembled just across from the federal parliament. Such demonstrations were not an everyday event in Communist Yugoslavia, but with the support of Milosevic, Serbian party chief, such events could be arranged. This time Solevic and his 'lads' hurled only abuse and invective, not rocks. For now, that was sufficient for Milosevic's purposes. The Kosovo Serbs demanded the abolition of Kosovo's autonomy, humiliating the federal Yugoslav leadership. Ivica Racan, a Croatian political leader, entered discussions that lasted for several hours, before the Kosovo Serbs eventually went home.

This episode was more than a display of anger by aggrieved Serbs. It highlighted the waning power of the federal authorities, who could no longer even keep proper order on the streets of the capital. It demonstrated that the normal political channels could be circumvented by physical force, or at least its threat. And it showed that when the nationalist mob howled, instead of dispersing it by force the authorities would instead listen and negotiate.

Milosevic's summer of plotting ended on 3 September 1987, when an Albanian army recruit called Aziz Keljmendi ran amok, shooting four soldiers dead and wounding six more. His victims included Muslims, a Slovene and a Croat, as well as one Serb, almost a microcosm of Yugoslavia, and its multi-ethnic army. Although army doctors ruled that Keljmendi had been mentally ill when he went berserk, the Serb media seized on the event, portraying Keljmendi's rampage as politically motivated. Zivorad Minovic, editor in chief of *Politika*, and a key Milosevic ally, knew what to do. *Politika* reported: 'Mindless rounds of the murderer Keljmendi, who, everything indicates, did not pull the trigger alone, will not and cannot shake our trust in our army.'[25] In one sentence are packed three messages: that Keljmendi killed his fellow soldiers on purpose; that he was part of an Albanian plot, and only the Yugoslav army could prevent future killings by Albanians. The Yugoslav army was being co-opted onto the cause of Serbian nationalism.

Thousands attended the funeral of the one Serb soldier killed in the rampage. Shouting nationalist slogans, they created such a furore that the dead boy's father demanded some dignity and respect for his son as he was being buried. In Belgrade Ivan Stambolic and Dragisa Pavlovic moved to stop the increasing hatred and xenophobia. Pavlovic, a sophisticated thinker, understood that a showdown was inevitable.

Just over a week later, on 11 September, he chaired a conference for senior media editors to try and calm the situation. He delivered a sober assessment of the situation in Kosovo, recognising that Serb nationalism was growing, and that Serbs were feeling increasingly beleaguered. He correctly recognised that the situation had deteriorated into a perilous zero-sum game. Any statement against Serb nationalism was immediately seen as support for its Albanian equivalent. Ill-considered words in public life, or in a newspaper, could lead to an explosion, he said:

> How many Albanian shop windows must be broken to convince us that anti-Albanian feeling does not exist only in the warnings issued in the highest [party] organs but in our streets as well ... Serbian nationalism now feeds not only on the situation in Kosovo, but also on the various ill-considered statements concerning Kosovo that appear in some of our media, public speeches and institutions of our system ... We must criticise Serbian nationalism today because, among other things, Serbian nationalists imagine themselves as saviours of the Serbian cause in Kosovo, without in fact being able to solve a single social problem, and especially without being able to improve inter-nationality events.[26]

The speech was a reasoned, well-judged and prescient analysis. It was also a powerful, barely-disguised attack on the Milosevic camp, and was seen by Milosevic and his supporters as a declaration of political war.

8

ET TU, SLOBODAN

Ousting Stambolic
August–September 1987

When somebody looks at your back for twenty-five years, it is understandable that he gets the desire to put a knife in it at some point.

Ivan Stambolic.[1]

As soon as Pavlovic's meeting with the editors was over, Dusan Mitevic went to see Milosevic. He was sprawled in an armchair, with his tie off and his feet up, watching a report on television. Pavlovic, said the reporter, had attacked a 'certain comrade' who 'made an anti-communist speech' which 'pretended to offer a solution to the Kosovo problem'. Everyone knew who he meant. But perhaps it was best this way. The battle lines had been drawn. On top of this, there was a personal grudge as well. When Milosevic had vacated the post of Belgrade party chief Ivan Stambolic had refused to allow Milosevic's candidate to take over, and had instead chosen Pavlovic. That had been over a year earlier, but Milosevic had not forgotten. All of these were more than enough ingredients to trigger a political war within the Serbian Communist Party.

Even so, it was Friday and nothing could be allowed to interrupt the cult of Pozarevac. The neighbours were waiting with their basket of stuffed peppers. Milosevic and Mira were packed and ready to go. He told Mitevic, 'OK, now I am leaving, and on Monday we are going to consider what to do.'[2] In the event, Milosevic did not wait until Monday. He telephoned Mitevic the next day. Mira had written an article that portrayed the dispute between Pavlovic and Milosevic as a political struggle waged by defenders of Serbian interests against those who would sacrifice them. Milosevic's ally Zivorad Minovic agreed to print the article in *Politika*. The problem was, nobody wanted to sign the piece. The Serbian party chief could not defend himself in print in such a manner, and nor could his wife. It would look demeaning. Dragoljub Milanovic, a sycophantic hack who walked around the *Politika* newsroom with a pistol in his belt, agreed to put his name to the piece.

When the article was published, all of Yugoslavia understood what was happening. The battle between the two factions began in earnest. Ostensibly it was about Kosovo. One side was led by Ivan Stambolic and Dragisa Pavlovic, who sought some kind of consensus, to be achieved through slow and patient negotiations with Albanian leaders. The Milosevic faction, in contrast, demanded rapid and dynamic action. But this was not the real issue. The Milosevic camp had their eye on a much bigger prize. They planned to bring down the whole partisan generation and the Tito-era figures who still ran Yugoslavia. Their method was the expedient exploitation of nationalism, populism and mob dynamics. At that time their objective was 'merely' winning domestic political power. But this cold and cynical decision ultimately helped set in motion a chain of events that led to four wars.

If Dusan Mitevic saw himself as a Balkan Machiavelli, Milosevic's other key ally at this time was more of a Serbian pitbull. A former manager of the Zastava car factory, Borisav Jovic was a senior party official: the archetypal Communist apparatchik who has tasted power in a one-party state and will resort to almost anything to keep it. Short and aggressive, he modelled his political style – quick, decisive, confrontational – on his master's and shared his taste for double-breasted suits. When Milosevic consulted Jovic about how to deal with Pavlovic, the answer was swift. 'I was categorical. That man must be expelled from the party. He [Milosevic] liked the idea, but he wasn't sure we could pull it off. This amounted to going for the President [Stambolic] himself.'[3] The split between the Milosevic and Pavlovic/Stambolic factions was symptomatic of the strains – political, economic and nationalist – now beginning to wrench apart the fragile Yugoslav state.

The Eighth Session of the Serbian Communist Party central committee, scheduled for 22 September, would be a major battleground. The usual preparatory political skirmishes were being fought. In party and government buildings apparatchiks huddled in smoke-wreathed cabals as they plotted their futures. It was increasingly clear to Pavlovic that he lacked the necessary forces to outmanoeuvre Milosevic at the session, so he decided to rebase on his own territory. He called a meeting of the Belgrade party and told those attending that Stambolic had written him a letter which declared that if Pavlovic was called to speak at the Eighth Session, Stambolic should be left to deal with the matter.

This was a blunder. Firstly, in Yugoslav politics to put things in writing was generally a mistake.[4] Secondly, Stambolic was the President of the Serbian republic, and the forthcoming Eighth Session was a meeting of the Serbian Communist Party central committee, not the Serbian government. The party was subordinate to the state, but like all political organisations, the Yugoslav Communist parties zealously guarded their territory from incursions, whether from the republic governments or federal institutions. Like British members of parliament who are perpetually dragooned into the voting lobbies by party whips, every now and again they rebelled against authority.

Ivan Stambolic's letter was not well received by Dusan Mitevic and other members of the Belgrade party committee: 'The letter said Stambolic was not expecting any discussion about Pavlovic, and the message was that we should shut up. This was unprecedented. I said immediately that I would do what I felt, that as a Communist I would not submit to this pressure.' Mitevic scented political blood. 'I also understood that they were losing. This letter was the proof. The president should never pressurise the party.' Nonetheless, at that meeting, the Belgrade party leadership did vote to support Pavlovic.

Milosevic then upped the stakes. On 18 September the presidency of the Serbian party met. There Stambolic tried to broker a deal between his two protégés. A reasonable and decent man, he repeatedly called for compromise and negotiation to defuse the political tension. He suggested that they meet for coffee every day. Or maybe even lemonade. Stambolic's touching suggestion showed how much the old-style compromiser was out of his depth. The time was long past for coffee or lemonade. Pavlovic was accused of impeding 'ideological unity' by the Milosevic camp. This was a catch-all phrase which essentially meant whatever the accuser wanted.

Still, Milosevic needed something more than this. He was wobbling. Mira telephoned him, to discuss how the meeting was progressing. She told her husband that there was no going back, he was too exposed. She was right. If Milosevic blew this, there would be no second chance. Dusan Mitevic went into action. He drafted a letter saying that he and four other members of the Belgrade party committee had been pressurised by Ivan Stambolic into supporting Dragisa Pavlovic.

The next morning, Milosevic, like Neville Chamberlain on his return from Munich, held in his hand a piece of paper. His face was thunderous as he took the podium. 'I thought the Russians had invaded, or the Third World War had begun,' recalled Stambolic. Milosevic spoke as though he had just read the letter for the first time.

> Comrades, I have hesitated for the last hour or two. We have received a letter. First I asked for it to be checked as authentic, that there wasn't some mistake. Then I doubted whether one could actually read out this letter at the Presidency itself . . .[5]

With the full attention of the four-dozen odd people at the meeting, Milosevic backtracked slightly. A little humility was in order before the final act in this brutal piece of political theatre. 'Maybe I will be making a mistake . . .'

By reading out the letter, Milosevic was arguing he had evidence that Stambolic was engaged in personal intrigues against the best interests of the party. Of course intrigue and plots were the lifeblood of the Serbian Communist Party, like every other political organisation. Milosevic seized the moment, and called for a vote to recommend the expulsion of Pavlovic. But only eleven out of twenty supported Milosevic. Five voted against, and four abstained. It was not a decisive enough victory over the Stambolic group. None the less Milosevic could not resist some parting words to his former friend: 'I sincerely hope, I believe it firmly, that Comrade Stambolic was manipulated and not guilty.'

Mitevic said that his letter was influential in saving Milosevic that day. 'The Central Committee was split . . . Stambolic's biggest problem was that he had not said he had written his first letter to us, so people got angry with him for acting behind the scenes. Even people who were against Milosevic said that they did not know this kind of thing was going on.'

Shortly before the actual Eighth Session was due to begin, a curious buzzing sound filled Milosevic's office. 'Milosevic hums to himself when he prepares for political battle. He paces up and down, alone, and hums like a guru or dervish,' said Mihailo Crnobrnja. But not all the guru's associates were happy with his new nationalist doctrine and the attack on Pavlovic. Crnobrnja had not taken part in Milosevic's attempt in 1986 to block Pavlovic's succession to his post as head of the Belgrade

Communist Party. 'In a sense he let me off the hook then. He did not
ask me to support him, because that would have put me in a very difficult
position. He did not talk to me about nationalism because he knew I did
not agree with it. I liked Pavlovic very much and he was a good friend
of mine. On the other hand, the message was that I should not make a
show of defiance.'[6]

The opening day of the Eighth Session, 22 September, would prove to
be a pivotal event in Yugoslav history. The meeting was supposedly about
economics, but that was merely a pretext for the political assassination
of Pavlovic, and, by extension, of Stambolic. Dusan Mitevic prepared
to broadcast the events on live television. Thirty years earlier Tito
had exploited the radio for live broadcasts of the party meeting that
considered the fate of the dissident writer Milovan Djilas. Now Milosevic
was learning the power of having the broadcast media under his control.
He could speak directly to the nation, and reach straight into the homes
of the Serbs.

Milosevic was playing for high stakes. Once he went public with
the new, 'nationalist' line – even if voiced in Titoist language – there
would be no going back. If Milosevic triumphed it would be the end
of the ancien régime. But if he and his group failed, Stambolic and his
allies would have no option but to crush them politically. Milosevic's
career would certainly be over, and if he went down, all his allies would
follow. They might even be sent to prison on some or other charge. In
a Communist state such things are easily arranged.

When the session opened Milosevic immediately attacked. He heaped
praise on Tito as a leader who had brought unity to Yugoslavia, then
accused Pavlovic of being against Tito and Yugoslavia. The charge was
absurd. Pavlovic had for weeks tried to maintain brotherhood and unity
between Serbs and Albanians, and calm the very nationalist hysteria that
Milosevic was fostering. But there was no place for logic. In the Alice in
Wonderland world of Serbian Communism, anti-logic ruled. For this was
a show trial, part of a tradition that stretched back to Stalinist Russia and the
Spanish Inquisition. The grand inquisitor might be Milosevic in Belgrade,
Vishinsky in Moscow, or Torquemada in Spain, but the ritual was identical:
some or other arbitrary standard was set, theological or ideological, which
the accused could never meet. Pavlovic could just as well have been charged
with secretly reading the Torah in Catholic Granada, thought-crime against
Stalin, or stealing chocolate from Serbian schoolchildren.

The dry words of party rhetoric spoken by Milosevic were long drained of any meaning. He proclaimed: 'We expected trouble from the Kosovo separatists. But we didn't expect it from party members here. Those who obstruct our reforms violate party discipline. They can't deny it.'[7] Stambolic proved to be a tough opponent. He attacked Milosevic for calling for party unity, while actually fostering dissent. Milosevic, he said, should try and avoid conflict. The country watched transfixed as the battle played out on its television screens.

The small minority of liberals at the session were not taken in. They were outnumbered, but they could still speak, for the historical record, if nothing else. A young historian called Ljubinka Trgovcevic accused Milosevic of 'using methods which were abandoned long ago'.[8] Milosevic canvassed every possible vote at the Eighth Session, including the leader of the Kosovo Albanians, Azem Vllasi. 'Milosevic said, "Azem, get me the Kosovo delegation's votes. Help me out on this one." I said, no way!'[9] Vllasi's refusal sparked a tirade of abuse from Milosevic, who was not used to being thwarted. Milosevic called him a 'cunt'. Vllasi retorted that Milosevic was 'a liar and a cheat'. Some delegates carried two speeches in their pockets, depending on how the vote went, recalled Trgovcevic. 'The atmosphere was terrible. People were standing and biting their nails. Everyone turned greyer and greyer.'

Pre-arranged telegrams of support poured in from provincial leaders, and from the Kosovo Serbs. The Milosevic bandwagon was now unstoppable. Milosevic himself stuck to Orwellian double-speak. It was not acceptable, he said, for the leaders of the Serbian Communist Party to be threatened with accusations of nationalism.

> Serbian nationalists would do the greatest harm to the Serbian people today by what they offer as being allegedly the best thing, namely isolating the Serbian people . . . No one can label us Serbian nationalists because we want to, and really will, resolve the problem of Kosovo in the interests of all the people who live there.

Film of the Eighth Session shows Stambolic's gradual realisation of what was happening to him and Pavlovic. Like a bull in a Spanish arena, he is first wounded by the picadors as they advance to pierce and stab his skin. A Milosevic ally, Dusan Ckrebic, accused Stambolic of 'behaving like a dictator'. He replied: 'I don't understand. Why do you accuse me of being a dictator. It's not my problem, I'm not the dictator.' Then the matador – Milosevic himself – moves in for the kill.

Milosevic called the vote. Dragisa Pavlovic was expelled from the Serbian party presidency. Milosevic savoured the moment. The lonely Pozarevac schoolboy, whose mother dressed him in a white shirt and tie before he set off for the classroom each morning, had come a long way.

The course of Yugoslav history might have taken a very different turn had Pavlovic not been defeated at the Eighth Session of the Serbian Communist Party's central committee. He was the kind of thoughtful political leader who understood that, with the approaching end of Communism, Yugoslavia needed to move towards social democracy and political liberalisation. With some nudging, and enough political support, Stambolic too might have eventually moved in this direction. Pavlovic left political life and died nine years later. A few days after the Eighth Session, Stambolic met with Milosevic and General Nikola Ljubicic, one of Milosevic's key backers in the army. Stambolic was allowed to continue as Serbian President until 14 December 1987. He then followed Milosevic into the world of international banking. The new president of Serbia was a retired general, a hawk-faced former partisan called Peter Gracanin.

Stambolic was a tragic figure, who made the fatal mistake of believing that his friendship with Milosevic was protection enough. In the rural, patriarchal Serbian society from which he came, a man's word was his bond. It was simply unthinkable, something outside his mental universe, that his *kum* could betray him. Others saw what was coming. Zivorad Kovacevic had warned Stambolic about Milosevic. At a farewell lunch after his appointment as Yugoslav ambassador to the United States in 1987, Kovacevic asked Stambolic:

'Ivan, what are you going to do with this man? Don't you see that he is preparing something against you, behind your back?' Milosevic had his people everywhere, especially in the media, but they were leaky. Stambolic said to me, 'I believed that you would be the last man to succumb to rumours like those, which are completely groundless.' I said, 'Ivan, you are a fool'. He was a bit offended, but said nothing.[10]

Kovacevic recalled a later conversation with Stambolic: 'I asked him, "Ivan, do you remember what the last words I said to you were?" He said, "Yes, you told me that I am stupid." I asked him what he thought now. He said, "Well, there is some truth in that".'

Stambolic's life was soon touched by a far worse tragedy. Early in 1988 his daughter Bojana was killed in a car crash. Milosevic attended the funeral. He and Stambolic embraced. Ivan's wife Katja, for whom Milosevic had once brought back so many gifts from New York, refused to acknowledge Milosevic's presence. The friendship between Milosevic and Stambolic was over, forever.

With hindsight it is clear that sending Milosevic to Kosovo was one of the biggest political mistakes of Stambolic's career. Yet how apparent was it then that Kosovo would become such a pivotal issue? In a sense Kosovo was Yugoslavia's Northern Ireland, continually rumbling in the background, and every now and again exploding into violence. Riots and demonstrations had erupted sporadically for years, and Kosovo was a long way from Belgrade.

According to Mitevic, Stambolic should have negotiated with Milosevic. Mitevic claimed that Pavlovic, not Stambolic, was the target.

> Stambolic showed that he was not a capable politician, he should not have taken anyone's side. He should have tried to make a deal with Milosevic . . . Milosevic did one thing that foreigners don't understand and that we forgot. During the 1980s there was a change of generation happening in Yugoslavia. A lot of old people, war heroes, were still in power. They kept everything for themselves. Milosevic was the only young man, from our generation, with a chance to break that generation. Everyone supported him.

Milosevic's toppling of Stambolic was supported by several factions within the party that would later turn against him. His triumph was not the result of some kind of diabolical manipulation. Certainly it was testimony to his powers of organisation, but he also understood the zeitgeist. Mihailo Crnobrnja said: 'In those days, unfortunately, most of the people felt that Milosevic was right. There was an impatience, and an underlying sense that Serbia was getting a raw deal, and that Stambolic was not doing enough. He was working slowly and patiently to change attitudes and views by balancing political forces, not by forcing people's arms.'

The Eighth Session was a battle between the generations, said Mira Markovic. 'The conflict had arisen before it began. The older generation did not have any feelings about reforms. I don't mind that, you cannot expect someone who is seventy to have the same view as a man of

forty. They lived in a different world. They had fought the battles of
the revolution, they had one view. I respected that, but their times
were over. That was nice and good in the 1950s, but not then.'[11] Ivan
Stambolic was a man of that era, as far as Mira was concerned. 'Those
leaders had long arms that reached into my husband's young generation.
Ivan Stambolic represented the old ways, a world and opinions that time
had passed by. He did not see things like my husband did, even though
he was only a few years older.'

By writing the letter that Milosevic had waved with such drama at
the Serbian party presidency meeting, Mitevic had ensured that the
vote went Milosevic's way. That victory helped set the future path of
Yugoslav history. Mitevic later said he had no regrets.

> I don't look at history that way. At that time Stambolic and Milosevic
> were both the same, just going after power. I think we did the right
> thing. We were pressurised and I did not like that. Stambolic was not
> a clever politician. He acted like it was his first day in politics. He took
> everything personally, which is not good for politicians. The Serbian
> ministers were behind Stambolic. They were the state and we were
> only a party central committee. They had the power, but they could
> not keep it. They were dilettantes.

Tahir Hasanovic, Milosevic's 'young lion', then leader of the pro-
Milosevic faction in the party's youth wing, was away at the time doing
his military service. With hindsight, he admitted that it was fortuitous
timing. 'Now I know I was lucky. My position then and my beliefs
were that I would have supported Milosevic at the Eighth Session.'[12]

In 1987, Hungary's Communist rulers, like their Yugoslav comrades, also
considered the future of their country in a changing world. Hungary's
leader was Janos Kadar, an elderly Communist of Tito's generation.
Like Tito, he had ruled with a soft touch. 'Goulash Communism', as
his era was known, was not quite as easygoing as Yugoslavia, but was
the most liberal in the Soviet bloc. Kadar made a pact with his citizens:
they would receive work, a home and holidays, even occasional travel
to the west, in exchange for social peace. His motto was: 'Those who
are not against us, are with us.' In 1988 Kadar was kicked upstairs to be
party president, a largely ceremonial post.

But Kadar was haunted by the violent events of thirty years earlier when the country rose up against the Soviets. The Hungarian revolution began on 23 October 1956. Its leader was Imre Nagy, an old comrade of Kadar's. Nagy was appointed prime minister of revolutionary Hungary, and Kadar was one of his deputies. Nagy promised a free and democratic Hungary, and the withdrawal of Soviet troops. For a week Nagy and Kadar were together every waking hour as their countrymen battled the Soviet troops.

It became increasingly clear that, alone, the Hungarians could never defeat the Soviets, but no military aid was coming from the West: a free and independent country on the border of the Soviet Union would destabilise the cold war balance of power. Like Belgrade in 1987, Budapest during the 1956 revolution was also a time to choose. Kadar changed sides and went over to the Russians. The Soviet tanks rolled in. The brave and quixotic Hungarian revolution was crushed. Bodies lay in the streets, and tens of thousands fled across the Austrian border. Imre Nagy, symbol of Hungarian freedom, took refuge in the Yugoslav embassy. Kadar eventually persuaded him to leave with a false promise of immunity. Nagy was then arrested and taken to Romania. After a secret trial, Nagy, together with other leaders, was executed in June 1958, under Kadar's personal authorisation.

Nagy and the others were buried in unmarked graves in a distant unkempt area of a Budapest cemetery, known only as plot 301. And then, for thirty years, silence. The words unspoken were the most eloquent of all. Three months before he died in 1988, Kadar appeared at a meeting of the party central committee. In a rambling, incoherent speech he repeatedly referred to his 'responsibility'. Kadar could not say the name of the man whose execution he had ordered. Instead he talked only of a 'the person who had since deceased'. Some said that Kadar in his dotage spent his nights wandering through his Budapest villa, looking for the seal with which he had authorised Nagy's death warrant.

Was Milosevic similarly troubled? At the end of their friendship in the summer of 1987, Stambolic, it seems, was in some kind of state of denial about Milosevic. But before that the men's lives had been interlinked for two decades, since their time at university. To sign someone's death warrant, whether actual or political, especially a close friend's, exacts a high psychological price. Hitler had suffered emotionally after he ordered the Night of the Long Knives massacre in 1934 when the SS had wiped out the leadership of the rival SA, the brownshirts. The SA leader Eric Rohm was one of

Hitler's oldest friends and allies, but was still shot dead in his prison cell.

According to Mira, Milosevic and Stambolic were not particularly close. 'They were not such great friends. People have made that up, we were not even family friends. We did not visit each other. I could spend three days denying all the things that were written about us. I mentioned that name [Stambolic] because of the Eighth Session. This was the point when the two concepts of social development were in conflict, and parted. And that is the substance of the Eighth Session. It was not Kosovo or nationalism. That was the second topic on the agenda.'

Even without bloodshed, political assassination can trigger an obsession, a need to explain and rationalise such a deed. In 1988 Zivorad Kovacevic returned home to Belgrade from Washington, D.C. for a visit. He paid a courtesy call on Milosevic. 'Milosevic immediately started saying that he expected me to say something about the Eighth Session. I said I didn't see why, because I am just an ambassador. He told me that "Well, you are not just an ambassador. It would mean something." Milosevic wanted me to make a statement of support for him.'

This time, Milosevic did not get what he wanted. 'I told him I was disgusted by it.' Milosevic remained silent.

Meanwhile, the writers and intellectuals associated with the SANU Memorandum watched and waited. Such men were not Communists but they perfectly well understood the spectacle that had taken place at the Eighth Session. They knew that even those who seek to construct a new world must still draw on the methods of the old. The vicious infighting was clearly part of Serbia's political heritage, said the nationalist dissident and author Dobrica Cosic at the time, but where it would lead was not yet clear.

If one would consider this conflict from the national-anthropological perspective I would say that it illustrates the worst political traditions of the Serbian people – radical politics, power-seeking, nepotism, careerism, political vassalage from its general founder Milos Obrenovic up to the prince of the contemporary Serbian bureaucracy . . . But Milosevic's intentions remain a big question. Is this present victor a democratic reformer or a new political chief who threatens to draw upon the conservative essence of the League of Communists and a deluded and desperate people? I'm not acquainted with him. We will see.[13]

9

THERE ARE NO
FRIENDS ANYMORE

The Reform Commission and the Yoghurt Revolution
1988

Hilmi's position was doubly difficult. Not only was he responsible to the [Western] powers for the proper introduction and administration of the reforms, but he was also held responsible by his lord and master, the Sultan, for their successful non-introduction.

Reginald Wyon on Hilmi Pacha.[1]

It was a grandly titled grouping with far-reaching ambitions. The Serbian Presidential Commission for Economic Reforms had thirty-three members, all of them high-ranking individuals. The President of the Presidential Commission was of course Slobodan Milosevic. Its General Secretary was Mihailo Crnobrnja. Other members included the Serbian prime minister and the president of parliament. There were titles aplenty, but also some innovative proposals.

The Milosevic reform commission – as it was known – began work in January 1988. Here was the voice of Milosevic the banker, the pro-western reformer. The aim was to start the process that would lead to the introduction of a market economy in Yugoslavia. Western diplomats hailed its first papers as the start of a new era, which would bring Yugoslavia into the European market and begin the process of democratisation. After the party turmoil of the Eighth Session, perhaps now Milosevic could transform into a Balkan Gorbachev. When the Soviet leader himself visited Belgrade in March 1988, Milosevic toasted him with the words: 'In spite of all the difficulties, which it meets on a daily and historical basis, Socialism is the most progressive society of our era.'[2]

Even so, Milosevic admitted it needed some tuning-up. The reform

commission's work was a natural follow-up to the victory at the Eighth
Session, said Mira Markovic.

> I supported him in the need for economic development, and the
> reforms that were badly needed. It is very important, and everybody
> forgot this, that in the late 1980s my husband stood for major social
> reform in Serbia. The first should have been economic reform. But
> economic reforms are not enough. They need to be followed by
> social reforms, the transformation of the political system, changes
> in the socialist party and democratisation, allowing other political
> opinions to be expressed. That would have been an introduction
> to the multi-party system in Serbia, which would have led to a sense
> of a new, more modern and developed socialism.[3]

Thus Mira in 2002. At the time, the reality was very different. After
the Eighth Session Milosevic launched a purge of Stalinist efficiency,
although the victims were sacked rather than shot. The policy was
known as 'differentiation'. During late 1987 and through 1988 thousands
of officials, managers and other workers lost their jobs, as Milosevic began
his great project of re-engineering Serbian society and consolidating his
power. No workplace was too mundane to escape Milosevic's attentions.
Even the head waiter at the Serbian government villa lost his job,
replaced with a Milosevic loyalist. For many in Serbia there was a
feeling of profound insecurity, as a new nationalist order was built. In the
increasingly feverish atmosphere of Serbia in the late 1980s, the victims
of Milosevic's purges were seen by his loyalists as tainted. The message
was clear: Those who were not with Milosevic, were against him

Among those marked for the sack was Braca Grubacic, the editor
at the Mladost publishing house, who had previously met Milosevic
to discuss the controversial memoirs of General Jaksic. Grubacic and
Milosevic bumped into each other in the lift at the headquarters of the
Serbian Communist Party and chatted briefly. Milosevic was polite to
Grubacic's face, but adopted a different tone when he thought he was
out of hearing.

> Milosevic was in the lift with a couple of his people, and when I left
> I heard him comment about me to them. He said 'Oh, yeah that
> yellow-haired guy.' He was very dismissive. I got the impression
> that he behaved very differently when he was with you, than how

he actually felt about you. He is someone who will flatter you, but doesn't care at all about you, a man who will use people.[4]

Grubacic was fired on 1 January 1988. He was young, and comparatively resilient. Jug Grizelj was less so. In many ways Grizelj symbolised the best of Tito's multi-national Yugoslavia. A Croat by birth, he was president of the Serbian journalists association. He was also a friend of Zivorad Kovacevic, then still serving as Yugoslav ambassador to the United States. 'Grizelj's position tells you something about the conditions of Yugoslavia at that time. But then he was ousted and it was very dirty. He was very hurt and he needed some time, so I invited him to visit me in Washington,' recalled Kovacevic.[5]

But Milosevic had a spy in the embassy. One of Kovacevic's own officials, whom he had personally brought with him to Washington, D.C., was sending back a stream of reports. On a visit back home to Belgrade Kovacevic was questioned by two of Milosevic's flunkies. 'One asked me why I had invited Jug to Washington. I asked him how he knew. He told me not to be naïve, that my work was "followed" over there. I told them I invited Jug because he was one of my closest friends. The other one said, "Ziko, don't be silly. You are either with us, or against us. There no friends any more".'

And there was not much Brotherhood and Unity either. On television, across the pages of newspapers and magazines, the chorus of propaganda resounded ever louder. Its theme was simple: the Serbs are victims. Victims for centuries of Turkish oppression, and victims now of Albanian terror in Kosovo. Victims of Croat genocide during the Second World War, victims too of sneaky Slovenes who were creaming off Yugoslavia's riches. The role of the media in fostering the twin senses of victimhood and accompanying hate was vital. Out of cynicism, belief or just the need to feed their families, many writers followed the Milosevic line and churned out articles calculated to incite hate. Their morbid influence cannot be overestimated. Although Yugoslavia's press had been lively and sophisticated, and newspapers such as *Politika* had pushed the boundaries of free speech, the vast majority of Serbs, outside the Belgrade metropolitan elite, simply believed much of what they saw on television or read in the newspapers.

The tradition of dissent or scepticism was comparatively weak. Even anti-Communist figures such as Dobrica Cosic or Croatia's Franjo Tudjman were nationalists, rather than liberal humanists. Milovan Djilas,

Tito's former comrade turned dissident, had long been released from prison and was acclaimed as one of Yugoslavia's greatest intellectuals. His principled refusal to ride the nationalist wave brought him respect, but no great constituency.

Milosevic's propagandists deliberately fostered a national sense of self-pity and bitterness, knowing what a powerful chord it would strike in the Serbian national psyche. For these were troubling times. It was clear that Yugoslavia was in a state of growing political and economic chaos. Serbs – indeed all Yugoslav nationalities – were right to be fearful for their future if the country fell apart. To be a Serb was no longer just a nationality, or ethnic identity. Threatened on all sides by malevolent, inchoate enemies, being a Serb became a full-time occupation. The Croats and Slovenes had their national leaders, and the Serbs too needed and sought a protector. In Milosevic they believed they had found one.

Milosevic was also aided by Yugoslavia's unique political structure. Political power was steadily dissipating from the Yugoslav federal state to the six republics. The growing confusion about the role of the federal authorities was creating a power vacuum. The republics took ever more control. As Serbia became more powerful, its political elite increasingly switched from Titoism to Milosevicism. Even among some of the older, partisan generation, it seemed that Serb patriotism had deeper roots than Yugoslavism. The fundamental structure of the power networks did not alter, their personnel merely changed loyalties. Few had any moral or ideological qualms. Not just in Yugoslavia but across the Communist world, political and economic self-interest had long ago replaced any vestiges of Marxist idealism. State ownership was seen as a licence for institutionalised corruption and creaming off as much as possible for personal gain. Milovan Djilas's prescient analysis remained as valid as ever. During the 1950s he had described how, under Tito, Yugoslavia had been ruled by a new class of professional bureaucrats and privileged officials who sought only their own advancement through their 'unscrupulous ambition'.

> Party members feel that authority, control over property, brings with it the privileges of this world. Consequently, unscrupulous ambition, duplicity, toadyism and jealousy inevitably must increase . . . Careerism and an ever-expanding bureaucracy are the incurable diseases of Communism . . . The only thing that is required to

get on the road is sincere and complete loyalty to the party or the new class.[6]

The only difference was that under Milosevic the professional Titoists became professional Serbs. The transition did not prove troubling. Milosevic would not interfere with their privileges.

Milosevic's next target was the leadership of the northern Serbian province of Voivodina. Voivodina stretched from the Hungarian border, down to the capital Novi Sad, perched on the Danube, an hour's drive from Belgrade. Historically the region had not been part of Serbia, but of the Austro-Hungarian empire, ruled from Vienna and Budapest. It had been awarded to Yugoslavia after the collapse of the Habsburg empire in 1918.

The province still considered itself part of Mittel-Europa. Its cosmopolitan ethnic mix included Hungarians, Czechs, Slovaks, Bosnians and Croats, as well as Serbs. Its people were independent minded, proud of their multi-cultural tradition. Novi Sad was a pleasant city with a historic centre of fine secessionist buildings, and an open main square lined by terrace cafés. The local Serbs were not seduced by Serbian nationalism, and looked down on the post-war immigrants whom Tito had brought north from Montenegro and southern Serbia to fill the houses of the expelled ethnic German minority. They were more narrow-minded and insular.

The Voivodina leadership, such as senior party official Bosko Krunic, were wary of both Ivan Stambolic and Milosevic. They feared that they were Serbian centralisers who wanted to reduce, or abolish, the autonomy granted to Voivodina in the 1974 constitution.

But they had not anticipated the methods that Milosevic would use to achieve his aims on the fateful night of 6 October 1988. An angry mob, at least 15,000 strong, had surrounded the Voivodina government building, pelting it with rocks and yoghurt and demanding that the entire Voivodina leadership resign. In a one-party state such violent and frightening events were unheard of.

Bosko Krunic recalled:

It was clear that this had been carefully planned. The placards and the demonstrators' rhetoric were vicious and dangerous. It was as if Milosevic himself was talking about Serbs and Serbia. Under my window alone there were two hundred people, all shouting that we were traitors and thieves, and to kill Azem Vllasi [the Kosovo Albanian leader]. During the evening the crowd grew bigger. There was a group of people from Cacak waving placards saying they had come to sort things out. The demonstrators were roaming across the city.[7]

Over a hundred windows were broken. Frightened staff inside took refuge in the basement, fearful that the mob would storm the building. The police were unable, or unwilling, to hold the crowd back and several dozen were injured in the melée. The leadership consulted Yugoslav President Raif Dizdarevic. He insisted that they resign. According to Krunic:

> Some in the Voivodina leadership were opposed, because they knew that Milosevic was organising this, and this was not a reason to step down. They wanted a proper meeting, with discussions and political debates, not something that was decided by a mob on the street. I thought by resigning it would take the pressure off, as I was one of the most attacked, and the political situation would then settle down. I thought it would be a good tactic so that we could then have further debates.

Milosevic had won. Toppling the Voivodina leadership was the first of what became known as the 'anti-bureaucratic' revolutions. At the Eighth Session Milosevic had exploited the widespread feeling in the party leadership that it was time for the old generation to stand down. The anti-bureaucratic revolution took that revolutionary dynamic, the righteous anger of those who feel their time has come, a stage further. Political battles were now fought not by anonymous, unaccountable apparatchiks in closed, smoky rooms, but by the people, on the streets. It was intoxicating and it was dangerous.

Next to be targeted was the southern republic of Montenegro, the homeland of Milosevic's parents. The majority of Montenegrins are culturally very close to Serbs, worshipping in the Orthodox faith and sharing the same cultural heritage. Many of them anyway favour union with Serbia. Milosevic's brother Borislav had declared himself of Montenegrin nationality, while Slobodan decided he was a Serb. Milosevic found easy recruits there for his nationalist, centralising campaign. On 7 October, two days after Voivodina's yoghurt revolution, demonstrators poured onto the streets of the capital Podgorica to protest against police repression, after police had broken up a gathering of striking steel workers. For the next three months a young Communist official named Momir Bulatovic organised a relentless political campaign against Montenegro's leaders, eventually forcing their resignations. Such was the deference and servility the thirty-four-year-old showed to Milosevic, he was soon nicknamed 'the waiter'.[8] But by spring 1989 the waiter was giving orders, not taking them.

Those who tried to resist Milosevic's advance such as Zivan Berisavljevic, the former Yugoslav ambassador to London, and an influential figure in Novi Sad, paid a high personal cost. Milosevic wanted Berisavljevic 'on-message', after the Eighth Session but the two men had not clicked when Milosevic had visited London as president of UBB. So Milosevic sent his envoy, Milan Milutinovic, a smooth talker who would later become Milosevic's ambassador to Greece, and eventually president of Serbia. 'Milutinovic said in essence Milosevic could offer me whatever I wanted, as long as I would be under his command. I told Milutinovic to pass my best regards to Milosevic. But I was never in the habit of regularly meeting and talking with Milosevic. In particular I didn't have the feeling that he was the kind of person to promote me. I told Milutinovic to advise Milosevic to ask the people in Voivodina first, before I would make a deal. If they agreed, then I might agree. But otherwise, I would not be Milosevic's tool and Serbia's man in Voivodina.'[10]

A propaganda barrage was immediately unleashed against Berisavljevic. His years of service to his country counted for nothing and his reputation was systematically shredded by a stream of poisonous articles in the national and local media. Berisavljevic's wife, a completely innocent party in this exchange, was also savaged and her career destroyed. Berisavljevic recalled: 'Day by day the articles claimed I was a traitor to the nation. I was demonised and great pressure was put on my family. My wife was an eminent banker, she was vice president of Voivodina Bank, in charge of foreign currency. She was sacked, and attacked in these articles as if she was corrupt and a thief. We had no possibility to defend ourselves. No one would publish our answer, no judge would dare to accept a libel case and even prominent lawyers were afraid to defend me.'

The campaign lasted two years. Its bitter legacy remains. 'There were death threats, people telephoned late at night threatening my daughter would be killed, my car was damaged in the presence of the police. You can still feel strong traces of this demonisation here in public opinion, which is logical if you read for years that someone is anti-Serb, that he is a secessionist or even a British spy. This was how Milosevic frightened, blackmailed and marginalised a lot of people. They followed him not because they were his supporters, but because they were scared.'

Milosevic's roving circus of protests, known as 'rallies for truth', took place all over the country during 1988 and early 1989. The demonstrators demanded unity for Serbia, support for the Kosovo Serbs, and the abolition of autonomy for Kosovo. These events gave Milosevic a direct, almost visceral connection to ordinary Serbs, as he simultaneously fostered and exploited their deepest fears for the future. This was classic populism, allowing Milosevic to sidestep the discredited bureaucrats and officials that represented the old order. 'Down with the armchair sitters,' his supporters shouted.

Although the rallies were presented as an expression of the 'spontaneous will of the people', they were nothing of the sort. They were highly planned and organised by Milosevic and the Serbian secret service, the SDB, designed to maintain a delicate balance between inciting fear and intimidation and actual violence. (It was a deliberate choice to provide demonstrators with pots of yoghurt, as well as rocks, for example.) Milosevic did not want the mob to physically attack opposition leaders: That would have triggered a backlash, and brought in the federal authorities to restore order.

An ethnic Hungarian called Mihalj Kertes played a key role in organising the Novi Sad protest. Kertes was connected to the SDB, and would soon become one of Milosevic's most important allies. He was Milosevic's answer to those who claimed he was a Serbian nationalist. Kertes declared that if he, an ethnic Hungarian, had nothing to fear from Serbia, then neither did anyone else. Milosevic had taken control of the Serbian SDB soon after he became head of the Serbian Communist Party in 1986. Each of the six Yugoslav republics boasted its own secret service. (There was also a Yugoslav SDB, reporting to the Federal Presidency.) In a one-party state, the ruling party and the secret services are entwined in a symbiotic relationship. The party needs the secret service to guard against any threats to its rule, while the secret service needs the ruling party to guarantee its privileges and power. During the late 1980s the growing political power of the republics was reflected in the increasing strength of their security services.

The man who ran the Serbian SDB, in effect Milosevic's intelligence chief, was Jovica Stanisic. He was from the same town as Mihalj Kertes, Backa Palanka in Voivodina. His family was of Montenegrin origin, one of the inner immigrants who had moved to Voivodina after the Second World War. Born in 1950, Stanisic studied political science and law in Belgrade, and joined the secret service after leaving university. A keen mind and highly-developed political sensors helped him rise quickly up the intelligence hierarchy to a senior position, and he became one of Milosevic's most important allies, playing an extremely significant role in the Serbian leader's consolidation of power. Stanisic is a highly secretive person, rarely seen in public. According to one source, his former classmates could not even trace his telephone number to invite him to a university graduation reunion.

Eastern European secret policemen are often assumed to be unimaginative robots. A Communist-era joke goes like this: Why do secret policemen go around in threes? One who can read, one who can write, and one to keep an eye on the two dangerous intellectuals. This is quite wrong, at least among senior officers. One reason for the endurance of the Communist regimes is that high-level intelligence officials were often sophisticated and clever individuals, who understood how the world really worked. This did not mean they were ethical or moral people, but they were efficient. The man who, more than any other, brought Mikhail Gorbachev to power was Yuri Andropov, chairman of the KGB. Milosevic was no Gorbachev, but he understood the value of accurate information. Buoyed by his triumphs in Voivodina, Milosevic turned to Kosovo. On 17 November 1988, the entire Kosovo party leadership was simply sacked. A group of miners from Trepca marched fifty-five kilometres to Pristina in protest. There they joined students for a demonstration that lasted days, demanding that their leaders be reinstated, to no avail.

Two days later the biggest ever public gathering was held in Belgrade. Serbian media claimed that up to one million people attended the 'meeting of all meetings'. The rally purported to celebrate 'Brotherhood and Unity'. But its true purpose was to celebrate and reinforce Milosevic's control over Kosovo. Across Serbia employees were directed by their bosses to take the day off, and enjoy the free food, drink and transport supplied to ferry them to the capital. Milosevic addressed the rally: 'Every nation has a love which warms its heart. For Serbia it is Kosovo. That is why Kosovo will remain in Serbia.'[10] The poet Milovan Vitezovic proclaimed: 'The people have happened'. It became the catch phrase of the Serbian nationalist renaissance.

In his exploitation of mob violence and his deft manipulation of national grievances, Milosevic was reminiscent of Mussolini, the Italian

Fascist leader. There were some historical and cultural similarities between Italy and Serbia. Both states were comparatively young, the result of nineteenth-century unification of culturally very different provinces. Milan, like Novi Sad, had been part of the Habsburg empire. Italy's southernmost province of Sicily had, like Kosovo and indeed most of Serbia, once been under Islamic rule. Mussolini and Milosevic had both started their political careers as left-wingers: Mussolini was at one time editor of *Avanti*, the Socialist Party newspaper. Both leaders understood the importance of controlling the streets. Mussolini deployed his Black-shirted *Fasci di Combattimento* (Fighting Leagues), and while Milosevic did not have Blackshirts, he did have Miroslav Solevic and his Organising Committee for Participation of Kosovo Serbs and Montenegrins in Protest Rallies Outside of the Region (to give his group its full title).

The Blackshirts did not hesitate to use violence against left-wing and liberal opponents. The cult of violence was an essential part of the Fascist creed. Fascism was modern, dynamic, focused and swept all opponents from its path. Like the Blackshirts, Solevic's 'lads' were also ready to provoke a riot at a moment's notice, and operated through fear and intimidation. Mussolini and Milosevic both understood that before they could take power nationally, they needed a local and regional base. Milosevic had his 'rallies for truth' taking place all over Serbia. As well as breaking up strikes, and attacking socialists, Mussolini's fascists also overthrew elected local councils.

However, Milosevic was subtler than Mussolini in the way he deployed his nationalist crowds. His aim was not to overthrow the regime but to control it. The anti-bureaucratic revolutions were presented as the will of the people, which would no longer be obstructed by enemies of Serbia. This was classic populism. But backed up by Solevic, and his 'lads', the 'crowd crystals' of Elias Canetti's study of mob power, it worked. Solevic recalled: 'To say we put him in power is wrong. But that we made a real leader out of him, sure!'[11]

All through the episode of the anti-bureaucratic revolutions, Milosevic presented an entirely different persona to the West, especially diplomats of the United States. To them he exuded charm and sophistication. It was a continual bravura performance for a select audience of diplomats and foreign correspondents.

On 29 November 1987, two months after the Eighth Session, Dessa Trevisan, the London *Times* Balkan correspondent, attended a Belgrade reception to celebrate the Day of the Yugoslav Republic. This was a federal, not national, holiday. The first person Trevisan saw was Draza Markovic. She walked over to greet the former partisan. Unaware that Markovic was the uncle of Milosevic's wife, Trevisan told him that the political situation after the Eighth Session was 'very interesting'. Markovic replied: 'Interesting. This is a catastrophe for Serbia. This is the worst person who could have been chosen to lead Serbia at this moment and I am afraid for the future. I warned Stambolic that Milosevic was the wrong person. He has no patience, he has all the qualities that will lead us to disaster.' Trevisan looked on in amazement as Markovic continued. 'I know this because he is our son-in-law. We call him "Rumenko" [ruddy-faced].'[12]

Trevisan, now better informed, left Markovic to talk to Stambolic, but he told her, 'Now is not the time.' Trevisan then approached Milosevic who did have time. 'He was in the corner of the room, standing all alone and being ignored. I introduced myself to him. I said, "Well, Mr Milosevic, I would like to meet you and talk." He said: "Sure. Let's have lunch." This was such a difference from ordinary officials. He didn't say to call his secretary, but he gave me his home number.' More surprises followed. 'Jack Scanlan, the American ambassador, came up and embraced Milosevic. I thought, this is the end of the world, to see an American ambassador kissing the head of the Serbian Communist Party. Jack Scanlan said to me that they were old friends, and so was Larry Eagleburger [former US ambassador].'

Over the next two years Trevisan had five lunches and one dinner with Milosevic, usually at the Intercontinental Hotel in New Belgrade, the post-war suburbs on the other side of the Danube. Milosevic was always pleasant company, easy-going and agreeable over the food and wine. 'He would listen, and make it sound as if he agreed with us. To me the most interesting thing was that he did not seem to be a nationalist. He was very pro-American, he knew the United States very well, and he knew all the bankers.' The affection was mutual, it seemed. 'In 1988 Milosevic told me that Larry Eagleburger had been in Belgrade and had gone to see him. Eagleburger had stayed four hours, according to Milosevic. He had told Milosevic that, whichever way the elections go, Republicans or Democrats, it will be all right for Serbia because he would get the job at State. I was amazed that Milosevic was so indiscreet as to tell me this.'

Even as Solevic's mobs toured the country, Milosevic maintained his connection with Trevisan. Like many Balkan politicians, used to operating in a political culture where the press is an arm of government policy, Milosevic doubtless believed that as a correspondent for *The Times*, Trevisan had the ear of important diplomats and politicians. Curiously enough, she had his ear, and tried to influence him. In 1988 Milosevic invited her to meet him in Dubrovnik, where he was staying at Tito's villa. The doughty Trevisan confronted the Serb leader. 'I said to him: "Mr Milosevic, you have so much power, you have the whole nation behind you. You have to make a speech of reconciliation." He listened to me, and he said, "You mean a conciliatory speech." I said, "No, no, one of reconciliation." He said it was a good idea. He would always agree with you. Whether it was Lord Owen, or Cyrus Vance, or Richard Holbrooke, he would agree, and do nothing. He is like an eel, he would look at you with those piggy eyes, he would flatter you and make it seem like he is listening, that what you say is going in, and then he would do the opposite.'

But the flattery and politeness was reserved for those who could help him. Those who placed themselves outside the charmed circle were treated with less diplomacy. Around this time Milosevic had announced plans for a customs-free zone on one of Belgrade's river islands. As a former mayor of Belgrade, Zivorad Kovacevic believed he could contribute his expertise to the project, but he believed it was being discussed in too grandiose terms. Milosevic had announced that a billion dollars would be invested in the scheme, but a very modest pilot project in Novi Sad had proved successful and was a better model, Kovacevic told Milosevic on a short visit to Belgrade from Washington, D.C. Milosevic was not used to getting advice. 'I said to him, "Slobo are you serious? You are a banker and you know how much money this is. Why not follow the Novi Sad idea, start with a modest project and enlarge it." He was so angry. He said, "You came from the West to tell me what I am going to do?" I told him that it was just well-intended advice. He asked me crossly if there was anything else.'

There was. The director of Belgrade airport, a good friend of Kovacevic's, was being vilified in the Serbian press. Kovacevic accused Milosevic of running a dirty campaign to oust him. 'I told him that the newspapers were full of innuendos and insinuations. I told him that he knew this man was doing his job well, and that Milosevic was doing this just because he had said in a restaurant that he would do something if his friend Ivan Stambolic was touched. Milosevic denied it. I said to him,

"Don't tell me that anything can be done without you. You can stop this with your little finger." He said he would not meddle in the affair, but doesn't believe that the man can keep his position.'[13] The airport director was fired a few days later.

Kovacevic was a veteran of Yugoslav politics, someone whose achievements had been recognised by his appointment as the country's ambassador to the United States. He was both efficient and popular among Washington diplomatic circles. Yet he admits that he failed to grasp what kind of man Milosevic was. Schooled in a softer, more humane politics, Kovacevic was not the only figure of his generation to underestimate Milosevic's ruthlessness.

'These episodes showed me that Milosevic was a different kind of man, and I had misjudged him. I had been frank, and it was not necessary to tell him what I thought about the Eighth Session. I gave him a piece of advice, and he did not need advice and I dared to question some of his moves.'

In 1989 Kovacevic was recalled to Belgrade. He retired from the diplomatic service and became a lexicographer. 'I was Yugoslav ambassador, but I could not have been Milosevic's ambassador, and defend a policy I was against. It was better that it happened sooner than later. When I published my first dictionary, I said in an interview that I should probably have included Milosevic in the acknowledgements, for giving me the necessary free time.' Kovacevic received a gesture of support from a surprising quarter. 'I was walking down the street and I saw Milosevic's brother Bora on the other side. I didn't want to embarrass him, so I looked the other way. But he came over, and said, "Ziko, I just have to tell you that I was against you being recalled from Washington, but my crazy brother insisted on it."'

10

CORONATION IN KOSOVO

1989 and All That

*Six centuries later we are again involved in battles, and facing battles.
They are not battles with arms, but these battles cannot be excluded.*

Slobodan Milosevic, speaking to a rally of over half a million
Serbs at Kosovo Polje on 28 June 1989.[1]

D essa Trevisan planned a soirée on a riverboat restaurant for herself,
Slobodan and Mira, but nobody told her that Mira liked meatballs.
The *Times* correspondent had hoped for a sophisticated touch of pre-war
Belgrade, dining on the river Sava, enjoying the cool breeze and the
twinkling lights of the city's panorama. This was the world that the
writer Rebecca West had described in the 1930s, in her book *Black
Lamb, Grey Falcon*, a city of terraced cafés under chestnut tree awnings,
grandiose sculptures in the landscaped gardens of Kalemegdan fortress,
and fine restaurants.

But Trevisan's evening had got off to a shaky start. 'I told Mira that I
went to great trouble to get some caviar. She said she didn't eat caviar.
I told her the restaurant specialised in fish. She said she didn't eat fish.'[2]
Even so, the evening was certainly fascinating. Mira rarely appeared at
social occasions, and she made quite an entrance. 'I was amazed that she
accepted. She wore a black dress, black stockings and high heels and
her hair was black. She had a plastic flower in her hair, and she wore
a yellow winter coat. Throughout the evening she kept talking, talking
and talking. She said things like "there is no more private ownership in
the West anymore". I watched Slobodan all through this. He did eat
fish, but he said very little. He just kept nodding and nodding.'

In later years, Mira was mocked as the 'Red Witch of Belgrade'. She
was portrayed as a dark manipulator, pulling the strings of the hapless
Slobo, at least over domestic issues. Her girlish voice, black clothes and
frumpy demeanour were satirised in newspaper cartoons and in skits

and plays. One cartoon showed Mira zipping herself into a Milosevic body suit.

Those who have known the family for a long time, such as Milosevic's university era friend Nebojsa Popov, saw Mira as a 'Pygmalion' figure, working behind the scenes to turn Milosevic into a malleable political leader. According to Mihailo Crnobrnja, Mira was the driving force behind Milosevic's triumph at the Eighth Session. 'She was the triggering mechanism. She wanted Ivan Stambolic out, and Milosevic in. The only instrument available to do that was Serbian nationalism. It might sound simple, but I feel that is how it was.'[3]

Unlike his wife, Milosevic has never presented himself as an intellectual, or a thinker. Many believe that he is somewhat in awe of Mira's intellectual pretensions. Milosevic has always taken immense pride in her books. Asked about her influence on her husband, Mira replied:

> I do have an influence and he has an influence on me. But what does that mean, 'having influence'? Communication between people means having influence. If we had lunch three times you would have some influence on me, and I would have some influence on you. This is communication. If I tell you about the books I have been reading, and you keep that in mind, that is an influence.[4]

Certainly the devotion Milosevic displayed at university had not lessened. At this time senior Yugoslav officials had a special, private telephone line that bypassed their secretaries. It was known as the 'girlfriend line'. Whenever Milosevic's 'girlfriend line' rang, it was his wife or children calling.[5]

Although her academic work was moored firmly in a Marxist tradition all but abandoned in the rest of eastern Europe, Mira Markovic is a rare creature in the Balkans: an outspoken supporter of women's liberation. It is unusual for a Serbian woman to insist on keeping her maiden name, and Mira refuses to open letters addressed to 'Mrs Milosevic'. In the Balkans the word 'feminist' has decidedly negative connotations of militant harpies who threaten the supremacy of the male. Many of Mira's thoughts would have sat quite happily on the *Guardian* women's page. 'I want women's position in society to be changed. I am always on the side of women. Even more, I am against equality of gender. I think that women should be more than equal for the next few centuries. They should be superior. Then they can settle the account,' she has said.[6]

In fact her analysis of feminism is an orthodox leftist one, that women's problems can only be solved within the context of overall social change. To focus on women's issues is a deviation from the main struggle.

> Feminists are stupid. They think that the status of women in society can be solved with the women's movement. That is not possible. The position of women in society can be changed only with the efforts of the whole society, both men and women. Everybody has to help. Educated men want educated women to be educated as well. I stand for a position that women should have all rights, to work, to be educated, to be political personalities and to be important in society.

Mocking Mira rather than her husband also fits classic patterns of Balkan misogyny. Across the region there are historical myths featuring malevolent females who encourage their husbands to greater feats of blood-letting. Hungary has Countess Bathory, a Transylvanian noble-woman who reputedly bathed in virgins' blood and ordered an errant Gypsy servant to be sewn into a horse's stomach. Serbia's version features Jerina, the wife of a fourteenth-century nobleman, who forced her husband to build a giant fortress at the cost of a massive toll in human lives.

Mira argued:

> The criticism against me comes from the residue of this medieval consciousness. These minds see a woman as someone who should stay at home. This is a peasant way of thinking. There is something else very much alive in every culture. The idea that there is a perfect male. He admits that he has some bad sides, and makes some mistakes. But behind them is a she. If there was not a she, he would have been a great person and would not have made any mistakes. The easiest 'she' to blame is a wife. She cannot be defined as a mother or daughter, because such people are blood relations. But a wife is an outsider. She entered his life, she made him do such things, to bring the nation to war, to call for elections, or not to call for elections. That is what she is guilty of.

Even so, Mira herself admitted that she barely had any female friends.

'I have worked, learned, thought, by socialising with men. That's why I always stress they are my reference group. And most, in fact almost all of them, have always been at my side. The only men who have been intolerant to me were those with inferiority complexes, or those with obvious endocrinological abnormalities.' But Mira was perhaps more Balkan than she admitted. Asked how she, as a feminist, got along with her head-of-state husband, she replied, 'If a wife is a feminist, it doesn't matter whether she is married to the president, a violin-player, a polar-bear hunter, a bank clerk or a famous astronomer. There are only two options, he will be enchanted with her thoughts, her outfits and her tears – or there'll be war.'[7]

Perhaps Milosevic did not say much at dinner because he had his mind on matters further south. Kosovo was proving troublesome again.

In February 1989 the Kosovo miners had barricaded themselves into their pits and threatened to blow themselves up unless the Kosovo Albanian leader, Azem Vllasi and others were re-instated. At a heated meeting of the Federal Presidency, Milosevic demanded that the army be sent in to restore order. The Slovenian leader, Milan Kucan, was implacably opposed to this. He recalled: 'With Milosevic you can never relax. Show him a finger and he will have your arm off.'[8]

The Slovene leader's career paralleled Milosevic's. Both men were born in 1941 and chose to study law, in Kucan's case at Ljubljana university. In 1978, when Milosevic took over Beogradska Banka, Kucan was appointed president of the Slovene parliament. Eight years later, when Milosevic was appointed head of the Serbian Communist Party, Kucan took over the Slovene Communist Party. A thoughtful man, with notably large blue eyes, Kucan always carefully considered both his words and his options.

Presidency meetings were becoming increasingly rancorous. The Serbs accused the Croats and Slovenes of supporting the Kosovo miners with food and money. Croatia and Slovenia in turn feared that imposing martial law on the rebellious southern province could trigger an explosion. It was becoming increasingly clear that the centre could not hold. Slovenia in particular was implacably opposed to sending tanks into Pristina. Kucan recalled: 'Milosevic said: "We Serbs will act in the interest of Serbia whether we do it in compliance with the constitution or not, whether we do it in compliance with the law or not, whether we do it in compliance with party statutes or not." We feared that after Kosovo, we would be next.'[9]

Kucan decided to go public with his support for the Kosovo miners. On the night of 27 February 1989 the whole of Slovenia watched Kucan, together with rest of the leadership, speak to a public meeting at Ljubljana's concert hall called in solidarity with the Kosovo miners. Arguments and political conflicts previously confined to closed meetings of the federal leadership were suddenly blown wide open. Slovenia's leadership was very publicly drawing a line in the sand, or rather Alpine snow, against Milosevic's advance. The slide into a state of emergency and 'a bloody civil war' had to be stopped. The Kosovo miners were defending Yugoslavia, said Kucan:

> All of us therefore feel that the tragedy of the [Kosovo] miners would also be our own defeat, that it would also be a very vocal indication that minority peoples and national communities were now being squeezed, first to the margins, and then out of the country, or even who knows where.[10]

In Belgrade Dusan Mitevic, Milosevic's Machiavellian spin-doctor, was watching Kucan speak on Slovenian television. If Kucan was prepared to up the stakes, then so was he. Mitevic decided to broadcast the rally, complete with Serbo-Croat subtitles. The media war broke out. Mired in nationalist self-pity, Serbia was electrified at the effrontery of the Slovenes. A tactless claim by one speaker that Kosovo Albanians were in a similar position to Jews in the Second World War provoked particular rage. Increasingly Serbs intellectuals were drawing comparison between the martyrdom of the Serb people and that of the Jews. Many prominent figures joined the new Serbian Jewish Friendship Society, set up by a Belgrade dentist called Klara Mandic. The society's aim was to promote links between Belgrade and Israel and exploit the tendency among many Jews outside Yugoslavia to sympathise with the Serbs. Belgrade's own Jewish community watched this politically manipulated surge of philo-Semitism uneasily. [11]

Meanwhile Serb television reported that 'Milan Kucan was deliberately provocative. He was defending separatism in Kosovo – and in Slovenia.'[12] That night Milosevic went into action. He decided to use the Slovenian protest as an excuse for a showdown with the federal authorities. Milosevic would take over the capital and show that Serbia, not Slovenia, decided the fate of Yugoslavia. The federal security service reported to the Yugoslav President Raif Dizdarevic that Serb workers were being given a holiday and bussed into town, under orders from

Serb party officials. Zoran Todorovic, a guest at Marija Milosevic's twentieth birthday party, was co-ordinating events. He was nicknamed *kundak*, meaning rifle-butt.

This was a rerun of previous meetings when Miroslav Solevic's 'lads' – the rock-throwers of Kosovo – had protested in Belgrade, but on a far larger scale. By the next morning hundreds of thousands of protestors had gathered outside the federal parliament. There was one name on their lips. This was what Elias Canetti calls a 'baiting crowd'.

> The baiting crowd forms with reference to a quickly attainable goal. The goal is known and clearly marked, and is also near . . . It is so easy and everything happens so quickly that people have to hurry to get there in time. The speed, elation and conviction of a baiting crowd is something uncanny. It is the excitement of blind men who are blindest when they suddenly think they can see.[13]

The goal of this 'baiting crowd' was to crush the Kosovo miners, strengthen Serbia and canonise its leader, Slobodan Milosevic. With Belgrade on the edge of anarchy, Milosevic struck. He delivered an ultimatum to Yugoslav President Dizdarevic: the Federal Presidency must declare martial law in Kosovo. If not, then Dizdarevic could try and disperse the crowd himself.

Like Mussolini over sixty years earlier, Milosevic had deployed a mob before presenting a weak government with an offer it could not refuse. Mussolini's Blackshirts had gathered outside Rome in October 1922. The Italian prime minister had called for a state of emergency and martial law, but King Victor Emmanuel III refused to sign the order. The Italian army, which might have stopped Mussolini, remained in its barracks. Mussolini won.

So did Milosevic. There was at this time growing opposition within the military to Milosevic's use of Serbian nationalism and the toppling of the partisan generation at the Eighth Session. But army generals were divided over Milosevic. The high proportion of Serbs in the military leadership gained Milosevic a natural sympathy among many officers. Others recognised that Serb nationalism could eventually destroy Yugoslavia, the state they had pledged to protect. However, because the Yugoslav military leadership was top-heavy with Serbs, anti-Milosevic officers were not trusted by the very people they needed to topple him, the republican leaderships of Croatia and Slovenia. There was little appetite for a military coup. As a Communist army, the JNA – the Yugoslav National Army – was heavily indoctrinated with the idea that it was always subordinate to civilian control. But attempts to outmanoeuvre Milosevic at a federal level also failed.

With all of downtown Belgrade filled with protestors calling for the Serbian leader, Milosevic knew that only he could calm the situation. More than blackmail, this was outright sedition. It was also a dangerous gamble by Milosevic, and he was playing for the highest stakes. This time the 'anti-bureaucratic revolution' had been brought to the very capital of Yugoslavia. The sheer numbers of the 'baiting crowd' meant the odds were in Milosevic's favour. If he lost, Milosevic could have faced arrest. Had the federal police, and even the army, been called in to take back control of the capital, the course of the next few years might have been very different.

But Milosevic had bulldozed his way through the Yugoslav power structure, leaving his opponents feeling weak and vulnerable. Dizdarevic did his best. He was a Bosnian, and a decent man who believed in federal Yugoslavia. He bravely stepped outside to address the crowd, but was howled down. The head of the Yugoslav state retreated, shaken and upset.

Fearful that the crowd could destroy the capital, the Yugoslav leadership voted to send the army into Kosovo. For the first time Milosevic's Serbia had used force to triumph over federal Yugoslavia. More than this, the Yugoslav army was now an instrument of Serbian policy, in effect of Milosevic's policy. A state of emergency was declared in Kosovo.

After keeping the crowd waiting for twenty-four hours, Milosevic finally emerged. 'Milosevic was like a saint to them, not an icon, but a living saint, they believed his every word and would not go home until he spoke to them,' said Borisav Jovic.[14] The living Serbian saint called for Serbia to fight for its rights, and demanded peace and unity for Yugoslavia. The crowd roared its approval. Protestors demanded the arrest of Azem Vllasi, the Kosovo Albanian leader.

Soon afterwards, the tanks and armoured personnel carriers rolled into Pristina. The miners' strike was over. Azem Vllasi was arrested and imprisoned. The Serbian parliament abolished the autonomy of both Kosovo and Voivodina, and finally achieved Milosevic's aim of a unified Serbia. Even though twenty-two ethnic Albanians, and two policemen were killed in the ensuing protests, 28 March 1989 was declared a Serbian national holiday. By bringing the capital to the very brink of chaos and anarchy, Milosevic had forced the federal leadership to deploy troops against their own citizens. An ominous precedent had been set.

Three months later to the day, on a bright summer morning, Milosevic stepped into a helicopter. Neatly dressed in a sober dark suit and matching tie, with a white shirt, his hair brushed back, he carefully took his seat as the pilot got the all-clear before take off. The machine shuddered and shook, and lifted up into the clear skies over Belgrade. Spread out in the morning sun, the city's squares and avenues offered an eye-catching panorama, the waters of the Danube and the Sava glinting blue under the ochre stone of Kalemegdan fortress. The helicopter banked and headed south. There, on the Kosovo battlefield known as Gazimestan – Turkish for 'place of the warriors' – over half a million adoring Serbs awaited their leader.

28 June was the Serb holiday of Vidovdan, St Vitus's day, and the six hundredth anniversary of the battle of Kosovo Polje, the pivotal event in Serbian history. On that day, according to Serbia's national legend, which resonated through the centuries, the Serbs had defended Christendom against Islam, and their defeat had tragically opened the door to centuries of oppression by the Ottoman Turks. This historical legend of a 'heavenly people', stubborn, proud and ready to fight to the death, had been developed for the modern world by such figures as the nationalist theoretician Ilija Garasanin and the poet Petar-Petrovic Njegos, composer of the *Mountain Wreath* epic ballad. The enduring power of Serbian patriotism had been noted by the American foreign correspondent John Reed, who wrote the classic account of the Russian Revolution, *Ten Days That Shook The World*. Reed covered the Balkans during the First World War, and observed in his book *War in Eastern Europe* that:

> Every [Serb] peasant soldier knows what he is fighting for. When he was a baby, his mother greeted him, 'Hail little avenger of Kosovo!' . . . When he had done something wrong, his mother reproved him thus: 'Not that way will you deliver Macedonia!'. The ceremony of passing from infancy to boyhood was marked by the recitation of an ancient poem: 'Jam sam Serbin', it began, 'I am a Serbian, born to be a soldier, Son of Iliya, of Milosh, of Vaso, of Marko'.[15]

In fact by 1389 the Ottoman empire already controlled large swathes of the Balkans, including areas inhabited by Serbs. Several local Serb chiefs had allied themselves with the Sultan, as a means of defeating their local rivals. When the nineteenth-century ruler Milos Obrenovic had sent the stuffed and skinned head of his rival Karadjordjevic to Istanbul on a plate he was merely following in this tradition of expedient vassalage. Serb soldiers, too, fought in the armies of Sultan Murat. In military terms the battle was more of a draw than outright defeat for either side. The fortress of Belgrade did not fall for another sixty years.

Yet why did the details of a conflict that took place six centuries ago matter? For many, the resonance of Balkan history is a mystery, its power enough to gather hundreds of thousands of people to wait for hours in a muddy field to hear Milosevic speak. But elsewhere in Europe, the memories of ancient battles also retain the power to mobilise communities, as the summer marching season in Northern Ireland shows.

By 1989 Serbia and all the Yugoslav republics were feeling increasingly insecure. Milosevic's strategy of weakening federal power through the anti-bureaucratic revolutions and the February demonstration in Belgrade had worked. Yugoslavia was increasingly reduced to an idea – and an ideal for many – but that was not enough. Communism was beginning to collapse all over eastern Europe, and the idea of Yugoslavia with it. While one belief system was crumbling, another needed to be constructed. So it was not surprising that in such turbulent times nationalism, with its comforting, familiar pageantry of medieval legends and symbols provided a welcoming embrace. At Gazimestan, myth and modernity were deftly fused. The design of the podium from which Milosevic spoke was firmly in the socialist-realist tradition: grandiose and overbearing, but simple. Giant numbers behind Milosevic spelled out '1389' and '1989'.

Milosevic knew when he stood behind the banks of microphones, that this was one of the most important days of his life. Although he generally disliked public speaking and addressing rallies, he realised that if all went well this would crown him the new king of Serbia, inheritor of the spirit of both Prince Lazar and Tito. He was relaxed and confident as he spoke. At Gazimestan there was no danger of votes going the wrong way or unscripted events disrupting the day's plan. Old-fashioned socialist planning and the Serbian secret service had taken care of that. His speech blended the wooden language of Marxist exhortation with older strands of myth and legend, and the possibility of future war. What was Mira's role in this pivotal event in Milosevic's evolution as a Serbian leader?

Many believed that while this section of the speech was written by
Milosevic himself:

> The battle of Kosovo contains within itself one great symbol. That
> is the symbol of heroism. It is commemorated in our songs, dances,
> literature and history . . . Six centuries later we are again involved
> in battles, and facing battles. They are not battles with arms, but
> these battles cannot be excluded. But regardless of what form they
> take these battles cannot be won without decisiveness, courage and
> sacrifice, without those good characteristics which long ago were
> present on the field of Kosovo.[16]

The distinct voice of Mira Markovic can be heard in the next
sentences:

> Our main battle today is for the realisation of economic, political,
> cultural and general social prosperity, and the successful advance
> towards the civilisation in which people will live in the twenty-first
> century.

Milosevic's Gazimestan speech has entered history. Extracts were even
used by the prosecution at the Hague tribunal as a means of trying to
prove that as early as the summer of 1989, Milosevic was planning war.
Mira denied that there was any belligerent intent.

> There is a mystification about this speech. So many people gathered
> there because ten years before Serbs were oppressed by the local
> Albanian community. Serbs were moving out of Kosovo. They
> were ill-treated and Serbs tolerated it because that older generation
> of politicians had the following policy: 'Serbs are the biggest nation
> in Yugoslavia and they have to endure and tolerate everything.' It
> was not a celebratory speech, it was just a ceremonial speech for the
> occasion. There is nothing that could hurt anyone in that speech.[17]

Even so, the Yugoslav federal officials on the podium next to
Milosevic looked increasingly uneasy as Milosevic laid out his vision
of Serbia's future. In the distance Pristina shimmered in the summer
heat, under a haze of pollution. The city's dusty unpaved roads and

cracked concrete tower blocks were silent. This was a day for Albanians to stay at home. The crowd roared and cheered. The presence of the Serb Patriarch German symbolised the Orthodox Church's blessing. The day was celebrating a battle against the Ottomans, but ironically it was the Ottomans themselves that intentionally strengthened the power of the national church as a bastion of national identity. Under the 'millet' system religious authorities were granted substantial autonomy, charged with raising their own taxes and running their own communal affairs. Orthodox churches, like the Serbian Church, are 'autocephalous'. An autocephalous church can appoint its own synod and leaders. Such national religious autonomy is seen as an expression of nationhood itself. Where the Church's writ runs, so does the nation's. This means that unlike in western Europe or the United States, there is no concept of the 'separation of church and state'. On the contrary, Orthodox churches have been one of the main engines of integrating church and state. The very idea of 'srpstvo', which roughly translates as 'serbness', is inextricably linked with the Serbian Orthodox Church.

Many demonstrators bedecked themselves in Orthodox and Chetnik regalia, to show their support both for the Church and for the Serbian nationalist movement that had fought Tito's partisans as much as the Nazis. The sight of Chetnik paraphernalia, redolent with the symbolism of war and Serbian ultra-patriotism, sent a nervous shudder through the other Yugoslav republics. The Serbian foreign ministry had laid on a special train for western envoys, but they proved unwilling to give to stamp of legitimacy to Milosevic's rally: the only envoy to attend was Turkish, and he noted wryly that as the Ottoman empire had won the battle of Kosovo Polje, it was remembered rather differently in Istanbul. Milosevic was furious at what he perceived as a snub from the diplomatic community, and blamed the US ambassador Warren Zimmerman, whom he refused to meet for months.

Zimmerman's recollections of his meetings with Milosevic offer an intriguing insight into the Serbian leader's outlook. Milosevic told him:

'Kosovo has always been Serbian, except for a brief period under World War II. Yet we have given the Albanians their own govern-ment, their own parliament, their own national library, and their own schools. We have even given them their own Academy of Sciences. Have you Americans given your blacks their own Academy of Sciences?[18]

As Zimmerman points out, in fact Kosovo was under Ottoman rule for 523 years, and by the time the conversation took place – after Milosevic's six month sulk through the latter half of 1989 – Albanians in Kosovo no longer had their own government or parliament.

The Gazimestan pageant was not an isolated event. From the Baltic to the Black Sea, marches and protests increasingly heralded the end of the old order in 1989. In many countries, there was a growing desire for some kind of catharsis, a need come to terms with Communism and its effects on those who had to live under a one-party state. While statues of Marx and Engels were being torn down, to be replaced with older national heroes, more thoughtful politicians and writers, such as Czechoslovakia's Vaclav Havel, attempted to recognise the ethical cost of personal compromises many people had been forced to make under a Marxist regime, and of the moral corruption that had tainted the whole Communist system. But self-knowledge demands a certain courage. It exacts a price that proved to be too high for some. Milosevic also understood that the end of the cold war presaged the dawn of a new era but he took another path: denial. Serbs and Serbia had done nothing wrong, he proclaimed. In fact they were victims of others' misdeeds.

Milosevic presented himself – or arranged that he be presented – as Serbia's national saviour. This fitted neatly into the south Slav cultural tradition of epics and heroes. In Orthodox lands the Communist cult of personality draws on Slavic traditions of royal-worship. As the *babushkas* used to say in Stalin's Soviet Union, 'We have a new Tsar now'. And the Tsar should maintain a certain distance. Zivorad Kovacevic recalled: 'For Milosevic it was always important that every appearance should be an event. Everything was prepared and he would not permit any improvisation. There was nothing casual, or showing any human features. This impresses people. His speeches were full of generalities and platitudes.'[19]

In June 1989 the Kosovo pilgrims held a picture of Milosevic in one hand, and one of Prince Lazar in the other. This too was no coincidence. Long preparations had preceded Milosevic's arrival by helicopter on the medieval battlefield. In the winter of 1988 the remains of Prince Lazar, hero and victim of the battle of Kosovo, were exhumed and sent around Serbia on a tour. Wherever his bones came to rest, however briefly, thousands of jubilant Serbs turned out to greet the remains of the country's most revered historical figure. Only Milosevic, Serbs believed, could guard the prince's heritage. After Gazimestan Milosevic was unassailable in Serbia. His opponents were vilified by a hysterical media. The June 28 rally at Kosovo Polje had anointed Milosevic as a modern king-saint for the post-Communist era. Draza Markovic recalled: 'At that time at those meetings there were pictures of Karadjordjev, St Sava and Slobodan Milosevic. There were no taxis or buses without a picture of Slobodan Milosevic. Myself and Ivan Stambolic were accused of being traitors. At that time I felt good when this word was used.'[20]

Milosevic though added a new twist to the cult of personality around him. He publicly discouraged it. The Serb leader presented himself as thoughtful and unassuming, a man of the people, who understood their concerns. This was perhaps partly genuine, as Milosevic was more comfortable operating in the corridors of power than in front of the crowds, but it also earnt him extra points with his adoring populace.

The Serbs are a naturally ebullient people, vivacious, proud and stubborn. They share an easy informality and Mediterranean joie de vivre with a passionate loyalty to both friends and relatives. Such qualities are engaging, especially to visitors from colder, northern climes. A Serb home is warm and extremely hospitable, as any visitor will testify. An endless supply of coffee, cigarettes, *rakija* (brandy) and food appears as if by magic, even in the midst of war. As the British foreign correspondent Reginald Wyon noted at the beginning of the twentieth century 'the peasant of the Balkans, be he Albanian or Serb or Montenegrin or Bulgar is hospitality personified, and his full-blooded energy is a pure delight to those who are weary of the Western detrimental.'[21]

But there is a dark side too to the Serbian character, a tendency to morbid self-pity, and a certainty that through the centuries no nation has suffered like the Serbs, except perhaps the Jews. Milosevic exploited this. While neighbouring countries looked forward to a future of freedom and democracy, he deployed the mechanisms of the one-party state – a pliant media, social control, secret police and fear – to steer the Serbs down a nationalist cul-de-sac. Once walled in by centuries of mordant history, he ensured that the Serbian response to the changing world situation was not a call for a change in leadership, but a demand for its strengthening – under his guidance.

There were alternatives to all of this. Neighbouring Hungary shared with Serbia a taste for choreographed national pageantry, a relic of both nations' Communist heritage. In June 1989 Hungary also organised a giant spectacle: the reburial of Imre Nagy, leader of the failed 1956 revolution. Imre Nagy and Tito were both country boys, born at the turn of the century, who had discovered Communism, somehow survived the perils of 1930s Moscow and returned home to build the one-party state. Both had broken with the Soviet Union.

So Hungary too had its psychic scars, although it was perhaps easier to find closure for a national trauma rooted in 1956 than 1389. The same month that Serbs gathered at Kosovo Polje, Nagy's coffin, and five others, had been displayed in Budapest's Heroes' Square, just a few yards from the Yugoslav embassy where Nagy had found brief refuge before his execution. The national heroes were then reburied with due pomp and circumstance. An attempt at least to lay Communism's ghosts to rest.

Meanwhile Milosevic's reformers watched the Serbian leader with increasing dismay. He no longer spoke in two voices. The recommendations of Milosevic's reform commission had fallen into the federal political limbo that was home to so many proposals from six republics. Mihailo Crnobrnja began to distance himself. 'I sensed more and more of this was coming, that my utility as an economist was decreasing.'[22] He left Belgrade for Brussels, for a post as Yugoslav ambassador to the European Union.

I I

WAR NO.1, SLOVENIA

Small War in Slovenia, Not Many Dead

1989–91

The Slovenes opened the door to the Yugoslav crisis. Although I can't say they were the only ones to blame.

Slobodan Milosevic.[1]

Milosevic's nationalist drive, and the subsequent weakening of federal authority, was having a rapid knock-on effect. Slovenia was thinking about leaving for the European Union. Its most popular slogan was 'Europe Now'. Slovenia was a country of tidy farms and Germanic work ethic. Unlike Belgrade or Sarajevo, the capital Ljubljana had never been occupied by the Turks. Ljubljana boasted pretty piazzas, arched bridges over the river Ljubljanica and fine secessionist architecture. The alpine republic was Yugoslavia's richest. Its sensible, reliable and industrious citizens enjoyed something approaching western levels of prosperity.

The Slovenian language was different from Serbo-Croat, and was not fully understood across Yugoslavia. Overwhelmingly Catholic, and sharing borders with Italy, Austria and Hungary, Slovenia saw itself as part of Mittel-Europa, not the Balkans. In the nineteenth century, Slovene culture had faced extinction and, in 1918, the Slovenes sought security within the framework of the Kingdom of the Serbs, Croats and Slovenes. In truth, many Yugoslavs considered Slovenes smug and just a tiny bit boring, unlike their more flamboyant neighbours to the south.

Milosevic's Serbian nationalism ensured that during the late 1980s, such feelings of cultural alienation were reciprocated. The youth magazine *Mladina* published sensational articles that broke Yugoslav taboos by criticising Tito and the army. A rock group called Laibach, the German name for Ljubljana, exploited Nazi imagery. Artists around the NSK

(New Slovenian Art) movement used radical and avant-garde symbolism. Even the British television programme, the *Rough Guide to Europe*, filmed an episode in Ljubljana, rhapsodising over its hip street-scene.

'*Burek, nein danke*,' proclaimed a slogan sprayed on a wall in Ljubljana in the late 1980s. A *burek* is a southeast European delicacy, a pie made of flaky pastry that may be filled with cheese, meat, spinach or potato. But a *burek* is not just a snack. It is, as critical theorists might say, a signifier. The layered pastry and stuffing brings in its wake a whole set of cultural and historical assumptions, especially for Slovenian graffiti artists. For them *burek* means Balkan, and an implied heritage of sloth, corruption and devotion to a godlike national leader. The Ljubljana graffiti writer had used German, daubing his slogan at a time when the slogan *Atomkraft nein danke*' (Nuclear Power No Thanks) was ubiquitous across Europe. But the choice of language on a Ljubljana wall was deliberate. What the slogan really meant was 'Yugoslavia, no thanks'.

As the country moved inexorably towards independence, the Slovene leader Milan Kucan had attempted to turn Milosevic's tactics against himself. In March 1989 the Slovenes had watched Milosevic rewrite the Serbian constitution to abolish the autonomy of Kosovo and Voivodina, so that the provinces were brought under central control. Kucan demanded the power to alter the Slovene constitution so that federal Yugoslav authorities could no longer interfere in Slovenian internal affairs. The Slovenes merely asked for similar powers to those Milosevic had already taken for Serbia. What could be fairer than that?

Milosevic refused outright. Instead he discussed with Borisav Jovic and the federal defence minister General Veljko Kadijevic whether martial law should be imposed on the alpine republic. Not yet, was the answer. Kadijevic, a former partisan of mixed Serb-Croat origin, was a career military man. As a loyal JNA (Yugoslav National Army) officer he believed in Yugoslavia, not Greater Serbia. But the JNA was a Communist army, thoroughly indoctrinated with the idea that military authority was absolutely subordinate to the politicians. General Kadijevic believed that if Slovenia left, Yugoslavia would collapse. Over the next few years General Kadijevic would be increasingly persuaded by Milosevic's arguments that as Yugoslavia could only be defended by force, it was necessary to go to war against the republics that wished to secede.

Those were the dog days of federal Yugoslavia, and times of great tension between the republics. Serbia was not an island, but one of six Yugoslav republics. Milosevic's politics – of crowds and power, demonstrations and intimidation – were fomenting an atmosphere of menace through the neighbouring states. Everywhere there was a sense of uncertainty, tinged with fear for the future. The symptoms of imperial terminal decline were brilliantly described by the Hungarian writer Sandor Marai, in his novel *Embers*. The book is set at the turn of the century, during the last years of Austro-Hungary, but change the nationalities and it just as well describes Yugoslavia:

> The inhabitants – Ukrainians, Germans, Jews and Russians – lived in a kind of turmoil that was continually being smothered and contained by the authorities; something seemed to be fermenting in the dimly lit, airless apartments, some uprising or perhaps just an ongoing seditious muttering and wretched discontent, or perhaps not even that, merely the uneasy disorder and permanent restlessness of a caravanserai.[2]

Through the months of constitutional wranglings as Kucan and his officials tried to stop, or at least stall, Milosevic's centralising drive, there ran an undercurrent of apprehension. Kucan feared being arrested, or even eliminated. When he and the Slovene leadership flew to Belgrade they took separate planes, in case of assassination attempts. They made plans for emergency evacuations, via the Bulgarian border, to exit Yugoslav territory as quickly as possible before returning home.

At an epic meeting in Belgrade at the end of September 1989 Kucan and the other Slovene leaders had come under intense pressure from both the Serbs and the Yugoslav army to back down from their plans. Borisav Jovic threatened Kucan that 'all means' would be used to stop the Slovenes altering their constitution to remove the power of the federal authorities. When Kucan asked what that meant, Jovic replied, 'Ask your lawyers, I'm not going to explain the law to you.'[3] After their return to Ljubljana, on 27 September, the parliament of the Slovenian republic voted itself the right to secede from Yugoslavia, as 'an independent sovereign and autonomous state'. The Slovene MPs cheered and sang songs. Milan Kucan went home to sleep. The parliament vote was not a declaration of independence, not yet anyway.

Milosevic's rise and consolidation of political power was greatly aided by Yugoslavia's parlous economy. Soaring inflation and increasing economic instability fuelled a sense of insecurity, boosting nationalism. State-run industries were uncompetitive and ineffective. The value of the dinar, once one of the more resilient currencies in eastern Europe, had plummeted. In 1987 prices rose by 120 per cent, and in 1988 by 194 per cent. The Yugoslav economy was being kept afloat by IMF loans, which also helped subsidise a near western standard of living for many, and ensure a ready supply of western consumer goods. But loans ultimately had to be paid back. By 1987 Yugoslavia's foreign debt stood at $22 billion. There was no realistic hope of repaying this, especially when Yugoslavs – understandably in such uncertain times – preferred to keep their hard currency in foreign not domestic banks.

By the end of December 1989 inflation had reached 2,600 per cent. The devaluation of the dinar was having a profound effect, not only in financial terms as dinar savings became worthless, but also in psychological terms. The dinar was the national currency, in use in all six republics, and so could be seen as a symbol of the multi-national state. The weakening of the currency seemed an awful portent of the eventual collapse of the whole country. There were echoes of Weimar Germany, of an economic collapse that was fuelling a dangerous nationalism.

Liberals and reformers rallied around Ante Markovic, the prime minister of federal Yugoslavia. A genial Bosnian Croat, Markovic (no relation to Mira Markovic) was a popular leader. With Markovic at the helm, many Yugoslavs believed, their country could still follow the Hungarians, Czechs and Poles into western peace and prosperity. And might even stay together. But Markovic faced an unsolvable dilemma. He was prime minister of Yugoslavia, but federal power was increasingly irrelevant. The six republics, especially Milosevic's Serbia, were calling the shots.

Economics also helped fuel the republics' independence drive. Both Slovenia and Croatia were increasingly unwilling to have their financial fortunes tied to the whole of Yugoslavia, especially the poorer southern regions. If a factory in Slovenia was showing a good profit, then why did it have to subsidise Macedonia and Bosnia? Two million Slovenes produced nearly one third of Yugoslavia's hard currency exports. In fact such arguments failed to recognise that the Yugoslav economic structure greatly subsidised the prosperity of Slovenia and Croatia. Both countries enjoyed easy supplies of cheap labour, subsidised raw materials and a captive market in the rest of Yugoslavia.

Markovic fought back with a programme of austerity measures. He also called for the introduction of a western-style economic and political system of political democracy with full freedoms and human rights. The old dinar was converted to the new dinar, at a rate of 10,000 to one, wages were frozen and the powers of the National Bank of Yugoslavia were boosted. A new arrangement was negotiated with the IMF and inflation began to fall. Perhaps Markovic could yet pull a western rabbit out of Tito's battered old hat.

Many of Markovic's ideas were similar to those first proposed by Milosevic's 1988 Presidential Reform Commission. But Markovic would get no help from Milosevic. By autumn 1989 Milosevic had abandoned modernisation for nationalism. For the Serbian leader a healthy economy, freedom, human rights and democracy would be an absolute disaster. Milosevic knew he would never be able to retain power in a modern Yugoslavia of six republics that peacefully co-existed. Ante Markovic had to be stopped. Here Milosevic found allies in both Ljubljana and Zagreb, as nationalists united to stop the Markovic reforms, as a prelude to breaking up federal Yugoslavia.

Ljubica Markovic recalled:

> Ante Markovic was the last big opportunity to reform the Communist state we had. Not only Milosevic brought him down, but also Slovenia and Croatia. They didn't want to hear what he said, they hated it. His was a completely modern approach that was so different from everything else we heard all those years. Markovic said ideology is not important, the economy is important, we have to work, produce and open to the world because we are part of the world. Milosevic hated this, it was the opposite of what he said.[4]

Milosevic attacked the reforms from a bizarre but effective angle. He evoked the spirit of Gazimestan for Serbia's shoppers. 'Markovic began importing cheap food and other goods from the west,' said Ljubica. 'You could get cheese, ham and oil at a low price. So Milosevic immediately went on television and started attacking these imports. The televisions, the kitchen and bathroom equipment you could get, Milosevic attacked everything for being third class.' Considering that the Serbian economy would spin into a black hole would make even professional economists shake their heads in wonder, this was the darkest irony.

Milosevic needed to provoke more tension between Belgrade and Ljubljana, and decided to deploy his favourite weapon: the roving band of Kosovo Serbs. In the winter of 1989 Belgrade announced plans for a 'Meeting of Truth' in Ljubljana. The Serbian leadership claimed this was necessary so that the Slovenes could be properly informed about Kosovo, as though this was still the issue at stake. The Kosovo Serbs headed north again.

Kucan hit back. The 'Meeting of Truth' was banned by the Slovene authorities. Geography was also a useful ally. To get to Ljubljana Milosevic's demonstrators had to pass through Croatia, Slovenia's inter-mittent ally in the struggle against Belgrade. The trains were stopped at the Croatian border and the demonstrators turned back. A few dozen Serbs already living in Ljubljana turned out to demonstrate but were bundled into police vans.

In December Belgrade announced that all economic ties with Slovenia would be cut, and that Serbs would launch an economic boycott of the alpine republic. Less than two months after the Berlin Wall had come down, Milosevic was building a financial one, inside Yugoslavia's frontiers. On one level this was a surprising decision: the Serbs and the Serb-dominated Partisans had fought the Croatian Ustasha in the Second World War, and had struggled with the Albanians for mastery of Kosovo for six hundred years, but there was no history of conflict or real antipathy between Slovenia and Serbia. Despite their cultural differences, the countries had got on reasonably well. During the war Serbs had sheltered thousands of Slovene children from the Nazis. Milosevic's move also made no economic sense, since Slovenia was Yugoslavia's most economically successful republic. Dozens of Serbian companies were forced to break off their contracts with Slovenia.

At this time the community of interest between Kucan and Milosevic crystallised. Kucan needed the failure of federal economic policies, and the weakening of federal authority to facilitate Slovenia's departure from Yugoslavia. For Milosevic the departure of Slovenia was greatly to be desired: it presented no strategic problems. Its fate did not greatly affect Serbian interests. The country was ethnically homogenous. There was no shared border, substantial Serbian minority or history of Serb settlement. Not even the most fervent irredentists, of which there was no shortage in Belgrade, could claim that Slovenia was ancient Serbian territory.

When Milosevic launched a political and economic offensive against Slovenia, he knew that such heavy-handed tactics would only strengthen the nascent Slovenian independence movement. This suited Kucan, as he could argue he was being forced down a path he wanted to take in any case. At the same time Slovenia's drive for independence also boosted Milosevic: by refusing Slovenia's demands, he could present himself as the defender of Yugoslavia, even as his Serbian nationalist policies were leading to its break-up. Kucan and Milosevic were *de facto* allies.

Even so, like every divorce, the departure of the Slovenes was marked by anger, bitterness and no small emotional toll, on all sides. On 23 January 1990 the fourteenth – and last, as it turned out – congress of the Yugoslav party had been held in Belgrade's Sava congress centre, its modern hall and conference rooms once the pride of the Tito era. By this time Slovenia and Croatia, like other former Communist countries, had already announced their first multi-party elections to be held that spring. Even Romania had toppled the hated Ceausescus. A new era was dawning – except in Serbia. Every Serb speaker expounded the Milosevic line, emphasising the primacy of the party, the need for a strong central authority, and making demands phrased in the kind of Leninist rhetoric that was now barely heard in eastern Europe.

As a good Bolshevik, Milosevic knew that the chairman of such a gathering, especially in the age of electric microphones and loudspeakers, had a vital position, controlling who spoke and for how long. Momir Bulatovic, the moustachioed president of Montenegro dubbed 'the waiter', was chosen for the job. The waiter delivered. Every single Slovene proposal on the future of Yugoslavia was voted down. The Slovenes threatened to walkout.

Dusan Mitevic broadcast the three-day event live on television. It was as rancorous as the end of any forty-five-year marriage could be, even thought the betrothal had been an arranged one. Serbs and Slovenes accused each other of being 'national socialists'. The Yugoslav Communist Party was dead, and with it the idea of a multi-national Yugoslavia. Milan Kucan recalled:

> The atmosphere was horrible. There was whistling, chanting, insults and cursing. I would not want to live through that again. We knew that we could never identify ourselves with such a political organisation. We left the congress. By doing that we also knew that the state, which was so closely bonded to the party then, could not be our state.[5]

Cyril Ribicic, a Slovene delegate, walked up to the microphone and dolefully declared: 'Under these circumstances, we have to leave the

Communist Party of Yugoslavia.' Many Serbs applauded, believing they had won a victory. Months later, Milosevic would mock his former Slovene comrades, accusing them of being more concerned with their hotel bills than their country. 'It was a dirty game, but I could see right through it. They'd checked out of their hotels. Those stingy Slovenes saved a night's bill. They'd left their bags at reception.'[6]

At the time Milosevic had not been quite so cocky. His manipulation of the Serbian bloc vote at the congress had engineered the Slovene walk-out. But until then Milosevic had won all his major triumphs – from the toppling of Ivan Stambolic to the adulation of the masses at Gazimestan – within the Serbian political arena. Now he was actually engineering the break-up of federal Yugoslavia. Television footage shows Milosevic looking uncertain. Huddled with his allies in a corner, his head swivelled back and forth across the congress. He appeared aware that he had to take control or the congress would collapse. Striding up to the microphone, he suggested that the delegates should be counted to establish a new quorum. It was a holding move.

Milosevic then lobbied the Croat delegation, led by Ivica Racan, who told him that a Yugoslav party without the Slovenes was not acceptable. 'Milosevic went quiet. For the first time, I saw him worried. His charm deserted him.'[7] The Croats then followed the Slovenes and walked out. The break-up of the Yugoslav Communist Party heralded that of the country itself. Congress Chairman Bulatovic called a quarter of an hour break. It lasted, he later noted, 'through history'.[8]

Now the Slovenes had the excuse they needed to press ahead with plans for full independence. Yet the walk-out from the fourteenth congress was not without personal cost. Some Slovene delegates filed out in tears. 'As children we had grown up in the second [federal] Yugoslavia, both in good times and harsh times, and there were many good times. The sudden realisation that our country had collapsed was not easy. This did not happen without emotions,' Kucan remembered.

What had been political issues soon became military ones. With new coalition governments taking power in Slovenia and Croatia, it was clear that the northern republics were headed for independence. But they would not be allowed to fight for it. Under Tito each of the republics had its own national territorial defence organisation (TO), as well as garrisons for troops of the Yugoslav army (JNA). In May 1990, General

Kadijevic ordered the JNA to take steps. Troops, under the control of the general staff in Belgrade, would stay in Slovenia and Croatia, while Slovene and Croatian TOs were disarmed to prevent them transforming into the armies of any future independent republic.

In response, Slovenia's interior minister, Igor Bavcar, and the defence minister, Janez Jansa (a former *Mladina* journalist), launched a clandestine arms-buying programme. Within three months the nascent Slovene army had 20,000 soldiers under arms. It is highly unlikely that the JNA, which at this time retained all its barracks, garrisons and intelligence organisations within Slovenia, was unaware of this. In October Slovene television showed film of Slovene troops blowing up a tank. Still no order came from Belgrade to halt Ljubljana's armaments drive. In December the Slovenes voted overwhelmingly for independence in a national plebiscite.

Slovenia's momentum was now unstoppable. Milosevic did not object, as long as he could benefit from events. Kucan recalled, 'Milosevic had said to me we should reach some agreement on Slovenia's desire to leave Yugoslavia. He said he would not stop us, and that the others didn't understand what the whole thing was about anyway. But he said he cannot let Croatia go, because Croatia was bound to Serbia by blood.' On 23 January 1991, Milosevic and Kucan headed a meeting of two delegations in Belgrade. Flanked by their aides, the two men eyed each other warily across the table. It was decision time.

Asked whether there was a community of interest between Slovenia and Serbia at this time, Kucan replied: 'One could say that. At a certain period of time Slovenia and Serbia had a common interest for reforming the society, but obviously based on completely different principles. This created the "community of interest" in that Milosevic's Yugoslavia had no room for Slovenia and Slovenia did not want to be in Milosevic's Yugoslavia.' Like Kucan, Milosevic knew exactly what he wanted. After lengthy negotiations, a joint communiqué was issued. Serbia would respect 'the right of the Slovene nation and the Republic of Slovenia to their own path and their stance regarding the form of future ties with other Yugoslav nations or republics'.[9]

What was the deal? Milosevic's price was hidden in the small print: 'Slovenia respects the interest of the Serbian people living in one state and ensures that the future Yugoslav government must give proper consideration to this interest.' Behind the bland diplomatese lay the rationale for the coming wars. Yugoslavia was a balancing act of six *republics*: Serbia, Croatia, Bosnia, Macedonia, Montenegro and Slovenia. But because of Yugoslavia's ethnic jumble – mirrored across the Balkans – the *nations* did not all live within the borders of their republics.

While Yugoslavia remained united this did not matter. Croatia and Bosnia were not independent republics but part of Yugoslavia, so the Serbs did indeed live in one state: Yugoslavia. But Milosevic argued that if Yugoslavia broke up and its constituent republics became independent states, then all Serbs, as part of the Serbian *nation*, should also have the right to live in one republic: Serbia. At first this sounded reasonable enough. If all the Slovenes had the right to live in one state, then why should the Serbs be denied something similar? The answer, of course, was that while over 90 per cent of Slovenes lived in Slovenia, the Serbs were also spread through Croatia and Bosnia. There were 600,000 Serbs in Croatia, and they made up 31 per cent of Bosnia's population.

Milosevic was introducing a new and highly dangerous principle: the primacy of *nation* over *republic*. This was a deliberate act of political destruction. It invalidated the borders of the republics within federal Yugoslavia. It was a recipe for chaos, uncertainty and, ultimately, war. Yugoslavia was an ethnic patchwork. As well as Serbs in Croatia, there were, for example, Albanians in Macedonia, Muslims in Serbia and Montenegro, and Croats in Bosnia. There was no way to satisfy each ethnic group's territorial demands. Milosevic, however, was concerned only with the Serbs. How would he bring them all into one state? By moving the borders, that is, by invading and annexing territory. This was Milosevic's plan for a Greater Serbia.

But Slovenia did not share a border with Serbia, and so could be let go. Slovene officials deny that the January 1991 meeting endorsed Milosevic's plan for Greater Serbia. They point to another sentence in the communiqué, which declares that while the Yugoslav nations do have the right to self-determination, that right must also take into account the equal rights of other nations. Thus Serbia cannot just slice off a chunk of Croatia or Bosnia because Serbs live there. None the less, the fundamental principle that led to the redrawing of the Yugoslav borders had been established.

On 25 June 1991 Slovenia declared independence from Yugoslavia. The Yugoslav flag was taken down, and the Slovene one raised. Slovene border and customs guards sent their Yugoslav predecessors packing. It was daring and audacious, and it triggered the first of four wars that would tear Yugoslavia apart. Milan Kucan denied that by leaving

Yugoslavia when it did, Slovenia bore responsibility for later events. Although Milosevic and Kucan had agreed a form of words about Slovenia's future development in their January communiqué, it did not provide for outright independence. There was no agreement to simply surrender Yugoslav strategic assets such as Ljubljana airport, and federal border crossings.

> Slovenia invested a lot of effort into reforming the Yugoslav federation. We first proposed an asymmetrical federation. Then, we proposed a confederation as a transitional arrangement until either the dissolution or the reintegration of the country. Finally, we proposed an agreement on the dissolution of the country, knowing that the whole thing could end in tragedy. When it became clear that none of the proposed solutions would be adopted, we had to focus on our responsibility towards our own nation. I have heard this allegation several times. I have asked others what they would do in the same position. Would they primarily consider the interests of others and not those of their own nation? I never got an answer.

For Milosevic, everything was going to plan. By declaring independence for the Slovene nation, and arguing that all Slovenes should live in one country, Ljubljana was setting a useful precedent. But Milosevic played his usual double game: although he had no real objection to Slovenia leaving Yugoslavia, he publicly presented himself as the defender of Yugoslavia. He could not be seen to sit back contentedly and watch Yugoslavia's richest republic stroll off into the European dawn. Milosevic needed the support of the army generals, who believed in federal Yugoslavia, and who were fervently opposed to the break-up of the country. By getting the JNA to fight to keep Slovenia within Yugoslavia he set a second precedent: that the army would go to war to prevent secession, which he could later exploit in Croatia and Bosnia.

There were two war options. Plan A involved 670 police and customs officers, accompanied by 2,000 troops being deployed to retake the border posts and the airport. In Plan B the 63rd Airborne Brigade would spearhead a full-blown invasion of Slovenia, backed up by the JNA's Fifth Military District. Martial law would be declared and the independence movement crushed. There would, the generals warned, be 'heavy casualties'.

Plan A was implemented. In the early hours of 27 June, Kucan was informed by his chief of staff that the JNA was moving through the country. At 5.00 a.m. he summoned his war cabinet. Two-day-old Slovenia had two options: to fight back or surrender.

Slovenia went to war. The Slovene militia surrounded the JNA bases and cut off the water and electricity. A JNA helicopter flying over Ljubljana was shot down. Pieces of charred machinery and two men's bodies lay on the streets of the capital, while pedestrians looked on in awe and fear. There was no going back from this. If anything, Slovenia had declared war on the JNA. The 35,000-strong Slovene army, highly motivated and well trained, proved superior to the lightly-armed JNA troops, most of whom had no idea why they were fighting.

In Belgrade Milosevic watched the generals rage at the JNA's humiliation. It was all falling into place. The JNA was involved, but it couldn't win without going to Plan B. The generals demanded authorisation to pour in the troops and put down the uprising. But Milosevic and his allies would never allow this, because he wanted Slovenia to secede. Borisav Jovic recalled: 'I put it bluntly. We didn't want a war with Slovenia. Serbia had no territorial claims there. It was an ethnically pure republic – no Serbs. We couldn't care less if they left Yugoslavia . . . We would have been overstretched. With Slovenia out of the way, we could dictate terms to the Croats.'[10]

Forty-four JNA soldiers were killed and 187 were wounded in ten days of fighting. Slovene casualties were in single figures. The Yugoslav casualties were mostly frightened and bewildered teenage conscripts. This was the human cost of the 'community of interest' between Milosevic and Kucan. Seasoned officers like Colonel Vaso Predojevic were utterly confused by being ordered to fire on their former countrymen. Predojevic, a Bosnian Serb married to a Slovene, was stationed at the Fifth Military District headquarters in Zagreb. 'We couldn't believe it, because before we were friends, living together, and then we had to fight each other. It was very hard to understand, because I was a Yugoslav, an army officer, then all of a sudden I realised that there was no more Yugoslavia. It used to be one country and it would never be the same anymore. It was very difficult.'[11]

Predojevic soon retired from the JNA. When the Slovenian war broke out, he had told his superior officer that he would not take part. 'He told me not to worry, that there would not be an attack on any JNA army officer or soldier, and that not even a stone would be thrown. He said everything had been decided in Ljubljana and Belgrade.'

12

WAR NO. 2, CROATIA

A Joint Criminal Enterprise

1990—2

The outlook in Serbia is particularly unpromising.

Reginald Wyon, 1904.[1]

Despite its human cost, the war in Slovenia was essentially a sideshow. It was in Croatia and Bosnia that Milosevic and his allies were planning the 'armed battles' of which he had spoken at Kosovo in 1989. As Borisav Jovic had noted, the Serb leadership had no real interest in the fate of Slovenia. Croatia and Bosnia, with their substantial Serb minorities, were another matter. They would provide the *casus belli* that Milosevic sought to bring the Serb-populated areas of Croatia and Bosnia under his control, allowing, in effect, all Serbs to live in one state, the vision described as 'Serboslavia'. Well over a year before the brief conflict in Ljubljana, Milosevic, Jovic and the federal defence minister, General Veljko Kadijevic, had been discussing the likelihood of future war, as Yugoslavia began to disintegrate. The three men had met on 13 February, recorded Jovic in his diaries:

Sloba said: 'There'll be war, by God.'
I disagreed: 'We won't allow it, by God. We have had enough war and death in two world wars. Now we shall avoid war by all means!'
'There will not be the kind of war which they want,' said Veljko, 'but it will be the kind of war which it must be, and that is that we shall not allow them to beat us.'[2]

It is not clear precisely when Milosevic decided on war. Milosevic's secretive, authoritarian modus operandi makes it unlikely that there is a 'smoking gun': a single incriminating document, or even a paper trail, of the kind sought by the investigators for the Hague Tribunal. But Jovic's diaries are a valuable resource. The two men worked closely together during the collapse of Yugoslavia, and Jovic was one of Milosevic's most trusted allies. If Milosevic was discussing war in February 1990, by June he was talking about more concrete plans to carve off territory from Croatia, and was both redrawing the map of Yugoslavia and planning the necessary constitutional gerrymandering to ram his decisions through the federal power structure. In his diary entry for 28 June 1990 Jovic records that Milosevic proposed that:

> the cutting off of Croatia be carried out in such a way that the municipalities of Lika, Banija and Kordun, which have created an association, should stay on our side, and people should later decide if they want to stay or leave; second that [federal] presidency members from Croatia and Slovenia be excluded from the vote on this issue, because they do not represent that part of Yugoslavia taking the decision.[3]

Milosevic understood that war – especially the right 'kind' – cannot just be conjured up. It needs co-conspirators and extensive preparations. Which is one reason why Milosevic's indictment for war crimes in Croatia (and Bosnia) describes him as a participant in a 'joint criminal enterprise' to ethnically cleanse about one third of Croatian territory, as a prelude to setting up a Serb para-state. This demands great organisation. Milosevic knew that lines must be drawn on maps, men deployed, guns and ammunition distributed and the population roused. Broadly speaking, he needed to control three Serbian power-structures, and two within federal Yugoslavia. In Serbia these were: the Communist – later Socialist – Party, the media and the secret service. The party controlled the political process, the media shaped public opinion and the secret service supplied the weapons to the Serb rebels.[4]

Within federal Yugoslavia, Milosevic needed to control the Yugoslav armed forces and the Federal Presidency, the supreme commander of the military. While there was opposition within the military to Milosevic's policies, Milosevic was able to dominate the federal defence minister General Veljko Kadijevic – himself a Serb. It was Milosevic's luck and Yugoslavia's great misfortune that his ally Borisav Jovic had in mid-May

1990 taken over as president of the federal collective presidency, which was the supreme commander of the Yugoslav military. Jovic was a pugnacious Serb nationalist who set the tone of future meetings with a belligerent inaugural speech, after which he refused to offer the customary thanks to his predecessor, the well-regarded Slovene politician Janez Drnovsek.

By 1990 Serbian politics, the media and the secret service were all under Milosevic's control. He had brought in a new secret service chief, Jovica Stanisic. Stanisic was a high-flying career intelligence officer, and soon became one of Milosevic's most important allies. Like Lenin, Milosevic understood that an efficient security service was the most important bastion of any authoritarian regime. Together they turned the service into a proactive organisation: agents had helped organise the 'anti-bureaucratic revolutions' in Voivodina and Kosovo, as well as the massive Belgrade demonstrations. Stanisic was just one of many powerful allies Milosevic had at the time. He had widespread support in the Yugoslav power structure, according to Milan Kucan. 'A very large part of the federal administration was interested in having a Yugoslavia which in essence would be a Serboslavia. The entire army structure, especially the leadership, many people in foreign affairs, in the police, and in the security services supported this.'5

Milosevic and Stanisic deployed their key people to prepare for conflict: Mihalj Kertes, Franko Simatovic and Radovan Stojicic. Kertes had brought in the demonstrators during the Voivodina 'anti-bureaucratic revolution'. Simatovic, known as 'Frenki', headed the secret service's murky special operations unit. Radovan Stojicic, nicknamed 'Badza' (after the violent bully character in *Popeye*) was a commander of the police special forces, who had operated in Kosovo during the miners' strike in 1989. Together with Jovica Stanisic, these three men were the key figures in what became known as the 'military faction' within the all-powerful Serbian Interior Ministry (MUP). The MUP controlled the domestic intelligence service, the police, and the police paramilitary and special forces units (as distinguished from similar units in the regular military). The job of the military faction was to organise an armed uprising of the Serbian minority in Croatia against the Croatian authorities, in preparation for a de facto annexation of the territories to Serbia itself.

This is how they did it. In spring 1990 the JNA disarmed the Croatian TO, just as had happened in Slovenia, and kept the weapons. Belgrade's plan was to distribute the guns to Serb militants based in Knin, a dusty railroad town situated in the heartland of an area known as Krajina. Whoever controlled Knin controlled the roads and railways linking Zagreb to the coast. Many of Croatia's Serbs were concentrated in the towns and villages of this rocky hinterland, set back from the Italianate jewels of the Adriatic seaside. The Krajina had once been the borderland between the Ottoman and Habsburg empires.

The Knin Serbs were stubborn, hardy and nervous about Croatia's first multiparty elections, to be held in April 1990, and the prospect of living in independent Croatia. Memories were still fresh of the first Croatian state, the NDH, and the wartime massacres carried out by the Ustasha in the remote Serb villages. Many of the Knin Serbs were unsophisticated folk. When Milosevic sent men from Belgrade to warn that their lives were in danger, they listened. When Frenki and Badza offered weapons, they took them.

Encouraged by the Serb nationalist writer Dobrica Cosic, the Serbs in Croatia and Bosnia had set up their own political party, the Serbian Democratic Party (SDS), which replaced the old Communist Party. Although the name had changed, the political bosses remained the same. This was a familiar story, repeated all over post-Communist eastern Europe, but the SDS served a different purpose: it provided a ready-made weapons-distribution network. The links were later formalised in February 1991, when Milosevic submitted a law to the Serbian parliament establishing twenty ministeries, including the Ministry for Links with Serbs outside Serbia. This ministry was used as a channel to rebel Serbs in both Croatia and Bosnia.

Milosevic also built his own network within the JNA, known as the Vojna Linija, or 'Military Line'. This was an ad hoc group of pro-Milosevic officers, who saw that Yugoslavia was about to break up and wanted to arm the Serbs in Croatia and Bosnia, as a prelude to annexing territory to Serbia. The key figure in the Military Line was a Serb JNA colonel called Ratko Mladic. Stocky and intelligent, Mladic was also extremely violent. Everything about him exuded menace. The writer Misha Glenny recalled how Mladic offered round his home-distilled *rakija* at a morning interview session in early 1992. Some in the party demurred, but only temporarily. Mladic had boomed: 'For a moment . . . I thought you were going to refuse my home-made. Which is very funny, you know, because nobody refuses my home-made.'[6]

Together with the Serbian leadership, the Military Line group evolved a plan reportedly known as RAM, or 'frame'. RAM detailed the geographical outline of the future Greater Serbia and how it would include large swathes of Croatia and Bosnia inhabited by Serbs.[7] RAM was a modern version of the plan for a Greater Serbia first outlined by the Serb nationalist theoretician Ilija Garasanin in the mid-nineteenth century. Garasanin called for spies to be sent into coveted territory, and Serb agents to infiltrate and set up parallel military and police forces, in preparation for annexation. These were precisely the methods used by Milosevic and the Serbian secret service. Armaments and military equipment were placed in strategic locations in Croatia and Bosnia, and local Serbs trained as police and paramilitary forces, as a prelude to ethnic cleansing and appropriation of territory. Garasanin's spiritual heirs, the authors of the 1986 SANU Memorandum, claimed they had identified the problems of the Serbs. Four years later, the generals in the Military Line would provide what they saw as the necessary solution.

At this time, in 1990, the SANU intellectuals grouped around the writer Dobrica Cosic, the intellectual godfather of modern Serbian nationalism, enjoyed good relations with Milosevic. After his turn to nationalism Milosevic sought popular legitimisation from the revered writer. And when the Serbian Communist Party transformed itself into the Serbian Socialist Party (SPS), several senior SANU members joined. Dobrica Cosic did not join the SPS, but held a long meeting with Milosevic in March 1990, at which Milosevic informed him that Yugoslavia had outlived its usefulness.[8] Cosic noted that Milosevic was 'the first Serbian Communist who has a conception of economics, communication and development,' as well as 'an autocratic personality'. Milosevic's personality was that of a 'party organisational secretary', he recorded, perceptively enough, as this was precisely Milosevic's post at Belgrade University.

In June 1996 Jerko Doko, the former Bosnian minister of defence, testified at The Hague about the RAM plan.

Q. Do you know where this RAM plan originated from?
A. Well, the RAM plan originates from the Serbian Academy of Arts and Sciences, the so-called SANU, where it was drawn up together with the Serbian leadership, with Milosevic and some members of the General Staff of JNA – normally in strict secrecy.[9]

Rooted in nineteenth-century ideas, the 1986 SANU Memorandum was a symptom not a cause of modern Serbian nationalism. But the collapse of Yugoslavia provided an opportunity to realise an age-old dream, the SANU intellectuals believed, and Milosevic was the man for the job. According to a former senior official in the Serbian secret service, the political links between Milosevic and SANU stretched back several years. 'The dream of realising Greater Serbia first began in higher intellectual circles. When the academicians drafted the Memorandum, they were looking for someone to implement it. So they brought Milosevic to power through the Eighth Session. The role of the secret service was the realisation of the Memorandum.' As early as 1989, the former official says, he heard a chilling prediction from a Serbian intellectual: 'Slavonia will be the first to fall, which will open the road to Zagreb, and Osijek is going to be completely destroyed. At the same time, or later, we will burn all the forests on the Dalmatian coast; all the Croats will run away, and we will take it.'[10]

Meanwhile in the Croatian capital Zagreb, the new president Franjo Tudjman considered his country's uncertain future. A former partisan and historian, Tudjman was leader of the Croatian Democratic Union (HDZ) which had won the country's first multi-party elections. His fevered supporters presented the jowly nationalist as a quasi-deity. The HDZ slogan was 'God in heaven, and Tudjman in the homeland'. Like Tito, Tudjman was from Croatia's Zagorje region, just north of Zagreb. He shared Tito's taste for white suits, splendid brocades and sashes. Born in 1922, Tudjman became a career army officer. By 1960 he was the youngest JNA general. But he soon resigned, complaining that too many senior officers were Serbs, and Croats were treated unfairly. Increasingly active in nationalist circles during the Croatian Spring of the early 1970s, Tudjman was expelled from the Communist Party and later jailed.

Like Mira Markovic, Tudjman considered himself an academic. He looked to history, the favourite and most malleable of Balkan academic disciplines, for his inspiration. In the dusty textbooks and crinkled maps of long-vanished kingdoms, he found chronicled the centuries of injustice that had prevented Croatia from realising its glorious potential. Tito's mini-empire was only the most recent.

In many ways Tudjman and Milosevic were mirror images of each other. Both were authoritarian Communists who were psychologically unable to make a transition to genuine democracy. In fact the two men got on quite well. They would later engage in some complicated secret diplomacy whose cynicism shocked even their own supporters. But although Tudjman was a prisoner of history, he – unlike Milosevic – actually believed in nationalism.

With Tudjman in power, Milosevic hit the jackpot. The Croatian president's outspoken nationalism and hapless political style made him Belgrade's best recruiting agent. Lacking an equivalent of Milosevic's media-manipulator Dusan Mitevic, Tudjman soon blundered on the campaign trail. 'Thank God my wife is not a Jew or a Serb,'[11] he blurted out at one election meeting in a Zagreb suburb. And when questioned about the Ustasha regime, Tudjman equivocated. He declared that the NDH was 'not only a quisling organisation and a Fascist crime, but was also an expression of the Croatian nation's historic desire for an independent homeland.'[12]

One of Milosevic's most effective propaganda weapons was the Croatian constitution. When the impossibly intricate arguments advanced by Croatian nationalist theoreticians concerning who was a 'true' Croat were finally resolved, it was deemed that the country's 600,000 Serbs were not. Croatia was no longer defined as 'the national state of the Croatian nation and the state of the Serbian nation in Croatia', with two official scripts, Cyrillic and Latin, as it had been in Yugoslavia. The new Croatian constitution declared the country to be, first, the homeland of the Croatian nation. The Serbs living in Croatia were no longer a nation but a national minority, ranked with the Italian, Hungarian and other ethnic communities. Cyrillic was no longer an official script. The effect was to make the Croatian Serbs feel alienated and disenfranchised. Five seats in the parliament were reserved for the Serb minority. No Serb MPs attended the opening ceremony.

The new Croatian flag was also most helpful to Milosevic. Croatian politicians spent much time discussing the red and white squares that made up the pattern of the *sahovnica*, the Croatian flag. The *sahovnica* was the emblem of both the medieval Croatian kingdom in pre-Communist times and the wartime NDH. For Serbs, the NDH flag had the same resonance as the swastika for Jews. A compromise was reached after hours of wrangling. The *sahovnica* would indeed return, but the design would be altered slightly so that the end square was red, and not white as in the NDH flag.[13]

All this was seized on by the Serbian media. Newspapers pumped out a stream of propaganda articles about the rebirth of 'Ustasha terror'. Serbian television broadcast gruesome films of wartime Ustasha atrocities. But Franjo Tudjman was not Ante Pavelic. The new Croatia was not the NDH reborn. Not only was the comparison wrong, but it also degraded the real victims of the Ustasha genocide.

> It is not hard to provoke nationalism. If you are not immune to that state of mind, it can be induced in a multi-cultural society, [noted Mira Markovic]. This nationalism was scientifically induced. The Slovenes, Croats, Serbs and Muslims, in one moment everyone turned back to the fourteenth century. It was like a madness, people talking about ancient times, the battles of Kosovo, miracles, religion came back with all the hymns, priests and calendars.[14]

Mira denied that her husband wanted to bring about a Greater Serbia. She argued that his aim was to preserve Yugoslavia. 'Slobo did not support this. He wanted a big Yugoslavia, because Serbs lived in Croatia, Bosnia and Montenegro. Serbs were everywhere. No other nation was spread all over as the Serbs, and the place for all Serbs in one country is Yugoslavia.' Either way, Milosevic showed no concern for the human cost of his policies. The equation was simple enough: war ensured political power; political power demanded war. Milosevic simply compartmentalised his work life and his home life. 'I doubt that he was ever bothered by guilt,' said Mihailo Crnobrnja. 'He had a technique to shut out unpleasant things. I don't know how he did it. It was a psychological technique, a mechanism to pretend they don't exist.'[15]

Some have compared Milosevic's cold detachment to that of Stalin. Stalin had sat at his desk long into the small hours, the only sound in the room the scratch of his pen as he ticked off the names on the lists of those to be purged. But Stalin was a paranoid recluse who sent his tea-maker to Lubyanka prison after an open packet was found in the Kremlin larder. Milosevic was not, at least in the early 1990s. He sang French songs at the piano, he enjoyed shopping in New York, he had tried to find boyfriends for his daughter. He could be charming and entertaining when he chose. He could certainly inspire friendship and loyalty, even if it was not always returned. Ivan Stambolic himself said that he had once loved Milosevic like a brother.

Milosevic too felt love, but only for four people: his wife Mira, son Marko, daughter Marija and brother Borislav. In the evenings, the family sat around the kitchen table, and talked about their day. Milosevic changed out of his suit, and put on a sweater and comfortable trousers, just like any middle-aged father and husband. He downed a glass of Viljamovka pear brandy and lit a cigarillo. His brother Borislav said: 'He is a man of strong will, he has his own beliefs, his own positions, but on the other hand he is a man devoted to his friends and family, he is a very good paterfamilias. He is a very good father and he is not a cruel person, as he is portrayed.'[16]

For his children, Milosevic would do anything. He was proud of Marko, who had grown into a skinny sixteen-year-old with a flat-top haircut and a taste for fast cars and designer trainers. Milosevic feared, correctly, that his son was keeping bad company in Pozarevac, where he stayed for much of the week, even though he rarely attended school. Marko was extremely spoilt and selfish, a pampered child who could do no wrong as far as his parents were concerned. Marko told his father that he wanted to be a racing driver. He was about to grow into a rather sinister young man.

Marija had settled down after her brief marriage to the diplomat in Japan. She had worked as a journalist, first with *Politika Ekspress* and then at the Kosava radio station. Although she lacked a university education, she was intelligent and had some personal career ambitions. While Mira was closer to Marko, whom in classic Balkan fashion she smothered with maternal love and admiration, Marija was more of a daddy's girl.

But daddy was paying more attention to politics than his daughter. Like her paternal grandparents, Marija became prone to fits of depression, which would get worse over the next few years. Milosevic worried about her turbulent emotional life. After Marija had broken up with Tahir Hasanovic, her consorts appeared increasingly unsuitable. She thought that men were interested in her only because of her powerful family connections.

Out of the public eye, Milosevic enjoyed a classic Serbian boisterous lifestyle. Unknown to him, the Croatian secret service was tapping his telephone, preserving the inner dynamics of the Milosevic family for all time. Here is Slobo talking to Marko about his son's appearance. Marko called his dad from Italy, just before midnight on 15 March 1997 to discuss his latest idea: an operation to pin his ears back. Slododan is not keen.

Slobodan: Alright, my lovely. Listen, I've been talking to a doctor here and I did some thinking with my own head. You know why it looks that way to you? Because you're terribly skinny, and every geek your age looks that way. As soon as you fill out and, as they say, stabilise a bit, everything will fall into place. I looked even worse when I was thin.

Marko: Look, I agree, but I do not intend to start looking good in fifteen years.

Slobodan: Marko, what I want to tell you is that it only appears that way because you're skinny. Even a chicken has some fat behind the ears. And you have only bones, you see, so any violence against nature is stupid. Secondly, you are handsome as a doll, your father's image. So don't screw around.

Marko: But dad . . .

Slobodan: I'm against it and I am your parent. There you go.

Marko: Excellent. And I am in favour of it and I am of age.

Slobodan: Well, since you're of age, I am going to beat you up as soon as you show up here . . . I want to tell you this only because you're skinny. Your head is all drawn thin, your stomach is like a five-dinar coin (i.e. thin). Why don't you put some more fat on it?[17]

Yet outside his family, the rest of the world simply did not matter for Milosevic. The British diplomat David Austin spent hours negotiating with the Serbian leader in Belgrade. Milosevic was extremely charming, generously plying his guests with food and drink. He made sure to enquire about Austin's baby daughter, yet never mentioned the tragedy unfolding around him. 'Milosevic gave the impression he did not care about people as individuals. Nothing seemed to affect him emotionally; any kind of human suffering just did not register. He never once expressed any sympathy. Apart from his family, people were just nothing to him.'[18] For Milosevic the fate of nations came second to family affairs. He once ended negotiations at five o'clock sharp, recalled David Austin, because he had to go home for his daughter's birthday party.

Milosevic's lack of human empathy, or consideration for other's feelings, is echoed by the Croatian prime minister Stipe Mesic. 'I spent a lot of time with him at official meetings, dinners and lunches. At formal meetings he was quite hard and hardly ever moved from his position. But at informal occasions he was often quite relaxed and jocular. He would make jokes, but always at the expense of his staff. Whenever we talked together, especially if I was critical

of him, he always knew how to reroute his criticism to his associates.'[19]

Mesic was engaged in an attempt to stop Milosevic arming the Krajina
Serbs. Zagreb could do little. The country's territorial defence had been
disarmed and the Croatian police lacked the men or firepower to take
on what was evolving into Milosevic's rebel army.

As relations deteriorated, Mesic's trips to Belgrade became increasingly uncomfortable.

> When I came to Belgrade in the autumn of 1990, I asked Jovic
> why they were arming the [Croatian] Serbs. They could not solve
> their problems by force, or violence. Jovic told me that was what
> Milosevic wanted. I said the [Croatian] Serbs could only deal with
> their problems by negotiation. Jovic said: 'We are not interested
> in the Serbs in Croatia. They are your citizens, you can do what
> you like with them, you can impale them for all we care. We are
> exclusively interested in Bosnia-Herzegovina, which was, and will
> be, Serbian.'

Such statements, and the subsequent course of events during the
1990s in the Krajina Serbs' mini-state, reveal the cynical expediency
of Milosevic's policies. 'I saw quite clearly that there would be war,'
said Mesic. 'I also saw that they didn't need the Serbs in Croatia, that
they were deceiving the Serbs in Croatia, and their primary goal was
Bosnia-Herzegovina.'

Jovic and Milosevic played a game of 'good cop, bad cop' with Mesic.
Milosevic was the good cop. He always appeared conciliatory, ready to
meet with Mesic and discuss his grievances. For example, Mesic was
angry that when Croatian Serb delegations came to Belgrade, they did
not meet with him, even though he was Croatia's member of the
federal presidency. Instead they met Borisav Jovic, Serbia's presidency
member. For Mesic, this was not acceptable, and he asked to be present
at the meetings. Milosevic, who took great care to coat his manoeuvres
with a veneer of constitutional legitimacy, agreed. Mesic recalled: 'He
would say, "This is an untenable state of affairs, it will be corrected
right away." But it was Milosevic who had invited them to Belgrade
in the first place.'

In August 1990 the Croatian Serbs held a referendum on 'sovereignty
and autonomy'. This meant that they would not recognise Croatia, if

and when it became independent, even though they lived within its borders. Croatia's Serb population voted massively in favour. Everything was going to according to plan. The political leader of the Krajina Serbs, Milan Babic, travelled to Belgrade for consultations. Careful not to leave any hostages to fortune, Milosevic dealt with Babic at one remove, delegating Borisav Jovic and General Petar Gracanin, the federal interior minister, to meet the Krajina Serb leader. Babic recalled: 'We did not get a specific promise, but I was left in no doubt that Belgrade would help us.' He certainly got plenty of advice from Gracanin, himself a Serb and former partisan: 'I told them to put up barricades. I said if you can't get anything else, use hunting rifles. Patrol your streets at night. Guard against attack from the Fascists who run Croatia.'[20]

The Croatian Serbs proclaimed the founding of the Republic of the Serb Krajina (RSK). The RSK then announced that it would stay in Yugoslavia. Croatia's borders were being redrawn for it, just as Milosevic had predicted. Milosevic began his salami tactics, slicing away at the constitutional safeguards around the JNA as he turned the Yugoslav army into the ally of the rebel Serb forces. A series of stepped armed clashes were staged between rebel Serbs and Croatian police.

On 2 May 1991 twelve Croat policemen were killed by Serb militiamen in the village of Borovo Selo. The battle triggered uproar in both Belgrade and Zagreb. Milosevic's ally, the Serbian interior minister Radmilo Bogdanovic, boasted: 'Where was the opposition then? If we had not equipped our Serbs, who knows how they would have fared in the attack by the Croatian National Guard on Borovo Selo.'[21] The Serbian government blamed the Croatian interior ministry for organising an unprovoked attack on the village. In the Serbian parliament Milosevic's allies orchestrated a chorus of outrage. Speaker after speaker demanded to know why the JNA was not protecting the Serbs in Croatia from the 'Ustasha hordes'.

That month the federal presidency, under immense pressure from Milosevic and his allies in the Serbian parliament, granted the JNA formal powers to intervene in the fighting between the Serb rebels and the Croats. This soon turned into support for the Serbs. Events began to follow a familiar pattern. The rebel Serbs would provoke a battle with the Croatian forces to capture more territory for their mini-republic. The JNA tanks would roll down the middle of the front line. The fighting would stop. Behind the JNA armour the rebel Serbs would consolidate their new gains.

The departure of Croatia, Slovenia, Macedonia and Bosnia from the federal presidency meant all presidency decisions were now taken by the 'Serbian bloc'. This was headed by Borisav Jovic, representing Serbia, together with the pro-Milosevic representatives of Montenegro, Voivodina and Kosovo. Through the Serbian bloc, Milosevic finally had control of the Federal Presidency, commander-in-chief of the JNA. Just as Milosevic had planned, the JNA was now a de facto army of Serbia.

By the autumn of 1991 rebel Serbs controlled about one-third of Croatian territory. A new term for an age-old practice entered the vocabulary of 1990s Europe: 'ethnic cleansing', the use of murder and destruction to force an exodus of minority populations. This was not solely a Serbian practice. When Croatian forces recaptured territory, they too 'cleansed' villages, sending a stream of Serb refugees fleeing in terror. Serbs living in Croatia outside the war zone were increasingly harassed and intimidated. In the coastal towns of Split and Zadar, not far from the front lines, Serb shops and holiday homes were set on fire, their owners driven away.

Just as the above-mentioned Serbian intellectual had predicted in 1989, Osijek in eastern Croatia was indeed 'set ablaze'. To drive into besieged Osijek was to enter a ghost town of deserted streets, where buildings had their windows blown out and their facades peppered with shrapnel. The population fled underground as Serb gunners daily rained down shell and mortar fire. Osijek echoed to the crack of sniper fire, the boom of artillery and the sharp bang of incoming mortars. Trenches and bunkers lined the only safe route into the city, defences against any future land attack by the Serb forces just a few kilometres away. Dead cats and dogs lay under a grey winter sky, and blackened cars mangled by shellfire lay splayed across the roads.

Across Croatia – as was to happen later in Bosnia – cities such as Osijek evolved their own version of the highway code: when driving in the target area, switch the radio off and leave the windows open to hear the direction of the shelling. Unlock car doors, undo seatbelts and be ready to roll immediately. The Serb siege of Osijek set a morbid precedent for future attacks on urban populations. The hospital was hit so many times that everything was moved into the basement. Injured Croat soldiers lay wrapped in bloody bandages under heating ducts in rooms of bare brick. Nearby, the reserve ward was an eerie sight, full of rows of empty beds, each covered in clean white sheets.[21]

Milosevic had finally achieved the remarkable, if grisly, feat of deploying a modern European army against its own citizens. There was indeed 'War, by God.'

13

STREET PROTESTS

Ten Days That Shook Belgrade
March 1991

Slobo, Saddam! Slobo, Saddam!
Student demonstrators in Belgrade, March 1991.

Milosevic had a dream. More of a recurring nightmare, really. He saw the bodies of two elderly Romanians, their hands bound, their crumpled corpses lying in pools of their own blood in a military barracks. Nicolae and Elena Ceausescu were two Balkan Communist leaders who had also stood firm against the historic changes reshaping eastern Europe. When Romanian demonstrators had protested in the northern city of Timisoara, not far from the Serbian border, the dreaded *securitate* secret police had killed them. The violence triggered the bloodiest uprising of 1989. President Ceausescu and his wife were caught attempting to flee. Tried in secret, they were sentenced to death. The firing squad lined up on Christmas Day, 1989. Elena Ceausescu, Romania's real ruler, was defiant to the end. 'I was like a mother to you,' she declared, before the soldiers pulled the trigger.

Milosevic's media mastermind, Dusan Mitevic, had shown the Romanian revolution on channel two of Serbian television. After live broadcasts of the Eighth Session in 1987 and the Gazimestan mass meeting in 1989, Mitevic was now eastern Europe's pioneer in streaming news. Milosevic was happy for images of his political triumph and coronation as modern king-saint to fill Serbian television. But revolutions next door were something else. Milosevic was spooked by what happened in Romania, Mitevic said. 'We sent a crew there, and they broadcast everything, directly as it was happening; even the BBC took our feed from us. Milosevic was not happy that we showed the executions of Ceausescu. He said it was not a human or cultural event to show the execution of the president of another country. He was afraid that he would finish the same way.'[1]

For Milosevic there were some disturbing parallels between his rise and Ceausescu's. Before Ceausescu had visited North Korea in 1971 and descended into megalomania, he had been seen in the West as a potential moderniser. Massive loans had poured in to prop up the Romanian economy. Ceausescu too had exploited nationalism to build a populist base. He had greatly expanded the power of Romania's secret service, the *securitate*. But that had not saved Ceausescu from the revolutionary mob. In fact there were increasing rumours that the *securitate* had organised the revolution. Praetorian guards had a habit of turning on those they were supposed to protect.

Yet ultimately, even Milosevic could not keep Yugoslavia isolated from the massive political changes that destroyed the Soviet system and tore down the Iron Curtain. When the aftershocks of the end of Communism had arrived in Serbia, Milosevic had diverted them into nationalism, and preparation for war. In Berlin they had danced on the remains of the wall. In Belgrade they had left on buses for Gazimestan. None the less, Milosevic understood that Serbia could not stand alone against the tide of democratic reform. The trick was to ensure that the more things had the appearance of change, the more they stayed the same.

But the man he had charged with helping direct the shaky transition of the Serbian Communist Party into the modern age was not following the party line. During the late 1980s Milosevic had continued to sponsor Tahir Hasanovic, even though Mira's attempts at matchmaking his protégé with their daughter had failed. By 1990, after working as foreign secretary of Yugoslavia's state youth organisation, Hasanovic had become the youngest member of the presidency of the Serbian Communist Party. He realised that the only answer for Yugoslavia was a complete transformation into a modern democracy.

Milosevic helped me get my position looking after international relations. When I travelled to London and Paris, it opened my eyes. My goal changed, to build a capitalist Serbia, to have a market economy, with an open door for the next generation. Milosevic also helped me become a member of the Serbian party presidency, but he tried to use me, because I had international connections. I looked at France and Britain, and I saw that the Berlin Wall had fallen. But when I began to discuss my western experience, I became a problem because Milosevic was fusing Communism with nationalism.[2]

The key word here is 'Communist'. Mira Markovic would never allow the Serbian Communist Party to evolve into a genuine social democratic grouping. 'Mira was the main person who destroyed any idea of turning the Communist Party into a social democratic one,' Hasanovic said. 'She and the people around her destroyed the proposal of the 1988 presidential reform commission. She asked me personally, "My dear Tahir, even South Africa has a Communist Party. Are you saying that only Serbia – where thousands of people died in World War Two – should not have a Communist Party? Are you crazy?"'

In the feverish Serbian political atmosphere, which fused Communist methodology with nationalist ideology, arguing for democracy and liberal freedoms was nothing less than treachery. 'Mira asked us why we were ruining the history and the heritage of the Communist movement in Yugoslavia. First it was a question, then it became an accusation, that we were traitors. So that's how I became a traitor.' Even now, over a decade later, the accusations are still painful for Hasanovic:

> Between 1984 and 1990 I was a professional politician in Yugoslavia. I had a car, a driver, a good salary, friends from abroad. I had the complete package, with all the kinds of privilege that society granted. Then I was expelled from the presidency of the Serbian party. I was twenty-nine years old and they said I was out of my mind. Because of my beliefs, everything was ruined. I did not have enough money for a Coca-cola.

Hasanovic recognised that his Turkish background and his Muslim name probably helped make his choice for him. Plenty of other politicians, who may even have in their hearts preferred to see social democracy triumph, still climbed on the Milosevic nationalist bandwagon. But as the Serbian Communist Party became increasingly more Serbian and less Communist, it is not entirely certain that there would have been a place for him anyway. 'If I was called something Serbian, like Jovan, maybe I would have been tempted to shut up about social democracy. But because of my name I was saved from the temptation to stay with them, to see what was happening.' Either way, Hasanovic's political career – at least as Milosevic's 'young lion' – was over.

*   *   *

A compromise was reached in the Milosevic household. The Serbian Communist Party would evolve into the Serbian Socialist Party (SPS), which would be little more than a change of name. Meanwhile, Comrade Dr Markovic would have her own political party, known as the League of Communists – Movement for Yugoslavia (LC-MY). As Mira Markovic had said, any husband who knew what was good for him had better be 'enchanted' with his wife's ideas. The new party was a dogmatic Marxist grouping. Such hard-left parties, nostalgic for the certainties of the old regime, briefly sprang up all over eastern Europe. Under normal circumstances the LC-MY would be irrelevant. But while its membership was minuscule, it was certainly influential. As well as the wife of Slobodan Milosevic, it included the federal defence minister General Veljko Kadijevic, the chief of staff and many other senior army officers who wanted a unified Yugoslavia. The party was not formed until the end of 1990, but when Yugoslavia went to war, the LC-MY would be the political channel between the Milosevic household and the battlefield.

When Serbia held an election in 1990, the outcome was a foregone conclusion, which perhaps is why Milosevic's party campaigned under the slogan: 'With us, there is no uncertainty'. Balkan politicians are no more trustworthy than their western counterparts, but as campaign promises go, this turned out to be one of the more accurate. The Serbian Socialists had a head-start in the race for parliament: they controlled the television. In fact they controlled most of the country. Just as happened in neighbouring countries, the Serbian Socialists simply appropriated the property, membership, patronage, power and economic networks of the former Communist regime. These assets were extensive. Moreover, the country's relatively underdeveloped political culture meant that many voters, particularly in rural areas, would vote for Milosevic as he represented continuity.

Serbia's elections were free, technically. But Milosevic had no intention of being voted out of office. Belgrade Television offered the following report of an opposition rally in July 1990:

So it happened that on Republic Square, in the middle of the day, in public, it was shown that the united Serbian opposition has no legitimacy among the Serbian people. Not even the throwing of mud at the government or the flood of primitive anticommunism helped. The united Serbian opposition showed clearly that in the name of the struggle for power it would sacrifice both true democracy and the constitutional unity of Serbia, and even its territorial integrity.[3]

When opposition demonstrators gathered outside Belgrade Television to protest against this sort of coverage, they were attacked by police. This prompted wry reminders of Milosevic's promise to the Kosovo Serbs in 1987, that 'no one should dare to beat you'.

Milosevic's Socialists won 46 per cent of the vote when Serbia went to the polls in December. Under Serbia's new parliamentary system the SPS had 194 seats in parliament out of 250, enough for a comfortable overall majority. The main opposition party, the Serbian Renewal Movement (SRM), was not social democratic but nationalist, led by Vuk Draskovic, author of *The Knife*. This bloodthirsty novel of wartime Bosnia, published in 1984, had broken a long-standing taboo about the discussion of Serb victims of wartime genocide. With his long hair and straggly beard, Draskovic cut a charismatic figure, although Belgrade insiders claimed that his fiery and statuesque Montenegrin wife Danica was, in classic Balkan fashion, the real boss. Either way, with just 19 seats the SRM presented no threat to Milosevic. Draskovic was a mercurial figure, whose ideological zig-zags would weaken the domestic opposition to Milosevic over the next few years.

Just as the Socialists had promised, by December, after Milosevic's victory, there was no 'uncertainty'. At this time, neighbouring post-Communist countries were building up their institutions by, for example, introducing an independent judiciary, removing the police from government control and freeing state broadcast media. The new Serbian president was neither able nor willing to do this. The interests of party and state, government and nation, remained synonymous, just as they had been under Communism.

Milosevic's regime was a very particular type of post-Communist Balkan democracy, with almost none of the checks and balances of a western parliamentary system. Parliament existed, but it was weak and relatively powerless. Milosevic, now confirmed as President of Serbia, mainly ruled by executive order. The small print of the Serbian constitution granted him extensive powers, including the right to dissolve parliament, approve international agreements without parliament's ratification, appoint judges, and to declare martial law. Milosevic remained aloof and untrusting. He hated to delegate and took most important decisions himself. His most trusted advisor remained his wife.

Milosevic was a good organiser, and a perfectionist, said Dusan Mitevic. 'He never let other people take the initiative. He checked and checked everything, and it had to be perfect.' Cabinet meetings were short, sharp and to the point. There was little disagreement, because if a minister disagreed with Milosevic his career would be short-lived. 'The government meetings never lasted more than half an hour. Milosevic spoke for a few minutes, usually three or four. He would say what he wanted to say, ask if anyone disagreed or there were any problems, and say, no, well, thank you very much. There were no discussions.'

On the rare occasions when a minister disagreed with the boss, Milosevic would speak to the errant official privately. The Serbian leader often used the technique of the silent reply to keep his aides off-balance, recalled Mitevic. 'You could tell him something and he would not say one word. You could have a meeting with him, and he would not tell you anything about his opinion. So when you left, you were wondering if you had said the right thing, or the wrong one. But he would think about what you said and then maybe use it himself, later.'

Visitors to the presidential palace during Milosevic's rule recall, most of all, the silence. There were security checks to enter the building, but once inside there was none of the buzz and hubbub that usually surrounds heads of state. No telephones rang, no aides rushed in and out, no advisers presented draft papers on pressing matters of state. There was only Milosevic, and a single female secretary. The spirit of Ottoman autocracy lived on. Occasional visitors were received in the presidential palace's massive reception room. With its twenty-feet high ceilings, comfortable leather chairs, dark wood furniture and intricately patterned Turkish carpets, the room was a sort of Balkan gentleman's club. Even *Vanity Fair* described Slobodan's salon as 'tastefully and timelessly' decorated.

After their election victory the Socialists controlled every ministry. The Belgrade publisher Braca Grubacic, sacked in one of Milosevic's purges, looked back ruefully on this time as Serbia's lost opportunity.

Things could have been different. We are a country without strong institutions to limit the power of one person, but we had something from Tito's Communism. It was not fantastic, but still it worked. It was not Romania here. Milosevic completely bypassed the institutions and appointed his people. If you came here you would think, OK there are ministries here, etc. But Milosevic appointed the ministers. Eventually you would see that if Milosevic does not say yes or no, then nothing else matters. He gave the orders.[4]

Milosevic has often been described as a dictator, yet this is incorrect. The best description of his regime is 'nationalist-authoritarianism', as defined by Professor Eric. D. Gordy.[5] Such a regime uses nationalism as a means of legitimacy for its authoritarian structure. But it is not totalitarian. Unlike Romania under Ceausescu, Milosevic's Serbia never attempted to control every aspect of its citizens' lives. For example, the opposition press functioned reasonably freely. Ljubica Markovic and Aleksandar Nenadovic, the former editor of *Politika*, were able to launch an independent news agency, BETA. Milosevic's former schoolmate Seska Stanojlovic and the journalist Milos Vasic both worked at *Vreme*, a weekly news magazine whose columns were filled with coruscating and bitter attacks on the Milosevic regime.

Milosevic did not ban BETA or *Vreme*. They helped foster the illusion that Serbia was indeed a western-style democracy, with free speech. *Vreme* posed little threat, in any case, as its readership was mostly liberal intellectuals who already loathed Milosevic. Besides, there were many subtler ways of muzzling the independent media. The state supplier of newsprint would charge double the usual rate. The state distributor of publications would have 'difficulties' moving copies around the country. State companies and enterprises – an important sector of the economy in a post-Communist state – would restrict their advertising to pro-regime publications.

In March 1991 the tensions within Serbia finally exploded. Milosevic was nearly toppled in ten days of protests and rioting that saw protestors take control of the capital. The Belgrade protests were Serbia's version of the Prague Velvet Revolution, with a touch of Tiananmen Square. In Czechoslovakia the Velvet Revolution had brought down the Communist government. In Beijing the students demanding democracy had been crushed by tanks. In Belgrade there was something of both.

It began on the morning of 9 March. Vuk Draskovic, the fiery opposition leader known as the 'King of the Squares', called a demonstration to protest against state television's torrent of propaganda and the lack of airtime for the opposition. The demonstration was banned, but Serbian nationalists united with liberal students to take over Belgrade's city centre, dodging police road-blocks and cordons. Serbian nationalists saw Milosevic as a Communist, or at least the heir to the Communists who had squashed Serbian nationalism. By lunchtime perhaps 100,000 people were jammed into Republic Square, spilling over on to the Terazie, with its pavement cafés. Speaking from the balcony of the National Theatre, Draskovic demanded a free media and an independent judiciary. At this stage the demonstration was orderly.

Milosevic had other ideas. Police squads in full riot gear formed a cordon around the protest. The police surged forwards firing tear gas canisters and a water cannon. Draskovic shouted: 'Charge! Charge.' Not all the demonstrators were peaceful students. The crowd was ringed by the hard men of Draskovic's party, some of whose leaders had connections to Belgrade's underworld, such as a young gangster called Aleksandar Knezevic, known as 'Knele', who later became one of the city's most famous underworld figures. When the police attacked, they fought back.

Violent clashes erupted as the protestors tried to break free and the police struggled to contain them. Plumes of tear gas drifted down streets slippery from the water cannon. Belgrade erupted into anarchy as the protestors broke through the police cordon. From Republic Square the demonstrators marched on their two main targets: parliament and state television. They occupied parliament, but a cordon of police in armoured vehicles surrounded the television building. The Romanian revolution had begun with the capture of the television station. Milosevic was determined that the same would not happen in Belgrade. The Serbian interior minister, Radmilo Bogdanovic, ordered massive armed reinforcements. So heavy was the police protection that from then on Serbian television was known as 'TV Bastille'.

Milosevic, never known for his physical courage, was at an army compound outside Belgrade. At Dobanovci military base Milosevic knew he would be safe from the mob, even if Belgrade fell. There he used the secure military communications network to order the police and secret service to try and break the protest. But as the violence increased, perhaps inevitably, the police opened fire. Five demonstrators were wounded and an eighteen-year-old student was killed. Elsewhere a policeman also died in the riot. Together with over a hundred demonstrators, Vuk Draskovic was arrested at the parliament.

That evening Bogdanovic accused the independent television station

Studio B and radio B-92 of 'calling for resistance to the government'. Serbian police closed down the stations. But federal prosecutors refused to bring any charges, and the stations were back on air the next day. Milosevic broadcast an ominous warning on state television. 'Today in Serbia and in Belgrade that which is of greatest value for our land and nation came under attack – peace was threatened . . . the state organs of the republic will use all their constitutional authority to ensure that chaos and violence are not permitted to spread in Serbia.'[6]

This was code for sending the tanks in. Borisav Jovic rang around each member of the federal presidency, demanding authorisation for the army to crush the demonstration. Fearful of a repeat of Tiananmen Square, presidency members were initially reluctant to turn the army on the students. But as the chaos spread, Jovic eventually got his permission. Draskovic recalled: 'We were attacked by 15,000 policemen, very well armed, with armoured cars, tear gas, horses and dogs. In spite of that we destroyed them, without even a knife, and Milosevic was forced to call out the army.'[7] Yugoslav military intelligence recorded a conversation between Blagoje Adzic, the army chief of staff, and the Serbian police minister: 'When the army gets there, send in your police. Order them to attack the demonstrators. Go for them. Beat them until you are exhausted.'[8]

The demonstrators regrouped. Up to half a million people gathered in central Belgrade as people's power took over the capital. Students drafted and then read out their demands, including the release of everyone arrested on 9 March, the sacking of Dusan Mitevic and other television editors, and the resignation of Radmilo Bogdanovic. Demonstrations spread throughout the country. Milosevic was unnerved. He understood the power of crowds. He had deployed mobs all over Serbia during the late 1980s, but this time the opposition was launching its own 'anti-bureaucratic revolution'.

On 11 March Milosevic did something unprecedented: he agreed to meet a student delegation. This was less the stirrings of a democratic impulse than Milosevic's acute realisation that the demonstrations had to be defused, or civil war could erupt. It was almost a year and half since the fall of the Berlin Wall, yet Milosevic's tired language shows how his transition from Communist to Socialist had been in name only. 'People should not destabilise things at a time when we are trying to stop the resurgent Ustasha forces, Albanian secessionists, as well as all other forces of the anti-Serbian coalition which are endangering people's freedom and rights,' he proclaimed. The journalists Laura Silber and Allan Little detail the next few minutes:

> Tihomir Arsic, a young actor popular for his rendition of Tito, asked permission to open the window. The room was suddenly filled with the demonstrators chants of 'Slobo, Saddam' . . . Milosevic pretended not to hear. [Student leader Zarko] Jokanovic showed him the picture of Milinovic, the youth killed during the demonstration. 'Is there nothing human left in you?' The Serbian president turned deep red, but said nothing.[9]

Events then took a bizarre turn. Jovic appeared on television, summoning the members of the federal presidency to Belgrade the next day for a meeting at four o'clock. Many anticipated a military coup. The Slovene representative was too frightened to attend. Stipe Mesic, the Croatian presidency member, bravely turned up. By this time fighting had erupted in Pakrac, Croatia, between rebel Serbs and the Croatian police. Belgrade was in chaos, the Yugoslav wars had begun, and not surprisingly Mesic feared being arrested.

Arriving at the presidency building, Mesic and the other members were highly alarmed to find themselves herded on to army buses under military escort. They were eventually ushered into an extremely cold room, where a camera was openly recording events. The army, it seemed, had hijacked its own commander-in-chief, the eight members of the federal presidency. Army winter-issue coats were handed out to the shivering politicians.

General Kadijevic, the Yugoslav defence minister, then demanded that the members of the federal presidency declare a state of emergency. This would allow the imposition of martial law. In effect this would be rule by Milosevic's diktat, as General Kadijevic followed Milosevic's orders. Milosevic would then have carte blanche to send more tanks into the streets of Belgrade to crush the student protest, and order military action in Croatia and Slovenia. But he still needed the federal presidency to vote in favour.

Perhaps no incident better illustrates the strange nature of Milosevic's regime than this one. This was a mass kidnapping and attempt to intimidate the presidency into doing his will, yet all the while observing the necessary constitutional niceties. Jovic called the vote. He needed five votes in favour to 'legitimise' plans for martial law. Milosevic's placemen – the representatives of Montenegro, Kosovo, Voivodina, and of course Jovic himself – voted yes. Stipe Mesic and Vasil Tuporkovski, the American-educated, pro-western Macedonian presidency member, voted no. The vote stood at four – two. Yugoslavia's future at that moment hinged on the decision of Bogic Bogicevic, the Bosnian representative. Since Bogicevic was a Bosnian Serb, Jovic expected him to vote with the Serbian bloc. But Bogicevic was a Yugoslav first. 'Jovic started shouting,' Tuporkovski recalled. 'Vote, what is the problem. Vote yes, vote no, but vote, Bogic, vote.' He voted no. Enraged, Jovic closed the session and then resigned from the federal presidency.[10] The chaos on the streets was mirrored in the government.

Milosevic soon recovered his balance, and made enough concessions to defuse the protest. Vuk Draskovic was released on 13 March. Dusan Mitevic and other senior television editors were sacked. Radmilo Bogdanovic resigned. 'The biggest mistake was to put tanks on the streets when the demonstrations started,' said Mitevic. 'The students followed what happened in Prague, but the tanks showed that we did not know how to deal with them, because we had never had any experience of this, in Tito's time.' Milosevic gave Mitevic a pistol as a leaving present. Mitevic noted that after his sacking none of his former political allies called to see how he was. 'It was a very educational experience,' he said dryly.

The March 1991 demonstrations showed that Serbia had arisen against Milosevic a year and a half too late. By the winter of 1989, when the people had taken over the streets of Berlin, Prague and Bucharest, Milosevic had already been anointed by the Serbian masses at Gazimestan. By December 1990 Serbia was also a democracy, albeit a warped and authoritarian one. On the battlefield of Kosovo Polje, and through the ballot box, Milosevic had defused enough of the tensions that brought down the neighbouring regimes to ensure that his survived.

In later years Draskovic was often criticised for failing to seize the moment on 9 March, and take power. He recalled: 'We had elections in December 1990. At that time eighty per cent of Serbs regarded Milosevic as a national messiah. It was impossible and not very democratic to demand that Vuk Draskovic should be president, a loser, a man who had lost the elections.'[11] Either way, toppling a government takes more than a sit-down protest and the sacking of some key officials. Half a million people on the streets is an impressive demonstration, but the protestors' energy dissipated after winning some comparatively minor concessions. Whatever impetus there may have been for a revolution was lost in questions of broadcast media and government personnel.

With the protests ended, Milosevic pressed his advantage. Serbia's leader addressed his nation again. He declared that special reservists and militia units would be mobilised. He announced the de facto departure of Serbia from Yugoslavia. 'Yugoslavia has entered into its final phase of agony. The Republic of Serbia will no longer recognise a single decision reached by the [Federal] Presidency under existing circumstances, because it would be illegal.'[12]

This was not true, but together with Borisav Jovic Milosevic was simply driving a tank through the constitution. All of Serbia's mayors were summoned by dawn telephone calls to a meeting in Belgrade, where they were addressed by Milosevic. Slovenia and Croatia wanted to secede from Yugoslavia, he told them, but the Muslims did not have any reason to leave. He added: 'If we have to, we'll fight. I hope they won't be so crazy as to fight against us. Because if we don't know how to work and do business, at least we know how to fight.'[13] A very clear line had now been drawn.

Soon after, Milosevic met with a group of 200 students and teachers at Belgrade University. If his first meeting with his staunchest opponents had been uncomfortable, this was even worse. It is surprising that Milosevic, who usually planned precisely every public appearance, agreed to such an event, where he would face a hostile audience who controlled the meeting's agenda. But these were some of the weakest days of his rule in very uncertain times. Milosevic had opponents not just on the streets but in the other republics, the federal administration and the JNA. All of those could be dismissed as 'separatists', or 'anti-Serbian' or whatever invective Milosevic chose. The students though were harder to dismiss. Although they had not voted for him, they were the children of the people who had voted him into power. They were not Slovenes or Croats, but Serbs, who represented Serbia's future.

None the less, the students were given the same message as the mayors. Any country could leave Yugoslavia, but they would not take the Serbs living there with them. Milosevic said:

> It has not occurred to us to dispute the right of the Croatian nation
> to secede from Yugoslavia, if that nation decides of its own free
> will in referendum . . . but I want to make it completely clear that

it should not occur to anyone that a part of the Serbian nation will be
allowed to go with them. Because the history of the Serbian nation
in the Independent State of Croatia [NDH] is too tragic to risk such
a fate again.[14]

Milosevic had misjudged his audience. These were not mayors of
remote provincial cities, loyal party hacks whose only concern was to
keep the privileges they had accumulated under Communism. This was
the Belgrade generation that had holidayed on the Adriatic coast, had
Croatian friends and mocked nationalism as much as they laughed at
Communism. They read *Time* and *Newsweek* and listened to the BBC.
They had travelled abroad. They listened to rap music, the Sex Pistols
and the Clash as well as Yugoslav rock groups such as Electric Orgasm
and Fish Soup. In fact Milosevic's two hundred inquisitors were virtually
indistinguishable – apart perhaps from the number of cigarettes they
smoked – from their counterparts in Berlin, London or New York.

They spoke English, they wore American jeans, and they departed for
new lives in the West. That war triggered waves of refugees from the
killing fields of Croatia, Bosnia and Kosovo is extensively documented.
But Serbia's own great emigration is less well known. Milosevic's policies
caused a mass exodus of the young and the educated, of liberals and
moderates, of simply ordinary people, all the best of the old Yugoslavia.
Tens of thousands, perhaps more than 100,000 young Serbs left, most
never to return. The country could ill afford such a massive loss.

But Milosevic did not object. It seemed he had not misjudged his
student audience at all. He had spelt out his vision of Yugoslavia's future
to the core of his natural opposition. Their reply was to regroup across the
world, in London and Johannesburg, Berlin and Paris, Toronto and New
York. From there they watched the march of wars across their homeland
live on CNN. Bitter and disillusioned, they telephoned home. But they
were no longer demonstrating on the streets of Belgrade.

14

WHAT A CARVE UP

Preparing For War No. 3, Bosnia
1991–2

Wars are often waged by those who know each other well, at the expense of those who have never met.

Stipe Mesic, President of Croatia.[1]

Two men chatted animatedly as they strolled through the landscaped gardens of the Karadjordjevo hunting lodge. 25 March 1991 was a beautiful spring day. Verdant ivy climbed up the walls of the villa; red and purple flowers blossomed on the terrace. Only the ring of security men around the villa indicated that something out of the ordinary was happening at one of Tito's favourite retreats.

Slobodan Milosevic and Franjo Tudjman were quite at ease in each other's company, each holding a glass of fruit brandy. Film of the meeting shows Milosevic dressed in a dark-blue suit, with a white shirt and purple tie. Tudjman is dressed in grey. His silver hair, metal-framed glasses and febrile manner give him the air of a tyrannical university professor or a company chairman who has hung on too long. The two leaders lean towards each other confidentially as they walk through the grounds. Milosevic gesticulates with his arms wide open, while Tudjman nods and occasionally taps him on the shoulder. Milosevic, it is clear, is the boss.

How could the two leaders find so much to talk about, in such agreeable circumstances, when their countries were on the eve of all-out war? Fighting had already erupted between rebel Serbs and Croats in the Croatian town of Pakrac. While their troops exchanged fire, Milosevic and Tudjman exchanged pleasantries and ideas. They agreed that Yugoslavia was dead. They agreed that war seemed inevitable. But most of all they agreed that Bosnia had no right to exist, and should be divided up between them.

The Karadjordjevo meeting was the opening summit of the secret diplomatic line that, throughout the wars in Croatia and Bosnia, ran from Zagreb to Belgrade. Tudjman and Milosevic agreed on much more than Bosnia. The signals exchanged at the clandestine diplomatic meetings eventually decided the fate of Milosevic's rebel Serb protégés within Croatia itself. Tudjman and Milosevic believed in each other, said Stipe Mesic. 'One of them wanted a Greater Serbia and the other wanted a Greater Croatia. They trusted each other and they kept negotiating throughout the war. When Rudolf Hess landed in Scotland not even a non-commissioned officer wanted to see him. For several years Milosevic and Tudjman's chiefs of cabinet held negotiations and talked to each other.'[2]

Some argued that, even before war had started, there was a cynical community of interest between the two men. This thesis was based on the premise that Tudjman arguably wanted a struggle of 'national liberation' to forge his new Croatian nation-state. War and the threat of an external enemy would bind the Croat people together and legitimise the new regime. It is an old technique, but no less effective for its age. Milosevic was happy to provide the necessary conflict.

Certainly by the end of 1991 many questions about Tudjman's role in Slovenia and Croatia remained unanswered. Until Slovenia declared independence in June 1991, the Slovene leader Milan Kucan and Franjo Tudjman had worked together. The neighbouring northern republics were natural allies. But at the crucial moment, Tudjman backtracked. 'In the fateful times of preparation for the plebiscite and the declaration of independence we worked together closely,' said Kucan. 'But when the war started against Slovenia we did not receive the assistance we expected. When the Yugoslav tanks rolled out from the barracks in Croatia, I telephoned Tudjman, asking for help. The idea was for him to assist the people who were blockading the Yugoslav army barracks and so prevent the JNA tanks driving from Croatia into Slovenia. Tudjman's answer was that he would not let tanks get involved in a war in Croatia just because of Slovenia.'[3]

Kucan had been working closely with a Croat former JNA general, Martin Spegelj, who became Tudjman's minister of defence. When the war started in Croatia General Spegelj proposed that the Croat forces follow the successful Slovene strategy of blockading JNA army bases to hold the troops and vehicles hostage. 'General Spegelj was correct. He was thinking along the right lines as a soldier,' said Kucan. Tudjman rejected this outright, and humiliated General Spegelj in a cabinet meeting. He then resigned, and was advised to leave the country for a while.

Events in Zagreb certainly suggest some kind of understanding between Milosevic and Tudjman. While the city came under sporadic attack, the JNA made no serious attempt to take over the city and topple Tudjman's government. The presidential palace was bombed, but only once. Zagreb was never subjected to the rain of sniper- and shell-fire that came down on Sarajevo. Only one Serbian city – Sid, near Vukovar – was briefly shelled by Croat forces.

There was also the strange episode of the Hungarian arms smuggling operation. In October 1990 General Spegelj went on a clandestine arms-buying mission to Budapest. Hungary agreed to sell 30,000 Kalashnikovs at DM280 a piece, less than half the going rate. Spegelj also bought mines, ammunition, rocket-propelled grenades and anti-aircraft systems. The first two consignments crossed the border into Yugoslavia a few days later, monitored by agents of KOS, Yugoslav military counter-intelligence. At this time Croatia was still part of Yugoslavia, yet no order came from Belgrade to stop the arms smuggling. While in Budapest General Spegelj had also negotiated secretly with JNA officers, to persuade them to hand over weapons. His mission had been filmed by KOS agents with a camera concealed in a television. Milosevic ordered an edited version of the film broadcast repeatedly on Belgrade television. War hysteria erupted.

The siege and fall of Vukovar raised the most questions. The once-pretty Danube town was pounded into rubble by JNA guns during a three-month siege in which hundreds were killed. Vukovar became known as Croatia's Stalingrad. Not just in terms of destruction, but as a symbol of Croatian patriotism. Vukovar surrendered to the JNA on 18 November 1991. Two hundred and sixty Croat prisoners were then taken away under JNA supervision, shot and bulldozed into a mass grave. Just over a month later, on 23 December, Germany unilat-erally recognised Croatia. Understandably, Vukovar triggered substantial international sympathy for Croatia, diverting attention from unwelcome matters such as the human rights of Croatia's Serb minority, who were also being ethnically cleansed, but by Croat extremists.

Vukovar's defenders accused Tudjman of cynically abandoning the city for political gain. Its commander, Milan Dedakovic, known as 'the Hawk', said that his fighters could have held out.

I asked for two or three brigades and an armoured battalion, but they never arrived. Croatia had the resources and could spare fifty tanks which is what we needed. But Tudjman and the political leadership are more concerned with policy-making than with the war. I feel absolutely betrayed and so do all the people of Vukovar . . . I fought fiercely for Croatia and when both Tudjman and Milosevic saw Vukovar could be defended by such a small group it did not suit either.[4]

A furore had erupted after a busload of Croat policemen entered the Serb village of Borovo Selo on 2 May, to be met by a hail of bullets that left twelve dead and twenty wounded. The background to this was that the previous month Gojko Susak, an extreme émigré Croat nationalist from Ottowa and Tudjman's defence minister, had taken a night trip to the outskirts of the village. Accompanied by the local police chief, Josip Reihl-Kir, Susak, a former pizza parlour owner, had fired three rockets into the village. Susak's version of home delivery could not have benefited Milosevic more if he had ordered it himself. One of the unexploded shells was shown on Belgrade television as indisputable proof of Croat aggression. Reihl-Kir was horrified at the attack, which he described as a 'lunatic' action. The police chief was a brave and honourable man who spent months trying to defuse local tensions. Soon after this incident he was shot eighteen times by one of his own colleagues.

Milosevic and Tudjman were partners in a common project, said the Belgrade military analyst Milos Vasic. 'Whenever there was some sort of truce or easing in the field, either Milosevic or Tudjman would produce an incident, a little massacre here or there, to start it all up again. They have been collaborating together since the beginning.'[5]

Sometimes Milosevic and Tudjman communicated through the staging of incidents, and sometimes they spoke to each other directly, using 'ti' rather than the more formal 'vi'. But mostly the deals were cut through a man called Hrvoje Sarinic, one of the few Croatian officials at the March 1991 Karadjordjevo meeting. He recalled: 'I was together with Tudjman and Milosevic for just fifteen minutes. Then they went out from the house and went for a walk. There was speculation that they discussed Bosnia. I don't think this was speculation. It was an unavoidable subject between them. This project of partitioning Bosnia was both of theirs, and finally they agreed that Bosnia historically has no right to exist.'[6]

Tudjman sent Sarinic to Belgrade thirteen times. A technocrat, who was fluent in English and French, with extensive international business experience and good intelligence contacts, he proved the perfect envoy. Sarinic's secret mission was launched on 9 November 1993, when he was summoned to Tudjman's rooms. The President was lying on his bed, covered with a blanket, listening to the radio with his eyes closed. The Croatian leader had been thinking. He had a brilliant new idea: open a direct channel of communications with Belgrade. 'It may be good to talk about this with Milosevic.' Sarinic replied that he understood what Tudjman meant. 'Then ring up and see how Milosevic is breathing,' Tudjman instructed, meaning Sarinic should try and discover what was on Milosevic's mind.

Sarinic then contacted Milosevic's office. 'I asked if it would be possible to see President Milosevic.' Perhaps not surprisingly, Milosevic's staff were taken aback to pick up the telephone and find Tudjman's chief of cabinet on the other end of the line. 'President Milosevic is very busy,' replied the Serbian official. But the message was passed on. 'Milosevic's secretary called the next day,' said Sarinic, 'and told me he was disposed to meet with me, but it should be completely secret.'

Croatia and Serbia were at war, but secret diplomatic missions across enemy lines long pre-dated Sarinic's secret mission to Belgrade. Realpolitik – and business – knows no borders. Even at the height of the Bosnian war, shops in the Bosnian Croat town of Kiseljak, just outside besieged Sarajevo, were stocked with fresh kiwi fruit and German chocolate thanks to the black-market deals the Bosnian Croats made with the Bosnian Serbs, although they were nominally at war. In the beseiged government-held city of Bihac, Bosnian Serbs even sold arms and ammunition to their enemies across the front line.

Sarinic understood that parleying with Milosevic was a risky business. Under Milosevic's protection, his safety was assured, but enemies awaited at home in Zagreb. 'In war there are always battles parallel with negotiations. But this was not a popular mission. On the front line you risk your life, you fight and you know that your enemy is in front of you. People saw Milosevic as a black devil, and some regarded me as a traitor.' To underline the seriousness of Sarinic's mission, and to dispel opposition within the ruling elite, Tudjman promoted Sarinic to Major-General. He reported only to Tudjman.

A few days later, on 12 November 1993, Sarinic landed at Batajnica military airport, just outside Belgrade. The venue for the meeting was not disclosed until the last moment. 'I was picked up in an old Mercedes.

The police escort did not know where we were going. They were given instructions by radio along the route. Everything was very polite, very secure and very secret.' Sarinic saw a city broken and decaying before his eyes. It was dark, cold and sombre. Sanctions had brought the economy to the brink of collapse. Sarinic began to see why Milosevic was so eager to meet. Even in Milosevic's sparsely furnished office on Andriceva Street in Belgrade there was no heating and one modest bookshelf. The freezing toilet was kept locked. Sarinic travelled with three bodyguards, but they were disarmed on arrival. 'They had to surrender their guns to the Serbian secret police. I asked, "What use are bodyguards without guns?"' Sarinic was searched for wiretaps and then was ushered through. He was met by Mira Dragojevic, Milosevic's secretary, who said that the president was waiting for him.

The two men got on well. 'When Tudjman charged me with being the contact man I worried that Milosevic would not accept me, because I was not on his high political level. But he accepted it very well. I can't say that we had a friendly relationship, but it was a good one. Sometimes he told me a funny story, or a joke.'

But in Bosnia, well into its second year of war, they weren't laughing. When Croatia declared independence in July 1991, Bosnia had two choices. The republic could remain in a Yugoslavia dominated by Belgrade as a Muslim quasi-colony of 'Serboslavia' or it could declare independence. But independence almost certainly meant war, since most of Bosnia's Serbs – one-third of the population – were utterly opposed to living in an independent Bosnia, and wanted to remain in Yugoslavia, which they saw as the best protector of Serb interests.

Bosnia was often referred to as a mini-Yugoslavia. Nowhere else was the ethnic and religious mix as pronounced. Its population of about 4.3 million was composed of 44 per cent Muslims, 31 per cent Serbs, 17 per cent Croats and just over 5 per cent declaring themselves as 'Yugoslavs'[7] This was partly a result of its geography. Bosnia bordered Croatia in the north and west, Serbia in the east and Montenegro in the south. In medieval times Bosnia had been an independent kingdom, until the Ottoman invasion in the fifteenth century. It remained a province of the Ottoman empire until 1878, when it was placed under the administration of Austro-Hungary, before being annexed in 1908 and then ceded to Royal Yugoslavia after the First World War.

As the westernmost stretch of Turkey-in-Europe, Bosnia was

conservative, especially in its rural areas. But cities such as the capital
Sarajevo, Banja Luka in the north and Visegrad in the south boasted
some of Europe's finest Ottoman-era architecture, and a way of life that
was easy-going and civilised. Visegrad was the site of the bridge in Nobel
laureate Ivo Andric's most famous work *Bridge on the Drina*, a complex
chronicle of the march of empires across the provincial city. When the
Ottomans came they built mosques, bazaars, baths and religious schools,
as well as bridges. The great sixteenth-century governor of Sarajevo,
Ghazi Husrev Beg, is immortalised in this Sarajevo folksong:

> I built the medresa *[school]* and imaret *[public kitchen]*
> I built the clock tower by it a mosque
> I built Taslihan and the cloth market
> I built three bridges in Sarajevo
> I turned a village into the town of Sarajevo

The new faith with its civilised comforts proved attractive. The great
majority of Yugoslav Muslims are Slavs who converted to Islam, which
brought a privileged status. A Muslim urban elite emerged. Bosnia wore
its Islam with a comparatively light touch. 'Go to Bosnia if you want to
see your wife' was one Turkish saying. After the partisan victory Tito
had refused the demands of Serb and Croat nationalists that Bosnia be
divided between Belgrade and Zagreb. Bosnia-Herzegovina – to give
the republic its full name – was seen as a necessary counterbalance to
the two strongest republics, Serbia and Croatia. Eventually Tito granted
Yugoslav Muslims the status of full nationality. But Serb and Croat
nationalists rejected this. Some claimed that Bosnian Muslims were
merely Serbs or Croats who had converted to Islam. Others decried
their Muslim neighbours as 'Turks'. There is of course a contradiction
here: Bosnians could not be both converted Slavs and Turks.

In November 1990 Bosnia, like its neighbouring republics, had gone
to the polls. A coalition government of the three ethnically based
parties was set up: the Serbian Democratic Party (SDS), the Croatian
Democratic Union (HDZ) and the Party of Democratic Action (SDA)
for the Muslims. Meanwhile, Milosevic played his usual double game.
Even as he planned to dismember the country, he tried to woo the
Bosnians into staying in Yugoslavia. Milosevic understood that talking
up the need for Bosnia to stay would reduce the influence of those in
Bosnia who wanted to arm themselves. Who needed to prepare for war

when there was no danger of war? Milosevic exploited the attachment many Bosnians felt to Yugoslavia, and especially to Tito, who had given them a republic and nationality status.[8] Several years into the Bosnian war it was still common to see Tito's picture on Bosnian walls when he had disappeared everywhere else.

In March 1991 Milosevic had proclaimed that he thought that the Muslims did not have any reason to secede from Yugoslavia. 'Some of them have been indoctrinated, but most of the Muslims want good, tolerant and I would say civic and friendly relations with the Serbs and other nations in Yugoslavia.'[9] This was in marked contrast to Milosevic's rhetoric about 'Ustashas' and 'Albanian terrorists'. Few in Bosnia believed that war was possible, and many – tragically including much of the Muslim leadership – had faith in the JNA as a neutral peace-keeping force, not understanding that it was under Milosevic's control. The JNA was allowed to disarm *all* troops in Bosnia (except its own) along with the Bosnian Territorial Defence Organisation as a means of preventing war. The Bosnian Croat and Muslim militias and paramilitaries were already vastly outnumbered and outgunned. This only weakened them further, and left the country defenceless against the Serbs.

Local Serbs were supplied with arms, and plans were drawn up to take over the local police forces and municipal administration. Just as in Krajina, the Bosnian Serbs declared SAOs, or Serb Autonomous Areas. Belgrade and local Serb television then launched a barrage of lies and propaganda about the coming horrors of a reborn Islamic state, under the rule of Alija Izetbegovic, the Muslim leader.

In any case, the progress of the war in neighbouring Croatia and the distribution of weapons gave events their own dark momentum. As JNA artillery pounded Croatian cities and streams of displaced refugees fled the fighting, it was hard to believe that Bosnia would escape the same fate. In mid-October 1991 the Bosnian parliament met to discuss whether the republic should become sovereign, a precursor to full independence.

Izetbegovic was a well-meaning but ultimately tragic figure who was no match for the ruthlessness of either Milosevic or Tudjman. An Islamic dissident under Tito, Izetbegovic was put on trial in 1983 for 'counter-revolutionary acts derived from Muslim nationalism'. He was sentenced to fourteen years in prison, of which he served six. He had already made his position clear in February 1991: 'I would sacrifice peace for a sovereign Bosnia-Herzegovina, but for that peace in Bosnia-Herzegovina I would not sacrifice sovereignty.'[10] The Muslim and Croat political parties were in favour of sovereignty. The Bosnian Serbs were not. Their political leader, Radovan Karadzic, offered the following chilling forecast:

> Do not think that you will not lead Bosnia-Herzegovina into hell, and do not think that you will not perhaps lead the Muslim people into annihilation, because the Muslims cannot defend themselves if there is war – How will you prevent everyone from being killed in Bosnia-Herzegovina?[11]

Like Milosevic, Karadzic is of Montenegrin origin. Born in 1945, he moved to Sarajevo where he qualified as a psychiatrist and treated the Sarajevo football team.[12] Some of his psychiatric advice was unconventional: when one young couple went to Karadzic for counselling on their troubled marriage, he told the husband to beat his wife more. With his bouffant hair and hyperbolic manner, Karadzic also fancied himself as a poet. Four volumes of his mordant works were published. For example:

> I hear misfortune walking
> Vacant entourages passing through the city
> Units of armed white poplars
> Marching through the skies[13]

Loud, dishevelled, possessed of Balkan delusions of grandeur, an inveterate gambler, the Bosnian Serb leader saw himself as a mini-statesman who would shape Serbian history. Although Karadzic was Milosevic's appointment, in many ways the poet-psychiatrist was more similar to Franjo Tudjman. Unlike Milosevic, both Tudjman and Karadzic actually believed in their own nationalism. Karadzic's refusal to follow the demands of realpolitik would later bring him into conflict with Milosevic. Meanwhile, he loved nothing more than to pore over maps, working out plans for the division of Sarajevo. He lapped up the attention of the world's diplomats and media who treated him with reverence, respectfully listening to his lies and bombast. Karadzic was little more than a literate crook. He had served time in prison for corruption.

But his warning to Alija Izetbegovic was accurate. A month earlier, in September 1991, Karadzic had consulted Milosevic about the progress of setting up the Bosnian Serb mini-state. His telephone was tapped by Yugoslav intelligence, who passed the transcript to Ante Markovic, the last prime minister of federal Yugoslavia. In a well-targeted but ultimately futile attack on Milosevic, Markovic released the transcript to the press:

> Milosevic: Go to Uzelac [JNA commander in northern Bosnia], he'll tell you everything. If you have any problems, telephone me.
>
> Karadzic: I've got problems down in Kupres. Some Serbs there are rather disobedient.
>
> Milosevic: We can deal with that. Just call Uzelac. Don't worry, you'll have everything. We are the strongest.
>
> Karadzic: Yes, yes.
>
> Milosevic: Don't worry. As long as there is the army no one can touch us ... Don't worry about Herzegovina. Momir [Bulatovic, Montenegrin leader] said to his men: 'Whoever is not ready to die in Bosnia, step forward five paces.' No one did so.
>
> Karadzic: That's good ... but what's going on with the bombing in ...
>
> Milosevic: Today is not a good day for the airforce. The European Community is in session.[14]

Markovic told his cabinet:

> The line has been clearly established. I know because I heard Milosevic give the order to Karadzic to get in contact with General Uzelac and to order, following the decisions of the meetings of the military hierarchy, that arms should be distributed and the territorial defence of Krajina and Bosnia be armed and utilised in the realisation of the RAM plan.[15]

This transcript is highly significant. It details the military-political triangle that linked the JNA, Milosevic and the Bosnian Serbs. It shows that Milosevic is the political mastermind behind the military strategy. The transcript also highlights Milosevic's keen awareness of the need to respond to the international diplomatic situation. The

Yugoslav airforce would not be used while diplomats were meeting. It is also clear that the southern republic of Montenegro was completely under Milosevic's control. Through the following months, the signs of coming war in Bosnia became ever louder and clearer.

Yet while Izetbegovic took his country down a path that would lead to war, he made almost no preparations to fight one. His doomed strategy was to hope for intervention by the United Nations or the United States, to prevent conflict. According to one gloomy joke, Izetbegovic put his faith in a magic fish: Izetbegovic, Milosevic and Tudjman go fishing one day. They catch a magic fish, which grants them each one wish. Milosevic asks that independent Croatia be crushed. The fish agrees. Tudjman requests that Serbia be defeated. The fish agrees. Izetbegovic asks the fish if Croatia has really been crushed and Serbia defeated. The fish confirms that this is the case. 'In that case, I'd just like a nice a cup of coffee,' says Izetbegovic.

On 9 January 1992 Karadzic declared the foundation of the Bosnian Serb Republic, later known as Republika Srpska, precisely modelled on the Serb Republic of Krajina. On the last weekend in February Bosnia went to the polls to vote for independence. The Bosnian Serbs boycotted the poll. They already had their own republic. On 6 April Bosnia declared independence from Yugoslavia. Milosevic was well prepared. He had anticipated that international recognition of Bosnia was inevitable, but also predicted, correctly, that the West would not go to war to save the country. Karadzic recalled: 'President Milosevic couldn't care less if Bosnia were recognised. He said, "Caligula proclaimed a horse a senator, but the horse never took its seat. Izetbegovic will get recognition, but he'll never get a state."'[16]

Milosevic had already ensured that when the fighting in Bosnia began, the balance of forces was massively in the Bosnian Serbs' favour. A UN investigative report detailed the clear chain of command between Belgrade and rebel Serbs in both Bosnia and Croatia:

The JNA adopted a new defence plan in early 1992 calling for the protection of the Serbian population outside of Serbia. [Serbian] territorial defence units in Croatia and Bosnia-Herzegovina were to be supplied with small arms, artillery, armour and missile launching systems. Moreover the Ministry of Defence of the Serbian Autonomous Regions (SAOs) of Croatia and Bosnia were to be subordinated to the Serbian Ministry of Defence. The JNA and the SAOs were to coordinate their defence plans and jointly protect their external borders and constitutional system.[17]

What this meant was that the Bosnian Serbs were not autonomous at all, but a client army of Milosevic and the JNA, whose overall strategy was controlled from Belgrade.

In early April 1992, when fighting broke out in Bosnia, the JNA had 80,000 troops deployed in the country. In early May the JNA was ordered to pull back to Yugoslavia. But Milosevic had already decided that all JNA troops born in Bosnia could stay on in the country. In addition, Bosnian Serb officers stationed elsewhere in Yugoslavia were redeployed in Bosnia. So 25,000 JNA troops left, but 55,000 Bosnian Serb soldiers remained. These were all transferred to the Bosnian Serb army. The Serb gunners laying siege to Sarajevo, for example, were now no longer soldiers of the JNA, but of the Romanija Corps of the Bosnian Serb army. But they were the same troops, firing the same guns from the same positions. They were still paid from Belgrade. For the citizens of Sarajevo, the distinction was purely academic as the shrapnel burst around them.

Milosevic then appointed General Ratko Mladic as commander of the Bosnian Serb army. But his army failed to capture Sarajevo. The defenders – drawn from all three ethnic communities, Muslim, Serb and Croat – beat back the Serb offensive as the heavy tanks got jammed in the narrow streets. For the next three years the General took a slow revenge. This is an intercept of one of his military communications to an officer commanding an artillery unit overlooking the city.

General Mladic here
Yes, sir
Don't panic. What's your name?
Vukasinovic
Colonel Vukasinovic
Yes, sir
Shell the presidency and the parliament. Shoot at slow intervals until I order you to stop. Target Muslim neighbourhoods – not many Serbs live there.
Look at all the smoke
Shell them until they're on the edge of madness.[18]

Shelled until they were indeed on the edge of madness, Sarajevo's inhabitants eked out a living in near-medieval conditions. Under the eyes of the world, live on television every day, a European city was turned into a giant concentration camp. Deprived of heating, electricity or running water, Sarajevans lived in a state of perpetual hunger and cold, surviving on food brought in by the intermittent UN airlift. High up in the bunkers in the surrounding hills, the Serb gunners picked off women filling buckets at a public spigot or lobbed mortars at children playing football. A simple journey across town became a deadly gamble: ducking in doorways, sprinting across open squares, and crunching a path across broken glass in abandoned buildings that offered meagre cover against incoming fire.

Still the city's inhabitants tried to live the semblance of a normal life. Women put on their make-up every morning before going to work in an office where there was nothing to do, their pride in their appearance a tiny gesture of defiance. Portly men with empty briefcases leapt across exposed intersections. Civic-minded citizens put up signs saying 'Pazi Snajper' (Danger – sniper). Even war could not interrupt the great Bosnian coffee ritual, except now customers placed their guns next to their cups. They chatted and tried to joke, but their hands twisted continually, fingers interwining, as one cigarette followed another. As the economy collapsed, cigarettes became a quasi-currency. Criminals and black marketeers soon cornered the market in pilfered UN aid and smuggled food, but the criminals had saved the city. So unprepared was the government of Alija Izetbegovic that when the war started the defence of the capital was led by mafia gangs, as they were the only ones who had weapons and knew how to use them.

Although Sarajevo did not fall, by the autumn of 1992 the Bosnian Serbs had captured almost 70 per cent of the country. The many months of detailed planning in Belgrade had paid off. The international outcry against the brutality of ethnic cleansing had done nothing to slow down the Serbian advance. Serbia, the nation that had suffered so much at the hands of the Nazis, set up its own network of concentration camps in Bosnia. Places such as Omarska, Keraterm and Trnopolje became bywords for a macabre horror not witnessed on mainland Europe since the Second World War.

Once again men starved behind barbed wire, while their captors tortured and killed them on a whim, often by knife or hammer so as not to 'waste' bullets. The slightest infraction of camp 'rules' was enough to be beaten to death. A kind of insanity descended, said Dr Milan Kovacevic, a former hospital director who had helped set up Omarska.

> What we did was not the same as Auschwitz or Dachau, but it was a mistake. It was planned to have a camp for people, but not a concentration camp. Omarska was planned as a reception centre . . . But then it turned into something else. I cannot explain the loss of control. I don't think even the historians will find an explanation in the next fifty years. You could call it collective madness.[19]

How much did Milosevic know of what was happening at the camps? Several thousand miles away, President George Bush certainly knew. On 3 August 1992, after news broke of the Omarska camp, State Department spokesman Richard Boucher told reporters that administration officials had been aware that 'Serbian forces are maintaining what they call detention centres', and also knew about the 'abuses and tortures taking place'.[20]

Belgrade and Omarska had until recently been part of the same country. The chain of command between Belgrade and the Bosnian Serb army and political leadership was such that it is inconceivable that Milosevic did not know what was happening in Bosnia. The transcript of the telephone conversation between Milosevic and Karadzic in September 1991 details how Milosevic was overseeing war preparations, and deciding whether or not to use the Yugoslav airforce. Milosevic was the apex of a triangle that linked the Serbian Intelligence Service and the Bosnian Serb military and political organisation. Belgrade supplied the weapons and uniforms of the Bosnian Serb army that captured the territory on which the camps were set up. It even paid their wages. Serbian intelligence supplied detailed briefings to Milosevic about the situation on the ground. Certainly by 6 August Milosevic, like the rest of the world, knew about the camps, as news of Omarska had been broadcast around the world by British Independent Television News.

Not all the victims of the 'collective madness' were Muslim or Croat. Many Bosnian Serbs lived on the 'wrong' side of the lines, in Bosnian Croat or government-controlled territory. Radmila was a Serb lawyer from the picturesque Ottoman-era city of Mostar. When in spring 1992 the JNA began bombarding Mostar, she covered the walls of her home with pictures of Tito. But her Yugoslav gallery of loyalty could only ever be a quixotic gesture. 'All through the war I tried to keep my identity as a person, not by nationality or religion. I did not want to leave my city and my friends. I never felt like a Serb, but they decided for me.' Harassed and intimidated by Bosnian Croat forces, Radmila and her husband – a JNA officer – fled to Belgrade. The departure was full of pain and heartache. 'How can you decide what to pack when you flee from your home? Should you pack the slippers your baby first walked in, or the ones he needs now? The furniture we left behind is not important, but the memories are.'[21]

Over 250,000 Bosnian refugees found sanctuary in Serbia, including some Muslims. Belgrade retained enough of its cosmopolitan spirit to take them in. But whatever their nationality, on a personal level many Bosnian refugees found they were not welcomed. Milosevic's idea of all Serbs in one state was fine in theory, but the practice it seemed was different. Radmila was unable to find a job. 'When I apply for jobs even as a secretary and they hear my Bosnian accent, they put a little mark on the form and nobody asks to see my qualifications.'

In Zagreb, President Tudjman watched all this with envy. Croat and Muslim soldiers had fought together against the JNA and the Bosnian Serbs. But Tudjman saw the establishment of Republika Srpska in Bosnia as a signal from Milosevic that he would permit Zagreb to do the same. He was correct. Tudjman had tremendous respect for Milosevic, said the British diplomat David Austin. 'Milosevic had plenty of self-confidence. Tudjman did not, at least in his dealings with Milosevic. Tudjman thought they were working to the same agenda, the division of Bosnia. But that was not Milosevic's real agenda. It was fine if Bosnia was divided, but all Milosevic cared about was Milosevic. He did not have a bigger agenda than that.'[22]

Tudjman believed that Croatia needed to annex the southern part of Bosnia known as Herzegovina, a Croat majority area and home to hard-line nationalists. He looked back longingly at the pre-1939 maps when Croatia had encompassed large stretches of land now in Bosnia. 'Tudjman said Croatia is a crescent shape, and it is impossible to defend such borders,' remembered Hrvoje Sarinic. 'He asked me one day to calculate what is the length of the border per capita in Croatia and to compare it with France. I don't remember exactly what it was, something like 2.5 metres per inhabitant in Croatia, and 0.8 in France. He said that we should enlarge the part of Croatia in the south, by adding Herzegovina.'

Tudjman already had a Croat equivalent of Radovan Karadzic. Mate Boban was a hard-line extremist headquartered in the backwater town of Grude. He did not write poetry, but like Karadzic he had served time in prison, in his case for black-marketing. On 5 July 1992, under Boban's leadership, Croats in Herzegovina declared their own quasi-state, to be known as Herceg-Bosna. A separate Bosnian Croat army was set up, known as the HVO. Like the Bosnian Serb army, the HVO was nominally independent, but in reality it was armed, trained and financed by Zagreb. Tudjman and the HVO followed the pattern set by Milosevic and the Bosnian Serb army. Just as in Serb-occupied Bosnia, checkpoints were erected and the movements of Muslims controlled. The Bosnian flag was replaced by a new Croat flag; the Bosnian dinar was replaced by Croatian currency. Boban declared that Sarajevo's authority would no longer be recognised. Herceg-Bosna even issued its own car number plates.

Inevitably, in the autumn of 1992 fighting broke out between the HVO and Bosnian government troops, gleefully watched by the Bosnian Serbs. Tudjman's military cooperation agreement with Sarajevo was torn up. With Zagreb's support the HVO laid siege to Mostar. Lacking the UN airlift that kept the Bosnian capital alive, Mostar's conditions were even worse than those in Sarajevo. Mostar too was split into two: Croats on the west bank, Muslims on the east. Boban's army, like the Bosnian Serbs, wanted the Muslims swept away. Even Muslim soldiers who had fought with the HVO were arrested and sent to Bosnian Croat concentration camps such as Dretelj. There they were starved, beaten and killed on the whim of their jailers. The line of command went straight back to Zagreb and Tudjman's office. The Croat leader Stipe Mesic recalled: 'When I found out about the camps, I told Tudjman, "You know they have camps there." He said, "So what, the others have camps as well."' Eventually the Croatian camps, like their Serb counterparts, were disbanded under pressure from the international community.

As for Milosevic, he did not have a problem with Herceg-Bosna, said Hrvoje Sarinic. 'He told me one day in Belgrade, "Tell Franjo that with Republika Srpska I solved 90 per cent of the Serbian national question, just as he will solve the Croatian national problem with Herceg-Bosna".'

15

WAR NO. 3, BOSNIA

The Bosnian Serb Republic

1993

Milosevic himself asked me to send my fighters . . . Milosevic and his generals didn't give us orders, just 'requests'. 'We need your fighters in this or that place.' We didn't let them down.

Vojislav Seselj, Serbian ultra-nationalist politician
and paramilitary leader.[1]

Sitting at home one afternoon during the Bosnian war, Milosevic was chatting with Dusan Mitevic and Mira when the telephone rang. Mira answered and Milosevic and Mitevic looked on in amazement as she snapped down the telephone: 'Please don't call him at home, call him at the office.' She turned to her husband. 'It's that Chetnik Karadzic. Don't have him phone here again.'[2]

As the proud daughter of a partisan mother, Mira never concealed her loathing for the Serb nationalists Milosevic used as expedient allies. The civil war between the Serb nationalist guerrillas – the 'Chetniks' – and the partisans lived on in her mind. 'Those people like Karadzic who are now indicted, Mira never liked,' said Mitevic. 'She never wanted to have them in the house. Milosevic could never meet them at home. The people that were allowed in were mutual friends, or her friends, but never Milosevic's friends.'

The contradiction between Milosevic's exploitation of nationalism and Mira's resolute anti-nationalist, pro-Yugoslav beliefs is one of the enduring mysteries of their lives. On one level Milosevic's relationship to nationalism is similar to his relationship to Communism. He understood the political power that both bestow, and exploited both for his own advantage. But Communism is more than an idealistic ideology. It also provided Milosevic with a methodology of power management for his authoritarian democracy. Nationalism is based on emotion. Milosevic was hardly an emotional person. He skilfully exploited Serb history and patriotic sentiment, but he never descended into the type of bloodthirsty rabble-rousing of Radovan Karadzic, who had warned Bosnian President Izetbegovic that he was leading the Muslims into hell and destruction. Milosevic always delivered the message he wanted, but with inbuilt plausible deniability. It was 'on the one hand, but on the other hand' stuff. At Gazimestan in 1989, for example, Milosevic had warned: 'Six centuries later we are again involved in battles, and facing battles. They are not battles with arms, but these battles cannot be excluded.'[3]

In the diary that she wrote for the Belgrade magazine *Duga*, Mira is highly critical of her husband's Serb nationalist protégés. She slammed Radovan Karadzic for his criticism of the old Yugoslavia as a 'dictatorship', and she was scathing about the comparison between Karadzic's Bosnian Serb Republic and the old Yugoslavia, where 'Serbs, Muslims and Croats were able to live side by side' without being broken up into different ethnic groups. She wrote: 'How come under that dictatorship citizens were able to educate their children, travel abroad, vacation at the seaside, and follow fashion without the existence of a black market, whereas in this democracy, in occupied Sarajevo, they have less to eat every day than the inmates of Auschwitz.'[4]

The more racist the Bosnian Serb statements, the angrier Mira became. The vice-president of the Bosnian Serb Republic, Biljana Plavsic, caused a scandal when she said openly that she could not live with Bosnian Muslims, and that they should be confined to a tiny sliver of territory. For Mira this was 'Nazism pure and simple'. Such a statement, she wrote, 'should have sparked off a storm of protests here in Serbia, both from the right and the left, both from those in power and from those in the opposition, from everyone'.[5]

The contradictions here are acute. The most obvious, of course, is that the man who was running Serbia, who was in constant contact with the Bosnian Serb military and political leadership that was overseeing the ethnic cleansing, was her husband. At the same time, Mira is also calling for the reflexes of a western civil society, of 'a storm of protest', although she herself is a staunch believer in an authoritarian one-party state. Dusan Mitevic observed: 'She had a much more Communist mentality than Milosevic. She would explain to Milosevic sometimes that someone was saying something bad about the family. But Milosevic said, "So what, I can't just put them in prison." She thought nobody should be able to do such things.'

Some in Belgrade thought Mira was simply in denial. Milosevic certainly was. He repeatedly stated that 'Serbia is not at war', even as the death notices of Serb soldiers killed in Bosnia filled up newspapers and were pinned to trees all over Yugoslavia. He proclaimed: 'We are not supporting any military action in Bosnia-Herzegovina.'[6] Others suggested that, rather than denial, Milosevic was caught in the 'Ceausescu Syndrome': surrounded by flunkeys and acolytes who are too cowed to deliver unwelcome news, victims of the syndrome lose touch with events in the real world.

Milosevic had certainly cynically exploited nationalism since 1987 to build his power base, but perhaps only he and Mira know if he ever really believed in it. It is quite likely that he did not, at least in regard to the wars in Croatia and Bosnia. Kosovo, which came later, seems to have aroused stronger feelings. Mira Markovic has always denied that her husband was a nationalist.

They attributed to him the easiest sin they could, which is that he is a nationalist. I think an educated man cannot be a nationalist. I frequently remember a sentence written by our Nobel Prize winner, Ivo Andric, that the more primitive you are, the bigger Serb or Croat you are. Slobodan is not a nationalist. But I must say that Slobodan has strongly developed patriotic feelings.

She explained the difference: 'Patriotism means loving your own country. Nationalism is having a too strong feeling for your own nation, and the inability to cope with other nations.'[7]

Of course such absurdities were noticed by Belgrade's writers. Radivoje Lola Djukic demanded to know: 'Well, who came to power and began to lead us down that path. Where have you been, Madame and Comrade Markovic? Why are you addressing world opinion instead of asking your husband during a dinner, why he permits the children of Serbia to be sent to die in such a war?'[8]

Relaxing at home over dinner, the last thing Milosevic wanted after a hard day's war was a discussion of politics, claimed Mira:

My husband received a lot of foreign and other delegations, and we never spoke about them. He was eager to come home and speak about other things. Not politics. I don't know where the ideas come from that we jointly planned things together. That is totally ridiculous.

When he came home we would talk about ordinary things, like home, our children, have friends for dinner or go out. Would it really be possible for a man who dealt with disastrous politics for ten hours a day to speak about that and then plot some more things with me for the next day? Even if he wanted to he had no strength to speak about it. Maybe in the first year I was interested, but later on I simply didn't care about those people and what they said, and I didn't ask.

This was not the view prevalent in Belgrade or western capitals. But in the end Mira, like her husband, simply believed what she wanted to. Her leftist beliefs did not prevent her from going weak at the knees when she met Lord Owen, after he was appointed the European Community negotiator for the former Yugoslavia in 1992. From Belgrade Lord Owen and his wife Debbie had taken a helicopter flight along the Danube to join Slobodan and Mira at one of Tito's former retreats. There the two couples enjoyed a long lunch. Lord Owen suspected her husband of 'playing the nationalist card'[9]. Mira soon put him right: 'I am an internationalist. I told Lord Owen, "You can be sure that my husband is not a nationalist, because if he was, I could not live with him. I am the main guarantee to you that Slobo is not a nationalist. I am a leftist, and I could not live with a monarchist. We have the same political opinions. We cannot have different political opinions and live together."'

Milosevic certainly understood the power of nationalist hate. War fuelled hate, and vice versa. For Milosevic hate was a weapon as sure as sniper bullets and artillery shells. Hate could be spread through words and deeds. Milosevic's appointees at Belgrade Television were inducing war hysteria among the Bosnian Serbs. It was significant that in northern Bosnia, for example, site of some of the most brutal ethnic cleansing of the war, television transmitters were retuned to broadcast programmes from Belgrade rather than the capital Sarajevo.

Deeds were more complicated. The problem for Milosevic and the Bosnian Serb military leader General Ratko Mladic was that Bosnia's ethnic mosaic meant that many soldiers on opposing sides knew each other. They had gone to school together, they had lived next door and dated each other's sisters. Even during the war, they chatted on the radio, traded goods – sometimes even weapons and ammunition – across the trenches, and often negotiated local ceasefires on largely static frontlines.

Bosnian Serb villagers, like their Muslim and Croat counterparts, might take up weapons to defend their homes, but building an ethnically homogenous Greater Serbia demanded more than this.

A wedge of hate had to be driven between Serbs and Muslims and Croats. The concentration camps were one means of achieving this: few of the Muslims who survived Omarska or Keraterm would consider returning to Bosnia. The use of rape as a weapon was another. The UN Special Rapporteur on Bosnia, Professor Cherif Bassiouni, testified to a US Congressional hearing that in the Serb-occupied eastern Bosnian city of Foca alone, there were three sites where women were kept to be raped. They were: the town's Partizan hall; a place where 'women were kept for the satisfaction of the soldiers coming in from the field on a 15-day rotation basis', and a house where eighteen women and girls, aged between eleven and seventeen, mainly daughters of prominent Muslims, were kept for between eight and ten months.

Professor Bassiouni testified: 'I interviewed a fourteen-year-old girl and a fifteen-year-old girl who had been raped, respectively, for eight and ten months, consistently by their guards. I saw an eleven-year-old girl in a fetal position in the psychiatric hospital in Sarajevo, having given birth to a child, having completely lost her mind.' He also noted that when the commander of one such centre was killed, a Bosnian Serb officer protected the women with a machine gun until they were released, and threatened to kill the guards who wanted to rape the captive girls once more. 'There have been many instances of really decent actions by individual Serbs who helped victims, and we should not overlook that.'[10]

Milosevic knew where to look for recruits to carry out the dirty work of the Bosnian and Croatian wars: among ultra-nationalists, criminals and football fans. These were the core of the paramilitary groups who carried out many atrocities. The UN Bassiouni report identified eighty-three paramilitary groups fighting in Bosnia and Croatia: fifty-six were Serb, fourteen Bosnian Muslim and thirteen Croat.[11] On the Serb side the two most significant, and notorious, were the Tigers run by Zeljko Raznatovic, better known as Arkan, and the Chetniks, commanded by Vojislav Seselj.

The son of a colonel in the Yugoslav air force, Arkan was a former juvenile delinquent turned bank robber. His exploits made him a folk hero for many Serbs. He had escaped from prison in Belgium, the

Netherlands and Germany. He was also allegedly linked to several killings of Yugoslav émigrés abroad. Back in Belgrade in the early 1980s, Arkan used his security service connections to reinforce his position in the world of organised crime. Whenever Belgrade police arrested him, they used to count the minutes that went by until someone from the Yugoslav secret service came to intervene on his behalf. Arkan lived the high life. He ran the fan club of the famed Red Star Belgrade football club, and was often seen in casinos and nightclubs. His fortune was built on smuggling oil into Serbia and selling looted goods on the Belgrade black market. These helped pay for a large house in the upmarket Belgrade suburb of Dedinje, where the Milosevic family also lived. Cold-blooded and ruthless, Arkan was also an intelligent individual who had spent time in both Britain and the United States. He enjoyed holding court to foreign journalists and spoke good English.

Many of the young unemployed men whom Milosevic deployed on the 'rallies for truth' in the late 1980s were hard-core football fans. The same slogans and nationalist flags appeared at both soccer matches and the demonstrations. The same chant was heard at both: 'Serbian Slobo, Serbia is with you.' Football, war and patriotism merged into an intoxicating cocktail. Fans of Partizan Belgrade, the greatest rivals of Red Star Belgrade, chanted: 'Partizan, Partizan, that's a Serbian team. Slobodan Milosevic is proud of them.' The response of the Red Star fans was: 'Partizan, Partizan, well-known Muslim team, Azem Vllasi [Kosovo Albanian leader] is proud of them.'

Even in present-day Britain football provides a powerful tribal identity and opportunities for ritualised violence. In the increasingly aggressive nationalistic atmosphere of Yugoslavia it was an easy progression from fighting on the field of play to that of battle. Arkan was a strict boss as he turned unruly hooligans into soldiers. 'From the beginning I insisted on discipline. You know what football fans are like, they're noisy, they like drinking, clowning. I put a stop to all that at a stroke. I made them cut their hair, shave regularly, stop drinking and it all took its course.'[12] Some even date the start of the Yugoslav wars to a notorious match between Dynamo Zagreb and Red Star Belgrade on 13 May 1990 in the Croatian capital. The game ended in a riot, as the fans attacked each other. Arkan himself said in an interview, 'We began to organise immediately after that . . . I could see war coming because of that match in Zagreb, I foresaw everything and I knew that the Ustasha daggers would soon be slaughtering Serbian women and children again.'[13]

In November 1990, Arkan was arrested in Croatia after a secret midnight meeting with the leaders of the Krajina rebel Serbs. Croatian police found weapons in his car, and he and his companions were held in prison. Curiously, after six and a half months, Arkan was released, just before war broke out in Slovenia. He immediately returned to Belgrade, boasting, 'You'll never take me alive.'

Milosevic needed Arkan to help channel the nationalism that he was unleashing. Milosevic understood that energy, once released, needs to be focused in the right direction, or it can spin out of control. For example, Serbian intelligence agents had been active as provocateurs in the March 1991 student protests in Belgrade. By writing their own slogans and infiltrating the leadership of the protest, they channelled the crowd in certain directions. They may even have ensured that protestors' main demands were merely tactical, such as the release of Vuk Draskovic and the sacking of television editors, rather than bringing down Milosevic.

For most governments violent football fans are a problem. For Milosevic, they were a solution. The deal was simple: Arkan would bring the rowdy nationalist football hooligans under control, and impose tight discipline. Because of his ties to the intelligence services, which had almost certainly helped Arkan escape from foreign prisons, Arkan was considered a 'reliable' nationalist. In exchange the Serbian intelligence service would provide him with a military training camp, and all necessary weapons and equipment for the Tigers' militia. With the help of the Serbian interior ministry, and Radovan Stojicic ('Badza'), the Tigers' training main camp was set up in Erdut, in eastern Croatia in autumn 1991. UN officials later deployed in the region believed that the militia was between five hundred and a thousand strong. They reported seeing the fighters speed-march around the compound every morning at 7.30 a.m., carrying their weapons. These included sniper rifles, AK-47s and Scorpion sub-machine guns.[14]

The Tigers instituted a reign of terror in the region around Erdut. Milosevic's indictment for war crimes in Croatia details how on 9 November 1991 Arkan, together with Serb rebel fighters, arrested a number of ethnic Hungarians and Croats in the Erdut region. They were taken to the Serb rebels' military headquarters. Twelve of those arrested were shot dead the next day, including Franjo and Mihajlo Pap, and Josip and Stjepan Senasi. Several days later, two other members of the Pap family, Franjo and Julijana, asked about the fate of their relatives;

they were immediately arrested and subsequently shot. Their bodies were dropped down a well. Over the next few months, Marija Senasi, a woman in her mid-fifties, bravely persisted in enquiring about Josip and Stjepan Senasi. On 3 June 1992 she was arrested by rebel Serbs and members of Arkan's Tigers. She too was shot, and her body thrown into a well.

The connection between the Serbian government and Arkan was outlined by interior minister Radmilo Bogdanovic. Milosevic ensured that everything was given the necessary legal approval. A law was passed on national defence, with an amendment allowing the organisation of volunteer units to be put under the command of the JNA, or the Territorial Defence organisation. 'Thus, Arkan got started,' said Bogdanovic. 'At first with forty volunteers, later with some more. I oversaw that initially as President of the Security Council, and then it was taken over by General Simovic and other generals. Other volunteers, not only Arkan, were set up that way, that is as a component of the JNA or of the Territorial Defence on that territory.'[15]

General Tomislav Simovic was Serbia's minister of defence. He also confirmed the links between the government and the Tigers. 'As far as I know, the aforementioned Arkan is acting with the direct blessing of the Serbian government in the areas of Slavonia, Western Srem and Baranja. It is also known that they are not the only volunteers. I would not differentiate between criminals and patriots, but rather between those who contribute to the interests of their nation and those who do not, and one knows where criminals fit in.'[16] Dobrila Gajic-Glisic was General Simovic's secretary. In her autobiographical book *Serbian Military*, she notes that General Simovic had a hotline to Milosevic. The two men spoke daily and also met privately. After consultations with Milosevic, the Ministry of Defence authorised the training of paramilitary units, and the funding of their equipment and salaries.[17]

In the field, it was often a different story. Many JNA officers were outraged at the brutality of the paramilitaries and angered by their direct line to Milosevic, which cut through traditional military chains of command.[18] The paramilitaries were, in effect, a parallel army, responsible not to the military leadership but to the State Security Service. Professional army officers tolerated the paramilitaries only when they had to, said Dragan Vuksic, a former army officer who is now an MP in the Serbian parliament. 'The paramilitaries were supported politically by Milosevic. Some officers opposed this, and they were released from the army. Some officers were even beaten by Arkan and the paramilitaries when they asked them who they were and what they were doing in their area of responsibility.'[19]

Arkan was a bank-robber, but Vojislav Seselj was an intellectual, an ideologist, and a genuine believer in the idea of Greater Serbia. His relationship with Milosevic would become more problematic over the years. A former teacher at Sarajevo University, he had been awarded the youngest PhD in Yugoslavia, for his thesis on Marxism and civic democracy. Bosnia and Montenegro, he claimed, were 'invented' nations which had no right to exist. Formulating this theory in an unpublished manuscript in 1984 earned Seselj twenty-two months in Zenica prison. There he was brutally treated. He emerged with a loathing of Muslims and Croats so visceral that many questioned his sanity. The US diplomat Warren Zimmerman described him in his book *Origins of a Catastrophe* as 'a psychopathic bully.'[20]

Initially Seselj had formed a political party together with the nationalist writer Vuk Draskovic, but no one organisation could contain two such titanic egos and it split. Seselj founded the Serbian Chetnik Movement, soon renamed the Serbian Radical Party. The Chetnik paramilitaries had been active in eastern Croatia, at the time of the attack on the busload of Croat policemen in the village of Borovo Selo. Seselj boasted on Belgrade Television that his Chetniks would gouge out Croatian eyeballs with rusty shoehorns. While Arkan's Tigers were fit and athletic, Seselj's Chetniks were slovenly and belligerent, out of condition, drunk, and often overweight, like their leader. For a while Seselj marched around in combat fatigues until he was mocked for looking like a pregnant frog. He carried a pistol, and intimidated his political opponents even within the Serbian parliament.

Mira openly loathed him and the feeling was mutual. She and Seselj personified Serbia's wartime schism between the monarchist Chetniks and the Communist partisans. Seselj repeatedly claimed that Milosevic was henpecked by his wife and once suggested on Belgrade Television Mira was not really a woman. Milosevic merely regretted that his wife was being insulted, but Mira accused Seselj of 'inciting others to fight in a war in which he did not have the guts to take part' and of being so afraid of men that he had to bully a woman. 'No, Seselj is not a Serb,' she wrote. 'He is a Turk, in the most primitive historical edition. Or perhaps he is just not a man.'[21]

For Mira's husband, however, Seselj had his uses. His Chetniks, like

Arkan's Tigers, were supplied with weapons, ammunition and transport by the Serbian government. As Seselj told the author Tim Judah:

> Milosevic organised everything. We gathered the volunteers and he gave us a special barracks, Bubanj Potok, all our uniforms, arms, military technology and buses. All our units were always under the command of the Krajina [Serb army] or [Bosnian] Republika Srpska Army or the JNA. Of course I don't believe he signed anything, these were verbal orders. None of our talks was taped and I never took a paper and pencil when I talked with him. His key people were the commanders. Nothing could happen on the Serbian side without Milosevic's order or his knowledge.[22]

Milosevic's alliance between the JNA, Arkan's Tigers and Seselj's Chetniks was cemented in the attack on the Bosnian city of Zvornik. Perched on the banks of the river Drina, which is the border between Bosnia and Serbia, Zvornik was an Ottoman-era town that lay under a medieval Turkish fortress. Control of Zvornik was a vital element of Belgrade's plan for Bosnia, as it lay on the routes from Belgrade towards both Sarajevo in the south and Tuzla in the north.

The attack on Zvornik is the clearest evidence that Milosevic's claim that Serbia was not involved in the Bosnian war is a lie.[23] Early in 1992 the JNA organised extensive military training exercises exclusively for local Serbs, who were also provided with arms. By March JNA tanks, artillery and anti-aircraft units were in position in the Zvornik region. The JNA emblems were eventually replaced by the Serbian flag, but otherwise everything stayed the same. Similar ordnance was in position on the other side of the Drina, in Serbia proper.

In the attack on Zvornik, Seselj's Chetniks and another paramilitary group known as the White Eagles were under the command of two JNA officers. Seselj's men were recognisable by their characteristic beards, fur caps and bandoliers of ammunition worn across their chest in a cross shape. Members of these two paramilitary groups looted and murdered at will. In contrast to the shambolic, ill-disciplined Chetniks and White Eagles, Arkan's Tigers (a.k.a. 'Arkanovci') had close-cropped hair, woollen caps and military uniforms. 'The Arkanovci, and in particular Arkan himself, are unanimously described as the key figures in the attack. During the attack operation, Arkan's standing was reportedly above that of the commanders of the JNA, as well as that of the leading figures of the local SDS [Serbian Democratic Party],' records the UN Commission of Experts report.[24]

Arkan arrived in Zvornik on 8 April, but some of his fighters had been in position since the end of March. By this time many Serbs had left Zvornik, especially women and children, often warning their Muslim friends and neighbours that they should leave as well. After Arkan's arrival 'negotiations' were opened with the Muslim leadership on the future of the town, in effect a demand for instant surrender. Snipers located in Mali Zvornik on the other side of the Drina opened fire, and a mortar barrage began. Negotiations continued the next day in Mali Zvornik. This was a local version of Milosevic's overall Bosnian strategy to keep the Muslim leadership talking, even as the Serbs took the safety catches off their weapons. The lightly-armed Muslim fighters did not stand a chance against the JNA and the paramilitaries. By 11 April Zvornik had fallen, although a group of Muslim fighters held out at the fortress of Kulagrad for another fortnight. The dates are important because the Bosnian Serb army was not officially founded until early May. The attack on Zvornik was carried out by JNA troops that were legally part of the Yugoslav armed forces. By this time, the only republics left in Yugoslavia were Serbia and Montenegro.

The same day that Zvornik's Muslims were fleeing in terror, Jose Maria Mendiluce, the most senior official of the United Nations High Commission for Refugees in former Yugoslavia, was in a meeting with Milosevic in Belgrade. Milosevic sat and lied straight-faced to Mendiluce as the UN official asked him to rein in his Bosnian Serb protégés. 'Milosevic told me, as he did throughout the conflict, that he didn't have any control over the Bosnian Serbs, but he would try to use his moral authority.'[25]

The actual result of Milosevic's 'moral authority' was the blood all over the road on which Mendiluce's jeep skidded when he arrived at the outskirts of Zvornik on his way back to Sarajevo, and the smoke and flashes from the guns positioned on the Serbian side of the river Drina. Mendiluce was detained for two hours by the Bosnian Serbs as they finished their work. 'I could see trucks full of dead bodies. I could see militiamen taking more corpses of children, women and old people from their houses and putting them on trucks. I saw at least four or five trucks full of corpses.'[26]

The capture of Zvornik had been planned in Belgrade, the paramilitary leader Vojislav Seselj said. 'The operation had been planned for a long time. It was not carried out in any kind of nervous fashion. Everything was well organised and implemented.'[27] Seselj and the paramilitaries, like virtually every one of Milosevic's allies, soon found themselves abandoned when they had outlived their usefulness. In 1993 Milosevic's Socialist Party attacked Seselj for abetting war profiteers and war criminals. Even Belgrade cynics looked on in amazement at the campaign Milosevic organised against his former ally, whose rampaging paramilitaries had been under the command of either the Serbian intelligence service, or the JNA. Those who had volunteered to fight for a Greater Serbia were also unceremoniously dumped by Milosevic. The War Veterans Association complained that it had no response to the three letters it had sent to Milosevic complaining about the poor treatment of both JNA soldiers and 'volunteers'.

One of the last serious interviews Milosevic gave the western press was in 1993 with Peter Maass, a former correspondent of the *Washington Post*, and author of the book *Love Thy Neighbour*. Maass asked Milosevic about Bosnian Serb ethnic cleansing. Milosevic sounded concerned, and said: 'I was discussing that problem with them and they said to me there was absolutely not any policy to press any Muslim to leave their cities. For example in Banja Luka there are a lot of Muslims living equally, equally treated to the others.'[28]

The Bosnian Serb leadership instituted a reign of terror in Banja Luka and its surrounding villages. The thousands of Muslim and Croat refugees expelled into nearby Croatia were comparatively lucky, escaping the horrors of northern Bosnia's network of concentration camps. In Banja Luka the Bosnian Serbs had also committed a cultural war crime: they systematically demolished sixteen mosques, many dating back to the sixteenth century. The stone blocks once hewed by Ottoman masons were used to build a car park, or dumped outside the city. If Milosevic had wanted to know what was happening in Banja Luka, he need only have asked his wife.

On 24 May 1993 Mira Markovic wrote in *Duga* magazine:

The mosques in Banja Luka have been torn down. Banja Luka falls within the territory of the [Bosnian] Serbian Republic . . . In the middle of the 1980s, cases of vandalism and desecration of Serbian cemeteries, monuments and monasteries in Kosovo perpetrated by ethnic Albanian extremists from Kosovo shocked Yugoslavia . . . And now it is very hard for me to understand how, just a few years later, a segment of that selfsame Serbian nation is doing to another nation the selfsame things that were considered dishonourable and barbaric when happening to them.[29]

An autocrat who was not used to being questioned by well-informed outsiders, Milosevic was rattled by Maass's questions about the contradiction between the reality of his policies and Mira's writings:

Maass: I've notice that your wife in her articles in *Duga* has expressed opinions that are quite different from your own.
Milosevic: How do you know that?
Maass: Because I have had translations and people have told me about it.
Milosevic: But how do you know that she is expressing different opinions?
Maass: Because she seems to be very critical of Mr Karadzic and critical of the way that the Bosnian Serbs have conducted themselves.
Milosevic: Are you critical of something which is happening in the United States?
Maass: Yes.
Milosevic: Of course. Any civilised intellectual has to be critical of life as it is. Do you think that I am not critical of many things which are happening here and all around Yugoslavia and Serbia. We have a lot of problems.

With his Croatian confidant, Tudjman's envoy Hrvoje Sarinic, Milosevic was more relaxed. When Sarinic met Milosevic in Belgrade on 12 November 1993 he asked the Serbian leader about Arkan. Milosevic laughed loudly, and said: 'I too must have someone to do certain kinds of dirty work for me.'[30]

16

MILAN PANIC

The Two Republics of Federal Yugoslavia
1992–3

Shut up.

> Yugoslav prime minister Milan Panic, to Serbian president
> Slobodan Milosevic at the London Conference on Bosnia,
> August 1992.[1]

And then there were two. After Slovenia, Croatia, Bosnia and Macedonia declared independence and departed from Yugoslavia, only Serbia and Montenegro were left. In April 1992, these two republics formed a new state, formally known as the Federal Republic of Yugoslavia. This time Milosevic did not call for the word 'Socialist' to be moved to the front. Here finally was, in effect, 'Serboslavia', a Yugoslavia controlled by Serbia, subordinate to Serbian interests, as decided by one man. Montenegro was little more than a pliant puppet, at least at this time. Its president was Momir Bulatovic, the man dubbed 'the waiter' for his servile obedience to Milosevic. Unconstrained by troublesome republics seeking independence, the Serbian president was able to totally dominate the new mini-Yugoslav state.

Milosevic ensured that the old federal structures and ministries remained in place. He argued that this Yugoslavia was the legitimate inheritor of its predecessors, and so could keep the assets of the old Yugoslavia, and the Yugoslav seat in the United Nations. Perhaps most importantly, Milosevic also used this opportunity to cement his control over the military. Supreme command of the army now rested in the new Supreme Defence Council. This had three members: Milosevic, President of Serbia; Momir Bulatovic, President of Montenegro, and the next President of Yugoslavia.

The question was, who should that be? A new country demanded

a fresh face at its head. Milosevic turned to Dusan Mitevic. Although
Mitevic had been sacked from his position at Belgrade Television a
year earlier, behind the scenes he remained a key Milosevic adviser.
'Milosevic asked me who we should have as president. I said nobody
from the Socialist Party. He said, then who should we have, if not one
of us? I said let's take someone from the opposition. I suggested Dobrica
Cosic.'[2]

It was an imaginative idea. At this time there was talk of Otto
Habsburg becoming president of neighbouring Slovenia. Within Serbia
the nationalist revival had reawakened interest in the country's own royal
family. History, and tradition – these would coat the third Yugoslavia
with a veneer of legitimacy. Still Milosevic had doubts. Cosic was
the intellectual godfather of Serbian nationalism. What would Mira
say when he went home and told her this? And would Cosic accept?
After a brief honeymoon in 1990 the intellectuals had fallen out with
Milosevic, realising that at heart Milosevic was an autocrat motivated
by power, not a Serb who believed in patriotism and the glories of
the 'heavenly people'. Mitevic recalled: 'I told Milosevic that difficult
times were coming, that we were a country in transition, we should
think democratically, and get someone who will not put us in prison
later. Apart from Milovan Djilas, we only had one dissident in the last
thirty years, and that was Cosic.'

Milosevic considered his position. He knew that he was in trouble
on both the diplomatic and home fronts. With two wars on its borders, its economy collapsing under sanctions, its nascent democratic
institutions wrecked, this third version of Yugoslavia was not a very
mighty construct. Its citizens were tired, confused and weary of war.
International outrage about the brutality of Serb ethnic cleansing was
turning Yugoslavia into a leper state. Germany, in particular the foreign
minister Hans-Dietrich Genscher, had forced through the diplomatic
recognition of Croatia and Slovenia, over the heads of other EU
countries. Croatia was eternally grateful to its former wartime ally.
Croats sang along to a new popular song, 'Danke Deutschland'. The
Café Genscher opened in the Adriatic port of Split. Clearly, the world
was changing, and perhaps Serbia should change with it.

Increasingly, Serbs were simply not willing to fight in Milosevic's
wars. The JNA had been wracked by desertions. One soldier drove
his armoured personnel carrier back to Belgrade and parked it in front
of the parliament. Another shot himself in the head in front of his

commanding officer. Others stripped off their uniforms and escaped through the borderland woods into Hungary. In March 1992 the Serbian patriarch, seen as the country's spiritual father, held a mass at Belgrade's St Sava church for the victims of the street protests a year before. When the service was broadcast live on Belgrade Television, Milosevic ordered the programme taken off air.

Angry and ashamed, many Serbs began to turn against their leader. Protestors took to the streets, pitching tents in downtown Belgrade. Milosevic was unnerved, fearing a rerun of the street protests of March 1991. Crowds were one of Milosevic's favourite political weapons, but he knew that a mob could be a two-edged sword. Like a pack of wolves, crowds sensed weakness in their prey. 'Just you wait, Slobodan, Ceausescu awaits you,' the protesters chanted in Belgrade. Students and young people used imaginative agit-prop to get their message across: the parliament was wrapped in a giant black ribbon to protest against the siege of Sarajevo. Parents joined the demonstrations, calling for the return of their sons from the frontlines in Bosnia. Milosevic even appeared on television to try and calm the situation and proclaimed that Serbia was not at war, and no Serbian soldiers were serving outside the republic. Perhaps a part of Milosevic even believed it. In Belgrade, some began to question his grip.

Confronted with the disastrous reality of his policies, Milosevic reverted to denial, outright mendacity and fantastical talk of wonderful economic opportunities. Warren Zimmerman's last meeting with Milosevic, on 19 April 1992, was a vintage encounter. The US ambassador came to dinner with a carrot as well as a stick. Washington was prepared to consider 'potential' international acceptance for Yugoslavia if Serbia reversed ethnic cleansing, and withdrew the JNA from Bosnia. The meeting started at 7.30 p.m. Meanwhile servants laid out dinner in the adjacent room – grilled lamb, plates of vegetables and bottles of wine and fruit brandy.

Just ten days before, the Bosnian city of Zvornik had fallen to a combined force of JNA troops and paramilitaries. Milosevic, initially conciliatory, listened carefully to Zimmerman's arguments of Serb and JNA involvement in the ethnic cleansing of Bosnia. He then claimed: 'No armed Serb irregulars have crossed into Bosnia.' Eventually Milosevic admitted that Arkan was indeed in Bosnia, but only as a 'bodyguard' for one of the Bosnian Serb leaders. And so it went on. Milosevic claimed that: 'Violence in Bosnia is not in Serbia's interest;

we have no territorial pretensions in Bosnia. We favour the European Community negotiations. Those shelling Sarajevo – if the shelling is really happening – are criminals.'[3]

It is hard to know what Milosevic was thinking. Did he really believe that the ambassador of the most powerful country in the world, with extensive intelligence services, and spy satellites that could read a car numberplate, did not know what was happening in Bosnia and who was responsible? Perhaps Milosevic, like many Serbian politicians, was suffering from 'a concept deficit.'[4] At one press conference in Geneva a journalist had asked the Bosnian Serb leader Radovan Karadzic about the first priority to rebuild the country. 'We will need a lot of glass,' replied Karadzic. 'We have many broken windows.' At a previous meeting with Zimmerman, on 6 April, Milosevic had also flatly denied that a single Serb was serving in Bosnia. He had described Arkan – among whose many business interests was an upmarket patisserie – as a 'simple sweetshop owner'. Little wonder that Zimmerman dubbed Milosevic the 'Teflon dictator'.

After three and a half hours of hard talking, Zimmerman, Milosevic and their officials retired to eat. The lamb was now coated with cold fat, and the vegetables had wilted. Still, Milosevic waxed lyrical about Yugoslavia's economic potential. 'With its efficient agriculture, energy resources, and key location for transportation – plus a free market – it will be in a strong position to attract foreign investment. Why only this week we were approached by French businessmen about a project for building a high-speed train.' At the end of the meal, Milosevic, perhaps made sentimental by his memories of New York, made a plea for friendship with the Americans. 'I'm not so bad, am I? Am I such a black sheep?'[5] Zimmerman was speechless.

Milosevic had a sentimental attachment to the United States. Fuelled by Viljamovka pear brandy, he often recalled his days as a banker in New York and his shopping trips on Fifth Avenue. Although Milosevic was a Balkan bully, part of him craved the respect of the most powerful country in the world, and its envoys as well. Not long after their dinner, Zimmerman was recalled to Washington, D.C., in protest at Milosevic's policies in Bosnia. Perhaps that snub brought back the anger Milosevic had felt in 1989 when no western ambassadors attended the Gazimestan spectacle. Zimmerman's leaving party was marred by an unpleasant incident: his garden was invaded by a gang of sinister hoodlums who began spraying insecticide all around.

*   *   *

Meanwhile, the more Milosevic thought about Dusan Mitevic's suggestion, the more it made sense. His natural instinct was to exclude everyone
outside his immediate circle from any position of power or influence.
But co-opting Cosic would be more subtle. Cosic was second in stature
perhaps only to the Serbian Patriarch. His appointment would legitimise
the third Yugoslavia, and help defuse domestic opposition. Persuaded by
Milosevic's arguments that he would be doing his Serbian patriotic duty,
Dobrica Cosic accepted.

As Serbian president, Milosevic controlled the Serbian government
and the Serbian parliament. He also controlled the Yugoslav parliament
through his loyalist MPs, who would ratify his choice of Yugoslav
president and prime minister. Milosevic asked Dusan Mitevic if he had
any ideas for suitable prime ministerial candidates. Mitevic suggested
Milan Panic, an émigré Yugoslav cycling champion who had defected
in 1955. Arriving in the United States a penniless immigrant. Panic
had built up a successful pharmaceutical business, ICN, based in
California. Panic had invested heavily in Serbia, buying up the Galenika
pharmaceutical factory.

Mitevic introduced the two men to each other. 'It was love at first
sight. Panic is an open and good-hearted man. Milosevic was a banker
who understood business. Milosevic was telling Panic how important
privatisation was.'[6] Mitevic saw Panic's appointment as a chance for
Serbia to democratise and move away from one-party control. 'I thought
we should work peacefully with the opposition parties. That's why I
brought in Panic. My idea was that instead of presenting ourselves as
a Communist country, we would have a rich American imperialist as
prime minister.' After a long drunken dinner, Milosevic offered Panic
the prime ministership of Yugoslavia. After ensuring that he could keep
his US citizenship, Panic accepted.

Milosevic's plan was that Panic, with his contacts in Washington and
the business world, would be the modern, western, face of Yugoslavia.
The sun-tanned capitalist would be Milosevic's front-man, whom he
could use to defuse the growing international outcry over Serbia's
actions in Bosnia. Milosevic was wrong. Before Panic was even officially
inaugurated as Yugoslav prime minister he demanded that Milosevic
resign. He proposed that the Milosevic family move to California,
where Milosevic would take up his old profession of banker, on a
fat salary with plenty of perks. For a while, Milosevic appeared, or
more likely pretended, to consider this. This proposal was not well

received at home. Mira was not willing to sacrifice her Balkan intrigues for *Baywatch*.

Panic picked a cabinet of pro-western, reform-minded ministers for his new Yugoslav government, although Milosevic ensured that a few of his loyalists were also appointed. The Yugoslav minister of justice was Tibor Varady, an ethnic Hungarian from Novi Sad who had studied law at Belgrade University with Milosevic. He recalled: 'At some point Milosevic felt that the threats of western military intervention, of bombing Serbian positions around Sarajevo, were becoming serious. So he needed to pull a rabbit out of his hat, and offer a gesture to the world.'[7]

The new Yugoslav Prime Minister was not willing to be a front-man for ethnic cleansing. In his inaugural speech to the Yugoslav assembly in July 1992 Panic called for the recognition of Croatia and Bosnia, the lifting of sanctions against Yugoslavia and the withdrawal of all Yugoslav military units, including paramilitaries, from Bosnia. He said he would order Serb leaders in Bosnia to close the concentration camps.

Panic's plan was to offer the West the removal of Milosevic, in exchange for sanctions being lifted. It seemed a simple enough quid pro quo. Panic saw this as essentially a business deal between two partners who both had something to trade. But he was not as well connected in Washington as either he or Milosevic thought. James Baker, US Secretary of State, was not disposed to get involved in what he thought was a European problem. President George Bush, facing an election campaign, was not very interested. The word in Washington was the United States 'did not have a dog in this fight'. Sanctions were anyway a matter for the United Nations, not the United States. And the Brahmins of the State Department regarded Panic as a wild card. He was neither a professional diplomat nor a politician, but someone out of their control.

Panic was certainly out of Milosevic's control. In July he flew to besieged Sarajevo to meet with Bosnian President Alija Izetbegovic. There he condemned 'cheap politicians who have played on nationalism and created a civil war', a clear shot at Milosevic. He went to Pristina and met with Kosovo Albanian leader Ibrahim Rugova, and called for human rights for ethnic Albanians. He also sacked Mihalj Kertes from his post as deputy Yugoslav interior minister. Kertes was working for the Serbian secret service, and his involvement in Milosevic's dirty tricks dated back to 1988 when he had bussed demonstrators into Novi Sad to throw rocks and yoghurt. He had also played a role in distributing weapons to the Serb rebels in both Croatia and Bosnia.

Panic and Milosevic were soon running competing governments. Milosevic controlled the Serbian government, the Serbian parliament and the Yugoslav parliament – now composed solely of MPs from Serbia and Montenegro. But he did not control the Yugoslav government, whose ministers increasingly existed in a curious constitutional limbo. Tibor Varady observed: 'This was an odd structure as the Yugoslav government was clearly European and western-minded. So as minister of justice I was writing laws according to my own taste, but none had the slightest chance of getting passed in the Yugoslav parliament, and none ever did.' The Serbian secret service, under the control of the Serbian interior ministry, even tapped the telephones and monitored the movement of Panic and his ministers. If the Yugoslav minister of justice wanted to talk to the Yugoslav prime minister, both had to leave their offices, in case they were bugged. As Varady noted: 'This was not a position of power.'

Even so, for Milosevic, the Panic experiment was turning into a nightmare. It was true that Panic spoke English with a heavy accent, mangled his Serbo-Croat and sometimes seemed eccentric. He could be a loose cannon, but he was also a shrewd businessman, with an instinct for the practicalities of a deal. His multi-million dollar international pharmaceutical empire was proof of that. The man was irrepressible. He cut through the complications of diplomacy, history and politics that had befuddled the Balkans for so long. Panic was revitalising the previously dormant Yugoslav government and turning it into a counterweight to Serbia. Milosevic realised that he had spawned a monster.

At the end of August 1992 the international community made another in its series of failed attempts to bring peace to Yugoslavia. Panic, Milosevic and other representatives of the Yugoslav and Serbian governments headed for the London Conference on Yugoslavia. The conference was supposed to stop the Serb onslaught on Bosnia, reverse ethnic cleansing and bring about a solution to the Yugoslav crisis. The plan was to caution Milosevic, who would then stop the war and return home chastened and reasonable. Milosevic, of course, had other ideas.

Europe's attempts to stop the fighting so far had been a dismal failure. When the Yugoslav conflict had first broken out in the summer of 1991 Jacques Poos, the foreign minister of Luxembourg, had foolishly declared that 'the hour of Europe has dawned',[8] meaning the new united continent would be able to sort out the challenge of disintegrating Yugoslavia. But there was no new dawn, only a descent into a long, dark night. The August 1992 London conference followed attempts the previous October by the former British foreign secretary, Lord Carrington, to broker a peace deal in negotiations at The Hague, under the auspices of the European Community (not yet then transformed into the European Union). It was a measure of the EC's lackadaisical approach at the time that Lord Carrington remained as chairman of Christie's, the London auction house, while trying to bring peace to Yugoslavia.

Nonetheless, the Carrington Plan could have provided the basis for a peaceful settlement. It made major concessions to the Serb minorities in both Croatia and Bosnia, granting them administrative autonomy, their own education system, their own parliament, police force and judiciary; in short, a virtual state within a state. Milosevic rejected it, probably because the Carrington Plan would apply all through Yugoslavia, so the same rights would have to be granted to the Albanians in Kosovo. This was unthinkable. The only surprise was that Momir Bulatovic, the Montenegrin president, broke ranks and voted to accept the Carrington Plan, tempted by the promise of an aid development programme for Montenegro worth millions of dollars. A campaign of intimidation, and a barrage of media accusations that Bulatovic was a traitor, quickly ensured that he backed down.[9]

Supremely arrogant at this time, Milosevic even turned down a proposal from his old colleague, Mihailo Crnobrnja, then Yugoslav ambassador to the EC, that he grant an interview to the *Wall Street Journal Europe*. At this time Serbia was being pilloried in the international press for its onslaught on Croatia. Crnobrnja recalled: 'I told him, so far everybody is antagonised by the Serbs, what better forum could there be to explain the Serbian and his position? He said, "I don't give a damn, the truth will prevail." He felt so superior he did not feel the need to explain himself.'[10] Crnobrnja was not willing to represent the third, Federal Yugoslavia, and in May 1992 he resigned his post as ambassador.

On the plane to London Milosevic was pleasant enough to Tibor Varady, even though he was one of Panic's ministers. A bout of turbulence had forced Varady to take the nearest available seat as they descended to land. It was next to Milosevic. There was a long embarrassed silence, at first, recalled Varady. 'There was obviously a difference between us and neither of us wanted to address it.'

Milosevic was rude when he wanted, but he could also turn on the charm. There was no point arguing with Varady about politics or the Yugoslav-Serbian rift, especially on an airplane full of eavesdropping journalists. 'Tibor,' he enquired, 'Whatever happened to Edit?'

Summoning up Edit was Milosevic's exit strategy from a potentially embarrassing encounter. Milosevic gave orders to generals, carved up neighbouring countries, negotiated with world leaders. But sticky social situations were another matter. And strapped in for a bumpy descent, there was nowhere else for him to go. 'I was thinking hard what to say, and he probably was too,' recalled Varady. 'Milosevic spoke like it was only yesterday that we had been drinking coffee together, although we never did. Edit was the only other Hungarian in our law class at Belgrade University, so mentioning her was a gesture.'

Varady had little news of Edit, but did know that she was working in Belgrade. Milosevic thought for a while: 'Edit was a very good student, very talented.' He paused. What else was there to say? 'She would probably be a good mother as well,' he threw in for good measure. Milosevic then asked some more questions, but Varady did not know the answers.

Varady recalled the bizarre moment: 'We were both afraid to leave Edit as a topic. But neither of us had any interest in poor Edit, and we ran out of information.' Silence, and the prospect of the upcoming conference on Bosnia loomed before them.

But Milosevic could always think on his feet. He had a brainwave. The past conditional came to the rescue. He asked Varady, if Edit had stayed at law school as a professor, what subject would she have chosen? Varady recalled: 'Since we no longer had a foothold on reality, we moved to the hypothetical. I said I thought civil law. He said I might be right, but she could have been very good at legal history as well. So we talked about Edit until we got to London.'[11]

At the London conference Milosevic for the first time experienced the kind of public humiliation that he used at the 1987 Eighth Session to destroy the career of Ivan Stambolic. When Milosevic asked to speak, Panic handed him a piece of paper. He had written on it, 'Shut up'.[12] In case any of the diplomats watching were wondering what was happening, Panic then told the conference that Milosevic was not authorised to speak

Panic argued strongly – and correctly – that Yugoslavia was the

internationally recognised state, not Serbia. Serbia was merely a constituent republic of Yugoslavia. As Panic was the head of the Yugoslav
government, he, not Milosevic, should speak for the country. Milosevic
was stunned. Ever since his university days, he had been a master at
making and breaking protégés and alliances, forming and dissolving
factions, using intimidation, force and public humiliation to advance
his interests. Now he was on the receiving end, in front of all the world's
statesmen, diplomats and media. This was a declaration of war by Panic.

The London conference followed the usual pattern of international
diplomacy in dealing with Milosevic at this time. Self-congratulatory
communiqués and press releases were issued. The closing declaration
called for the closure of the concentration camps; rejected ethnic
cleansing as 'inhuman and illegal'; called for more peace talks in Geneva;
demanded that international treaties be respected, and called for the
despatch of human rights observers to Kosovo and Voivodina. The
most serious threat was of 'stringent sanctions' that would lead to
'total international isolation'. In addition, the UN announced that
peacekeeping troops would be despatched to Bosnia. Crucially, even
though the pictures of the horrors of the Bosnian Serb concentration
camp at Omarska had been broadcast around the world, there was no
mention of the use of force against the Bosnian Serbs.

Milosevic took little notice of these demands, except perhaps a clause
about a proposal for a war crimes tribunal. Back in Belgrade he acted
swiftly against Panic. Late one Saturday night in October Mihalj Kertes,
the Serbian secret service agent inside the Yugoslav interior ministry
whom Panic had sacked, took his revenge. Masked and armed Serbian
police commandos took over the Yugoslav interior ministry while Panic
and Dobrica Cosic were in Geneva. The building was sealed off, and its
files were systematically boxed up and removed to the headquarters of the
Serbian secret police. Milosevic had gambled that Panic would not order
the Yugoslav army to retake the building for fear of sparking civil war.
He was correct. It is likely that Panic could have mobilised disaffected
elements of the Yugoslav security services to retake the building, but he
chose not to do so. Panic was seriously weakened by this episode.

Earlier that year, under pressure from the opposition and the student
protesters, Milosevic had agreed to call elections in Serbia. Many
believed that Dobrica Cosic would stand and beat Milosevic. The
date was set for 20 December. The handful of Milosevic loyalists in
Panic's Yugoslav government resigned. Panic was smeared as an agent

of foreign powers. The great Serb patriot Dobrica Cosic prevaricated. He then announced that he would not run against Milosevic.

Panic announced he would stand against Milosevic for Serbian president. Little Lenin went to work, using every trick in the Communist book. Immediately, a stream of pseudo-legal and constitutional difficulties were conjured up to obstruct Panic's campaign. The Serbian Electoral Commission announced that Panic could not run because he had not been resident in Serbia for a year. When opposition parties threatened to boycott the poll the Constitutional Court eventually overruled the requirement, which had anyway only been introduced the previous month. There was even talk of death threats.

Belgrade Television was an open propaganda weapon for Milosevic. Panic was not even allowed paid advertisements. He was smeared by implication as an American agent. Even the weather forecast was press-ganged into service, said Tibor Varady. 'It went like this: "Tomorrow we are expecting snow flurries around Belgrade. Now dear viewers we would like to tell you how the weather will be in Knin, where our Serb brothers are suffering under Croatian fascism. But since our prime minister Mr Panic wants to recognise Croatia and does not care about our Serbian brethren we cannot tell you how the weather is there."'

Milosevic's propaganda attacks could not prevent Panic from receiving a warm welcome all over the country. Over 100,000 people attended his last election rally in Belgrade. However Milosevic's gerrymandering of the electoral rolls and other tricks such as closing the borders, and issuing students (many of whom were strong Panic supporters) with their grant cheques on polling day, thus preventing them from travelling home to vote, helped ensure that he won.

Milosevic took 56 per cent of the vote and Panic 34 per cent. Despite his unpredictable ways, the sun-tanned Californian Serb had brought hope to a country made grey and miserable by war and economic sanctions. The tightening of sanctions did not help Panic. On 17 November a naval blockade of the Danube and the Adriatic was introduced. Many Serbs felt that if the country was going to be punished anyway, then they would stick with Milosevic. None the less, had the election been honest, it is quite possible that Panic could have stopped Milosevic getting the 50 per cent of votes needed to win outright in the first round. 'If there had been a run-off and a second round, Panic would have won, because Milosevic's myth of invincibility would have been broken,' said Tibor Varady.

Panic had fought well but he lacked proper backing from the West to defeat a leader who had hijacked the whole country's media and political infrastructure. Milosevic did not like being crossed. He took his final revenge when Panic eventually left Yugoslavia in January 1993. He was held at the border for five hours before being allowed to cross into Hungary, even though he was still technically the head of the Yugoslav government. Dobrica Cosic was removed from office in June. There would be no more experiments with 'rich American imperialist' front-men for the Milosevic regime.

17

MEANWHILE, ON THE HOME FRONT

Hijacking the Yugoslav Economy

1992–3

You cannot achieve anything in Serbia through honest business or fair work.
People cannot live normally on a salary of DM100 a month. Better to have
everything than nothing.

Belgrade gangster.[1]

Ljubica Markovic was having trouble at the Belgrade post office. After a long illness, her father Moma Markovic had passed away, and she wanted to send a telegram to Mira. She wrote out, 'Father has died', and addressed it to Dr Mirjana Markovic. But the clerk would not accept the telegram. He demanded: 'What is this text, is it a provocation?' Ljubica recalled: 'I said, "How can you ask me such a thing, this is a personal message."'[2]

Eventually the telegram was sent. Ljubica Markovic had thought carefully before contacting her half-sister. It was August 1992, and Mira had not seen her father since they had quarrelled about Milosevic's policies in 1989. Moma had told Ljubica, she said, that he did not wish Mira to attend his funeral. But Ljubica decided he did not really mean it. 'I thought about what to do, because informing her about his death was against my father's will. But somehow I felt, would have agreed anyway. She was his daughter too, and I thought that was the right thing to do.' Later that afternoon Milosevic telephoned to confirm that he and Mira would attend the funeral. 'It was the first time we had heard his voice for years. My father asked to be buried without ceremony, as it was the middle of the war,' said Ljubica. 'They came very late, they stayed ten minutes with their bodyguards, and then they left. They did not say a word to anyone.' Ljubica noticed that her sister's dress sense had changed. 'She used to dress in a modest manner, and now she was wearing expensive clothes. She had snakeskin shoes.'

By 1992 any boots, let alone snakeskin ones, were out of reach of most Serbs. In June inflation topped 100 per cent per month. But Milosevic ensured that he and his family were living in comfort. The previous year, he had signed a contract of purchase for number 33 Tolstoyeva Street, a three-storey house that was more than three and a half times the size of the family's previous home: the modest flat on 14 December Street in downtown Belgrade.

In fact the Milosevic family had already lived in the house for three years or so, since the defeat of Ivan Stambolic at the 1987 Eighth Session. That had been a turning point, not just for Serbian politics, but also for Milosevic's status and prestige. 33 Tolstoyeva Street had been renovated, redecorated, and kitted out with the latest security equipment. The villa was located in the smartest part of Belgrade, a plush and exclusive suburb known as Dedinje, surrounded by woods and parkland. Tito had lived in Dedinje, as did the nationalist writer Dobrica Cosic, and Arkan, the paramilitary leader. The outbreak of the Croatian war spurred Milosevic to formalise his ownership. The price was 7.3 million dinars (£197,000), and a monthly repayment of 15,977 dinars (£430).[3]

Milosevic understood money. He could have used his knowledge of capitalism to introduce free market reforms and privatisation. Instead he ran the Serbian economy the same way he ran the Serbian state, setting up a network of trusted loyalists who either took over, or sidestepped, the established financial institutions. At the apex sat Borka Vucic, the Beogradska Banka official who, back in the 1970s, had accompanied Milosevic to IMF meetings in Washington, D.C., and insisted on pressing his trousers. Vucic was ferociously loyal to Milosevic. Apart from Mira, she was the only woman admitted to his inner circle.

Vucic was based in Cyprus as head of Beogradska Banka's offshore subsidiary, before returning to Belgrade in 1998. In Cyprus she ran a multi-million dollar international financial network stretching from Serbia to Switzerland, Lebanon, Russia and Greece. Suitcases full of money were flown in and out of Cyprus to fund a complex sanctions-busting operation to pay for the wars, and enrich the business-political elite around Milosevic. According to one diplomatic source: 'Borka Vucic was Milosevic's chief financial officer throughout the whole of the Milosevic era. She played a critical role. She was the principal person making payments to Cyprus, running all the financial aspects. She was head and shoulders above everyone else.'[4]

Cyprus was chosen because it was near to Serbia and offered offshore banking secrecy. At the same time, Orthodox Greece was one of Serbia's few allies in Europe, a sympathy shared by Greek Cypriots. At one stage there were 7,500 offshore Yugoslav companies registered there. 'All the banks did the same to survive,' said Vucic. 'A lot of people were taking money into Cyprus. There were other people on airplanes carrying the money, but not with me. If someone was taking money without the permission of the bank or the companies, it's not my responsibility.'[5] Borka Vucic also defended her role as a patriotic duty: 'We had no other resources. We urgently needed medicine, hospital equipment.'[6]

While Vucic was setting up in Cyprus, Milosevic was cooking the books. National monetary policy was under the control of the Yugoslav National Bank, but each republic also had its own bank. Serbia was fortunate enough to control the Voivodina Bank as well. In December 1990 these two institutions suddenly conjured up the equivalent of 18.3 billion dinars (£1 billion). These 'grey dinars' were either issued as new banknotes, or simply distributed as credits to favoured companies and institutions. The following month, the books were balanced, sort of. Suddenly injecting an extra 18.3 billion dinars into the economy obviously devalues the dinar, so the official DM exchange rate was altered from 1:7 to 1:9.

The next step was simply stealing funds from Serbian citizens. Because so many Serbs had worked abroad as guestworkers in Germany, Austria and other western countries, substantial amounts of hard currency had entered Serbia. The Serbian state froze foreign currency accounts worth almost 7.5 billion DMs. The money was returned later, but only as dinars.

After that the regime targeted the actual hard currency that people had hidden at home. Two methods were used: state-induced hyperinflation, and state-sponsored pyramid banking schemes. Hyperinflation was triggered simply by printing more and more money. The dinar was soon barely worth the paper on which it was printed. In 1993 a banknote was introduced with a face value of 50,000,000,000 dinars. By January 1994 Serbian inflation was running at a monthly rate of over 310 million per cent, which meant 62 per cent a day, or 2 per cent an hour. On 10 November 1993, a kilogram of potatoes cost 4,000 dinars. By 17 January 1994 it cost 8,000,000,000,000,000 dinars.[2]

Yet while the dinar banknotes were virtually worthless, state-owned shops that provided staples such as bread and cooking oil – and petrol – would not take hard currency. This meant that in order to live, citizens were forced to sell their dollars and Deutschmarks to the state, in exchange for devalued dinars. The shady characters on every street corners whispering the word '*devize, devize*' (foreign currency) at passers-by were part of a 'grey market' run by the state itself, and were state employees.

Milosevic's Serbia deliberately impoverished its own citizens, said Aleksandar Radovic, president of the Investigating Commission of Economic and Financial Abuses of the Milosevic Regime (ICEFA), which is now attempting to track the missing money, estimated to total $30 billion. 'One cannot behave like a naïve French maid, but anyone would be shocked at this. The first aim of these policies was the extreme impoverishment of Serbia. When you have poor people struggling to survive, you can buy them for nothing. They need to make a deal with the regime.'[8]

Initially at least, the imposition of sanctions, intended to weaken Milosevic, to some extent rebounded. Even liberal Yugoslavs were angered at the isolation in which they found themselves. Academics could not get their papers published abroad. Foreign books could no longer be imported. Medicine and medical equipment became scarce. Milosevic himself said that sanctions were the price the country had to pay for supporting the Serbs outside Serbia. Serbs adopted a Balkan version of the 'Blitz spirit' of wartime Londoners. They dug for victory, and grew their own food. Radovic said: 'Milosevic did not want anyone else to corrupt Serbia, so if one man was happy to have sanctions it was him. People think Milosevic was a mediocrity, but in this he was an absolute master, to achieve such things on such a level is unprecedented.'

Sanctions also significantly accelerated the impoverishment and criminalisation of Serbian society. A parallel economy sprang up, rooted in pre-existing Communist era smuggling and black market networks. Previously upstanding citizens found themselves engaged in dubious deals with criminals and smugglers. Obscure border villages suddenly turned into boom towns, made rich on the proceeds of contraband. Hyperinflation also brought strange benefits as the dinar became worthless. Gas, electricity and even telephone calls became free, in effect. State utilities could not keep up with hyperinflation. Nor could banks.

Milosevic's mortgage was now just the equivalent of a handful of Deutschmarks.

The collapse of the economy could be measured with figures and statistics. The wider impact of this was harder to quantify, but no less significant. Economies can be rebuilt, but the regime's destruction of the foundations of everyday life in modern European society – the value of money, of honest work, ethical behaviour, even common courtesy – had a profoundly corrosive effect on Serbian society, from which it has yet to recover.

The next stage was setting up pyramid schemes. These date back centuries. They are a financial juggling act, paying very high interest rates that are funded by new deposits. But the scheme only works as long as gullible new investors are willing to pay in their money to keep the scheme going. When that stops the scheme collapses. Pyramid schemes are symptomatic of a primitive capitalist economy: they also operated in Russia, Romania and Albania.

Hijacking a whole country's economy demanded substantial organisation. But not everyone was willing to take part in the state-sponsored plundering. As one of Yugoslavia's best-regarded bankers, Aca Singer, who had worked at Ljubljanska Banka in the 1970s, was asked to lend his expertise. He refused. 'They asked me to help them obtain money, first from the people. Milosevic knew there was a lot of money in people's houses, especially those who had families abroad. There was a lot of confusion and corruption at that time. But I refused to cooperate. Thank God I was not involved.'[9]

Milosevic and Vucic's front-man for the pyramid schemes was a former television importer called Jezdimir Vasiljevic, who was also known as Gazda Jezda, or Jezda the Boss. Although Vasiljevic had no experience in banking, he was given permission to set up a credit and savings co-operative, which opened in Milosevic's home town of Pozarevac in 1990. This evolved into the Jugoskandik bank, which then offered interest rates up to 10 per cent on short-term foreign currency deposits. With the open support of the state-controlled media, the scam initially worked very well. Large amounts were invested into Jugoskandik, from where funds were transferred to the National Bank, and the state granted Jezda a concession to import cigarettes and petrol. This was priceless. During the Milosevic regime, especially under sanctions, petrol and cigarette smuggling developed into complex industries worth hundreds of millions of dollars a year.

Much of the cigarette-smuggling business ran through the southern republic of Montenegro. It was there that Gazda Jezda organised one of the more bizarre events of the Yugoslav wars: a sanctions-busting chess match in autumn 1992 between the eccentric American player Bobby Fischer and the Russian Boris Spassky in the extremely luxurious seaside resort of Sveti Stefan, which gave the Milosevic regime a much-needed domestic PR boost. The Boss also financed the Serbian Socialist Party, helping pay for its election campaign in 1992.

In March 1993 Jugoskandik followed the inevitable path of every pyramid scheme and collapsed. Gazda Jezda fled abroad, first to Israel and then on to Ecuador. Over DM 100 million simply disappeared, the life savings of many gullible Serbs. There was little public reaction, mainly just a weary resignation.[10]

Milosevic's perverse monetary policies played on the naïveté of many Serbs. Over four decades of Communism − of life in a society where work, home, holidays and a decent income were provided by the state − had produced a certain passivity. If the state media said your money was safe in Jugoskandik, then surely it would be. Socialist Serbia was run by the same people as under Communism. Corruption was anyway institutionalised. Poverty-stricken Serbs found little support for their plight among officials of the ruling Socialist party, as they struggled to survive collapsing pyramid schemes and hyperinflation. Borisav Jovic declared in September 1993 that 'the cause of poverty in Serbia is the great quantity of money which citizens have at their disposal.'[11]

Soon after the launch of Jugoskandik a more ambitious version, known as the Dafiment Bank, was set up. It says a lot about the Milosevic regime that the woman selected to run Dafiment, Dafina Milanovic, had been imprisoned for financial malpractice. Like Gazda the Boss, Milanovic was trumpeted by the state-owned media as the answer to the financial problems of both Serbs and Serbia. She appeared on television waving fistfuls of Deutschmarks, and when Jugoskandik went bust she took television cameras into the vaults of her bank to prove it was still solvent. There also seem to have been links between Dafiment and the Serbian secret services. Mihalj Kertes, the key Milosevic loyalist and Serbian intelligence agent, started his career working with Milanovic's husband and knew the family well. 'He called Dafina "little sister" and she called him "little brother",' states the ICEFA report.

Milosevic used Dafiment as a kind of ad hoc treasure chest to boost state funds when they ran low. He tapped the bank for a 'loan' of

DM40 million to carry out repair work on the railway network. Not surprisingly, the French businessmen of whom Milosevic had spoken at dinner with the US ambassador Warren Zimmerman had not come through with their plans for a high-speed rail link through Serbia. Milanovic's connection to Milosevic did not prevent Dafiment from also going spectacularly bust, soon after Jugoskandik. Dafiment's loss was estimated at between DM500 and DM600 million.

Some time before it collapsed, Milanovic's husband and two of her children were killed in a car accident in Hungary. Milanovic herself, though, was prevented from leaving the country. In the dark world where high finance and politics met in the Milosevic regime, the tragic deaths of her relatives spawned a myriad of conspiracy theories. The Serbian leader was the driving force behind Gazda Jezda and Dafina Milanovic, said Dusan Mitevic. 'They were not real bankers, they were unsophisticated people. Milosevic gave the idea to them, he taught them how to do it, and then created the environment in which it could happen. Milosevic was an absolutely key person for them. Without him they would not have been able to work for three minutes. Milosevic and his regime were stealing the people's money.'[12]

Milosevic ran the economy – if it can be so called – the way he ran the country, by micromanaging. It appears that, sitting in the presidential office, Milosevic in effect worked out sums on the back of an envelope to keep the country running. It was under his instructions that the dinar was devalued in 1995 by over 200 per cent. When funds ran low, whether to pay pensions or paramilitaries, he called up his associates such as Dafina Milanovic. After the fall of his regime in October 2001, Mira Markovic, Marija Milosevic and Borislav Milosevic all had their Swiss bank accounts frozen, together with several other aides.[13] Yet it appears that apart from purchasing property at a bargain rate, Milosevic personally did not vastly enrich himself. No hoards of banknotes, jewels or valuables were found at the Milosevic residence. Nor did Milosevic acquire fleets of luxury cars or yachts. His currency was power, the only thing which he wanted to acquire.

However the political-business-criminal élite that ran Serbia was allowed to enrich itself, as long its members stayed loyal. 'Under Milosevic the links between crime and politics were very close. He practically constructed his regime on those links,' said Budimir Babovic, a former head of the Yugoslav Interpol bureau, who resigned in 1991. 'Well-known criminals such as Arkan became MPs, but that was not the worst problem. As all levels of society became criminalised, public morality was completely destroyed. We had apparent freedom of speech to criticise the government, but when you have no public morality to correct wrongdoings, this freedom is worth nothing.'[14]

Milosevic's allies took over key sectors of the economy. Directors of major companies became government ministers, and vice versa. 'If I am a minister you cannot compete with me, because I know which law will be adopted and how it will be drafted, so I can take every possible advantage from my position as a minister to help my business,' said Babovic. Or a Milosevic ally would take over a successful state-run company and set up his own private company, run from the same office. The accounts and the customers of the state-run company would be steadily redirected to the private company, until the state-run company went bankrupt.

Milosevic was a master at pushing boundaries to undreamt-of extremes, but then knowing when to stop. Which was the cue for Dragoslav Avramovic, a Serb who had spent twenty years working at the World Bank in Washington, D.C. Milosevic invited Avramovic back to Belgrade in December 1993 to sort out the mess. On 24 January 1994 Avramovic announced that hyperinflation would stop. The old worthless dinar was replaced by a new dinar, pegged at one to one with the Deutschmark. 'Super-grandpa', as Avramovic was dubbed, had done the trick. When Milosevic ordered the presses to stop printing money, the economy stabilised. Inflation did indeed stop for several months, although by the end of 1995 it had climbed back up to 119 per cent.

Meanwhile, Marko Milosevic was keeping some questionable company. Marko had left Belgrade and moved back to Pozarevac when he was sixteen. He visited the capital regularly, as he was technically enrolled at a Belgrade school, studying humanities as a private student.[15] While Slobodan nagged Marko to study hard, Mira was more easygoing. 'My mother is very soft with me. I am her only son.' But he did not want to live with his parents, he said in an interview in 1993. 'I have a different, dynamic temperament. I'm not used to living within a family.' It was much more fun to live in Pozarevac. 'Probably most people my age would do the same thing. I could not combine the nice things of life, like going out, with serious studies and being a very good student.' Marko lived at Mira's family home, but he was annoyed by the ever-present guards, and the policeman in front of the house. 'It degrades me. I think that my value is greater than this 180-year-old house.'

Milosevic at school in Pozarevac during the 1950s. For many young people these were times of great hope and idealism.

Milosevic and Ivan Stambolic (*left*), his closest friend and former mentor, shake hands in 1986. Just one year later Milosevic would oust him in a ruthless act of betrayal.

Milosevic addresses a crowd of over half a million at Gazimestan in Kosovo on 28 June 1989 to mark the six hundredth anniversary of Serbia's defeat by the Turks at the battle of Kosovo Polje. The event crowned Milosevic as the unrivalled leader of the Serbs.

Croatian President Franjo Tudjman together with Milosevic in Belgrade in April 1991. The two men's nations were descending into war, but they readily agreed on the need to divide Bosnia between them.

A Bosnian man mourns the loss of his wife and daughter at the Lion Cemetery, Sarajevo, June 1993.

Two boys rummage through the remains of the Bosnian state library, destroyed by Bosnian Serb artillery. Serb gunners deliberately targeted cultural and religious institutions as they laid siege to the city.

Marko Milosevic sits in his racing car before the start of the Belgrade summer race, August 1994.

The Milosevic family, *left to right*, Slobodan, Marija, Mira and Marko.

Mira greets Slobodan on his triumphant return from Dayton in winter 1995. The man previously condemned as a warmaker was now acclaimed by the United States and the West as a bastion of Balkan stability.

Belgrade, March 1999. A newspaper seller in downtown Belgrade hawks copies of the Yugoslav newspaper *Telegraf* a few hours before NATO airstrikes are expected to begin. The headline reads 'Stop the war'.

Kosovo Albanians survey the centre of Djakovica, days after Yugoslav army and interior ministry police troops destroyed the city in early summer 1999.

Reuters/Popperfoto

Serb paramilitary leader 'Arkan', Zeljko Raznatovic, fires a machine pistol in the eastern Serbian village of Zitoradje, birthplace of his bride, Serbian folk singer Ceca Velickovic.

Mark H. Milstein/ Northfoto

Serbs dance on the wing of a United States Air Force F-117A stealth fighter jet, March 1999. The plane was downed the previous night in Budjanovci, twenty-five miles west of the capital Belgrade.

The endgame begins. The opposition rally against election fraud outside the Yugoslav parliament in Belgrade on 5 October 2000.

The thin lines of riot police are eventually swept aside as the crowd storms in and takes over the parliament building.

Marko's was an unusual arrangement by Serbian standards, where family relations are close. In these crucial, formative years, Marko was, in effect, being brought up by bodyguards. So perhaps it was not surprising that at the age of eighteen his main interests were cars and guns. His favourite car was a Peugeot 205 GTI, which he nicknamed 'Cira'. 'That's the car of my life. I treat it as someone else treats a dog, a pet,' he said. 'Cira' was one of the first of many vehicles that Marko would crash. While driving in Belgrade he hit a tram. He sold 'Cira' soon after, as the sanctions were anyway making it impossible to obtain enough petrol.

Guns had been a long-standing enthusiasm. Back in 1986, ensconced with Marija at the Milosevic family home in Belgrade, Tahir Hasanovic had been alarmed to hear several gunshots coming from the neighbouring room, as Marko fired off a few rounds. His favourite weapon was a Ruger GP 100357 Magnum. Marko told his *Vreme* interviewer: 'You know how kids like guns. When a kid is watching a movie he likes guns. As time goes by, some people lose that feeling, others don't. I do have a passion for that.' Guns were a hobby, he said, and he did not need one for security. The security guards were for the Milosevic home, not him. 'I go everywhere without bodyguards. I'm not isolated, I never had any problems.' He worked part-time at a bar called Rolex.[16]

Around this time Marko was signed up for a car-racing team by Vlada Kovacevic, nicknamed 'Tref', who was one of the country's most famous racing drivers. Backed by Tref, Marko did well. On his twentieth birthday, 4 July 1994, driving a BMW M3, he won first place in his class at a race in Kraljevo, and held a party to celebrate at a café in Pozarevac. Mira recorded her pride in her diary. 'Early this morning, very early, with the first rays of the early morning sun, my son came into my room and announced with a radiant smile: "Mama, I'm twenty years and one day old now." I know, as did he, that he was being facetious. Incorrigibly cheerful, sometimes sad without reason, walking on clouds, wrapped up in his dreams of adventure, he will never grow up. He will be for ever young, like Peter Pan.'[17] Tref was sixteen years older than Marko but the two became close. Marko looked up to Tref, who ran a successful business empire, and Marko was a prize recruit for the Tref team, as his family name opened many doors, not all of which were legitimate. Tref supplied Mitsubishi four-wheel drive vehicles to the paramilitary leader, Arkan, for use in Croatia and Bosnia.[18] As Marko's eyes opened, he too began to realise the business opportunities that his name brought.

Marko's fascination with guns was not unique. Weapons had always been a part of the region's culture. For a Balkan man it was a matter of pride to be able to physically defend his family, and village. The Titoist doctrine of territorial defence – that Yugoslavia should be prepared for invasion from either East or West – was rooted in this tradition. The cult of the gun was given new impetus by the inevitable spillover from the wars in Croatia and Bosnia. Soaring crime, the atomisation of society and a general collapse in morality all combined to brutalise Serbia. When the state itself robs its citizens, 'ordinary' criminals no longer feel constrained by any notions of crime or punishment. Serbia descended into crime and anarchy, a world worthy of Mira Markovic's favourite author, Dostoevsky. Raskolnikov, the hero of *Crime and Punishment*, who killed an old woman to see if he had the courage to transgress moral law, would have felt quite at home in early 1990s Belgrade.

'Weekend Chetniks' drove across the border into Bosnia on Friday nights, spent the weekend fighting and looting, before returning to the factory or neighbourhood bar. Others fought turf battles in the mafia wars that broke out across the city. Weapons were easily available. A Kalashnikov could be had for £150 ($220), a pistol for much less. The gangsters' motto was '*Pistolj, Pajero and Plavusa*', *Pajero* was a four-wheel drive car, and *plavusa* a blonde. They listened to a raucous and patriotic music known as turbo-folk. The best known turbo-folk singer was Svetlana Velickovic, a.k.a. Ceca, who later married Arkan.

This was 'Weimar' Belgrade, dancing on the edge of total meltdown. The hero of the hour was a young gangster called Aleksandar Knezevic, known as 'Knele'. All over Belgrade youngsters adopted Knele's style. He wore a Gucci tracksuit top tucked into trousers, open to the neck to show off several thick gold chains with heavy medallions. Knele had been one of the hard men in the front line of the March 1991 street protests against Milosevic. In March 1992 he was shot dead in his room in Belgrade's five-star Hyatt hotel.

The Milosevic gangster generation respected nothing of the old rules. During the 1980s, the Yugoslav authorities had come to an arrangement with their gangsters: they turned them into criminal guestworkers. State security provided passports in exchange for 'favours', such as the elimination of troublesome émigré politicians. A former secret service official explained how it worked: 'They stole in western countries, and came back to Yugoslavia with plenty of money so they didn't need to steal anything here. There was peace here in Yugoslavia with this kind of system. They spent their foreign currency here, and when they had spent it, they went back to the west for another salary.'[19]

Many of the older criminals came home once war broke out in 1991. But they soon discovered that old territory divisions were irrelevant. What the new generation of criminals wanted, they took, by force. Violence exploded across the streets of the capital. The police looked on, unable to stem the tide of crime, which added to the growing sense of anarchy. A mafia leader known as 'the Duke' lamented: 'This young generation is unbelievable. We could divide everything, have enough for everyone, and all have money. But they are not interested.'[20]

The nihilistic *weltanschauung* of 'Weimar' Belgrade was captured in an extraordinary documentary of criminal life, called, aptly enough, *See You in the Obituaries*, made by the independent B-92 station. Mihailo Divac was twenty-eight, a member of a gang that operated in the concrete tower blocks of New Belgrade. Like many of those interviewed, he was open about his life of crime. 'I don't know a different kind of life. Everything is interesting for me, to live like this. It is a challenge, and I won't withdraw because of pussies. It is bullshit to say that you can leave this kind of life. Once you are in this kind of life, you never give up.'

Divac soon took his own place in the obituaries. He was shot dead in 1995, one of three gangsters interviewed to be killed before the programme was even broadcast.

Another man featured was Goran Vukovic, a legendary figure in the Belgrade underworld who had survived five attempts on his life, including one in which an anti-tank missile was fired at his car. Vukovic had plenty of enemies because he had killed a former head of the Belgrade mafia. 'There is a list of mafia leaders prepared by the state, of who should be killed,' he said. 'I know this list exists and my name is on it. I will defend myself. If they start to kill us we will kill them. There are enough weapons for a war, we will defend ourselves. I don't say we can, but we will try.'[22] Vukovic was shot twenty-five times leaving a Belgrade restaurant in December 1994.

For the Milosevic family, the increasing criminalisation of Serbian society was having unexpected side-effects. Marija also boasted to women's magazines about how she looked good with a pistol on her hip. But the increasing atmosphere of menace and intimidation was affecting Marija's business. At the end of 1995, she phoned her father about problems she was having at her Kosava radio station, where an advertiser was refusing to pay his airtime bill. Marija's boyfriend wanted to get heavy. Milosevic was not a fan of his, describing him as 'a scoundrel and a nouveau riche'.

Marija says: 'Hi there, there is this guy threatening Kosava, says he will buy us all, that we can all go to hell, that he has the court, the police and the SPS [Socialist Party] and that he will fuck us all. Says he [the advertiser] will buy us all. I mean he might have a lot of money, he came from Bosnia, a crook. Says we can suck his dick because he's got everything.'

Milosevic gave his daughter some financial advice but was not very supportive. 'Next time don't play commercials for someone who hasn't paid up front. Huge debts are a problem of every company in Yugoslavia. OK let's not talk further, I can tell you are very busy.' He advised his daughter to file a lawsuit. 'OK Marija, don't spread this further, it might end up looking like someone is threatening to kill us, for Christ's sake. He won't pay? Big deal. Sue him. Everything's OK.'[23]

Milosevic sounded rattled. Earlier that year a hand grenade had exploded not far from the Serbian presidency building. The vacuum left by his destruction of state institutions was being filled by forces over which he had no control. During the next few years some of the Milosevic family's closest associates would be picked off, one by one, in professional assassinations.

18

WEATHERING OPERATION STORM

NATO Bombs the Bosnian Serbs

1994–5

Hrvoje, what is this? What did we waste all these hours for? You shouldn't have done this. The shelling has to stop.

Slobodan Milosevic on the telephone to President Tudjman's secret envoy Hrvoje Sarinic in May 1995, as Croat forces attack Serb-held Krajina.[1]

After a few visits to Belgrade, Hrvoje Sarinic was getting the measure of Slobodan Milosevic. 'When you spend thirty-eight hours with someone tête-à-tête, you start to know the person, whatever his mode of presenting things is. You know what he is hiding.'[2] The two men fenced verbally, but Milosevic just ducked and weaved. Sarinic challenged Milosevic: 'I said to him once, "President Milosevic, you have said wherever a Serb is, that is Serbia." He said, "I never stated that, who told you that?" But it was generally known that it was his policy.'

So widespread was the belief that this was Milosevic's policy, it spawned this mordant joke: in a last-ditch attempt to save the old federal Yugoslavia, a team of astronauts is sent to the moon: a Bosnian Muslim, a Croat and two Serbs. When the rocket lands, the astronauts get out and immediately start squabbling over which republic's flag to raise. The Croat says: 'Look at all the mountains and rocks, it's just like Croatia.' The Bosnian says: 'No, no, look at us, a Muslim, a Croat and Serbs all together, it's just like Bosnia.' Then one Serb takes out a gun and shoots the other. He says: 'A Serb has died here. This is Serbia.'

Beneath the word games, Milosevic's objectives were far more realistic. At this time the Serbian leader had two main objectives: in the long term, to get sanctions lifted, and in the short term to acquire as much oil as possible. Sarinic noted how cold it was in Belgrade, and the lines of bedraggled vendors hawking bottles of petrol or logs for firewood. When he accused Milosevic of taking the Serbs back to the Middle Ages, he merely said, 'I know'.[3]

Milosevic saw that sanctions were substantially eroding his support. Factories were closing for lack of oil. The parlous state of the economy, a massive increase in crime and poverty, and hundreds of thousands of refugees from Bosnia and Croatia were threatening Serbia's social stability. And while Milosevic outmanoeuvred the international community on a day-to-day basis, he knew that to stay in power some kind of settlement would have to be reached eventually.

Milosevic was thinking of recognising Croatia and normalising relations, as a step to easing Serbia's economic and diplomatic isolation. He was in any case losing patience with the Krajina Serb leadership. The Napoleonic policeman Milan Martic and the baby-faced dentist Milan Babic refused to consider the proposals put forward by international mediators that would offer some kind of autonomy, within the borders of Croatia. Martic and Babic insisted on 'independence' for their quasi-state. The Krajina Serbs were becoming a financial millstone, and an obstacle to Milosevic's efforts to present himself as a peacemaker.

In addition, the Serbs in Knin were allying themselves not with Belgrade but with Karadzic's increasingly hard-line Bosnian Serbs in their mountain stronghold of Pale. Karadzic was also refusing to follow orders. Milosevic had not one but two monsters on his hands, who were ganging up on their Frankensteinean creator. Meanwhile the military intelligence reports landing on Milosevic's desk reported that the Croatian army had become a powerful military force, while the creaking JNA was demoralised. The UN arms embargo had done nothing to prevent Croatia acquiring a plentiful supply of weapons, while western powers turned a blind eye. The question was, what should he do about it?

Milosevic and Tudjman had temporarily settled the Croatian question in January 1992 by agreeing to the Vance plan, named after Cyrus Vance, the American mediator appointed by the UN. By the end of 1991 rebel Serbs held over a quarter of Croatia. The fighting and the front lines had more or less stabilised. At that time Milosevic knew that the war in Croatia was deeply unpopular at home. The JNA had been wracked by desertions, and many officers were unhappy about the Serbianisation of the once multi-national institution. Milosevic understood that for now at least, it was time to call a halt.

The Vance plan institutionalised Serb gains in Croatia. The Serb-occupied areas were designated UNPAS, UN Protected Areas, divided into sectors: north, south, east and west. Sectors North, South and West were roughly contiguous, a crescent of occupied territory nudging the coast near the Adriatic port city of Zadar, and stretching along the Bosnian border. Sector East was separate: an area around Vukovar overlooking the Danube, which was the border with Serbia. The Vance plan called for the JNA and the paramilitaries to withdraw, a ceasefire to be implemented, and the return of refugees. It was a clear victory for Milosevic. The government of the Republic of Serb Krajina remained in place. The paramilitaries were not disarmed, and there was no realistic right of return for Croatian refugees who wanted to go home. Milosevic had finessed the UN into enforcing the division of the country, and ensuring that the Serb rebels kept control of the territories they had seized. There were no open transport or communication links between the UNPAS and the rest of Croatia. UN troops sat at heavily guarded checkpoints, controlling all access into the UNPAS. Crucially, the UN would not actually administer the areas, merely monitor their administration.

The international community presented this as a diplomatic triumph. Perhaps it was, considering the diplomats' response to the situation so far. Admittedly, on 12 November 1991 the European Community had resolutely 'condemned the further escalation of attacks on Vukovar, Dubrovnik and other towns in Croatia', but even the most resolute condemnation was poor defence against a barrage of 155 mm artillery shells. In Sector East Arkan's Tigers remained in place, murdering those who questioned their actions.[4] The JNA did withdraw, which anyway suited Milosevic as he had other plans for the Yugoslav troops, in Bosnia.

Milosevic – and Tudjman – understood the significance of the Vance plan. There was no political will in the international community to enforce a military solution to the Yugoslav conflict. The way Milosevic saw it, Belgrade could take as much territory as it wanted, stop fighting when it needed, and then sit down at the negotiating table and present itself as a peacemaker. At which point a grateful international community, spared the problem of taking difficult decisions, would send in UN troops to consolidate the Serbs' gains. Milosevic was correct.

UN aid-workers would engage in relief work for refugees, and UN troops would help enforce an already agreed peace, but they would never impose one by force of arms. Tudjman realised that the Vance plan in effect gave him the green light to go ahead with his planned annexation of southern Bosnia. If Milosevic could get away with it in Croatia, then why shouldn't he in Herzegovina?

By the end of 1994 it was clear that the UNPAS were not a viable long-term solution. Sarinic's secret missions to Milosevic were increasingly focused on one question: how would he react if Croatia attacked the rebel Serbs? Everything hinged on this, said Sarinic. 'We wanted to know would Milosevic be involved, would he defend his Serbs, because he pushed them to revolution. We knew the ratio of forces, and if the Serbian army intervened it would be a different story.'

The diplomatic dance began. First, Milosevic asked Sarinic for support in lifting the economic blockade. Maybe, said Sarinic, for a price: Belgrade should recognise Croatia, within its internationally recognised borders. Sarinic pushed harder. If not, Croatia would attack Knin, the headquarters of the rebel Serbs, and anyway take back its territories by force. Milosevic tried to stall. But he specifically warned Sarinic off attacking eastern Slavonia, known as Sector East, which was under the control of Russian UN troops who made no secret of their sympathy for their Orthodox brothers, the Serbs.

Sector East was notoriously corrupt. It was the centre of a flourishing black market in smuggled petrol. Sarinic recalled: 'Milosevic told me not to touch eastern Slavonia, because it was on the border with Serbia. I told him, "Be careful, Mr President, because if the battle starts for eastern Slavonia, then war could come to Serbia, which did not happen before." I saw that Milosevic's situation was not as easy and comfortable as it had been two or three years before. I told him that time was not working in his favour any more.' When Sarinic quipped that Milosevic would have to put the SANU Memorandum – that many saw as the blueprint for Greater Serbia – in a drawer, Milosevic replied, 'Well everyone thinks about better times.' Sarinic reported all this back to Tudjman. His own assessment was that Milosevic would not step in to save the Krajina Serbs. The Croat military stepped up its preparations to attack.

Milosevic enjoyed his meetings with Sarinic. One took place at Milosevic's remote mountain holiday home near the Romanian border. Sarinic travelled there by helicopter with Thorvald Stoltenberg, a former

Norwegian foreign minister who was now the UN's special envoy to Yugoslavia. Together with his European Community counterpart, Lord Owen, Stoltenberg co-chaired the International Conference on the Former Yugoslavia (ICFY), which had been founded after the London conference, where Milan Panic had told Milosevic to 'shut up'.

The flight took an hour and a half. As the helicopter landed Milosevic came forward to greet his visitors. He was accompanied by a large dog, recalled Sarinic. 'He was very polite and gentlemanly. Milosevic said the dog used to be wild, but now he fed him, so the dog was his dog.' Ushered inside, Sarinic and Stoltenberg were directed to a reception room to wait for Milosevic. The UN's envoy was left alone to kick his heels while Milosevic consulted with Sarinic. 'Stoltenberg wanted to come as well, and after the meeting he was very curious as to what we had discussed,' Sarinic recalled.

Yet at times it appeared that Milosevic's grip was slipping. His consumption of pear brandy was rising. He usually took no notes of what was agreed, or said. He wanted to go on holiday. In one conversation with Sarinic, in January 1995, he seemed to try and convince himself that the wars were not his fault. Milosevic's words provide a rare glimpse into his inner thoughts, and the mass of contradictions therein. There is even a hint that he felt guilty. 'When all this was happening I was on vacation in Dubrovnik and I realised straight away what this was all about. I can't wait for all this to end so I can go to Dubrovnik again. I will do everything I can from my side to make this happen this year already. Some idiots were saying Dubrovnik was also a Serbian town. Serbia has no territorial pretensions, if you insist, not even towards Baranja.'[5]

Mira too was also a great fan of the jewel of the Adriatic. It was Dubrovnik which had 'stolen her heart for ever', she had written, reminiscing about a holiday the family had taken there in 1984, driving from Belgrade to the coast in their small Volkswagen. 'Towards evening, down below the highway, the lights of Dubrovnik came into view. Dubrovnik – sparkling, boisterous, all in flowers.'[6] Mira had written a poem on her seventeenth birthday for the city, and there seen *Hamlet* for the first time. Battered by a rain of JNA shell and mortar fire during the Croatian war of independence, it would be a long time before Dubrovnik welcomed the Milosevics.

Milosevic and Tudjman communicated through shells and infantry attacks, as well as envoys. In January 1993 thousands of Croat troops

attacked and captured the Serb-held area around the Croatian port of
Zadar, a strip of land that allowed the rebel Serbs to virtually cut Croatia
in two. The Croat offensive was condemned by the UN Security
Council. Two French UN peacekeepers were killed. None of which
stopped the Croat tanks from rolling across the UN lines. Tudjman
had learnt the lesson taught so well by Milosevic. The international
community had neither the will nor the ability to stop the warring
sides using force. Milosevic's message to Tudjman was unspoken but
no less clear for it. Belgrade did nothing.

Tudjman's next probe was far messier. In September Croat forces
launched an attack on rebel Serbs occupying an area known as the
'Medak pocket', and captured several villages. At least twenty-nine Serb
civilians were murdered by Croat troops, and five wounded or captured
Serb troops were executed. Many of the victims were elderly, women
and some were also handicapped. The operation was commanded by
Major General Rahim Ademi, a Kosovo Albanian who had graduated
from the JNA military academy and eventually joined the Croatian
army. Ademi was later indicted by the International Criminal Tribunal
for the former Yugoslavia at the Hague (ICTY). The attack on the
Medak pocket caused outrage, and Croatia withdrew under UN orders,
to allow the return of UN peacekeepers.

These events, and the revelations about the Bosnian Croat concentration camps, caused a substantial shift in world and diplomatic opinion.
Now Croatia was seen as an aggressor, and was threatened with sanctions.
That prospect, and growing domestic unease about Tudjman's policies,
caused a sea-change in Croatian public opinion that he could not ignore.

Enter the United States. Unlike George Bush's administration, President
Clinton's believed that the US did have a 'dog in this fight', even if
only to win a moral victory. The US supported a policy of 'Lift and
Strike', meaning lift the arms embargo against Bosnia and strike the
Bosnian Serbs. They delivered a clear message to Tudjman: stop the
war in Bosnia, close the concentration camps and forget about annexing
Herceg-Bosna. Otherwise Croatia would face international isolation. It
worked.

American diplomats saw that Tudjman was just as hypocritical as
Milosevic. Milosevic demanded self-determination for the Krajina Serbs
within Croatia's borders, but denied the same for the Kosovo Albanians
within Serbia's borders. Tudjman demanded that the borders of Croatia

be sacrosanct, and refused to consider some form of self-determination for the Serbs in Krajina. He backed the Croats of Herzegovina, financing their para-state and arming their militia, and called for the dismemberment of Bosnia. But Tudjman saw himself as a great Croatian leader, who would take his place in history. And Croatia, he boasted, was not an eastern Balkan state, with all that implied, but a modern western democracy. His version of democracy was pretty much what could be expected from a former general in a Communist army turned nationalist dissident. Still he understood that for his state to survive, it needed good relations with the West, especially with the United States, which was positioning itself as a Balkan power broker, to the annoyance of Europe.

In March 1994, Croatia agreed to form a Bosnian-Croat federation in the parts of Bosnia not under Serb control. The Croat statelet of Herzeg-Bosna was partially dismantled. The Bosnian Croat army once again joined forces with the Muslim-led Bosnian government army. The two sides had been allies, enemies, and now they were allies again. Too much blood had been spilt for it to be anything but a grudging and bitter alliance, but it held. Tudjman made it clear to the US there was a price for giving up his ambitions in Bosnia. He wanted a clear run to recapture the one-third of Croatia that had been occupied by the rebel Serbs in Krajina. He got it.

Watching the US court Tudjman, Milosevic understood that everything had changed, with serious implications. First, the fighting between Bosnian Croats and Muslims had stopped. The old principle of 'divide and rule' no longer applied. Bosnian Serbs would not be able to rent out their tanks for a day to either side, or accept commissions to fire their artillery to order. The United States had boldly gone where Europe had feared to tread.

European diplomacy had always been a stitched-together compromise. In Britain the Foreign Office was resolutely opposed to taking military action against Serbia. Its argument was that it would endanger the substantial number of British troops on the ground, to which cynics responded that the British UN troops – whose officers in fact took a vigorous approach to peace-keeping that often dismayed the Foreign Office grandees – had been deployed for that very reason. The Germans took a tougher line, but were hampered by memories of the Nazi era. The French, like the Greeks, were seen as being traditionally pro-Serb. All of this had provided Milosevic with much room for mischief and manoeuvre.

Courted by a procession of world statesmen and diplomats, Milosevic positively bloomed under the world's spotlight. There was a strong argument that European diplomats, such as Lord Owen, somehow legitimised his regime. As the European envoy of the International Conference on Former Yugoslavia, Owen was an influential figure in Balkan diplomacy, who seemed to spend vast amounts of time sitting on Milosevic's sofa nodding sagely. At one meeting in Serbia Owen had delivered a clear message to Sarinic, Tudjman's envoy recalled. 'I remember very well, it remains with me to this day. Stoltenberg and Owen were there with their teams. We discussed how to solve the problem of Krajina and occupied Croatia. Owen told me, "Don't think you are going to get on the green table what you lost on the battlefield." You can imagine such a statement from an important representative of the international community, it encouraged Milosevic.'[7]

Neither Owen nor Milosevic lacked self-belief. The good lord had, as one of his domestic critics pointed out, 'Balkanised' a few political parties himself. Sarinic had once asked Milosevic if it was true that Lord Owen had written the introduction to Mira's book, which had recently been published in Russia. Milosevic said: 'Owen is our good friend, Mira's and mine, but he did not write the introduction, although he did make some suggestions. The Russian edition alone brought Mira 340,000 Deutschmarks.' Sarinic replied: 'You married well.' Milosevic could only agree: 'I can't complain.'[8]

Tibor Varady, Yugoslav Minister of Justice in the short-lived pro-western government of Milan Panic, recalled: 'For many years we implored western leaders not to negotiate with Milosevic. In order to create the impression that legality matters, I said why don't you negotiate with the man who is entitled to speak, the Yugoslav prime minister, Radoje Kontic. He would have called Milosevic every five minutes on the telephone, but it would have been something.'[9] Varady believes that negotiating with Milosevic became a kind of badge of pride for many politicians. 'I am not entitled to guess their motives, but for western diplomats speaking with Milosevic was some kind of achievement. It was very important for their careers, to have negotiated with this mighty, ruthless ruler. To say, "I was there with Kontic", well, who on earth is Kontic? But Milosevic, that was more manly as well. Diplomats are also human.'

Varady recalled how in August 1992, he and Milan Panic had dined with Lord Owen, after the envoy had lunched with Milosevic. 'Owen said, much to my surprise, "Now it is clear that Milosevic really wants peace." That is what he came up with after his lunch with Milosevic. I could not be rude, so I told him he was not the first person to come to this conclusion.'[10]

Mira was certainly taken with Lord Owen when she and Milosevic had a double-date for lunch with Lord Owen and his wife Debbie in March 1994. 'He left an impression of a civilised and very cultured person, close to me in many things regarding the wars in Yugoslavia itself, and in general questions of civilisation. It was an easy conversation. He was absolutely close to my stance.'[11] But Mira was piqued to discover Lord Owen's recollection of their lunch in his book *Balkan Odyssey*. 'I was astonished to see what he wrote, that I in our conversation had been against the market economy, when I was not. Secondly, we did not speak about that. He is a doctor and he does not know the first thing about economics.'[12]

Lord Owen, and arguably the whole panoply of European diplomacy, were anyway about to become irrelevant. The US government had engineered the Croat-Muslim Federation agreement. Now it was going to re-organise its armies. The future of the former Yugoslavia would be decided on the battlefield, not at the dining tables of diplomats. Like its post-Communist neighbours, Croatia wanted to join Partnership for Peace, the entry-salon for eventual NATO membership. All PfP members were required to bring their Warsaw Pact era forces up to NATO standards. This was a massive undertaking, requiring extensive re-training in current western military techniques, familiarisation with NATO weapons and a total re-organisation of the defence ministry.

This called for US military assistance, much of it channelled through private contractors. US military aid was almost certainly Croatia's reward for forming the Croat-Bosnian Federation in April that year. There were reports that Croatia also agreed to the building of a CIA base on the island of Krk to operate unmanned 'Predator' drones, and supported air-drops of weapons to the Bosnian army.[13]

The balance of power in the Balkans was about to change for good. At the beginning of May 1995 Operation Flash was launched. Over three thousand Croatian troops, backed by twenty tanks, recaptured Serb-occupied Sector West in less than two days. The Bosnian Serb leader, Radovan Karadzic, did nothing to help his brothers in arms. Nor did Belgrade. Analysts noted that Operation Flash was based on current western military doctrine, far in advance of the lumbering Soviet-era tactics used by the JNA. The Croatian armour and infantry were well co-ordinated, aided by good use of modern communication techniques and equipment.[14]

Although Milosevic had indicated that he would not deploy the JNA to aid the Krajina Serbs, he was still enraged when the attack started. He immediately called Hrvoje Sarinic demanding a ceasefire. When Sarinic asked him to sack the Krajina Serb leader, Milan Martic, Milosevic responded furiously, if disingenuously: 'How can I sack him. I never appointed him there, so I can't sack him,' he shouted, before slamming down the telephone. But, crucially, the JNA troops stayed in their barracks. The rebel Serbs fired Orkan rockets fitted with cluster bombs into downtown Zagreb, killing eleven civilians, a cowardly act that made no difference to the military outcome, for which Milan Martic was indicted by the Hague Tribunal for war crimes.

Faced with the capture of Sector West, the international community proposed a plan known as Z4. Considering the future events of that summer of 1995, Z4 offered unimaginable benefits to the rebel Serbs, including self-determination, their own flag, police, parliament and a president. Milosevic supported the plan, as did Tudjman although with reservations. In a decision of quite remarkable stupidity, the Krajina Serb leaders, Milan Martic and Milan Babic, rejected Z4 outright. Instead they despatched troops to join the Bosnian Serb army's attack on the Bosnian-government-held city of Bihac.

Bihac, cut off by besieging Serbs, had been declared a UN safe area, like Srebrenica. When Srebrenica fell in July, the Bosnian Serb military leader, General Ratko Mladic, launched an attack on Bihac. Unlike Srebrenica, Bihac had been fairly quiet for years, thanks to the region's massive black market from which all three sides profited. So quiet, in fact, that the Bosnian Serb army sold considerable amounts of weapons to their supposed enemies, believing they would never be used. The Bosnian Serbs were wrong. The Croat and Bosnian Croat army attacked the besieging Serbs from behind, while the Bosnian Croat and government forces inside Bihac broke out. The Serbs were caught in the middle. 'Welcome to Bihac,' said the Bosnian army commander Atif Dedakovic, when the Croat forces broke through. 'We have been waiting for you.'[15]

The liberation of Bihac marked the end of the Republic of Serb Krajina. At dawn on 4 August, Operation Storm commenced. With

200,000 troops, the Croat forces outnumbered the Krajina Serb army five to one as it advanced on the rebel stronghold of Knin. Many Serb soldiers, and their political leaders, simply fled. Few were willing to risk their lives for a 'republic' that had offered almost nothing to its citizens except the chance to live under Serb rule. The economy barely functioned, there was little work and no investment.

Ethnic cleansing turned out to be a poor foundation for a state. The Republic of Serb Krajina collapsed overnight. By 10.00 a.m. on 5 August, the Croatian flag was flying over Knin castle. Between 150,000 and 200,000 Serbs ran from the Croat onslaught, often escaping only with what they could carry by hand, leaving meals half-eaten on the table and a trail of dropped possessions that littered the roads into Bosnia. It was the end of a historic European community that had stretched back centuries. As Hrvoje Sarinic had predicted, Milosevic did nothing to aid the rebel Serb statelet he had helped found.

How effective was US military assistance? Operation Storm was a brutal exercise in ethnic cleansing. Civilians and civilian buildings were shelled. But in the grim arithmetic of Balkan warfare, the level of atrocity was comparatively low compared to, for example, the Serb assault on eastern Bosnia. The aim seemed to be to expel the Serbs and prevent their return, rather than wholesale slaughter. None the less, at least 150 Serb civilians, many of them elderly, were executed. And if Serbs did want to return there was nowhere to go. For weeks afterwards Croat troops burnt down houses and farm buildings owned by Serbs, according to the war crimes indictment of the man in charge of Operation Storm, Major-General Ante Gotovina. Graham Blewitt, deputy prosecutor at the ICTY, said: 'Operation Storm is not being indicted, only the crimes committed within it. We have seen no evidence of indictment to war crimes from the US.'

The Krajina refugees poured into Belgrade on tractors, and on foot. Whole families were jammed into tiny cars. At best they found a grudging reception from mother Serbia: most Serbs were too wrapped in their own problems of trying to put food on the table to care about their brothers from the rocky hinterlands of Krajina. Many felt that the refugees from Krajina – and the increasing numbers from Bosnia – should have stayed and fought. Writing in *Duga* magazine Mira Markovic noted:

The patriots from Bosnia and Krajina living in Belgrade are not satisfied with the results of the war, and they express their dissatisfaction

aggressively. They are angry with the poor in Bosnia's and Krajina's rugged hills for not being more efficient . . . It simply does not occur to them that they must take part themselves in the war which they have launched with so much propaganda.[16]

Few had been more responsible for war propaganda than Milosevic's tame journalists, yet in Belgrade there was no media campaign demanding the defence of the Krajina. Belgrade Television showed a circus festival in Monte Carlo. *Politika* newspaper reported the next day: 'Serbs Withdraw: Military Command Moved to Reserve Positions.' Milosevic's abandonment of the Krajina was cynical, but also supremely realistic. By 1995 few young Serb men wanted to risk their lives for the opportunity to shell Croatia's Adriatic coast.

At the same time, there was no longer any dispute about Croatia's status as a former Yugoslav republic. If Serbia defended the Krajina Serbs it would be declaring war on an internationally recognised sovereign state. An all-out war with Croatia would certainly have triggered a furious diplomatic backlash. Milosevic wanted sanctions lifted, not tightened. He also understood that his regime was highly unlikely to survive a new conflict. And, ultimately, the Serbs in Krajina did not matter that much. As Borisav Jovic had told the Croatian politician Stipe Mesic back in 1990: 'We are not interested in the Serbs in Croatia. They are your citizens, you can do what you like with them, you can impale them for all we care. We are exclusively interested in Bosnia-Herzegovina, which was, and will be, Serbian.'[17]

More than this, Milosevic understood the importance of the entrance of the United States, both in diplomatical terms – with the Washington agreement on the Croat-Muslim Federation – and in military terms. For not just in Belgrade, but also in Washington, D.C., realpolitik triumphed over morality. The biggest single act yet of ethnic cleansing in Yugoslavia[18] had been carried out by an army trained – to whatever extent – by US military advisers and almost certainly aided by US intelligence. 'There is a lot of proof that the Americans cooperated with Croatia. The CIA was here all the time with General Gotovina, they knew everything, they sent special equipment for controlling intelligence and eavesdropping,' said Hrvoje Sarinic.

On the ground, the balance of power had been altered for good. It was time for Milosevic to forge his own Pax Americana.

AMERICA TO THE RESCUE

Sarajevo Relieved, Eventually

Summer 1995

Our army is very, very responsible. People, civilians as well as UN personnel, are completely safe and secure.

Radovan Karadzic, Bosnian Serb leader.[1]

Outgunned and outnumbered by the besieging Bosnian Serbs, the inhabitants of Sarajevo hit back with humour. One of the favourite themes of Sarajevo radio's Surrealist Hit Parade show was the increasing disobedience of the Bosnian Serb leader Radovan Karadzic. Not only was the wild-haired psychiatrist-poet one of the most accomplished liars in the Balkans, but he was also disobeying Milosevic's orders. He and the Bosnian Serb leaders repeatedly refused to sign up for peace plans that would end sanctions against Serbia. In a bedtime-story voice, the Hit Parade presenter narrates a very Balkan children's tale: 'Far, far away, in a tiny land, in a tiny village, in a tiny workshop, Slobetto the Toymaker has carved a disobedient puppet named Radovanocchio.' But Radovanocchio keeps getting his maker into trouble, and simply won't do what he is told. 'I'm going to make an orthopaedic brace out of you!' yells Slobetto at his wayward creation.[2]

Milosevic couldn't do that. But he could, and did, stand by as the Croats destroyed the rebel Serb statelet in Knin. A side benefit of which was the weakening of Radovan Karadzic. In Knin and Pale, the leaders of the rebel Serb statelets had succumbed to delusions of grandeur, believing they could survive without Belgrade's support. Their armies engaged in joint operations together, and their politicians preferred to consult each other rather than Milosevic. They issued grand communiqués about uniting their armies under one joint command, but forgot who supplied the bullets and guns to fire them: Belgrade.

Even by Balkan standards, Milosevic's tactic of using an enemy army to bring uppity satrapies under control was a masterstroke. His plan was to boost an alternative, supposedly 'moderate' (by Bosnian Serb standards) leadership, based in the northern city of Banja Luka, which he could use to break Karadzic's power base in the town of Pale, just outside Sarajevo. Milosevic told Sarinic: 'The Serbs cannot get more than fifty per cent of Bosnia, and Sarajevo cannot be a Serb city. A majority in the Pale parliament comes from the Banja Luka region and it is through them that I will topple Karadzic, but in return I will have to strengthen this part territorially.'[3]

Milosevic realised that he had to take control of Pale after the Bosnian Serbs had rejected first the Vance-Owen peace plan, and then its main successor, known as the Contact Group plan. The 1993 plan devised by Cyrus Vance and Lord Owen claimed to support the idea that Bosnia should be a single state, and refugees would have the right to return. Bizarrely, this was to be achieved through dividing the country into ten semi-autonomous provinces, each of which would be 'predominantly' either Serb, Croat or Muslim. There would be a weak central government with no army, and no means of enforcing the right of return for refugees. Which are just a few of the reasons why Milosevic and Tudjman welcomed the Vance-Owen plan. Ironically, the maps delineating the cantons triggered a fresh outbreak of fighting in central Bosnia, as the Bosnian Croats attempted to grab the lands marked as Croat cantons. The Bosnian Croats joked that the initials of their army, HVO, now stood for 'Hvala Vance Owen', meaning 'Thank you, Vance Owen'.

The plan was to be considered by the Bosnian Serb assembly. To make sure they got the message, Milosevic summoned Montenegro's leader, Momir Bulatovic, and the president of Serbia, Dobrica Cosic, to help draft a letter to the Bosnian Serbs. Among its many haughty paragraphs was one which said:

Now is not the time for us to compete in patriotism. It is the right time for a courageous, considered and far-reaching decision. You have no right to expose ten million citizens of Yugoslavia to danger and international sanctions merely because of the remaining open issues which are of far less importance than the results achieved so far.[4]

The Yugoslav foreign minister, Vladislav Jovanovic, was woken up and despatched by helicopter to read the letter out to the Bosnian Serb assembly. He was not welcome. Biljana Plavsic, the hard-line vice-president, responded: 'Who is this Milosevic, this Bulatovic, this Cosic? Did this nation elect them? No it did not.'[5] The Bosnian Serbs voted against the Vance-Owen plan.

Milosevic then attempted to exploit Greece's traditional pro-Serb sympathies. The Greek prime minister, Constantin Mitsotakis, hosted a two-day summit in Athens at the beginning of May to discuss Vance-Owen. There, under intense pressure from Milosevic and the international community, Karadzic signed the plan, although he had no intention of sticking to it. The whole circus then moved from Athens to Pale, where Milosevic planned to speak to the Bosnian Serb assembly and persuade them to ratify Karadzic's decision. But Karadzic had not survived years at the top of the Bosnian Serb leadership without knowing a few tricks himself. Like Milosevic, he used the media to get his message across. Risto Djogo, the newsreader on Pale Television, pretended to commit suicide on television by shooting himself in the head. He announced: 'The Serbs of Bosnia are not about to commit suicide.'[6]

When Milosevic arrived, Biljana Plavsic refused to shake his hand. Milosevic, Mitsotakis and Cosic all called for the Bosnian Serbs to accept the plan. Karadzic prevaricated, and played his trump card, General Mladic, who produced two maps, one showing current Serb-controlled territory, and the other illustrating how much would have to be given up. This time the assembly voted 51–2 against acceptance, with twelve abstentions. Biljana Plavsic earned Milosevic's eternal loathing for her acute observation: 'He was not normal. This could be seen on his face and on his hands . . . He did not know how to behave himself in parliament, because he never attended parliamentary sessions.'[7] The Pale performance was one of the worst setbacks of Milosevic's career. He was tired, angry, and perhaps uncomprehending. Even worse, Milosevic's defeat had been observed by diplomats, foreign ministers and the world's media.

He prepared a slow revenge. Over the next few months Radovan Karadzic was no longer lauded by the pliant Belgrade media as a national hero. Instead there were repeated allusions to black marketeering and war-profiteering, and the Serb statelets in Bosnia and Croatia were portrayed as obstacles to peace. On 7 June 1994 the Yugoslav President, Zoran Lilic, announced in an interview: 'Ten million citizens of

Yugoslavia cannot be held hostage to any leader who came from the territory of Yugoslavia, neither Republika Srpska, nor Republika Srpska Krajina.'[8] The warning to the Serb leaderships in Knin and Pale could not have been clearer.

The Contact Group, whose plan followed Vance-Owen, was composed of representatives from Britain, France, Russia, Germany and the United States. Their plan split Bosnia into two: 51 per cent for the Croat–Muslim federation, and 49 per cent for the Serbs. This was fine for Milosevic, for whom the only thing that mattered was the lifting of the sanctions. The Sarajevo government agreed grudgingly, knowing that they would be blamed for prolonging the war if they refused, and gambling that it didn't really matter because the Bosnian Serbs would reject the plan. Which they did, for the third time, on the night of 3 August 1994.

Milosevic immediately blockaded the border between Yugoslavia and Bosnia. Even telephone lines were cut off. Biljana Plavsic spoke for many when she said: 'No one would have expected such a dagger in the back.'[9] Milosevic's media machine went into overdrive. Even by Milosevic-era standards, Yugoslav President Zoran Lilic's attack on Pale was a tour de force. 'How many times have they promised that they would not shell Sarajevo, and perpetuate the agony of civilians in this city? How many times have they promised to arrest the bands and paramilitary units which are terrorising civilians and besmirching the honour of the Serbs?'[10] Lilic, of course, did not mention who had supplied the shells landing on Sarajevo and armed the paramilitary units now revealed to be 'terrorising civilians and besmirching the honour of the Serbs'.[11]

A terrible few days in July 1995 changed everything. On 11 July General Mladic announced that he would give Srebrenica as a 'present to the Serb nation'. The town had been designated by the UN as a 'Safe Area'[12] since French UN General Philippe Morillon had barged his way through the Serb lines in March 1993, and raised the blue UN flag, declaring Srebrenica to be under UN protection. His brave, quixotic gesture sent UN diplomats in New York into fits of anguish as they struggled to find a formula that would prevent any genuine commitment to defend the enclaves. The proposal by the non-aligned countries that Srebrenica be declared a 'Safe Haven' – obliging the UN to defend the town – was rejected after opposition from Britain, France and Russia.

Instead the term 'Safe Area' was agreed on, meaning that none of the warring parties should operate militarily within the enclaves. But while the Bosnian government troops inside Srebrenica surrendered many of their weapons, the Bosnian Serbs did not. There was neither the international will, nor the necessary UN mandate, to ensure that the enclaves were secure from attack. The 'Safe Areas' were some of the most dangerous places in the world.

Srebrenica was supervised by 110 lightly-armed Dutch peacekeepers, known as 'Dutchbat', who offered no resistance when General Mladic stormed in. Demands for air-strikes were somehow lost or delayed in the UN bureaucracy. Instead the Dutch troops – indeed the whole world – stood by and watched as the Bosnian Serbs separated men from women and children, and took the men off to their deaths. Srebrenica was indeed a bloody gift. Over the next few days, the fields and woods around the city became the site of the biggest single atrocity of the Bosnian war as Mladic's men killed more than 7,000 Muslim men and boys. Many died as they tried to trek through to Bosnian-government-controlled Tuzla in the north. The massacre triggered a worldwide wave of revulsion. Graphic accounts by survivors of how the Bosnian Serbs had lined up men before the machine guns evoked scenes of the Second World War, when Nazi *Einsatzkommandos* on the eastern front had shot rows of Jews into trenches.

Even now many questions remained unanswered about this darkest episode of the Bosnian war. Without air-support or proper reinforcements, Dutchbat certainly could not have held off General Mladic's men for long.[13] However, the question remains: if Dutchbat had resisted, would General Mladic have been prepared to kill 110 UN soldiers?[14]

The commander of the Muslim forces defending Srebrenica was Nasir Oric, who had once been one of Milosevic's bodyguards. Through the long years of siege, he had led night raiding parties through Serb lines to attack local villages and steal food. Many Bosnian Serbs were killed in these attacks, including civilians and the elderly, and their houses destroyed. The peculiar squalor of the conflict in and around Srebrenica was a throwback to the Thirty Years War. In the wake of Oric's fighters, a ragged wave of starving Muslims known as '*torbari*', or 'bag-carriers', would swoop down on the charred houses and pick over the remains for food or other valuables.

Before Srebrenica fell, Oric and his commanders had been pulled out under orders from Sarajevo, and forbidden to return. For the Bosnian leadership, Srebrenica was no longer a political priority. Many believed that Sarajevo was coming under increasing pressure from the West, especially Washington, D.C., to cut a deal with Milosevic and thought that a cynical pact had been made to exchange Srebrenica for Bosnian-Serb-held land around Sarajevo. Certainly, the fall of Srebrenica – or perhaps its removal as an obstacle to the new maps being drawn up in Washington – fitted in with US policy at this time. Sandy Vershbow, an advisor to President Clinton said: 'Well, already in June [1995], the fate of Srebrenica seemed pretty gloomy. We already then were considering some kind of swap for at least the smaller of the eastern enclaves for more territory in central Bosnia might be one of the things that would be wise.'[15] Milosevic doubtless would have seen this policy option as a de facto green light to capture the enclave.

But there is a difference between capturing territory and slaughtering every male inhabitant. The grim leitmotif of the Bosnian war was 'ethnic cleansing', that is, population displacement, not extermination. Even by the bloody standards of the Bosnian war, the Srebrenica massacre was unprecedented. Milosevic's precise relationship to the details of the fall of Srebrenica – and many other war crimes in Bosnia – remains unclear. The issue will be closely examined during the course of his trial at the International War Crimes Tribunal in The Hague under the terms of his indictment for genocide and war crimes in Bosnia. As one senior US official said: 'What remains unknown to me, and to everybody, is how direct a role he played at Srebrenica and the capture of the enclaves, and in the shelling of Sarajevo. Did he order it, did he approve it, what was his role?'[16]

Yet even through the fog of war, some contours of the command and control relationship can be distinguished. Two years earlier, in spring 1993, when it first appeared that Srebrenica was about to fall, Lord Owen had asked Milosevic to use his influence with the Bosnian Serb leaders to stop the attack. 'Milosevic believed it would be a great mistake for the Bosnian Serbs to take Srebrenica and promised to tell Karadzic so,' wrote Owen in his memoirs.[17] The Bosnian Serbs did then eventually pull back.

Western military analysts reported that there were strong links between General Mladic and Belgrade. Writing in *Jane's Intelligence Review*, Dr James Gow noted that Mladic 'communicates daily with both the defence ministry of the "Serbian Republic in Bosnia" and the Yugoslav Federal Ministry of Defence, conveniently located close to each other in the Serbian capital. It is from Belgrade that General Mladic appears to take his orders, although these seem to give him broad control at the operational level.'[18] The key phrase here is 'broad control at the operational level': Mladic exerted day-to-day command over his forces on the ground.

However the relationship between Milosevic and the Bosnian Serb leadership in July 1995 was very different from that of April 1993. After the rejection of the Vance-Owen and Contact Group Bosnian peace plans, relations had broken down between the Pale and Belgrade political leaderships. And so, when NATO launched pin-prick air-strikes against the Bosnian Serbs in May 1995, and Mladic responded by taking over 400 UN peacekeepers hostage, Milosevic despatched his trusted intelligence chief, Jovica Stanisic, to 'persuade' Radovan Karadzic to release the UN troops. Milosevic told the British ambassador Ivor Roberts, 'Stanisic will tell Karadzic that I will have him killed if he doesn't release the hostages. He knows I can do it.'[19]

Milosevic's main objective then was the lifting of sanctions on Serbia. There was no benefit in ordering a massacre of more than 7,000 prisoners, with all the ensuing anti-Serb backlash. The official report commissioned by the Dutch government into the massacre found no evidence of political or military liaison with Belgrade concerning the mass killings.[20] It seems more likely that, by this time, the Bosnian Serb military leadership was simply out of control, and General Mladic was unable to contain his blood lust.[21] None the less, the US diplomat Louis Sell notes that: '. . . throughout the Srebrenica crisis, Milosevic was in direct personal contact with Mladic.'[22] Sell also says that Carl Bildt observed Milosevic alternate 'between begging and giving orders to Mladic'.[23] When the author Laura Silber asked him what happened in Srebrenica, Milosevic replied: 'A moment came when you could no longer expect any kind of rational control. I don't exactly know what happened there.'[24]

What did the West know? The US certainly knew about the Serb preparations to take Srebrenica: U-2 spy planes were patrolling the area, and a stream of satellite intelligence was also being fed back to Washington. On 9 August 1995 Madeleine Albright, the US ambassador to the UN, presented two photographs of the area around Srebrenica to the UN Security Council. The first shot, of an empty field, was taken shortly before Srebrenica fell. The second showed the same field a few days later, with mounds of freshly turned earth – the mass graves where the victims had been buried. In addition, an extensive investigation published in the *New York Review of Books* suggested the US was aware of liaison between General Momcilo Perisic, chief of staff of the Yugoslav army, and General Mladic.

> A US military intelligence source who had access to the raw data coming out of Bosnia confirmed the existence of intercepted conversations about Srebrenica between Belgrade and Mladic. 'There's about a week's worth,' the source says, 'and basically it's Belgrade asking, "Hey [Mladic] you're not going to Srebrenica, are you?" And [Mladic] says, "Of course I am. I'm not done yet, I'm hitting Gorazde and Zepa, too."'[25]

Certainly if there was some kind of diplomatic understanding between the West and Belgrade over Srebrenica, it went horribly wrong over the fate of the inhabitants. One witness remembered Mladic surveying the rows of Muslim prisoners with satisfaction. It is cruelly ironic that the man who had directed the destruction of Bosnia's Islamic heritage then announced a 'meze': the Arabic word for a long feast of many small dishes. 'There are so many. It is going to be a meze. There will be blood up to your knees,' he said, according to Nedzida Sadikovic, a woman survivor. He then nodded at the many young women in the crowd and told his soldiers: 'Beautiful. Keep the good ones over there. Enjoy them.'[26]

One cause of Mladic's hunger for a blood meze was that soldiers operating out of Srebrenica had attacked his home village of Visnice, and burnt down its houses. The suicide of Mladic's daughter Ana, a medical student in her early twenties, had certainly hardened his heart. Encouraged by their commander, the Bosnian Serb soldiers descended into a frenzy of blood lust. The basic constraints of humanitarian behaviour – never very much in evidence in Bosnia – just snapped. But even if Mladic was out of control, ultimately some degree of responsibility still rests with his political masters in Belgrade.

Emboldened by their slaughter at Srebrenica, the Bosnian Serbs resumed the shelling of Sarajevo. On 28 August 1995 thirty-seven people were killed in Sarajevo's main market by five mortar shells fired from a Bosnian Serb position, in defiance of agreements by the Bosnian Serbs to pull back their heavy weapons. This time, NATO meant business. 'Finally the decks were cleared for a real military response, not some piece of garbage,' said Richard Holbrooke, the US diplomat who was about to become the key player in the diplomatic negotiations with Milosevic that would end the war in Bosnia.[27]

The shells that dropped onto Sarajevo's marketplace on 28 August were some of the many thousands that had fallen during the siege. They left the streets slippery with blood. Mangled corpses lay across the pavement or draped over the railings. Such gruesome scenes were common in Sarajevo: Serb gunners in the hills specifically targeted places at the time when they would be most crowded, such as Kosevo hospital during visiting hours, or the entrance to the tunnel that ran under Sarajevo's airport runway. But coming after the Srebrenica massacre, these were five shells too many.

Two days later, the inhabitants of Sarajevo watched in awe and wonder as the NATO jets screamed overhead, wondering why it had taken so long. Haris Silajdzic, the Bosnian prime minister, said: 'I must say that I enjoyed it. I must say that because those who killed so many people, those who aimed [at] baby hospitals, those who aimed [at] children who were playing, could finally feel what it means to be targeted, to be defenceless, and they deserved it.'[28] In rolling waves of air-strikes, combined with Tomahawk cruise missiles, NATO systematically destroyed much of the Bosnian Serbs' military and communications infrastructure over the next two weeks. A barrage of more than 500 shells from the Anglo-French UN troops ensured that Bosnian Serb guns never again fired on Sarajevo. Just as the 'laptop bombardiers' – those journalists who called for air-strikes to defend Bosnia – had predicted, the Bosnian Serb military crumpled under attack from NATO.

So did Milosevic. While NATO hit the Bosnian Serbs, he hit the bottle. He arrived at a meeting with the British diplomat David Austin and Carl Bildt, Lord Owen's successor as EU envoy to Yugoslavia, almost incoherent. Austin looked on amazed as Milosevic slumped in a chair and Milan Milutinovic, the Yugoslav foreign minister, took over.

Milutinovic was a suave operator, well versed in the niceties of diplomacy, although this was a new experience. As he presented the Yugoslav position, Milosevic would occasionally interrupt to say 'You've got to stop the bombing, it's intolerable,' before drifting off again into an alcoholic haze. 'Milosevic was really shocked that NATO had actually started bombing. Maybe he thought it would never happen. It was a good job for Milosevic that Milutinovic was there, because he carried the meeting,' said Austin.[29]

Milosevic, Austin and Bildt had spent the previous weeks in marathon negotiating sessions that often lasted as long as nine or ten hours. Milosevic was a gracious host, and always laid on plentiful supplies of lamb, veal, wine and fruit brandy. During the negotiations he spoke in English and almost always knew exactly what he wanted to say. There was no translator, no advisors and, apart from his chief of Cabinet, Goran Milinovic, the only other people in the building were the villa's staff. Austin observed: 'Serbia was run by one man. Milosevic gave the impression that he had nothing else to do but talk to us. He had an intellectual arrogance that nobody else in the country could do it. He knew the subject intimately. He took decisions, made concessions, and he never had to consult anybody. He just did it. This was a very odd way to operate. He liked a good argument and discussion and seemed to be enjoying it. He was good at it, although quite often he would marshal facts which were not facts at all.'

Milosevic's tried to charm Austin by finding a common link. 'Several times during the negotiations he compared the Bosnian Serbs to children. He would say "That Karadzic, I can't control him. They are like children. You know what it is like Mr Austin, trying to control children." Or he would call them bastards, he would mock Karadzic and Mladic, he was pretty insulting. It was part of the game, showing us how difficult they were to control.'

Underneath the bonhomie, Milosevic was always ready to remind the envoys who was in charge. One lengthy negotiating session took place at a villa that was forty minutes' drive from Belgrade. Milosevic insisted that it was too late for Austin and Bildt to return to the city, and ensured they were comfortable in their guest rooms. He then appeared and announced: 'Goodnight, gentlemen. I am going back to Belgrade.' Austin recalled: 'He was always a genial host, but he wanted to keep you off balance.'

Milosevic also took more practical steps. He summoned Karadzic and the Bosnian Serb leadership to Belgrade and gave them an ultimatum: either the Bosnian Serbs granted him full powers to negotiate a peace for them, or Serbia would impose a total blockade on Republika Srpska. 'It's crucial to stop the war immediately,' he said. 'How we do it isn't the issue. We could discuss details forever.' Milosevic, the former Communist and atheist even press-ganged the Serbian Orthodox Patriarch Pavle into service. The spiritual leader commanded immense authority: he sat down with Karadzic, and talked things over. He pronounced: 'Differences of opinion are inevitable. But never lose sight of the common interest.' Milosevic had won.[30]

At this time, September 1995, Milosevic was reeling. The NATO air strikes had a profound psychological effect on the Serbs. (Even General Mladic sent a long rambling fax to the UN Commander General, Bernard Janvier, declaring the NATO bombardment worse than the Nazis' levelling of Belgrade.)[31] The sanctions were still in place: there was no heating oil, and ragged hawkers sold watered-down petrol in milk bottles. Krajina had collapsed, and Serbia had now taken in almost 200,000 refugees from Croatia. The Croatian and Bosnian armies were pushing hard through northern Bosnia. The northern enclave of Bihac had been liberated. Well armed, highly motivated and properly equipped, the joint Croat-Bosnian force looked unstoppable.

So much so that by mid-September the two armies were within striking distance of Banja Luka, the northern Bosnian city that Milosevic was cultivating as an alternative power base. The Bosnian Serb leadership there was supposedly more 'moderate', though Banja Luka had been the epicentre of ethnic cleansing in northern Bosnia in 1992, and for Muslims and Croats it was a place of terror and murder. Now, however, it was the turn of the Bosnian Serbs to panic. The city prepared to evacuate as the advancing Croat and Bosnian forces stormed through the Bosnian Serb lines.

But Washington had decided that Banja Luka would not be allowed to fall. The city, and Milosevic, were saved by the Americans, in the bulldozer form of Richard Holbrooke. A career diplomat who had served in Vietnam, Holbrooke was appointed US special envoy to Yugoslavia in late 1994. He used his power as Clinton's man in the Balkans, and his gung-ho can-do American approach, to cut through the layers of diplomatic obfuscation. When Milosevic suggested to Holbrooke that he meet with Radovan Karadzic and General Mladic to discuss a ceasefire in Bosnia, Holbrooke agreed, but demanded there be 'no historical lectures, no bullshit'. When General Mladic had started his usual tirade about brave little Serbia, Holbrooke walked out, telling Milosevic: 'Mr President, you told us we were here to be serious. If we're not serious we have to go.'[32]

Milosevic relished this tough-guy approach. He too wanted to be serious, without 'historical bullshit' in which he had anyway never been very interested. Finally, he believed, he had found someone who could, and would, cut deals without having to get every full stop and comma authorised by the UN. Holbrooke and Milosevic enjoyed a personal chemistry that would be a significant factor in eventually bringing peace to Bosnia. Like every autocratic ruler who surrounds himself with yes-men, Milosevic was often bored. Secure in his position as the supreme ruler of Serbia, he enjoyed the chance to lock horns with an equal.

Washington believed, almost certainly correctly, that if Banja Luka fell then the whole Bosnian Serb Republic would collapse, bringing down Milosevic. According to this scenario, hundreds of thousands of Bosnian Serbs would pour across the border into Serbia. Milosevic would either be toppled in a military coup, or be forced to deploy the JNA in Bosnia to defend the Bosnian Serbs. This would trigger a full-fledged war between Yugoslavia and her successor states, which would threaten the whole Balkans. Momir Bulatovic, the Montenegrin leader, recalled Belgrade's warning: 'We told the Americans this huge exodus of refugees would radically alter politics here. Decisions would be out of our hands. We'd be forced to intervene directly.'[33]

The US needed Milosevic to broker a peace deal over Bosnia. Hrvoje Sarinic explained: 'The US saw that there were no results with the previous kind of negotiations. So they decided to change the rules of the game. There is no document, but they said if we change the ratio of forces involved, negotiations could be more successful. Our army was more than successful. We solved the problem of Bihac, which had been in a catastrophic situation. We – officially the HVO [Bosnian Croat army] – were twenty kilometres from Banja Luka and the evacuation started. We could have captured Banja Luka, their forces were panicking. But then Bosnia would have been split into several parts, and it would have been much harder to organise the Dayton agreement. So the US stopped our offensive.'[34] In his book *To End a War* Holbrooke argued that the fall of Banja Luka would trigger a humanitarian catastrophe of 200,000 Bosnian Serb refugees. He told President Tudjman: 'Mr President, I urge you to go as far as you can, but not to take Banja Luka.'[35] Tudjman agreed. Banja Luka was spared.

In Sarajevo, President Izetbegovic and his generals wanted to push on and liberate more territory. Holbrooke turned up the heat. In characteristically blunt language, he told Izetbegovic he was 'shooting craps' (i.e., playing dice) with Bosnia's destiny.[36] Izetbegovic understood that without Croatia's military support and Washington's back-up, Bosnia's offensive would anyway likely soon stop. Izetbegovic's price was to lift the siege of Sarajevo, and turn on the electricity, gas and water. It was paid. The siege of the Bosnian capital was over.

The US diplomatic cavalry had saved Milosevic. Less than three years later, the Kosovo Albanians would pay the price.

20

THE ONLY MAN
WHO MATTERS

Dayton

November 1995

You deserve Sarajevo because you fought for it and those cowards killed you from the hills.

Slobodan Milosevic ceding the Serb–occupied areas of the
Bosnian capital to Haris Silajdzic, Bosnian prime minister, at the
Dayton peace conference in November 1995.[1]

A month after the lights and heating went on in Sarajevo, Milosevic was at the piano, whisky in hand, regaling western diplomats with his version of 'Tenderly'. The site of this impromptu serenade was the Wright-Patterson US airbase in Dayton, Ohio. Milosevic, Franjo Tudjman, Alija Izetbegovic and their advisors had arrived on 31 October to thrash out the details of the final peace settlement for Bosnia. Now Milosevic was where he most wanted to be: at the centre of attention, recognised by the world as the only man who matters, whose imprimatur could stop, finally, the Bosnian war. Best of all, Milosevic was in his second favourite country, the United States.

Despite the hundreds of journalists outside the perimeter fence, the airbase was sealed off from the media, and the three leaders were virtually locked in. The message from Washington was clear: this was their last chance. Asked how confident he was that the talks would succeed, Milosevic had said on arrival: 'Well, I am [an] optimist. I believe the talks will succeed. We attach the greatest importance to [the] peace initiative of the United States.'[2] Warren Christopher, the US Secretary of State, had even coaxed the three leaders into a handshake for the cameras.

Nominally, the Dayton conference, as it became known, had three co-chairmen: Carl Bildt, the European envoy, the Russian Igor Ivanov and Richard Holbrooke. But in diplomacy it is the host country that counts, and everyone understood that this was primarily an American show, in the main run by Holbrooke. The Americans took the credit, but the Dayton conference was not conjured up out of nowhere. It was the final stage in the years of diplomatic wrangling that had marked attempts to bring peace to Bosnia, stretching back to Europe's involvement in the early 1990s when the Bush administration had taken a back seat, believing that the US did not 'have a dog in this fight'. But ultimately only America, it seemed, had the power and will to lock the Balkan leaders in an airbase – albeit a luxuriously fitted one – until they signed up for peace. The choice of venue was significant – a deliberate reminder of American air power, coming just a few weeks after NATO's air strikes against the Bosnian Serbs.

Milosevic came to Dayton ready to sign. He was weak on the military, diplomatic and home fronts. His control of Serbia's state broadcast media could not temper Serb anger about the disasters that had befallen them. Serbia was a comparatively small country, and many of its inhabitants had relatives or friends among the refugees from Croatia and Bosnia. In 1991 football fans had lauded Milosevic as a great Serb leader and defender of its people: The terraces swayed to 'Serbian Slobo, Serbia is with you'. Now they chanted 'Slobo, you have betrayed Krajina'.

Milosevic knew he could survive the fallout from operations Flash and Storm, but they still sent aftershocks through his government. When, after the fall of Krajina, the children of Yugoslav prime minister Radoje Kontic told him that they 'pissed on his premiership', Kontic had retreated to his office with a bottle of cognac. The massacre at Srebrenica had shown Milosevic that General Mladic was out of control. Who knew what horrors he might carry out next, and what the consequences might be for Serbia?

But first, it was dinner time. Holbrooke took Milosevic to the all-American on-base restaurant, Packy's All-Sports Bar.[3] The walls were covered with pictures of Bob Hope. Four giant television screens showed news and sports channels. This was the America that Milosevic had so admired on his trips to Wall Street and to the IMF meetings, where he had so dazzled the world's bankers with his command of capitalism. He was entranced by the slick technology, the smooth efficiency, the sheer luxurious availability of everything. Most of all, it seemed, he was impressed by a Tomahawk Cruise Missile, on display at the base museum. Just a few weeks before, a fusillade of the twenty-foot long projectiles had helped destroy much of the Bosnian Serb army's communications systems in western Bosnia. 'So much damage from such a little thing,' he said.[4]

At Packy's Milosevic turned on the charm. He soon had his own favourite waitress. He asked her name, and where she was from. Vicky became 'Waitress Wicky', as Milosevic pronounced her name, and always served the Serb leader. At more formal dinners at the Officers' Club restaurant, Milosevic even invited one of the waiters to come and work for him in Belgrade.

The Americans made great efforts to warm up the – unsurprisingly – glacial atmosphere between Milosevic and the Bosnian government delegation, with sometimes bizarre results. With hindsight it is clear that it may have been more tactful to stick to diplomatic rather than social business: the Bosnians were in no mood for socialising, especially with the man they saw as the killer of their country. When a dinner was organised at the Officers' Club, Holbrooke seated his wife, the Hungarian writer Kati Marton, between Milosevic and Izetbegovic. The Bosnian President could barely stand to look at Milosevic, let alone break bread with him. 'Three black women sergeants performed as the Andrews Sisters', recorded Holbrooke, 'and as they sang "Boogie Woogie Bugle Boy", Milosevic sang along, while Izetbegovic sat sullenly.'[5]

Milosevic's immediate concern was the lifting of sanctions. Six days into Dayton, Milosevic asked for twenty-three thousand tons of heating oil, and for natural gas supplies to be resumed. By this time winter had set in in Belgrade. Milosevic realised that if he was to sign away much of Bosnia, he needed to deliver something concrete for the home front. He also understood that the Americans would probably be willing to make this kind of concession – which was important for him, but relatively irrelevant to the overall Dayton strategy – as a goodwill gesture. Milosevic drafted unlikely allies for his request: Izetbegovic himself and the Bosnian prime minister, Haris Silajdzic. They agreed, pointing out that the 5 October ceasefire was supposed to turn the heating on in Belgrade as well as Sarajevo. After Milosevic's request, it did.

It seemed a good omen for the broader principles being thrashed out. The Dayton conference followed a period of intense US-led shuttle diplomacy through September 1995, after which Milosevic and Izetbegovic had agreed on a set of basic political principles to decide Bosnia's future. These were that Bosnia would remain a single, internationally-recognised state, with its borders intact. Zagreb would not annex Herzegovina, and nor would Belgrade carve off eastern Bosnia. The Bosnian Serbs and Bosnian Croats would stay within Bosnia.

The price, for President Izetbegovic and his government, was high, and one which is still being paid. Within its international borders, Bosnia would be split into two 'entities', as they became known: the Bosnian Croat-Muslim Federation, which would get 51 per cent of its territory, and the Bosnian Serb Republic, which would take 49 per cent. Both entities would remain nominally under the authority of a multinational government in Sarajevo, and one currency would be in use, the convertible mark. But the 'Federation' – as the Croat-Muslim territory became known – and the Bosnian Serb Republic would retain their own armies, police forces, political structures and judiciaries. This was the ultimate victory of the Bosnian Serbs, that a country where all three nations had lived in mixed towns and villages would now be divided into two, on ethnic lines. The Bosnian Serb Republic would remain in existence, would even keep its name of 'Republika Srpska' and its foundations of ethnic cleansing would be legitimised.

The European diplomats worked out the details of Bosnia's future constitution. The Americans oversaw the wrangling about the map. Bosnia-Herzegovina had been ruled by the Ottoman Sultans, the Habsburg emperors, the King of Yugoslavia, and then Tito. Now it was about to become – in effect – an international protectorate, its fate decided not in Istanbul or Vienna, but on an American airbase. Over the next week the brief co-operation over heating Belgrade evaporated. By day sixteen no agreement had been reached and time was running out. A major sticking point was the city of Gorazde, in eastern Bosnia. Gorazde was a government-held town surrounded by the Bosnian Serbs. Like Srebrenica, Gorazde was a UN Safe Area. Unlike Srebrenica, despite repeated attacks by Mladic's forces, Gorazde had not fallen. The city had been kept alive by a thin lifeline of weapons and supplies that were brought in down a perilous mountain track from Sarajevo. For years government soldiers had trekked nightly into the city past Bosnian Serb frontlines that were so near they could hear the enemy talking and see the red tips of their cigarettes glowing.

The Bosnian government had paid for Gorazde in blood, and would not surrender the city. But as Gorazde was an enclave, it needed a land-link, a safe corridor, to the capital Sarajevo. Corridor negotiations were the nightmare of any Bosnian peace plan. The length and width of the corridor were merely the starting point in the long litany of subsidiary questions. How many metres from the edge of the actual road would the territory of the corridor stretch? Would the road itself be dirt or metal? Would the corridor by supervised by UN troops? Would there be crossing points or junctions, and who would administer them, and so on, and so forth.

Holbrooke told Haris Silajdzic that Milosevic wanted to come over to his table to talk to him about Gorazde. Silajdzic refused. By this time Dayton had descended into an acrimonious 'zero-sum' game. Any concession, no matter how tiny, was seen as a defeat by those making it, and a victory for those receiving it. Silajdzic recalled: 'The fact that he comes to my table, gives him, in a way, a psychological advantage, that he is doing something, that he is making a concession and so on. So I said, no, I'll go to his table. These are our small Balkan ways.'[6]

The Bosnian prime minister and Milosevic eventually reached an agreement. NATO would build a road, under international control, linking the enclave of Gorazde to the main Federation territory. With agreement reached in principle on the corridor, the next question was its width: that is, how much territory would the Bosnian Serbs need to surrender? Which was the cue for the biggest video game in the world: known as 'Power Scene', a digital imaging system which had stored the whole topography of Bosnia in a 3-D 'virtual reality machine', as Holbrooke described it. 'We had an aerial photograph of the entire country and you could fly with the joystick over any part of the country, stop, look straight down, look sideways, go up, go down.'[7]

Milosevic arrived at 11.00 p.m. and was soon entranced with his virtual reality journey through Bosnia. Fuelled by considerable amounts of Scotch, he spent hours 'flying' around Bosnia as he discussed the future shape and size of the corridor. General Wesley Clark, who in three years' time would meet Milosevic in a much less agreeable atmosphere, drew up a plan for one version of the corridor. Milosevic proposed some alterations. Eventually, agreement was found. At 2.00 a.m. Milosevic knocked back his last glass for the night, shook hands all round and exclaimed, 'We have found our road.'[8] This was later dubbed the 'Scotch corridor'.

The personal chemistry between Milosevic and the Americans, especially

Richard Holbrooke, was a significant factor in finalising the Dayton accords. He was probably the most popular of the three leaders. Franjo Tudjman was seen as a febrile bore who lectured and hectored about Croatia's centuries of glorious history, glossing over his own tolerance of the rehabilitation of the symbolism of the Ustasha regime. Alija Izetbegovic sat dour and unforgiving. His severe countenance was a moral reproach to the western leaders who had stood by while Bosnia was being destroyed. He made people feel guilty, and uncomfortable.

Milosevic was much smarter. He was one of the guys. Milosevic knew and liked the United States and Americans, and understood how to interact with them. As one western official, present at the Dayton talks, noted: 'Milosevic was only instantly available to Richard Holbrooke. He even ate with the Americans, or on his own.' Milosevic took care to humanise himself, and behave like an ebullient, rumbustious Serb, instead of a sinister fanatic like General Mladic or Momcilo Krajisnik. This was clever, as there were some moral qualms about negotiating with the man dubbed by many the 'Butcher of the Balkans'.

His tactics were effective. 'Milosevic knew us very well as a people, he was able to play with us. He knew what our red lines and bottom lines were, maybe even more than we did. He learned this during his time in the US in dealing with us,' said one senior US official who had extensive dealings over the years with the Serbian leader. 'He had an uncanny ability to judge how serious we were, and in most cases he would be right. He was a real student of human nature. We might say ten times that he had to do X, Y and Z. He knew the one time out of ten when there would be consequences if he did not.'[9]

As Tibor Varady, once Yugoslav minister for justice, had noted, Milosevic exerted a powerful aura, which drew many diplomats into his orbit. When dozens of politicians and advisors are locked up together for weeks on end, the human factor can be decisive. Aware of the rivalry and intermittent tension between the Americans and the Europeans, Milosevic skilfully played off one side against the other. He chose a surprising but effective weapon: humour. Not only could Slobo sing, it seemed he could conjure up a whole range of impersonations as well. As ever, he picked his audience carefully, recalled David Austin. 'He took great pleasure in mimicking Carl Bildt and his Swedish accent, according to the Americans. But when he was with us, he would mock the Americans. He was playing a game with us all the time, and even then it was divide and rule.'[10]

The Bosnian government delegation was also weakened by 'small Balkan ways'. Its bitter internal factionalising did not help Sarajevo's cause. Izetbegovic had encouraged Silajdzic, who possessed a better sense of realpolitik, to negotiate alone with Milosevic over Gorazde. But he had not been pleased with the success of these negotiations, which boosted his prime minister's standing with the Americans. At the time, Holbrooke noted down that the Bosnian delegation is 'divided and confused. Silajdzic told me that he had not spoken to Izetbegovic in over twenty-four hours. They have let other opportunities for peace slip away before. It could happen again.'[11]

The most curious feature of the Dayton negotiations was the utter contempt with which Milosevic treated the Bosnian Serbs. Milosevic had forced Karadzic to give him a mandate to negotiate for the Bosnian Serbs, but they still sent their own delegation, headed by Momcilo Krajisnik, a sinister figure whose eyebrows met in the middle. Milosevic had loathed Krajisnik ever since he supported Radovan Karadzic's rejection of the Vance-Owen peace plan in 1993.

'Milosevic behaved abominably towards the Bosnian Serbs,' David Austin remembered. 'He humiliated them. Each delegation had one fax machine. Milosevic controlled access to the Serb fax machine, but would not let them use it.' When the Bosnian Serb General Tolimir wanted to send some documents back to Pale, he had to ask Austin to use his fax machine.

Krajisnik was allowed occasional input into comparatively minor questions such as the future Bosnian constitution. But the key, the map, was reserved for Milosevic. On the rare occasions that Milosevic wanted to consult with someone on his own side, he would talk to Momir Bulatovic, the pliant president of Montenegro, the junior partner in the third Yugoslavia. Austin recalled: 'Milosevic used to walk up and down the car park, with Bulatovic. That really rubbed it in to the Bosnian Serbs as well. Who was Bulatovic in this? He was completely irrelevant. Milosevic did this in full view of the Bosnian Serbs.' Krajisnik was so out of the loop' that he wrote to Holbrooke asking what was happening. Holbrooke showed the letters to Milosevic, and Milosevic threw them in the dustbin.

Milosevic's total control of the negotiations from the Serb side was most evident in the diplomatic battle for Sarajevo. The Bosnian capital was divided into two zones: government-controlled and Serb-controlled.

These were the siege lines from behind which the Bosnian Serbs had shelled the city for three and a half years. The Bosnian government would not budge on their key demand: that the Serbs surrender all the districts of Sarajevo that they controlled, especially an area known as Grbavica. During the war Radovan Karadzic had been quite open that his aim was to split Sarajevo into two separate zones, a sort of Balkan Berlin, complete with checkpoints and border guards controlling access from one side to another.

Momcilo Krajisnik demanded that the Serbs retain control of local councils and police in Serb areas of the city. This was essentially a demand to formalise the division of the city. Richard Holbrooke said: 'Krajisnik had gone up to the maps and, slamming them with his fist, had said, "I live here" – he's pointing to a farm he had in [the Serb-controlled district of] Ilidza, "and I'm never going to give this up".'[12] Milosevic broke the deadlock with a startling and unexpected offer: he simply gave the whole of the Bosnian capital to the government side. Momcilo Krajisnik's farm was lost, although the matter soon became academic as Krajisnik was arrested by NATO troops as a war criminal in 2000, and deported to The Hague. Silajdzic recalled Milosevic's proposal: 'He said, "You deserve Sarajevo because you fought for it and those cowards killed you from the hills", meaning the Bosnian Serbs.'[13]

This was Milosevic's ultimate gesture of contempt for the Bosnian Serb leadership. It was also part of the plan that he had outlined to President Tudjman's envoy Hrvoje Sarinic earlier that year, to strengthen the supposedly 'moderate' northern city of Banja Luka, against Pale. Of course there was a price: Milosevic wanted the strategically important northern Bosnian city of Brcko because it controlled access to the northern corridor of territory in Serb-occupied Bosnia that stretched to Serbia proper. He did not get it, but neither did the Bosnian government. After much wrangling Brcko was placed directly under international administration.

The US official argued that Milosevic gave away Sarajevo not to ease the path to a settlement at Dayton, but in fact to ensure that, ultimately, Bosnia would not function as multi-ethnic country. A ceasefire would be signed, but Serbs would never live alongside Muslims again. 'A cynic would say that Milosevic ceded Sarajevo to ensure Dayton would not work. For Dayton to work you would need an integrated Sarajevo. You need the Sarajevo Serbs to be living in the capital. By giving Sarajevo away, Milosevic ensured this would not happen. This willingness to abandon Serbs who have been on the front line fighting for Serbdom is an absolute characteristic of Milosevic. Once more, these were his protégés and then he walked away from them.'[14]

The real victor of Dayton was President Tudjman. With his victorious US-assisted army, Tudjman was negotiating from a position of strength. He and President Izetbegovic despised each other, but Izetbegovic understood that it was the Croat and Bosnian Croat armies that had altered the balance of power sufficiently to bring Milosevic to Dayton, ready to make a deal. Tudjman was not very interested in the minutiae of the Bosnian constitution. The area of Bosnia formerly known as Herceg-Bosna remained firmly within control of the Bosnian-Croat Federation. In Mostar his allies, the hard-line Bosnian Croats, remained in place, controlling much of the local government through violence and intimidation.

Tudjman's main concern was Sector East of Serb-occupied Croatia. Operations Flash and Storm had recaptured sectors North, South and West from the rebel Serbs. But the Croat army had not attacked Sector East, the area including Vukovar, known as eastern Slavonia, that was a centre of petrol-smuggling in and out of Serbia proper. With the prospect of sanctions being lifted in reward for his co-operation at Dayton, Milosevic was prepared to cut a deal with Tudjman over eastern Slavonia. In Balkan fashion, it was conducted away from the limelight: a series of meetings were arranged at which the two leaders addressed each other as 'Franjo' and 'Slobo'.

Tudjman understood that raising the Croatian flag over Sector East was not quite as straightforward as it was in the other rebel-Serb-held areas. His forces could certainly have swept through the UN ceasefire lines and retaken the area, but Vukovar – or what was left of it – lay on the Danube, the border between Croatia and Serbia. There was a chance that Milosevic might send Yugoslav forces across the river to defend the rebel Serbs, and that would re-ignite the war, which this time would be between two sovereign international states.

Eventually, Franjo and Slobo went for a walk, just as they had done back in March 1991 when they carved up Bosnia at Tito's hunting resort of Karadjordjevo. This time they marched round and round the parking area at Dayton, batting proposals back and forth. At first they shouted and gesticulated, but after an hour, they were in step, both in the parking area, and over Sector East. They would, they announced, agree to the proposal that Sector East would return to Croatia, after a period of UN transitional administration with guarantees of human rights for Serbs who wished to remain under Croatian rule. These were not properly implemented, but Tudjman still regained Sector East without a shot being fired.

In some ways Milosevic's presence at Dayton was an anomaly. Milosevic was the president of Serbia, one of the two constituent republics of Yugoslavia. Neither Yugoslavia, nor Serbia, was officially at war in Bosnia. Indeed Milosevic himself had repeatedly denied that Serb troops were fighting in Bosnia, although nobody believed him.

The real leaders of the Bosnian Serbs were Radovan Karadzic and General Mladic. But these two men were indicted war criminals and so could not be allowed on American soil. At a meeting in Serbia Richard Holbrooke had insulted Mladic by refusing to eat at the same table. But with hindsight it seems, Holbrooke had no qualms about dining and drinking with Milosevic, who had chosen Mladic as commander of the Bosnian Serb army, and provided the political and military means for Radovan Karadzic to build the Bosnian Serb Republic. Indeed, Milosevic's indictments for war crimes in Croatia and Bosnia describe him as a member of a 'joint criminal enterprise' along with other key figures in the Serb leadership in Belgrade, the Croatian Serb leadership in Knin and the Bosnian Serb leadership in Pale, in the drive to ethnically cleanse first Serb-occupied Croatia, and then Serb-occupied Bosnia.

So why was Milosevic feted as an international statesman in 1995, when the details of the wars between 1991 and 1995, and the extent of his role within them were thoroughly documented, not least by the American intelligence services? Because the demands of geo-politics, and American policy, meant that Milosevic was then seen as the linchpin of any deal that could bring peace to the former Yugoslavia. Statesman or war criminal: much of the difference, it seems, is in the eye of the beholder. It is also a question of timing. In the winter of 1995, Milosevic was seen not as the problem, but the solution. Flying him to Dayton was merely the logical next step after saving his regime from collapse by halting the Croat-Bosnian attack on Banja Luka.

But morality and realpolitik make a murky combination, especially when men seek to act as gods and decide the fate of nations. Mira Markovic argued: 'Now the Hague prosecution is saying that he did this in 1991 and 1992 and so on. Would they take such a man to Dayton? The West treated him as their ally, and as a factor of stability and peace in the Balkans. He was in Dayton because he knew that he could bring the Serbs on the other side of the river Drina to their senses. He was one of the people they relied on. They should be grateful to my husband for the Dayton peace accords and they well know that.'[15]

If Milosevic was a war criminal, then so was President Tudjman. Under Tudjman, the Bosnian Croats had also set up a network of concentration camps, and ethnically cleansed Muslims. Just three months earlier the United States had given the nod to Croatia to recapture the Krajina in an operation in which 200,000 Serb refugees fled or were expelled. Officials at the ICTY confirm that had Tudjman lived, he would have been indicted for war crimes and crimes against humanity.[16] So at Dayton Milosevic was at least in good company.

ENTER MIRA, STAGE LEFT

Setting up JUL

1995–7

> LADY MACBETH: *Only look up clear.*
> *To alter favour ever is to fear*
> *Leave all the rest to me.*[1]

Milosevic picked up the telephone. It was 13 January 1996, and his new strategic partner was on the line. President Clinton was flying to visit US troops stationed in southern Hungary, and in Tuzla in northern Bosnia. Just one month earlier, Milosevic had signed the Dayton peace agreement in Paris. President Clinton had said to him then: 'I know this agreement would not have been possible without you. You made Dayton possible. Now you must help make it work.'[2]

Milosevic was the man of the moment. On the phone Clinton outlined his hopes for the region's future. 'We support normalisation of relations and I know it cannot go ahead without you. We need that, but it only takes a small thing for everything to fall through. That's why I count on [Secretary of State Warren] Christopher's trip and then we shall see his report.'[3] Milosevic replied: 'That is really encouraging and I am glad to hear that. I am looking forward to receiving Mr Christopher, it can only lead to good. I am optimistic. Thank you for your optimism and your proposal.'

Greatly buoyed by his chat with Clinton, Milosevic then called the Yugoslav foreign minister, the urbane Milan Milutinovic, and told him about the conversation. Both men were somewhat in awe of Madeleine Albright, the US ambassador to the United Nations. Albright, who was of Czech Jewish descent, had spent some time in Belgrade during the Second World War. A powerful figure in the Clinton administration, with an intuitive understanding of the Balkans, she was also a classic

Slavic matriarch. She stood for no nonsense from errant males, even
Serbian presidents and foreign ministers. Milosevic and Milutinovic
were soon snickering like schoolboys:

> Milutinovic: It's a big thing Clinton dared to speak that way in front
> of Albright.
> Milosevic: Yes, he spoke really nicely.
> Milutinovic: He must have hid in the airplane's toilet.
> Milosevic: You're joking. You think he is afraid of Albright?
> Milutinovic: She's a real ——. You have no idea how it is.
> Milosevic: You know how he started the conversation? He was very
> polite, extremely nice, I simply cannot tell you.
> Milutinovic: You know why I'm laughing? The old —— has told
> me so many things and I have told her many things. She told me
> 'I like you so I'll tell you everything.'
> Milosevic: Well, I don't know if they were all with him.
> Milutinovic: Yes, yes they were. She was on the plane, and Holbrooke.
> That's why it makes it an even greater accomplishment.[4]

But Milosevic was not laughing the next day, when he saw how
Clinton's visit to Tuzla had been reported in *Politika*. The once-
respected newspaper was now a degraded mouthpiece for regime
propaganda. The man in charge, Hadzi Dragan Antic,[5] had not yet
grasped the new party line. This was surprising as Antic was very
close to both Marija Milosevic and Mira Markovic. As a family friend,
Antic should have known that the president of the United States was
no longer a warmaker, but a peacemaker. Instead the *Politika* report
claimed that Clinton had come to Tuzla to have his picture taken,
and dredged up old canards about Vietnam and Whitewater.

As soon as he saw the article, a furious Milosevic rang up Antic.
'Are you out of your fucking mind? I want to build something and
you demolish it as much as you can, you spit on everything and kick
everyone.'[6] Antic weedily protested that he did not know about the
report. Milosevic stormed on, making the unlikely claim that: 'Believe
me, this is a scandal without precedent . . . to insult an American
president for the positive thing that he is doing. You fuckers didn't
insult him so much when there was bombing . . . and then you
tell me how you support the peace policies.' Milosevic then issued
instructions for the next day's coverage. 'I will do it right away,'

said Antic, promising to report everything Clinton did as 'extremely positive'.

Milosevic had returned in triumph from the Dayton signing. Mira, Marko and Marija all waited for him at Belgrade airport, together with phalanxes of reporters and cameramen. Milosevic had won: he had brought the Bosnian Serbs to heel, but also kept the nationalists happy by ensuring that Republika Srpska, founded on terror and ethnic cleansing, was now institutionalised as one of Bosnia's two component entities.[7] True, there were some constitutional provisions for the right of return of Muslim and Croat refugees, but nobody – apart perhaps from the refugees – expected these to be implemented.

Yet as 1995 rolled into 1996, Milosevic became listless and depressed. His moment of glory had passed. In some ways Dayton weakened Milosevic at home. With the war ended, there were no more excuses for Serbia's collapsing economy and crumbling infrastructure. And where was the promised foreign capital? The sanctions imposed by the United Nations were lifted, but what was known as the 'outer wall' of sanctions, imposed by the US, were not, even though President Clinton was ringing up for goodwill chats. There could be no economic revival while the outer wall prevented Yugoslavia from rejoining the IMF and World Bank. Somehow, in the bonhomie of steak dinner and whisky sing-songs at Dayton, the precise details of which set of sanctions would be lifted, and when, had got lost.

The increasingly high profile of the UN's International Criminal Tribunal for the Former Yugoslavia (ICTY) was also making Milosevic jittery.[8] Since its foundation in 1993, its annual budget had increased almost one hundredfold: from $276,000 to $25,300,000. Radovan Karadzic and General Mladic had been indicted for genocide in Bosnia. It was now often implied that Milosevic might be next. Even worse, with Bosnia solved, the old issue of human rights in Kosovo was reappearing on the diplomatic agenda. Not surprisingly, Milosevic felt betrayed.

On top of all this, there was Mira. While Milosevic had been away at Dayton, Mira had gone into action. As Ivan Stambolic had learnt, anyone who became too close to Milosevic would eventually run up against Mira's possessive jealousy. Mira steadily replaced Milosevic loyalists with her own protégés. At *Politika*, for example, Zivorad Minovic, a long-term ally of Milosevic, was sacked in an unseemly episode reportedly involving a night-time visit from the secret police. Each of these small victories steadily increased Mira's power and influence over her husband, and Serbia itself.

Mira enjoyed another victory at the end of November 1995, when Milosevic called a meeting of the Socialist Party's executive committee. As Dusan Mitevic recalled, meetings chaired by Milosevic rarely lasted more than half an hour. This one was no exception. Milosevic informed those gathered that six senior figures – known as the 'nationalist' faction – were purged. They included the academic Mihailo Markovic, associated with the SANU Memorandum; Milorad Vucelic, the head of Belgrade Television; and, perhaps most significantly, Borisav Jovic, Milosevic's political hit man during the early 1990s. With the meeting's business out of the way, Milosevic invited those present for a drink to celebrate the triumph of Dayton.

It was common knowledge that all these six opposed Mira's influence over her husband. Jovic found out he had been sacked when a reporter rang him to ask for his comments. But he had seen it coming: the clipped, pugnacious official had just published his diary, *The Last Days of Socialist Federal Yugoslavia*, and it had caused a sensation. The rigorous, detailed account of his meetings with Milosevic included considerable details of the political planning for war. The diary was also doubtless being read with great interest in The Hague.

The purges within the Socialist Party had been signalled from within Mira Markovic's camp as early as the summer of 1994, when an official of her League of Communists – Movement for Yugoslavia (LC-MY) party had suddenly described Mihailo Markovic, Borisav Jovic and Milorad Vucelic as 'the greatest warmongers in the Serbian government'. The LC-MY was small in numbers, but influential. By emphasising its commitment to 'Yugoslavia' – as Mira did in her writings – it drew support from high-ranking military figures. However, in mid-1993 Mira engineered an inner-party coup, elbowing aside the 'military faction' in favour of a grouping led by herself and Zoran Todorovic. These apparently obscure manoeuvrings set in motion a chain of events that would have a profound impact on the Milosevic regime and ultimately on the fate of the Milosevic family.

Todorovic was known as 'Kundak', or rifle-butt. Born in 1959, he had left his home town of Sabac for Belgrade University, where he enrolled in the school of political science.[9] There he became secretary of the Communist Party's university committee. Youthful, committed and ideologically zealous, Kundak soon came to the notice of Mira, who brought him into the Milosevic family circle. He had attended Marija's twentieth birthday party.

With his well-trimmed beard, sharp suits set off by a well-chosen silk tie, and ebullient manner, Kundak was soon cutting an important figure in Belgrade's corridors of power. He was a key player behind the scenes at the Eighth Session in 1987, reportedly writing out himself the 'telegrams of support' that Milosevic claimed to have received from workers' delegations. He also helped organise the anti-bureaucratic revolutions of 1988, and bussed demonstrators into Belgrade.

Todorovic was as greedy as he was ambitious. He became the prototype of a new hybrid figure that flourished in the shadowy world where Serbian politics and big business met, the 'red businessman'. Such figures were not unique to Serbia, but the utterly degraded state of the country's institutions, the fusion of political interests with institutionalised criminality, and the rickety Serbian economy meant there were virtually no constraints on Todorovic's ambitions. Kundak ruled like a feudal lord. He used his political power as head of a Belgrade workers' organisation to sack the heads of key companies and put his own people in. He made many enemies, especially with his machinations at the multi-billion dollar Jugopetrol company. Kundak also used his political connections to obtain information about state companies that were in financial difficulties, which he then bought up on the cheap. He was soon one of the richest men in Serbia.

In March 1995 the LC-MY was relaunched in Belgrade as the Yugoslav United Left (JUL), under Mira's auspices. JUL was an alliance of twenty-one parties, mostly leftist or 'Yugo-nostalgic'. The levers of party power were controlled by Mira, who ran JUL's executive committee. There were two strands to JUL: the red businessmen such as Todorovic, appointed secretary general, and the intellectuals, such as party president Ljubisa Ristic. Ristic was an internationally acclaimed avant-garde theatre director, who had worked at the Riverside Theatre in London. Such figures saw JUL as a guarantor of the old Yugoslavia's multi-ethnic, and anti-imperialist, heritage. The party was strongly anti-nationalist, and virulently attacked Radovan Karadzic. JUL especially tried to woo young people. Its slogan – 'JUL je kul' (JUL is cool) – was the chorus of its raucous radio advertisement, and was also emblazoned on a lapel badge. Prized recruits among Belgrade's artistic community were given mobile telephones, if they also wore the badge. JUL knew it had really arrived on the Belgrade scene when the rock group Fish Soup released a satirical song dubbing Mira 'Baba Jula' (Granny JUL).

JUL was Markovic's creation, but it served two specific roles for Milosevic as well. First, it was a source of political functionaries, *personally* loyal to Milosevic and Mira, who could be placed in important political and economic positions, going over the heads of the Socialist Party, where Mira had many enemies. Like Chairman Mao and his wife during the Cultural Revolution, Milosevic and his wife set up, in effect, a kind of personal para-state. Mao had the 'Red Guards'; they had JUL. Second, with the Serbian leader disassociating himself from Serbian nationalism in the wake of the Dayton agreement, JUL provided a useful political alibi for Milosevic's new ideological line, that 'There is no alternative to peace'. JUL, for example, expended considerable effort in courting the Slavic Muslim community in the southern Serbian region of Sandzak.

But what JUL was really about, it seemed to many, was money. Mihailo Markovic, one of the Socialist Party leaders sacked in Milosevic's mini-purge, observed: 'There are amongst its leaders sincere leftists and honest individuals, but many of them are simply Mafiosi and war profiteers.'[10] JUL, or at least its leader, Mira Markovic, was also backed by the powerful Karic brothers. Like many businessmen, the four brothers, led by Boguljub, saw JUL as an open door to Milosevic. They began their careers as musicians at weddings in their home town of Pec in Kosovo before opening a business trading in farming implements. Through an adroit use of political connections – they were introduced to Mira Markovic through Dusan Mitevic – and considerable business acumen, they soon built a flourishing business empire that stretched from Serbia to Russia and North America, serviced by the Karic Bank.

The bank was soon followed by the Karic Brothers' private university and a television station, BK Television. One of Boguljub Karic's smartest moves was to support the publication of a book of Mira Markovic's collected diary columns. Another was to back the Kosova radio station where Marija Milosevic worked. According to Slavoljub Djukic, Mira travelled on Boguljub Karic's private jet to Crete, and he paid for the renovation of Marija's apartment.[11] Karic hedged his bets: the ultranationalist paramilitary leader Vojislav Seselj claimed that Boguljub had contributed 30,000DM to his party's election campaign in 1992.[12] Karic also set up an international charitable foundation, with branches in London, Nicosia and Moscow. The foundation was a co-organiser of Serbian Week in Israel and also worked with Borka Vucic in Cyprus, while she was running Beogradska Banka there, according to its website: www.karicfoundation.com., Karic sponsored several talking-head symposiums in Belgrade, of the kind beloved by Mira. These included the very apposite 'Role of Religion in the Peaceful Settlement of Conflicts' and even 'New Achievements in the Study of Consciousness'.

Mira Markovic and the other leaders of JUL never resolved the contradiction between the party's stated leftist aims and its wealthy backers. But then they did not need to. 'We could say that JUL was created as an econo–mafia structure which operated under the patronage of the Socialist Party,' noted the report of the Serbian Public Revenue Agency.[13]

In the summer of 1996 Milosevic was buoyed by the arrival in Belgrade of the former British Foreign Secretary Douglas Hurd, accompanied by Dame Pauline Neville-Jones, who as political director to the Foreign Office had served as Britain's head of delegation to Dayton. Since leaving the cabinet the previous year, Hurd had taken a highly-lucrative post as deputy chairman of NatWest Markets, where Neville-Jones also worked. The bank was interested in the privatisation of Serbian state utilities, in particular Serbian Telecom.

Hurd had joined the subsidiary of National Westminster Bank in October 1995. Neville-Jones had left the Foreign Office in January 1996, after which she had acted as a senior adviser to Carl Bildt, who had been appointed the international community's High Representative in Bosnia, in overall charge of implementing Dayton. But by July Neville-Jones had left Bildt's office and joined NatWest Markets. There was criticism in the press about this swift transition from the diplomatic to commercial sector, and the speed with which Hurd and Neville-Jones touted for business in such a sensitive area, of which they had such detailed inside knowledge. A question was even asked in parliament.

During his time as foreign secretary Hurd had been widely criticised by Bosnia's supporters. He had supported the UN arms embargo, which had guaranteed Serb military superiority. In the summer of 1993 Hurd gave a speech on Bosnia at the Travellers' Club. He attacked the media for their 'selectivity' in the way they reported Bosnia, saying, 'most of those who report for the BBC, *The Times*, the *Independent*, the *Guardian* have all been in different ways enthusiasts for pushing military intervention in Bosnia. They are founder members of the "something must be done" school.'[15]

Milosevic had attempted to exploit pro-Serb sympathies in Westminster and Whitehall. At the start of the Yugoslav wars in 1992 Belgrade made two payments, totalling £96,250, to Ian Greer Associates, the Westminster lobbying group with high-level connections to the Conservative Party.[16] Greer's lobbying work was usefully timed for Milosevic, then under diplomatic pressure after the revelations about the Serb concentration camps in Bosnia (although outrage about Omarska did not guarantee anything would be done: as Lord Owen had proclaimed at Sarajevo airport in December 1992: 'Don't, don't, don't live under this dream that the West is going to come in and sort this problem out. Don't dream dreams').[17]

On the cover of *Unfinest Hour*, the forensic dissection of Britain's Bosnia policy by the Cambridge academic Brendan Simms, is a picture of British UN Commander General Rose smiling and shaking hands with a laughing General Mladic. As demands grew in the United States for military intervention against the Serbs, General Rose had fulminated against what he called the 'powerful Jewish lobby behind the Bosnian state',[18] surely the first time in history when Jews had been criticised for being too pro-Muslim. Clearly, Klara Mandic's Serb-Jewish Friendship Society had not been working hard enough. It was also noticeable that much of the British left remained silent over Bosnia, wrongly believing that somehow Milosevic was Tito's heir.

General Rose was replaced as UNPROFOR commander in Bosnia by General Sir Rupert Smith. Under General Smith's command, finally, something was done. At the end of August 1995, Operation 'Deliberate Force' was launched against the Bosnian Serbs. The NATO air strikes, and the joint Croat-Bosnian offensive in northern Bosnia brought Milosevic to the negotiating table. He signed the Dayton accord, sanctions were lifted and Serbia was open for business, which is where Hurd and Neville-Jones came in.

A deal was eventually struck. NatWest Markets would broker the lucrative contract to part-privatise Serbian Telecom. Italian and Greek investors would take 49 per cent of the company. NatWest Markets reportedly was paid at least £10 million in commission. NatWest also

agreed to manage Serbia's national debt. The deal was seen hopefully
in the NatWest boardroom as the first of many privatisations of Serbia's
state utilities. Mira's interests were also represented. According to the
ICEFA report, JUL President Ljubisa Ristic then travelled to London
and subsequently assumed the responsibility for the concrete details
of the arrangement. The contract for Serbian Telecom was worth
$1 billion for the Milosevic regime. This was a massive amount of
money for a country that was wrecked economically. Five years later,
in the summer of 2001, Serb officials argued that the Telecom contract
helped Milosevic stay in power and helped keep his regime going long
enough to pay for the next war, in Kosovo.[19]

By this time Milosevic had been at the summit of Serbian politics
for almost nine years, since his triumph at the Eighth Session in
September 1987. He governed – or rather ruled – by a combination
of micro-management and diktat. But while this authoritarian approach
succeeded, after a fashion, in a wartime environment, it was less suited
to managing the peace, which demanded a more subtle, considered
approach. Milosevic was psychologically unable to adjust to the new
circumstances.

'Milosevic was not an ideologue. He understood that after Dayton,
he should go in another direction, and abandon Greater Serbia,' said
the Belgrade analyst Braca Grubacic.[20]

> But he was unable to accept democratisation. Milosevic also saw in
> neighbouring countries that whoever made the transition to democ-
> racy then lost power. He sacked the nationalists, but instead of going
> towards liberalisation, and real democratisation of the country, he
> switched to an outdated type of Communism, and JUL. He was
> more of a tactician, and Mira influenced his political strategy. He
> lost his own roots in the power structure as it rotted away. This was
> the influence of his wife.

Always haunted by the bloody Romanian revolution in 1989,
Milosevic himself began to fall victim to 'Ceausescu Syndrome'. He
was surrounded by yes-men and Mira's loyalists at JUL, and there were
increasing rumours that he was losing his grip.

In turning to JUL, Milosevic was following a well-established pattern.
He had for years sidestepped the established institutions and then set up

his own parallel or 'shadow network', which destroyed, or devoured, the original. At the Eighth Session in 1987 Milosevic had outmanoeuvred the faction around Ivan Stambolic with his cabal of loyalists. With the Communist Party under his control, Milosevic then took over Serbia itself, and finally Yugoslavia, where he controlled the Federal Presidency through his placement in the 'Serbian bloc' (the representatives of Serbia, Montenegro, Kosovo and Voivodina). Even the National Bank was less important than Borka Vucic, Milosevic's shadow finance minister, who ran her own autonomous economic empire, based in Cyprus. Milosevic had opened his own private diplomatic line to President Tudjman. All these moves were buttressed by one of Milosevic's key strategic decisions: the marginalisation of the federal Yugoslav intelligence services – especially the military branches – and their subordination to the Serbian domestic intelligence, the (by now renamed) RDB, under the direction of Jovica Stanisic.

The strength of the 'shadow' gambit is that it is dynamic and decisive. In a degraded political structure it brings short-term results. Its weakness is that ultimately, there is nowhere else left to go, it leaves a trail of embittered former allies in its wake, and the supply of suitable personnel eventually runs dry. Which was where JUL came in.

Mira certainly had no intention of democratising. She was increasingly inspired by China, which she had visited as part of a Yugoslav delegation. A curious Belgrade–Beijing axis was developing. So numerous were the Chinese immigrants that the Balkan capital began to boast its own Chinatown. The people-smuggling networks that brought illegal migrants into the West ran a line from Belgrade into Hungary, from where it was a short hop into Austria, and the borderless European Union. Belgrade wits dubbed JUL 'The Communist Party of China in Serbia'.

The hard-liners in both JUL and the Chinese Communist Party shared a similar neo-Marxist world-view, opposing what they described as the hegemony of the United States. China saw Belgrade as a useful counterweight to US policies in the Balkans. Mira's growing influence could be seen in the visit by Yugoslav President Zoran Lilic to China in November 1995, after which he praised its economy and society. Increasingly, Milosevic appeared to be following the Chinese model, at least domestically. In February 1996 the independent television station Studio B was taken over by the regime. Twenty journalists were sacked and a new emphasis was announced, on 'sport and entertainment'.

The move signalled Milosevic's determination to control the outcome of the local and federal elections in November. The three main figures of the fractious opposition had finally joined their parties in a coalition known as 'Zajedno', meaning 'together'. Zajedno was jointly led by Vuk Draskovic, leader of the Serbian Renewal Movement, Zoran Djindjic of the centrist Democratic Party, and Vesna Pesic of the liberal Civic Alliance. Zajedno did poorly in the federal election, winning just twenty-two seats in parliament, compared to sixty-four for the government coalition of the Socialists, JUL and the business-orientated New Democracy Party. Most surprising were the sixteen seats won by the paramilitary leader Vojislav Seselj's party.

But Zajedno won in over a dozen localities, including Belgrade, Novi Sad and the southern city of Nis. Zoran Djindjic was presented to a rally in Belgrade as the city's new mayor and declared to the crowd that, 'Serbia's friends will be able to say that Serbia is neither Cuba nor Korea.' It would be a while, however, before he took over Belgrade city hall. The local election results were annulled because of 'irregularities', and a third round of voting was announced. In Nis, the election committee simply awarded the city to the Socialists. Zajedno called for a boycott of the third round, which was widely observed. Robert Thomas notes that when Belgrade Television filmed Milosevic voting, the only other person in the polling station was Marko.[21]

Anger and outrage spread at Milosevic's blatant stealing of the election. By the end of November 1996 Belgrade was brought to a halt by daily demonstrations. Tens of thousands of protestors – many of whom were students, but there were also members of the disgruntled general public – took to the streets. They hurled rocks and eggs at the headquarters of *Politika* and Belgrade Radio and Television. Vuk Draskovic declared that Milosevic had come to power on 'yoghurt, and will go out on eggs', in a reference to the 1988 'Yoghurt Revolution' in Voivodina.

Zajedno's daily protests were innovative, and colourful. The streets became a giant political carnival. A new 'Serbian airforce' was inaugurated, when thousands of paper aeroplanes were launched at the Belgrade television building. Female demonstrators handed flowers to policemen, just as their predecessors had done in anti-Vietnam war protests. Many carried foreign flags, as a protest against Serbia's isolationism. After the first week of demonstrations as many as 200,000 people were on the streets in Belgrade alone, with satellite protests in cities such as Nis.

Meanwhile Serbian state television broadcast dreary Soviet-style reports about visits by delegations from Russia and Bulgaria. Eventually, in December, the regime reacted by denouncing the protesters as 'pro-Fascists'. The Serbian police announced that unauthorised demonstrations would no longer be tolerated. Mira, who had returned from a trip to India, also strongly criticised the protesters. Milosevic's tame journalists attempted to portray the protesters as tools of foreign powers, a classic Balkan smear tactic. The Serbian people were not so easily fooled. Almost every family in the country had someone on the streets protesting. The more lies the state media propagated, the more they discredited themselves. So much so that Aleksandar Tijanic, the government's own information minister, resigned.

Inevitably, the regime resorted to violence. A demonstrator called Dejan Bulatovic, a member of Vuk Draskovic's party, had operated a life-size Milosevic puppet, dressed in prison uniform, which always drew ironic cheers from the crowd. Bulatovic was arrested, beaten up by the police and sentenced to twenty-five days in prison for traffic obstruction. The opposition magazine *Vreme* ran a picture of Bulatovic on its cover, with Milosevic's claim to the Kosovo Serbs that 'No one should dare to beat you'.

Night after night the protestors braved the freezing Belgrade winter, and the police. There was a sense that the Milosevic regime was corroding and weakening. Strange allies came forward. The nationalist writer Dobrica Cosic addressed a Zajedno rally. Thirty members of the Academy of Sciences signed a declaration of support. And other messages of support came from exiled Prince Alexander Karadjordjevic, heir to the throne; Biljana Plavsic, who had replaced her old rival Radovan Karadzic as President of Republika Srpska; and even the Kosovo Albanian activist Adem Demaci.

The street protests were a symptom of the force of anger and resentment against the Milosevic regime. Serbs had simply had enough of war, privation, corruption and poverty. For a politician with a reasonably sophisticated grasp of international politics. Milosevic had a poor understanding of events in his own country. He saw 'conspiracies' everywhere, and blamed everything on malevolent outside forces. Under pressure, he took refuge in a bottle of Viljamovka. 'Milosevic could not handle the winter demonstrations. He was drunk a lot of the time,' said one high level source.[22] 'Milosevic was angry with America. He said, "I gave Clinton Dayton, I gave him peace, I gave him a second term. Why are they plotting against me, and trying to organise this against me?"'[23]

Here once again was the 'concept deficit' of a leader whose political methodology had barely evolved from 1986, when he had become president of the Communist Party. Zoran Djindjic recalled a conversation with Milosevic: 'I said, "You really have problems; there are one hundred thousand people on the street demonstrating against you." He looked at me and said, "You must be watching too much CNN. There aren't."'[24]

The West considered its next step. The Dayton peacemaker had reverted to a Balkan tyrant. The opposition made it clear that it was opposed to further sanctions, which would further impoverish the demonstrators. Attention focused instead on a new tactic, known as 'smart sanctions', which would selectively target the key people in the regime, hitting them in their pockets by freezing overseas assets and refusing visas for travel to the West. Over the next few years these sanctions would have a significant effect on the regime's power structure, triggering cracks that would eventually widen into deep fissures.

Marooned in the mindset of the late 1980s, Milosevic responded with the tactics, personnel, even the tired rhetoric of that time. Mihalj Kertes, organiser of the 1988 'anti-bureaucratic revolution' in Novi Sad, was ordered to organise a counter-demonstration in Belgrade on 24 December. The authorities promised 500,000 demonstrators. Just as in 1988, buses and supplies of food and drink were laid on. But the 60,000 government supporters who turned up were shocked to find themselves outnumbered five to one by Zajedno's demonstrators. A visibly angry Milosevic addressed his small, if adoring, crowd: 'What are the aims of all these [Zajedno] demonstrations? First it is to retard our economic development, and secondly to weaken us so as to threaten the integrity of Yugoslavia and Serbia. But Serbia will not be divided.'[25]

Milosevic had ignited wars in Slovenia, Croatia and Bosnia. Now it seemed he was turning Serb against Serb in a bid to stay in power. Fighting broke out between government and Zajedno supporters, one of whom was shot in the head. Another Zajedno protester later died from the beating he received from government supporters. Fifty-eight people were hospitalised.

Milosevic had also made another mistake. A delegation from the Organisation for Security and Co-operation in Europe (OSCE) was invited to Belgrade to see for themselves the results of the local elections. As these had been annulled by Milosevic for no good reason except his party lost, the OSCE delegation duly reported that the opposition had indeed won.

Buoyed by this, Zajedno pushed harder, and not just on the streets, where the protests continued. The coalition opened links to the army, where dissatisfaction with Milosevic's direction of the wars in Bosnia and Croatia was running high. After one elite unit expressed its support for the protesters, General Momcilo Perisic, the army chief of staff, met student leaders on 6 January 1997. Afterwards, one of the student leaders said: 'Perisic said we were on the same side. Both of us wanted to see the constitution respected.'[26] This significant meeting was followed by a statement of support from the Orthodox Church, condemning the 'Communist, godless and satanic regime'. Zajedno also used perhaps the deadliest weapon in the political arsenal: humour. Live sheep were brought to protests and placards were draped around their necks proclaiming 'We support the Socialist Party'. Protesters split into twenty mini-marches, which were harder to control by the police, and walked the streets blowing whistles and banging pots and pans. Instead of fading away in the winter cold, as Milosevic hoped, Zajedno's protests grew ever more dynamic.

Milosevic's own ranks began to split. Nebojsa Covic, the Socialist mayor of Belgrade, was expelled from the party. Milosevic conceded defeat in Nis, where Socialist Party members came forward with lurid details of ballot rigging and election fraud. Behind the scenes Mira Markovic clashed with secret police chief Jovica Stanisic, who was opposed to breaking up the demonstrations by force. None the less, on the night of 2 February eight demonstrators were injured by police using water cannons and clubs. The next night, though, the widely anticipated violence did not happen. The regime seemed confused. In early February Milosevic conceded defeat. A special law was rushed through parliament recognising Zajedno's victories in the local elections. Zoran Djindjic was inaugurated as mayor of Belgrade on 21 February.

This was a bad week for the Milosevic family. The previous day Vlada Kovacevic – nicknamed 'Tref' – the former racing driver who had sponsored Marko's racing career had been shot dead as he walked to his office in Belgrade. Bolstered by his association with Marko, Tref had moved into the highly-lucrative duty-free and import business, much of which was controlled by organised crime. It was observed with interest – in more places than Belgrade – that having the son of the Serbian president as a business partner was not protection enough.

22

WAR NO. 4, KOSOVO –
PART 1

Finishing Unfinished Business

1998

MACBETH: Oh full of scorpions is my mind, dear wife!

M arko had moved into a new house. He was only twenty-two, but he owned a spacious villa in Pozarevac, surrounded by a high fence, not far from his parents' residence. Quite an achievement when the average monthly wage was the equivalent of £50, if it was ever paid.

Marko earned more than that. He had gone into business with Mihalj Kertes. Kertes had organised demonstrations for Milosevic since 1988, and had another job. He was head of the Yugoslav customs service, controlling the flow of smuggled oil and cigarettes into the country. Marko controlled the import of the Philip Morris brand.[2] Each truckload of cigarettes brought in about $250,000. Of course, that had to be split down the line, but enough remained to pay for underfloor heating in Marko's house, and a swimming pool. But Marko was wondering, how warm should the water be? He called Dad for some advice.

Marko: Do you know the water in my pool is heated to 38 degrees Celsius?
Slobodan: You're a fool, man. That's not healthy.
Marko: Yeah, right. It should be 18 degrees. That's the real thing.
Slobodan: In any case, it should not be over 30 degrees. Why on earth are you fooling around?
Marko: Why not, I swim at 40 degrees.
Sloba gives up, passes him on to Mira.
Mira: Darling, my sweet puppy . . .

Marko: Mummy, I had the water heated to 38 degrees. If only you knew how wonderful it is.[3]

Like every good businessman, Marko was diversifying. He ran a bakery and a disco in Pozarevac called Madona (*sic*), one of the biggest nightclubs in the Balkans. He was thinking about opening a private luxury maternity ward for the mothers of Pozarevac. Slobodan advised him against. 'Don't fuck around. Stick to the Madona.'[4]

Radovan Stojicic (a.k.a. 'Badza') also smuggled cigarettes. Stojicic, together with Mihalj Kertes and others, had armed the rebel Serbs in Croatia. A violent man, skilled in martial arts, Stojicic prospered under Milosevic. By 1997 he was acting interior minister and chief of police. Word was, Badza was getting greedy. On the night of 10 April, he went to meet his son, Vojislav, and others at the Mama Mia Italian restaurant in downtown Belgrade. Located not far from the police headquarters, and the British and United States embassies, Mama Mia was a favourite hang-out of both cops and diplomats.

Sometime after midnight a man wearing a ski mask walked in. He ordered everyone in the restaurant to lie down, walked up to Badza and fired half a dozen rounds into him at almost point-blank range.[5] The police immediately sealed off the area, but the killer was never caught. Some suspected Milosevic had ordered the hit, for Badza knew where the bodies were buried, and who ordered them put there.

It was more likely, many believed, that Badza's former partners-in-crime were responsible. If this theory was correct, the crime barons now felt confident enough to assassinate the chief of police in public. State security, it seemed, could not even protect itself, let alone the country. 'This was a lesson. That was the first killing of its kind. Badza was killed by the tobacco mafia,' said one former regime insider. 'It did not matter how high a rank someone had. This looked like a political killing, but it was not.'[6]

There was heavy security at Badza's funeral. Slobodan himself stood in the front row, as well as Marija and Marko. Beneath the grief and bravado the black-draped mourners looked nervous. Mira did not attend. Arkan attended, together with his wife, the turbo-folk singer known as 'Ceca'. So did a man called Nikola Sainovic, who kept a low profile. He ran eastern Serbia for Milosevic, and the mining town of Bor. Sainovic had held a series of high-ranking government posts since his appointment as Serbian minister of mining and energy in 1991. Milosevic valued him for his discretion, and technical knowledge. He controlled much of Serbia's precious metals trade. According to the Serbian Public Revenue Agency report: 'He controlled the Pozarevac-Nis line, where the two strategic products, copper and gold, were exported. However, the amount of gold produced in Serbia was never known. According to an engineer at Bor, six tons were processed every year, according to official reports, three tons.'[7]

By 1997 Sainovic was Yugoslav deputy prime minister. But the death of Badza and Mira's purges left Milosevic with a personnel problem. He was reduced to appointing Vlajko Stojilkovic as Serbian interior minister. Like Milosevic and Mira, Stojilkovic came from Pozarevac. He was a dull-witted, brutal man, and a party hard-liner. His appointment triggered scathing comments in what was left of Serbia's free media, as well as several resignations in the interior ministry.

However, Zajedno was not very 'together'. Vuk Draskovic was furious because his wife Danica was not given the position of president of the Belgrade City government. Draskovic was a veteran of the anti-Milosevic movement, dating back to 1991. In street protests of 1993 both he and his wife had been arrested and severely beaten by police. Draskovic's injuries were so bad that he was subsequently hospitalised. When Danica had been hit, she had mocked the policemen for their 'bravery'. Draskovic, who now called for the restoration of the monarchy, wanted to stand as Zajedno candidate for president in the 1997 Serbian elections. His rival, Belgrade mayor Zoran Djindjic, was opposed.

Milosevic slid further into authoritarianism. By the summer of 1997 fifty-five local radio and television stations were shut down. Among them was Radio Bum in Pozarevac. Marko had paid Bum a visit. According to the Serbian writer Slavoljub Djukic, Marko had lined up the station's staff and screamed: 'Do you want me to tear out your antennae, destroy your equipment, and see to it that within two hours your station's shut down? I'll show you who you are fucking with.'[8]

The atmosphere of violence and intimidation, and the police beating of the Zajedno demonstrators, put off the few foreign investors who were considering doing business in Belgrade. Douglas Hurd's judgment was called into question for having brokered the deal to privatise Serbian Telecom. Buffeted by increasing criticism at home over his links with Belgrade, he justified his actions in a letter to the London *Times*, arguing that after Dayton, it 'seemed possible' the Yugoslav government had decided to 'move towards economic and political liberalisation'. Hurd wrote: 'It is very much in the interests of the West that they should do so. In those circumstances it was legitimate for an international western bank to offer to help in carrying through this programme.'[9] He also called on Milosevic 'to recognise fully the results of the Serbian Municipal elections'. That month National Westminster Bank cancelled a contract to manage Serbia's foreign debt that had been negotiated at the same time as the privatisation of Serbian Telecom. The bank cited Milosevic's failure to implement his promises of 'economic liberalisation and democratisation'. But the Telecom deal, the single most important privatisation at this time, remained in place.

In July the Socialist-led majority in the federal parliament voted in Milosevic as President of Yugoslavia. He had served two terms as President of Serbia, which was all the constitution allowed.

The appointment signified little more than a change of job title. Milosevic remained in charge. But the family had a new home: Tito's former residence. Situated on Uzicka Street, a couple of minutes' walk from Milosevic's property at Tolstoyeva 33, this was the grandest residence of all in the plush suburb of Dedinje, known as Belgrade's Beverly Hills. It was a long way from the squalid shanty towns around Belgrade, where tens of thousands of Serb refugees from Bosnia and Croatia huddled together in ramshackle dwellings without proper water or electricity supplies. 'Uzicka', as the residence was known, covered a whole city block. It included two houses, Tito's tomb, several small cabins Tito used for his hobbies such as metalworking, and extensive landscaped gardens. One house was a modern white villa, built for Tito in the 1970s. The other was a grand pre-war mansion, splendid enough to have been requisitioned by the German army commander during the Second World War.

Mira chose the mansion. But first, everything had to go. Paranoid that Tito's former residence had been bugged, Mira ordered the house stripped. The Persian carpets were burnt in the garden. The antique pianos were reduced to firewood. When some of the workers asked if they could at least take a carpet home, the foreman replied that Mira's orders were to destroy everything.

Once the renovation work was finished, Marko went to have a look. He immediately called his mother to offer: 'My deepest and sincere congratulations'. Mira's heart swelled with maternal joy. She wanted

Marko to see her study. But she was most proud of the colour scheme she had chosen for Marko's rooms. The bathroom had blue lights, to match the blue walls.

> Mira: Did you see you can go from the bathroom onto the terrace?
> Marko: No.
> Mira: Go have a look.
> Marko: Oh, that. Yes, I did; I did. [. . .]
> Mira: And the bathroom, like an entire flat, isn't it?
> Marko: When I walked in, I couldn't believe it, honestly.
> Mira: That's because your mommy chose everything . . . It had been closed for seventeen years, ever since Tito died. I threw everything out. Literally everything. Except a few chandeliers downstairs and one chandelier here. Look at our living rooms on the first floor. Look at the dining room, the kitchen. Also, go upstairs and to the penthouse.[10]

Mira and Marko had also been thinking about remodelling themselves. As JUL increased its profile, Mira began to appear in public. She dressed in Versace, the favoured label of Belgrade gangsters. Self-conscious about her looks, and her weight, she underwent liposuction at Belgrade's military hospital, according to Dusan Mitevic. 'She started to work on her image. They brought two Italian doctors to the army hospital, because we did not have the technical ability to do this.'[11]

Milosevic had other matters on his mind. In August, he invited Draskovic for talks at Uzicka to discuss the next month's Serbian elections. Draskovic was flattered at the attention. He claimed he was now 'leader of the opposition'. In response Belgrade mayor Zoran Djindjic called for a boycott of the elections. Draskovic pledged to take part. Their supporters were soon fighting each other – sometimes physically – instead of Milosevic.

Meanwhile neighbouring Albania was descending into civil war. After the collapse of Communism, the country barely functioned. Albania had the worst infrastructure in Europe, and considerable areas were wild and lawless, beyond the control of the central government. With no experience of capitalism and the free market, and no real understanding of how banks and economics worked, many Albanians had poured all their savings into murky pyramid banking schemes, just as in Serbia. When, inevitably, the pyramid schemes collapsed, disgruntled creditors broke into the national arsenals. Like Tito, Albania's Communist rulers had prepared for possible invasion from either NATO or the Warsaw Pact. The swindled investors stole the guns and fought pitched street battles. The country was flooded with weapons. Albania plunged into total anarchy, a development which would have profound consequences for Serbia later on. These weapons would later arm the nascent Kosovo Liberation Army. Milosevic had first built his power base on exploiting Kosovo, and initially funded his regime on pyramid schemes. The crash of their Albanian equivalents would bring the war to Serbia.

But up in Uzicka as far as Milosevic was concerned, everything was going to plan as the country went to the polls. The 'Left Coalition' of the Socialists, JUL and New Democracy won the election with 110 seats. Draskovic's party took 45 seats. Vojislav's Seselj's Serbian Radicals won 82 seats. In revenge for Djindjic's boycott of the polls Draskovic attempted to remove Zoran Djindjic as mayor of Belgrade. Once again Belgrade's streets filled with demonstrators. This time they were protesting not against Milosevic, but Draskovic. Squads of riot police fell on the demonstrators as they poured into Belgrade. Many were beaten, including Djindjic himself.

While Zajedno auto-destructed, Mira's JUL tightened its grip on the country's assets. Zoran Todorovic, a.k.a. Kundak, now ran Beopetrol, the second largest petrol company in Serbia, rivalled only by Jugopetrol. But just after 8.00 a.m. on 24 October Kundak was parking his car when a young man came running towards him.[13] He fired two short bursts into Kundak's head and back. Like the man who killed Badza, he was never found.

Kundak had epitomised the rise of JUL's red businessmen, who had treated the country as their personal holding, to be plundered at will. Mira had plucked Kundak from obscurity at Belgrade University and made him one of the richest and most powerful men in Serbia. Kundak was one of the Milosevic family's closest friends. He even wrote poems to Mira. Mira herself was on a visit to India when her adored protégé was killed. She was nearly hysterical when she heard of his death, and locked herself in her hotel room. Kundak's funeral was virtually a Who's Who of the Serbian elite. Mira sent condolences from India. Milosevic was seen to cry. But beneath the tears, the mourners were asking themselves the same question: first Marko's partner Tref, then Milosevic's ally Badza, and now Mira's protégé Kundak. Who would be next?

The following month Milosevic appointed secret service chief Jovica Stanisic national security advisor. From now on, all intelligence gathered by the four secret services – Serbian, Montenegrin, military and diplomatic – would land on Stanisic's desk.[14]

An increasing number of intelligence reports Stanisic saw confirmed there was indeed a serious threat to Serbian national security. Not from mafia hitmen, but from a military force with far deadlier potential. On 28 November a trio of masked gunmen appeared at a funeral of three Albanians in Kosovo who had been killed in a shoot-out with Serbian police. The cheers of twenty thousand mourners resounded across the valley, when the gunmen announced that only the Kosovo Liberation Army (KLA) could fight for the liberation of Kosovo from the Serbs. The shadowy organisation had now gone public.

Since Milosevic had revoked Kosovo's autonomy in 1989, the province had teetered on the edge of civil war. Milosevic had ordered a systematic repression to crush any political opposition to his nationalist drive, backed up by a heavily armed paramilitary police force that never hesitated to use violence. Albanian language newspapers and television stations were closed. Schools and colleges were shut down. All Albanian professors were expelled from Pristina University. Hundreds of thousands of workers, from doctors to dustbin men, lost their jobs in a massive purge of state employees. Arkan's Tigers set up headquarters in the capital Pristina and Arkan himself became an MP for Kosovo. He easily won elections, as the 80 per cent of the population who were ethnic Albanians boycotted the polls.

The leader of the Kosovo Albanians was Ibrahim Rugova, a bespectacled academic who during the 1970s had studied literary criticism in Paris under Roland Barthes. Rugova still wore his trademark scarf from his student days. His great passion was collecting rocks. He was president of the Democratic League of Kosovo (LDK), the main Albanian political party. Kosovo had declared independence in July 1990, although no country recognised it. During the 1990s, under Rugova's Ghandian policy of passive resistance, the LDK built up a complete parallel state, simply side-stepping the Serbian institutions. The LDK ran its own schools, hospitals (all Albanian doctors had been fired by the Serbs) and welfare organisations, and even collected taxes. Milosevic more or less tolerated this, as it saved the province from conflict and saved Belgrade from having to provide the usual services of government.

As the random arrests, beatings and prison sentences increased, a system of de facto apartheid set in. There was virtually no contact between the Albanians and Serbs. Children stopped playing together, and the evening *corso*, the social parade, was divided between Albanians on one side of the road and Serbs on the other. The few brave young lovers who crossed the ethnic divide had to meet in secret. To be seen together in public would merit a beating, or worse. Tito's modernisation had made little impact on Albanian society, much of which, especially outside the cities, remained deeply conservative and patriarchal. Women were expected to marry young and bear many children quickly. The traditional walled compounds behind which several generations of an extended family lived could still be seen in the countryside. Much of Albanian life was lived by the *kanun* of Lek Dukagjini, a body of laws dating back to the fifteenth century, which also regulated the laws that governed spilled blood.

Many families kept going on the wages sent home by their relatives who were guestworkers in German and Austrian car factories. Kosovo functioned, but only barely. Pristina was a dusty, oppressive city, ringed by shoddy Socialist-era tower blocks. The infrastructure was shaky and the economy was wrecked, although ironically many Kosovars enriched themselves by running sanctions-busting smuggling operations over the porous borders to Albania, Greece and Macedonia.[15] Some Kosovars were involved in organised crime networks in Europe. In the villages Serbs could be offered spectacular sums to sell their houses.

Fear and alienation fuelled widespread anti-Albanian racism. For many Serbs this was something more visceral than the prejudice they felt against Croats or Bosnian Muslims. If Croats were feared and Bosnian Muslims looked down on, at least they were Slavs, and spoke the same language (Albanian is unrelated to the Slavic tongues). The wars were a family affair, albeit a very Balkan one. Even sophisticated Belgrade liberals were often dismissive of Albanians, regarding them as primitive or backward. And, of course, most of the Kosovars were Muslims.

The wars in Croatia and Bosnia that brought those countries independence – at whatever cost – radicalised the Kosovo Albanians. There was anger that Kosovo had been ignored at Dayton, but the Albanians saw the benefits that secessionist violence had brought for the Bosnian Serbs. During the mid-1990s the nascent Albanian guerrilla forces in Kosovo's mountains had began to coalesce. Growing dissatisfaction with Rugova's passive resistance led many to believe that the time had come to take up arms. The KLA was born.[16] The KLA's support came from young radicals released from prison, former soldiers and police officers who had weapons training. Dissatisfaction was spreading with Rugova's approach. Rugova behaved like a president, and drove around Pristina in an Audi. People stood up when he entered a restaurant. But nothing changed.

By 1996 the increasingly frequent armed skirmishes between Albanian fighters and Serbian police had made some villages effectively 'no-go areas' for the authorities. The meltdown of central government in Albania provided the arms for the KLA. The guns 'liberated' by the angry former depositors in the pyramid schemes poured across the border. Kosovo was classic guerrilla warfare territory, providing a ready-made support network in the remote Albanian villages. Milosevic was a former Communist but had not, it seemed, much studied the works of the arch guerilla tactician Mao Tse-tung. The money was provided by the Albanian diaspora in Europe. In smoky bars and exiled cafés across Germany, Switzerland and Austria the hat went round for the homeland struggle. It was soon overflowing with cash.

The fighting stepped up. In February 1998 an American diplomat, Robert Gelbard, was despatched to meet Milosevic. Gelbard praised his 'significant positive influence' in Bosnia,[17] and then travelled on to Pristina. There Gelbard condemned the killing of three Serb police officers by the KLA as a terrorist act. He then described the KLA as 'without any questions, a terrorist group'.[18] Milosevic saw this as a message. On the morning of Saturday 28 February a KLA patrol was ambushed by Serb police. Two policemen were killed and two died later of their wounds. The police took their revenge by killing twenty-six Albanians. Many were executed at point-blank range. On 5 March the Serbs attacked the compound of the family of Adem Jashari, a veteran KLA leader, in the village of Donji Prekaz, with heavy artillery. By the end of the day the Jashari compound was a tangle of rubble, blood and bodies. Fifty-eight people were killed, including eighteen women and ten children under sixteen. The kanun of Lek Dukagjini declared that there was no going back from this.

The Kosovo crackdown and the international outcry against the massacre of the Jasharis began to trigger splits within the Milosevic regime. More moderate figures, such as Zoran Lilic, called for limited and precisely-targeted actions to reduce both civilian casualties and the possibility of international intervention. Lilic was an undistinguished former Yugoslav president who had previously been regarded as a Milosevic figurehead. But he spoke for many who wanted Yugoslavia to rejoin the international community.

From Washington, D.C. to Belgrade, it was widely understood that if Kosovo erupted into war, NATO would almost certainly intervene. Only the western military alliance had the necessary force of arms to stop the Serbs. NATO had bombed the Bosnian Serbs in 1995 and Belgrade would be next. The alliance's prestige was on the line, especially after the massacres at Srebrenica. General Momcilo Perisic, Yugoslav army chief of staff, and national security advisor Jovica Stanisic, began to distance themselves from Milosevic. General Perisic had promised the student protesters that the army would not intervene against the Zajedno demonstrations, and also told Milosevic as much. There were rumours that elements of the army high command were considering some kind of military coup. Stanisic, like Perisic, was increasingly concerned that, under the influence of JUL, Milosevic was leading Serbia into complete international isolation, war with NATO and eventual collapse.

These fears seemed to be confirmed when the new Serbian government was formed in March 1998, a coalition of the Socialists, JUL and the Serbian Radical Party, led by Vojislav Seselj, the ultra-national paramilitary leader. Just a few years earlier Milosevic's regime had accused Seselj of war crimes and he had returned the compliment. During the mid-1990s, Mira Markovic had written: 'No, Seselj is not a Serb. He is a Turk, in the most primitive historical edition. Or perhaps, he just is not a man. Although, to be honest, I think that he is neither one nor the other. Neither a Serb nor a man.'[19]

This did not prevent Seselj and his deputy from being appointed deputy prime ministers by her husband, nor Mira's colleagues from serving in the same government as her former *bête noire*. Seselj's Serbian Radical Party received sixteen senior government posts, and other ministries went to JUL. Seselj was quite open about his plans for Kosovo. Over 300,000 Albanian 'post-war immigrants' would be immediately expelled, and a swathe of territory between twenty and fifty kilometres wide along the border with Albania would be cleared. In April the regime organised a referendum over whether there should be foreign intervention in Kosovo. In true Communist style, the state media claimed that 94.73 per cent had voted against.

The Serb offensive in Kosovo that summer followed the tactics of siege warfare honed by General Mladic in Bosnia. There was a small Yugoslav army presence, but Milosevic's heavily armed police did the bulk of the dirty work, together with its notorious 'special units' that had been deployed in Croatia and Bosnia. The Serb police surrounded villages where the KLA was believed to be operating. After an intense artillery and mortar bombardment, they would sweep through, destroying houses and killing both fighters and civilians. Now-familiar pictures of the Balkans filled newspaper columns and television screens: burning houses, weeping women, terrified children and armed men swaggering over the corpses they left in their wake. By the summer of 1998 up to 250,000 Albanians had fled their homes, either to the mountains or neighbouring countries.

Still, the KLA was fighting an increasingly effective guerrilla war. The Serb police were not trained in counter-insurgency techniques. KLA snipers picked them off at checkpoints. The KLA soon established its own mini-statelet around the town of Malisevo, and took control of a section of the road to Pristina. Like the rebel Serbs in Croatia and Bosnia, the KLA set up its own police and administration, and even issued car licence plates. In areas under KLA control local Serbs were murdered, kidnapped and intimidated.

Pressure mounted on Milosevic to act decisively. The rebel Serbs in Croatia had been sacrificed, and Milosevic had turned against his former protégés in Bosnia. The Kosovo Serbs could not be so easily jettisoned. Kosovo was sovereign Serbian territory and part of Yugoslavia. Milosevic himself had exploited Kosovo to take power and topple Ivan Stambolic. He personally seemed to share the prejudices and emotions of many Serbs over Kosovo. In meetings with western officials such as the US ambassador Warren Zimmerman or Lord Owen, Milosevic lost the suave charm he deployed to discuss Croatia or Bosnia, becoming emotional and confrontational, and demonising the Albanians. He understood that the Serb leader who lost Kosovo would not long survive in power. NATO General Klaus Naumann, who negotiated with Milosevic over Kosovo in October 1998, recalled: 'It seemed to me that Bosnia did not concern him as much as Kosovo. He regarded Kosovo as Serbia's heartland. He told us that Kosovo is an integral part of Serbian history and culture, and he could not give it up.'[20]

All of which put Milosevic in a double-bind. He understood that if he agreed to independence for Kosovo, or even realistic autonomy, his increasingly narrow support base would collapse. But if he did not reach agreement, the war with the KLA would step up until he was forced to deploy the Yugoslav army, just as he had done in Bosnia and Croatia. If the Yugoslav army was deployed in Kosovo, NATO would almost certainly intervene. Perhaps the answer lay in Moscow. Concerned by increasing talk of NATO intervention, Boris Yeltsin invited Milosevic in June, but the Serbian leader received a frosty reception. Yeltsin did not like Milosevic, and described him as 'one of the most cynical politicians I have ever met'.[21] Under pressure from Yeltsin, Milosevic agreed to the deployment of observer missions in Kosovo.

As the ethnic cleansing continued, prompting ever greater public out-rage in the West that, once again, the Milosevic regime was getting away with murder, NATO prepared for intervention and launched an air operation deploying eighty planes over neighbouring Albania and Macedonia. Behind the scenes, plans were drawn up for a range of military options from air power to a full ground invasion of Kosovo. NATO's sabre-rattling sharpened the divisions within the regime. The leadership of the Socialist Party met in Belgrade. Milosevic appeared disorientated: like every bully, he lost his grip under pressure. When NATO had bombed the Bosnian Serbs, when Zajedno took over central Belgrade, Milosevic sought refuge in a bottle of Viljamovka. He was sober at the party meeting, but seemed 'tired and frightened . . . out of touch', said one source.[22]

A cycle of decay set in. As Mira, JUL and Seselj all increased their influence, the 'moderate' Socialists became increasingly marginalised and dispirited. This left a gap in the power structure . . . filled by JUL, Mira and Seselj. None of these had the will, experience or expertise to deal with the approaching crisis. Alarm further grew when Milosevic proposed that all decision-making powers within the Socialist Party should be handed to him and a cabal of fifteen loyal hard-liners, men such as the mining expert Nikola Sainovic, and the Serbian interior minister Vlajko Stojilkovic.

In October Richard Holbrooke arrived in Belgrade. He brought with him the threat of a phased air campaign if the Kosovo offensive did not end. Increasingly, Milosevic spoke and acted as if he wanted a war with the West. For the Serbian leader and his rapidly shrinking clique, NATO air strikes would be morbid confirmation that he had been right all along, that the world was and always would be dedicated to the destruction of Serbia. Milosevic said to a US airforce general accompanying Holbrooke: 'So you are the man who is going to bomb me?'[23] After three days of obfuscation from Milosevic, Holbrooke departed from Belgrade with no results.

While NATO authorised the orders that would allow Supreme Commander General Wesley Clark to begin air strikes, Serbian municipal authorities opened up bomb shelters that dated back to the Second World War. Holbrooke then returned to Belgrade. Milosevic backed down and agreed to withdraw Serb forces from Kosovo, and to allow more international monitors to be deployed. Milosevic also shut down two newspapers and banned the re-broadcasting of Serbian language broadcasts from the BBC, Radio Free Europe and Voice of America.

NATO General Secretary Xavier Solana, General Clark and General Klaus Naumann arrived in Belgrade to finalise the details of the Serbs' withdrawal. Ensconced in the White Palace, the former residence of Serbia's royal family, Milosevic reverted to his old tactics. NATO's delegation had come with hard intelligence about Serbian forces in Kosovo. Milosevic denied that the police units were there until he was presented with the evidence. Increasingly exasperated, General Clark spoke to him alone: 'Mr President, you are going to have to withdraw all your excess forces. Let's stop fencing about this. If you don't withdraw, Washington is going to tell me to bomb you, and I'm going to bomb you good.'[24] Milosevic replied: 'Well, General Clark, NATO will do what it must do.'[25] Clark was having none of this. A Vietnam veteran, he knew Milosevic from Dayton, where he had served as chief military negotiator. 'Get real, Mr President. You don't want to be bombed.' Milosevic replied: 'No, General Clark, I don't.'[26]

Milosevic offered some counter-proposals, which Clark presented to NATO. These were considered insufficient. Milosevic appears to have taken a much greater role in micro-managing the Kosovo war than in Bosnia or Croatia. As President of Yugoslavia Milosevic was the supreme commander of the Yugoslav military. According to General Naumann, Milosevic exercised his authority. 'General Perisic told us that Milosevic was the commander in chief for everything that was done, and all decisions were based on this. We were negotiating for two and a half hours on the reduction of Serb forces. But we only had a solution for one village. When we ran into an impasse with the General Staff, Perisic told us to see Milosevic. This for me is a clear indication that Milosevic was the commander in chief.'[27]

But the chief's grip was slipping. After hours of wrangling with Clark and Naumann, he handed round brandies. He waxed lyrical on his favourite discussion topic with westerners: Serbia's future economic potential. Then he suddenly flipped: 'You know General, we know how to deal with those murderers and rapists, these killers, killers of their own kind. We have taken care of them before. In 1946, in Drenica [a town in Kosovo] we killed them, killed them all.' He added: 'Oh, it took several years, but we eventually killed them all.'[28]

Milosevic finally agreed the details of the withdrawal of police units. By now, among Milosevic's loyal cabal there was increasing discussion of using the army to systematically ethnically cleanse Kosovo. But General Perisic was utterly opposed to this. The gap between the Yugoslav president and the army chief of staff was turning into a chasm. General Perisic had been present during some of the meetings between Naumann, Clark and Milosevic. When Milosevic had denied that certain units were deployed in Kosovo, Perisic had confirmed their presence. This was walking a dangerous high wire.

General Naumann recalled: 'When we met General Perisic he said he wanted to keep Serb forces out of the conflict. His aim was to prevent a military confrontation between NATO and Serbia. He understood that it would be very difficult to use a conscript army to cleanse Kosovo and he did not want to see this happen.'[29] Unusually for a senior army commander, General Perisic made his opposition public. He gave a speech in eastern Serbia calling for the resignation of the key officials directing Kosovo policy. Soon after, Perisic was sacked. He issued a public statement condemning his removal as illegal and unconstitutional. Perisic saw what was coming in Kosovo. Although he now presented himself as a democrat, Perisic was wanted for war crimes in Croatia and had overseen the Serb assault on Mostar.

National security advisor Jovica Stanisic was also fired. Stanisic had been seen as one of the most powerful individuals in the regime. As head of the Serbian intelligence service, Stanisic was deeply implicated in the war crimes carried out by Serb forces in both Croatia and Bosnia. He was named by the ICTY as a member of the 'joint criminal conspiracy' to carry out war crimes in both countries.[30] None the less, Stanisic was regarded in the West as a professional intelligence officer. After he was fired, Stanisic issued a public statement that he had always acted in accord with the policies of the Serbian president. The removal of Stanisic was followed by a purge of senior intelligence officers, including high-level analysts, who were replaced by JUL loyalists.

Milosevic also sacked the airforce chief and replaced Perisic with

General Dragoljub Ojdanic, who had commanded operations in eastern Bosnia in 1992, site of the bloodiest ethnic cleansing operations. Stanisic was replaced by Rade Markovic, a policeman for thirty years who had risen to become chief of Belgrade police, before joining the Serbian security service after the killing of Badza in April 1997. Both he and Ojdanic were members of JUL. Mira's loyalists now controlled the two most powerful institutions in the country.

Yet in a morbid symmetry, the more powerful Mira became, the more her husband's regime cracked and corroded. The appointment of Rade Markovic was seen as an ominous portent. Dusan Mitevic made preparations to take his family out of Serbia. Relations had steadily cooled since 1991, but after the period of the Zajedno demonstrations in winter 1996–7 Mitevic had completely broken with Milosevic and Mira. In spring 1999, after the sacking of Stanisic and his replacement by Rade Markovic, the office of ICN (Milan Panic's pharmaceutical company) where Mitevic worked had been raided by the police. Mitevic was thrown out, abused as a 'corrupt traitor' and a 'western lackey'. 'The regime was falling apart,' he said. 'If the chief of police is someone like Rade Markovic, when the police are supposed to protect you, it is better to leave the country. I realised that he was going to start getting rid of people.'

Darkness was falling.

23

WAR NO. 4, KOSOVO – PART 2

NATO Bombs the Serbs

1999

Here in the kingdom we have won
Our arms crossed on our breasts
We continue the battle

We continue it backwards

from 'The Warriors of The Blackbird's Fields', by Vasko Popa[1]

I t was 22 March 1999. Spring was in the air and so were NATO spy planes. Families frantically stocked up on food and basic items. Yugoslavia's president was also making a hurried purchase: another house. As a banker, he knew when to consolidate the family holdings. He had purchased Tolstoyeva 33 in July 1991, just as war was erupting in Croatia. The new place was small, but in a prime location, at Uzicka 34, just down the road from the presidential residence. A 94-square metre dwelling surrounded by one and a half acres of land, it cost Milosevic 84,221 dinars[2] (about £3,400), a fraction of its real value. The contract, signed by the Serbian finance minister Borislav Milacic, was legally questionable anyway as tenants of state-owned property could only buy one residence.

War was just two days away. Richard Holbrooke's October 1998 agreement with Milosevic to bring peace to Kosovo had collapsed. In mid-December the Yugoslav army had killed thirty-six KLA fighters infiltrating from Kosovo. Masked gunmen, presumed to be Albanian, then shot six Serb teenagers playing pool in the town of Pec. In January 1999 the KLA killed four Serb policemen. In retaliation, Serb forces killed forty-five Albanians at the village of Racak, including a twelve-year-old boy and two women.

Television footage of the twisted corpses lying in a ditch was broadcast around the world. The momentum for NATO intervention seemed unstoppable. The chief of the OSCE Kosovo verification mission, US diplomat William Walker, described the attack as 'an unspeakable atrocity', and blamed 'government security forces' for the killings. A former US ambassador to El Salvador, Walker had much experience of working in an environment where government security forces carried out 'unspeakable' atrocities: Washington had for years backed the El Salvadorean death squads.

Milosevic ordered Walker out of the country. He also refused to allow in Louise Arbour, Chief Prosecutor of the ICTY in The Hague, to investigate the Racak massacre. Increasingly nervous about his own likely indictment, Milosevic refused to co-operate with the ICTY, even though that had been part of the Dayton agreement. After news of the Racak massacre broke, generals Clark and Naumann were despatched to Belgrade. Milosevic was evasive, belligerent and cocky. He did not take the threat of NATO retaliation seriously.

General Naumann remembered: 'We confronted him with evidence of the massacre at Racak. He said again that Serb forces do not do this, that they fought cleanly. We had already told him in October that we had evidence to show the opposite. Milosevic said that NATO may be the world's most powerful alliance, but we had no right to bomb Serbia, and if we did we would be war criminals.'[3] Milosevic argued that the KLA were terrorists. Naumann recalled: 'I said I had seen terrorism in my country as well, but we never had the idea of surrounding a village with tanks and artillery, and shelling it while we looked for terrorists. I told him this should be a police operation.' Milosevic's idea of law enforcement, though, was rather different to Naumann's.

Despite the repeated threats by NATO, Naumann believes that in January 1998 Milosevic was not particularly bothered by the prospect of NATO bombing. The Serb leader had already sneered that he expected the bombing to 'be polite'. For years he had skilfully exploited the divisions within the western countries to prevent any serious military threat. Back in 1995, when it had seemed that Banja Luka was about to fall, bringing down Milosevic, Washington had ordered the Croat-Bosnian ground offensive stopped. Milosevic was saved.

The drive to war also had its own atavistic momentum. There was a sense, on both sides, that now, finally, some centuries-old unfinished business could be resolved. Asked how the police would deal with the

KLA, one Serb policeman quoted the title of a film about the Bosnian war, 'Ever seen *Lepa sela, lepo gore* [Pretty Villages, Burn Prettily]?'[4] Milosevic believed his regime could withstand some 'polite' bombing, which could even strengthen his domestic support. He also knew that, behind the NATO generals' threats, the alliance was deeply divided. 'In October Milosevic was concerned that we were serious. In January, he was not,' said Naumann. 'He thought NATO was not cohesive, and he did not believe that there would be any bombing. That was a tragic mistake on his part. It was also a big mistake on the part of certain NATO countries, who gave him hints that no bombing would happen.'

Fearful perhaps of being arrested as a war criminal, Milosevic did not attend the final diplomatic talks over Kosovo, held at the fourteenth-century French château of Rambouillet, just outside Paris. The KLA had demanded independence. Instead Rambouillet offered the Kosovar Albanians substantial autonomy, backed up by 30,000 NATO troops and the withdrawal of most Serb forces. However, 5,000 police and border guards would stay in place. Most crucially, Kosovo would legally remain part of Serbia and Yugoslavia. A final settlement was postponed for three years because no real compromise was possible over Albanian demands for independence. After two rounds of meetings, and under intense pressure from the United States, the Albanian delegation signed up for the peace plan in March.

The Albanians signed in much the same spirit that the Bosnian government had agreed to various peace plans – knowing that as the Serbs would reject them, they might as well take the diplomatic credit. The Albanian delegation was in any case deeply divided. The pacifist leader Ibrahim Rugova refused to support the KLA's armed struggle. He was intimidated by the KLA, in part because two of his closest aides had recently been killed, murders blamed on Albanian extremists. The attention diplomats paid to the KLA's political leader, Hashim Thaci, showed where the power was flowing. Thaci was on a high – through Milosevic's obduracy, luck and circumstance, a group condemned as 'terrorist' just one year earlier was about to drag NATO into war, on its side.

Led by the mining expert Nikola Sainovic, the Serbs had taken little interest in the negotiations. Instead they spent most of their time walking around the gardens, and holding boisterous parties, according to the US diplomat Louis Sell: 'On one occasion, the Albanians complained to their foreign hosts that the Serbs had kept them awake until the early hours of the morning playing the piano and singing nationalist songs.'[5]

But despite the convivial food and wine – notably superior to the fare at Packy's All-Sports Bar – and the beautiful gardens, Rambouillet failed. Milosevic refused to sign. In mid-March Richard Holbrooke returned to Belgrade for one last attempt. By this time Milosevic had sunk into maudlin defiance. He informed the US diplomat Chris Hill that, 'You are a superpower. You can do what you want. If you say Sunday is Wednesday, you can, it is up to you.'[6] This phraseology, with its invocation of a parallel reality, was also a favourite of Mira's. When she was later confronted by the BBC's Tim Sebastian about a report in the Croatian magazine *Globus*, which said Mira was angry about the events around Milosevic's arrest, she replied: 'Honestly, I've never heard of such a magazine. I don't know about its existence or what it says, and what you just said is like telling me it's Sunday today whereas it's actually Tuesday.'[7]

Locked on to his kamikaze course, Milosevic sacked the head of military intelligence, General Aleksandar Dimitrijevic, who had counselled against war with NATO. Holbrooke saw Milosevic for the last time on 22 March, the day the contract was signed for the purchase of Uzicka 34. Holbrooke chose his words carefully. As authorised by the Pentagon, he said the bombing 'will be swift, it will be severe, it will be sustained'. Milosevic replied: 'No more engagement, no more negotiations, I understand that, you will bomb us. You are a great and powerful country, there is nothing we can do about it.' Holbrooke replied, 'It will start very soon after I leave.' There was a long silence, until Milosevic said, 'There is nothing more I can say.' He then asked Holbrooke, 'Will I ever see you again?' Holbrooke replied, 'That's up to you, Mr President.'[8] The embassies of NATO countries closed; diplomats and their families left. US diplomats smashed their computers with sledgehammers.

Thirty-four hours later, NATO began bombing. The night skies over Belgrade lit up with the tracer bullets of the anti-aircraft guns that fired in vain at the NATO planes, flying high out of reach. The targets were military and communications installations. All were empty. Some believed that a spy within had tipped off the regime before the sites were hit. There was also a Balkan conspiracy theory that NATO had even known about the leak. Heavy casualties at this stage would have threatened the alliance's cohesion. A wave of stubborn patriotism swept through Serbia. For a time, political differences were forgotten. The country was under attack, and like Londoners during the Blitz, Serbs exhibited a stubborn pride.

Each night thousands of demonstrators congregated on the bridges over the Danube, daring NATO to bomb the bridges and them too. Some even wore T-shirts emblazoned with a target. There was much talk of '*inat*' (spite, derived from a Turkish word) and '*prkos*' (defiance), two perceived Serbian characteristics. The way they saw it, Serbs had defied the Turks, the Habsburgs, Hitler and then Stalin. Now they would defy NATO. The protesters were not bombed. But many other bridges were destroyed and crumpled into the Danube.

The regime used war to step up repression. Dusan Mitevic warned the opposition journalist Slavko Curuvija to leave Belgrade as his life was in danger. A tranche of restrictive new laws were passed. On 11 April Curuvija was shot in front of his house, dying in his wife's arms. His death bore the hallmarks of a state-sponsored operation, and the killing sent a wave of fear through Belgrade's opposition. Curuvija had once been extremely close to the Milosevic family, especially Mira. The previous October, together with Aleksandar Tijanic, a former minister of information, he had written an open letter, published in the magazine *European*, which was highly critical of Milosevic. The government had fined the newspaper £160,000 and confiscated its property.

Curuvija had then visited Mira to give her a piece of his mind, he said in an interview in November 1998. 'I told her that everything her husband had done was dramatically bad and that he had to do several things to save Serbia. I said: "If you don't stop what's going on, the end will be bloody, and many people will be killed and maybe some will be hanged on the Terazije".' Curuvija also predicted: 'If you make war in Slovenia, you can step back to Croatia. If you start a war in Montenegro, you can step back to Belgrade. When you start a war in Belgrade, you have nowhere to step back to except a trench around your house.'[9]

As NATO's bombs fell, Serb forces carried out ethnic cleansing on a massive scale. The age-old dreams of nationalist theoreticians for an ethnically 'pure' Kosovo were now becoming reality. According to Milosevic's indictment for war crimes in Kosovo, a total of 800,000 Kosovo Albanian citizens were forcibly deported: 'Throughout Kosovo forces of the FRY [Federal Republic of Yugoslavia] and

Serbia systematically shelled towns and villages, burned homes and
farms, damaged and destroyed Kosovo Albanian cultural and religious
institutions, murdered Kosovo Albanian citizens and sexually assaulted
Kosovo Albanian women.'[10] Compared to the grim precision with
which the Serbs had ethnically cleansed northern and eastern Bosnia,
Kosovo was a chaotic operation. While many Albanians fled, others –
as Tim Judah noted – 'were simply marched around the province, told
to go in one direction, then sent home, then sent elsewhere and then
finally expelled.'[11] Two districts of Pristina were purged, but others left
alone. The disorganisation showed that Milosevic was beginning to lose
control.

The dirtiest work was left to the paramilitaries and the special forces.
In an interview with two American journalists Milan (a pseudonym)
described how he was recruited by members of the Serbian Radical
Party (whose leader Vojislav Seselj was deputy prime minister), and how
his unit operated during the Kosovo war. There were twenty fighters in
Milan's unit, three of whom were former state security agents. Several
others were criminals. The unit was supplied with food, ammunition
and the necessary papers to pass checkpoints by a Yugoslav army officer.
Just as in Croatia and Bosnia, money was the main motivation for many.
Some members of the security services transported Albanian civilians out
of the war zone in their car boots for $2,700. Often, though, the Serbs
took the money and just killed their passenger.

Milan described how his unit entered a village where they believed
the KLA had been:

There was this village elder, some old Albanian guy, who refused
to leave. I mean the guy was just pathetic. We ordered him to go
to the border to Albania, but he just refused. So we put a bullet
in his forehead. The others were taken to the border while we
burned everything in that village. The whole village. We'd hear
what was happening to Serbs every day on the news. When you
see that NATO is bombing the centre of a town or the television
station in Belgrade, and every day friends, comrades, died, you don't
care about Albanians. Why should you? We lived off revenge. Sweet
revenge . . . Back then, revenge felt very good. Especially when we
killed the KLA. Now I can't sleep, I can't eat. It hasn't lasted.[12]

Also operating in Kosovo was the feared Special Operations Unit

(JSO), the praetorian guard of the Serbian intelligence service. Armed with state-of-the-art weaponry and communications equipment, the JSO was commanded by Franko Simatovic, a former intelligence officer who had also operated in Croatia and Bosnia. As a unit of the intelligence service, the JSO was responsible to Milosevic's intelligence chief, Rade Markovic. Simatovic is named in Milosevic's indictments for war crimes in Croatia and Bosnia as a member of the 'joint criminal enterprise'.

Despite the appearance of familiar uniforms in Kosovo, there was a notable difference between the Bosnia and Kosovo wars. As many as 200,000 people were killed in Bosnia. Before the air-strikes about 2,000 people were killed in Kosovo. Yet after Dayton Milosevic was hailed as a peacemaker. President Clinton called for a chat. Lord Hurd came by to privatise the telephone network. Was one Albanian worth one hundred Bosnians? High on the slopes of Sarajevo's Lions Cemetery, where rolling acres of grave markers stood in silent vigil, it certainly looked that way. NATO's aims in Kosovo were geo-political as much as humanitarian. Milosevic had to be stopped, not because his police and soldiers killed people and burned down their houses – as they had done, intermittently, since 1991 – but because he now represented a threat to western strategic interests.

By expelling the Kosovars Milosevic planned to completely destabilise the whole Balkan region. Albania barely functioned as a state and could not cope with a massive refugee influx. Macedonia was under pressure from its own ethnic Albanian minority. If enough Albanians poured across the border, the country could explode, as it very nearly did. Greece, although a NATO member, refused to recognise Macedonia, and Athens cast a greedy eye on the territories of the former Yugoslav republic. As soon as the air-strikes began, Serbs living in the Macedonian capital, Skopje, rioted. If Macedonia and Albania collapsed, Greece and possibly Bulgaria would get dragged in, and there might even be conflict between Greece and Turkey, both NATO members.

The world watched transfixed as thousands of Albanians were daily forced into trains, before being sent across the border. Commentators drew comparison with the Nazi deportations of the Jews, although the Albanians were not killed on arrival. As Milosevic by now lacked any basic democratic instincts, he did not understand – or care about – the importance of public opinion in shaping policy. Milosevic lived in a world of plots, cabals and conspiracies. His shrinking support base only fuelled his sense of paranoia. As the bombing continued he increasingly lost his temper, screamed and shouted. He gambled that under pressure of war, NATO would split: because he had no feeling for human suffering, he failed to realise that public outrage over Kosovo would hold NATO together. The bombing, said the West, would stop when the alliance's three basic war aims were met: all Albanian refugees to be allowed home; all Serb forces to leave; and NATO-led peacekeepers to take over.

According to one senior British diplomat, Milosevic almost succeeded in splitting the alliance.

> If Milosevic had done nothing when the NATO bombing started, if he had not expelled hundreds of thousands of Albanians, I think he could have split NATO. Initially alliance-cohesion was pretty weak. The Italians and the Germans were extremely nervous. There was a real sense of, 'Should we really be doing this?' But Tony Blair and the Americans said we have to stop this. We were really lucky that he did not split the alliance, and that he eventually gave way. It was touch and go. He potentially had a winning hand in Kosovo, but he played it very badly.'[13]

NATO's mistakes handed Milosevic a series of propaganda victories – especially when the victims were Albanians. Bombs were dropped on passenger trains, homes and other civilian buildings. The attack on the Chinese embassy in Belgrade – supposedly because Washington had accidentally used an out-of-date map of Belgrade – triggered fury in Beijing. Milosevic also scored a propaganda victory when the Yugoslavs shot down a top secret Stealth Bomber and it landed in a field. Demonstrators danced on the wing, some holding up signs saying 'Sorry, we didn't know it was invisible'. But the wave of Serb patriotism steadily curdled into a deeper anger against the regime. Unlike Croatia's President Tudjman, Milosevic was not known to have ever visited a front-line or attended wounded soldiers in hospital. But in mid-May, he made a gesture to morale by publicly praising police officers.

The Yugoslav army could not win against NATO. The Stealth Bomber was one of only two planes to be lost, out of 33,000 NATO missions. NATO destroyed more than 100 Serb planes: It became the KLA's de facto airforce. As the KLA gathered in strength and numbers, Serb forces had to concentrate *en masse* to prepare for large-scale operations. Bunched together, Serb troops were easier targets for NATO jets. The Serb forces had expelled Albanian civilians, but they could not destroy the KLA's rear bases in Albania proper. In late April, according to Louis Sell, the CIA and US Special Forces operating in the region began meetings with the KLA over co-ordinating military operations and exchanging intelligence.[14]

Meanwhile, NATO's military planners drew up blueprints for an invasion of Serbia. A ground war would be launched from either Greece, Albania and Macedonia, or even north from Hungary. On 3 June Milosevic blinked first. He told UN envoys Viktor Chernomyrdin and Martti Ahtisari that he accepted NATO terms. 'The end for Milosevic came when Tony Blair and others in NATO concluded that if the air campaign did not work, then there would have to be a ground war,' said the senior British diplomat. 'Then Milosevic truly realised the game was up. Because at that stage our will to see this through was greater than his, for the first time. He could not have withstood a ground war.'

Milosevic broadcast to the nation that 'We did not give up Kosovo'. This was true – up to a point. Although Kosovo would technically remain within Yugoslavia, it would become a UN protectorate. All Serb forces would be withdrawn. A week later NATO troops moved in. Behind them were the returning Albanian refugees, who wreaked a terrible vengeance. Now Serb houses were looted before burning prettily. NATO troops proved no protection for the Serbs, including elderly civilians, who were murdered by men in KLA uniform. Apart from a few isolated ghettos, Kosovo's Serbs fled, never to return.

NATO had set an interesting precedent in Kosovo. When Kurdish rebels in Turkey launched a guerrilla war for independence, and Kurdish civilians had been killed by the Turkish army, NATO had not gone to war in their defence. But then Turkey was a NATO member. When Russian troops had levelled the Chechen capital, Grozny, no cruise missiles had been fired at Moscow. While China tightened its repressive grip on Tibet, American companies fought for contracts in Beijing.

Mira Markovic argued that the loss of Kosovo followed the same pattern as the previous Yugoslav wars.

Nationalism was always here, although now they say that Slobodan invented it. With the support of those living abroad, that nationalism became organised terrorism. They could not have done anything by themselves. Then that terrorism was brought to its knees by the military and the police, who did their job, which is nothing unusual in Kosovo.[15]

The international community applied double standards, she argued.

The Albanians wanted to separate off. Every country would do something to prevent its territory being divided. But we were told not to do that, because then we were terrorists. When the police and the military succeeded in defeating the KLA, in 1998, then NATO said we are oppressing ethnic Albanians and we should be bombed.'

Bombs and cruise missiles were not the only weapons in NATO's arsenal. In May the European Union announced the names of 305 key people who were banned from travelling to, or doing business in, Europe. The United States, and most non-EU European countries, followed suit. Milosevic headed the list, followed by politicians such as his Kosovo envoy, Nikola Sainovic, and Serbian President Milan Milutinovic, together with Mira, Marko, Marija, Slobodan's brother Borislav and Marko's wife, Milica Gajic. Gajic, who had managed the Madona disco in Pozarevac, was an attractive raven-haired woman. After considerable pressure from his mother, Marko married Gajic, who gave birth to a son, Marko junior.

'The List' was a kind of financial-political Jiu Jitsu. It turned the regime's strength against it. The Milosevic regime was based on loyalty to the ruling couple, rewarded with a political or business position. In Serbia Inc. – as the country was dubbed – loyalty paid, handsomely. Ministers were directors of state companies doing business with their own ministries. The List sowed dissent among the senior ranks of the Milosevic regime, by hitting key figures in their pockets, and humiliated them by refusing them visas.

In public those named paraded their inclusion as a badge of patriotic pride. But very few – if any – of Milosevic's allies served at his court out of belief. Once their personal overseas assets were frozen, and there were no more weekend shopping trips to Paris, or even Budapest, many judged that loyalty demanded too high a price. Behind the scenes many made extensive efforts to have their names removed and made overtures to the West. Because Milosevic's support base was, by this time, so narrow, precisely-targeted names on the list had a disproportionate effect on the regime's stability. 'For the first time, members of Serbia Inc. are paying a high personal price, and it's hitting them square in the forehead,' said one senior US official.[16]

Also on the list was Dragan Hadzi Antic, the editor of *Politika* newspaper who had misreported Clinton's visit to Tuzla, back in January 1996, in Milosevic's peacemaker days. In December 1997 Antic had borrowed 865,000 Deutschmarks for a new house, which he then shared with Marija Milosevic and her gynaecologist.[17] Antic was in love with Marija. But she had announced that she had fallen in love with her bodyguard, a former criminal. When Antic and Marija eventually fell out over the house deal, Marija shot his dog.

Boguljub Karic, now minister without portfolio, was the first to feel the list's humiliating pinch. On 21 May Karic and his wife Milenka landed at Nicosia airport in Cyprus. The island was home to one branch of the Karic Foundation, as well as several companies controlled by Boguljub. Among his many ventures, Karic owned a bank there. He and his wife were refused entry and sent back to Belgrade. Karic then reportedly travelled to Budapest to meet with American officials. Somehow a transcript of that meeting landed on Milosevic's desk.[18] Karic's television station and other companies were then raided by customs officers and the tax police.

After the bombing, Serbian society began to collapse. Frightened and bewildered, many Serbs took refuge in the paranormal. The regime certainly had no more earthly solutions to offer. Witches and soothsayers gave dark succour. A rash of magazines about the occult suddenly appeared on newsstands. *The Third Eye* published Milosevic's astrological charts. 'The stars smile on Slobodan Milosevic. He has made many enemies, but that's only to be expected. He is the best of men, so it's normal that many wish to remove him from power. His birth chart is Leo and the chart of Yugoslavia is Taurus, which shows they cannot be separated.' *The Third Eye* also noted: 'There are difficult years ahead.'[19] An article in *Miracle* magazine explained how the devil himself is working to create a new world order, opposed only by Serbia and China.

Others looked for support from the ever-growing gangster class. A new phenomenon emerged: 'sponsor-girls'. Their sponsors were mobsters, who kept them in designer clothes, mobile telephones and meals in fancy restaurants. The age-old bargain was often struck at the riverboat restaurants that lined the banks of the Danube. Dressed in skin-tight skimpy dresses, the young women would sit at the bar. The mobsters would sit at a table, flashing their wallets and car keys. Eye contact would be made, nods exchanged, and the sponsorhip deal was done. But being a sponsor girl was a short-term option. There was an almost endless supply of young women to choose from. Once their protectors tired of their latest acquisitions, they traded them in for a newer, and younger model. A sponsor girl, said the *European* magazine was 'a symbol of the absolute commercialisation of sexuality, the newest manifestation of the subjugation of women. She is the target of malicious gossip and the dark subject of her fellow teenagers' dreams, the reason for her parents' distress.'[20]

As for Milosevic, there were no more deals to be made. On 27 May, during the bombing, Louise Arbour, chief prosecutor of the ICTY in The Hague, announced that Milosevic had been indicted for war crimes in Kosovo. So were the former mining minister Nikola Sainovic; Serbia's interior minister, Vlajko Stojikovic; Serb president, Milan Milutinovic; and General Dragoljub Ojdanic, Yugoslav army chief of staff. Graham Blewitt, ICTY deputy prosecutor, explained: 'As president of Yugoslavia, Milosevic was commander in chief of the army. In a *de jure* sense he was responsible. By May 1999 we had sufficient evidence of this beyond reasonable doubt, and so the Kosovo indictment was issued.'[21] Publicly, Milosevic was contemptuous of the indictment. Privately, he pondered how far he had fallen. No more whisky sing-songs and steak dinners with Richard Holbrooke, or long lunches with Lord Owen. Never again a glad confident morning, starting with a business breakfast with Lord Hurd.

For all Milosevic's sneers, his indictment had two profoundly important consequences. If the head of state was going down, his fall would drag many in its wake. Several of Milosevic's key associates soon made contact, generally through intermediaries, with the ICTY. Graham Blewitt said: 'Milosevic opened up other areas of interest. Once he was indicted for Kosovo, we could then bring indictments for Bosnia and Croatia, because people talked to us. Some people were trying to do the right thing, and some people wanted to do deals.' In addition, the indictment was a green light for the West to pour in support for the Serbian opposition. As one senior British diplomat explained: 'The indictment was the key moment. It gave us an excuse to build a policy around opposition to Milosevic. We could say the world is not against Serbs, and that Milosevic was the only thing stopping normal relations.'[22]

Perhaps wisely, Milosevic was concentrating his assets at home. There was a problem with the land at Uzicka 34. It was split into four pieces, making it difficult to obtain a building permit. The obliging mayor of Belgrade, Vojislav Mihajlovic, convened a closed meeting of the city council on 21 April, during the NATO bombardment, without the opposition party councillors. Those who attended were presented with a plan under which the four parcels of Milosevic's land would legally be merged into one, thus easing the path through the planning bureaucracy. The question soon became academic when a cruise missile hit the Milosevic presidential residence. No one was at home when NATO came knocking, but the lights went out for good in Marko's blue bathroom.

24

TOPPLING MILOSEVIC
FROM BUDAPEST

One Day that Shook the World
5 October 2000

Revolution is impossible until it is inevitable.

Leon Trotsky.[1]

When the US diplomat William Montgomery departed from Belgrade in 1978, Beogradska Banka president Slobodan Milosevic hosted his leaving party. Twenty-two years later, Montgomery returned the favour.

Montgomery ran the Office of Yugoslav Affairs (OYA) in Budapest. The OYA was a satellite of the US embassy. It opened in August 2000 and was a personal priority of Madeleine Albright, US secretary of state. Publicly, its aim was to aid democratic forces in Yugoslavia. Its actual function was to provide political and financial support (some of it covert) to the Serb opposition, in order to bring down Milosevic. During the Kosovo war, Albright had fought a turf war with Richard Holbrooke over Balkan policy. Albright was not interested in drinking Viljamovka and taking computer graphic trips around Bosnia with Milosevic. She said: 'We are making it clear that we don't see Milosevic in the future.'[2]

Milosevic had once snickered about Albright when he spoke on the telephone to his brother Borislav. But by the summer of 2000, Milosevic was in serious trouble. His indictment for war crimes on 27 May 1999 was the trigger the international community needed to orchestrate his downfall. Earlier that month Tony Blair had openly called for Serbs to 'cast out' the Milosevic regime, which he described as a 'corrupt dictatorship', guilty of 'hideous racial genocide'.[3] In July *Time* and *Newsweek* carried reports that President Clinton had authorised the CIA to commence covert operations against Belgrade to topple Milosevic.

These could include computer hacking against Milosevic's international bank accounts; funnelling cash to opposition groups and making contact with dissident elements within the regime.

The OYA was one point in a network that stretched from Budapest to the State Department in Washington, D.C., the Foreign Office in London, Paris and Berlin. Britain also maintained a small Yugoslav liaison office at its embassy in Budapest, which was in regular contact with the OYA, and the same Yugoslav opposition figures.

Broadly speaking, the West's plan was steadily to increase international political and economic pressure on the regime, while simultaneously supporting the domestic opposition that would undermine it from the inside. Eventually, enough force would be applied on two fronts to force its collapse. At which point prearranged clandestine deals with the Yugoslav army, police, intelligence services and special forces would ensure that when Milosevic called for help, none came. This part, known as 'blocking the response mechanism' was the most difficult to arrange. 'The aim was to isolate the regime and engage the people. This concept was adopted after the NATO air-strikes. There was a strong team effort to plan and see this through,' said one senior British diplomat.[4] Moscow was also kept informed by email, partly as a thank you for Russian co-operation – more or less – over Kosovo, and also to keep Moscow 'on-message'.

Washington, D.C. had long experience in toppling governments considered unhelpful to US interests, as the peoples of Guatemala, Iran and Chile could testify. In those countries the US had engineered the installation of dictatorships. In Yugoslavia the aim was to bring one down. 'Montgomery was running an embassy-in-exile. It was a very small, very tight operation of five people. Much of its work was reporting. A steady flow of people were brought in. There were also meetings in southern Hungary in Szeged, in Croatia, Bosnia and Montenegro. It was a regional effort,' said a senior US official. 'The beauty of having it in Budapest was that all the support systems could be organised by the embassy there.'[5]

There was no sign on the front door of the OYA. It was based in an anonymous office block on a narrow sidestreet in downtown Pest, conveniently located just a few stops away on the underground from the Yugoslav embassy. Milosevic knew something was brewing, and according to one source, Belgrade despatched over twenty people to find out what. The Hungarian capital filled with rival intelligence agents following each other around, while endangered opposition figures sought visas to the West. This was Harry Lime's Vienna, shifted east and fast-forwarded to 2001. Serbs did not need visas to enter Hungary, and the city's *fin de siècle* cafes were already crowded with chain-smoking, nervous exiles. But information is not always enough. By October 1917 the Tsar's secret service, the Okhrana, had thoroughly penetrated the Bolshevik party. Events still assumed their own momentum.

Since the loss of Kosovo, the aura of decay around Milosevic's regime had strengthened. Operation Allied Force was a harsh psychological blow for the man who for the previous decade had been courted by presidents. More significantly, the NATO air-strikes were a profound psychological shock to a nation that, despite ten years of neighbouring conflicts, had not confronted the harsh, direct reality of war. 'During the previous decade Serbia supported the wars in Croatia and Bosnia, but was never directly affected. Belgrade was a relatively acceptable place,' observed Braca Grubacic, publisher of the *VIP* newsletter. NATO bombs blew that complacency apart, he said. 'You can live in poverty, you can be humiliated, but war is the ultimate event.'[6]

Milosevic's own Socialist Party was demoralised by purges and politically marginalised by Mira's JUL and Seselj's ultra-nationalists. Figures such as federal defence minister Dragoljub Ojdanic remained loyal, but Ojdanic was an indicted war criminal. General Momcilo Perisic, sacked by Milosevic as army chief of staff, spoke for many in the military: 'The current state leadership must be removed by political means, and the people should be taken along the path of civic and democratic programmes, and not those of hatred and violence'.[7] As for the intelligence services, morale was low after the professional officers around sacked intelligence chief Jovica Stanisic had been replaced by JUL loyalists. 'Mira's people decided to take over everything, even though for this kind of work, you need professional skills,' said one high-level Serbian source. 'When I heard that one of the most important analytical intelligence positions was filled by someone from JUL, I knew they were on the wrong track.'[8]

Step by step, day by day, the West was ratcheting up the pressure. The broadcast media had helped keep Milosevic in power, so breaking the regime's information monopoly was a high priority. Radio Free Europe, Deutsche Welle, Voice of America and other western stations were beamed in from transmitters located in neighbouring states including Bosnia and Croatia. This was known as the 'Ring Around Serbia'.

Support was also funnelled to the network of independent radio stations within Serbia, in part through Britain's £3 million Independent Media and Civil Society Programme.

Not far from the OYA's office, in the riverside Hyatt hotel, British diplomats were nurturing a Yugoslav élite-in-waiting. Senior Serbian figures in fields such as the military, law enforcement and academia were brought to Budapest to design a blueprint for post-Milosevic Serbia, and prepare for the country's re-integration into Europe. This was the New Serbia Forum, an initiative funded by the Foreign Office, and organised by Sir John Birch, former British ambassador to Hungary. Serb opposition leaders were also brought to the Foreign Office centre at Wilton Park. Milosevic was feeling increasingly beleaguered by this international effort. In Belgrade, recent visitors to Budapest were liable to be pulled in by the police for questioning.

There was a lot of forward planning that summer, and not only in Budapest. Western officials were despatched to cities including Vienna, Banja Luka in northern Bosnia, and Pristina in Kosovo. Among their tasks were the opening of channels to dissidents within the regime, and ensuring that the response mechanisms were blocked. 'Some of these people, who worked behind the scenes, were heroes, the ones from small anonymous offices in London and Washington, D.C.,' said the Serbian source. Detailed preparations were also drawn up to ensure that the revolution would be broadcast live on television. 'Great importance was placed on the media. There were three different plans to ensure satellite access for CNN and the others, through different television stations.'[9] Germany too played a role. Squabbling Serbian opposition leaders were brought to Berlin, and money was channelled to cities with opposition mayors.

Force would be met with force. In the southern city of Cacak, an opposition stronghold ruled by fiery mayor Vladimir Ilic, the Democratic Opposition of Serbia (DOS) was building its own private militia of shock troops. Disgruntled army officers, policemen, karate champions, body builders and criminals trained for the final showdown. The football fans who had once chanted, 'Serbian Slobo, Serbia is with you', now chanted 'Slobo, save Serbia and kill yourself'.

As it degenerated, becoming more reliant on violence and intimidation, the regime slid closer to all-out dictatorship. Armed police stood on almost every corner, checking documents and demanding identification, often backed up by interior ministry troops. Men of military age were asked to report to the interior ministry to have their addresses confirmed. Milosevic, in true Ceausescu-style, was proclaimed a 'national hero'. Belgrade wits coined a new joke about ever-shrinking Serbia: Mira wakes up one morning and looks out of the window of their house at Uzicka. She is alarmed to see a checkpoint outside, ringed by armed men. 'Slobo, come quickly, there are gunmen in uniform outside the house!' Slobo rolls over and says, 'Oh, don't worry about them. They're just the new border guards.'

A series of killings, and attempted killings punctuated Serbia's steady darkening. On 3 October 1999 Vuk Draskovic, who had briefly served in Milosevic's wartime government, narrowly escaped death in a highly-suspicious road accident in which two bodyguards and his brother-in-law were killed. Draskovic, and many others, blamed the Serbian security services. Draskovic took refuge in Montenegro where he had another narrow escape the following summer, when a sniper's bullet grazed his forehead. In January 2000 Arkan was shot dead in the lobby of Belgrade's Intercontinental Hotel. The security conscious Arkan had not seemed alarmed when his killers had approached, indicating that he knew them. Some blamed the mafia. But many others believed the regime was responsible.

Arkan was an intelligent individual and probably understood that Milosevic's shelf-life was limited. There were repeated rumours that Arkan had been in touch with the Hague tribunal through intermediaries to try and cut a deal. Interviewed in 2002, Graham Blewitt, deputy prosecutor, said: 'We told Arkan's lawyer that we will deal with you when your client is standing in front of the tribunal.'[10] Arkan's killing was followed by the death of federal defence minister, Pavle Bulatovic, shot by a sniper while dining in a restaurant. In late April Zika Petrovic, the head of Yugoslav airlines and a childhood friend of Milosevic, was killed. As shooting followed shooting, rumours swirled in Belgrade of a group dubbed 'The Men in Black', darkest of all the forces that supposedly operated in the shadows of the regime.

Throughout his rule, Milosevic had cemented his power by finding enemies. He had led his people to war in Slovenia, Croatia, Bosnia and Kosovo, and he had lost every one. Many feared that Milosevic would now either start a civil war, or turn against the last republic remaining alongside Serbia in Yugoslavia: Montenegro. The home-land of Milosevic's parents was led by a pro-western reformer, Milo Djukanovic. Yugoslav army troops took over the airport at the capital

Podgorica. Belgrade implemented a complete trade embargo. Milosevic used the Yugoslav army to harass and intimidate the Montenegrin security forces, all the while broadcasting Serbian propaganda into the province.

Milosevic's newest enemy was the student movement Otpor (Resistance), founded at Belgrade University in autumn 1998. Emblazoned on T-shirts, leaflets and stickers, Otpor's clenched-fist symbol soon appeared on walls across the country, often accompanied by the slogan '*Gotov je!*' (He's finished). Otpor was dynamic, innovative and decentralised. Its members painted red footsteps on the ground to symbolise Milosevic's final departure from parliament. Cardboard telescopes offered passers-by a chance to watch a falling star named 'Slobotea'. When actors in a Belgrade theatre raised their hands in a clenched-fist salute, the audience gave them a standing ovation.[11] Such incidents gave strength and determination.

Eventually more than 70,000 young Serbs joined Otpor. Many were barely twenty. After the great exodus of the early 1990s, when tens of thousands of young people left Serbia, mostly never to return, it took eight or nine years for Milosevic's children to come of age. Because Milosevic was essentially an authoritarian centraliser, he was unable to grasp the principles behind Otpor's horizontal, non-hierarchical cell structure. Unlike Zajedno (Together), which had spearheaded the winter protests of 1996–7, Otpor could not be destroyed by splitting or arresting the leadership.

Cells operated out of a nationwide network of safe houses. Members kept in touch through mobile telephones and emails, often routed through servers abroad. Milosevic also had his own email address posted on the Yugoslav government website: Slobodan.Milosevic@gov.yu with an invitation to drop him a line, although he did not write back. The information war was one he could not win.

Increasingly, the regime hit back with arrests, intimidation and beatings. In Vladicin Han, a small town in southern Serbia, Otpor members were subjected to an orgy of violence by three drunken policemen. The activists were strangled until they were about to pass out. They were ordered to squat with outstretched arms. Anyone who moved was beaten. They were raised up above the floor and subjected to the 'bastinado': a severe pounding of the legs and feet. But in Vladicin Han, and across Serbia, whenever Otpor activists were arrested, threatened or beaten, they gave the same message: 'We are not afraid.'

Otpor leaders were brought to Budapest for instruction in techniques of non-violent resistance. Ensconced in the luxurious Hilton hotel that overlooks the Danube, they absorbed the principles of what was called 'asymmetric political warfare' – turning the regime's strength against it: the more the regime tries to crush opposition, the greater the backlash.[12] When a previously law-abiding son or daughter returns home battered and bruised from a police beating for wearing an Otpor T-shirt, his or her parents will be radicalised (as happened in Vladicin Han, where enraged parents demonstrated outside the police station).

Otpor activists translated sections from Gene Sharp's book *From Dictatorship to Democracy: A Conceptual Framework for Liberation*[13] and passed them from cell to cell. Sharp listed 198 methods of non-violent action, many of which could be employed in Serbia. The Milosevic regime was never quite an all-out dictatorship. Milosevic saw himself as a democratic and modern leader. Otpor operated in the space – albeit rapidly shrinking – the regime left open to claim it was a democracy. But the most important principle was simply to stop being afraid.

American newspapers reported that over $70 million was eventually paid to the Serbian opposition. Much was handed over in cash in Budapest, and then smuggled across the border. As a new NATO member, the Hungarian government was keen to help. A senior British diplomat admitted: 'There was so much money pouring into the opposition that Milosevic would have been justified in cancelling the election on the grounds of outside interference.'[14] In public, however, Otpor and the West kept their distance. 'It was important that the Serbs got rid of Milosevic. Otpor did not want to be seen as anyone's lackeys. Everyone was very conscious that the US government must not topple Milosevic or be seen to topple him, especially because of who the Serbs were and their proud history,' said a US official.[15]

Former allies of Milosevic also began to invest in the future. 'Who was behind Otpor? The United States and Britain. But also Greece, and money and business in Serbia. Some of these companies are now very successful. They needed a movement out of control of the political parties, but where they had influence,' said the Serbian source.[16] Athens had supported Milosevic throughout the Yugoslav wars, to the West's growing anger. One hundred Greeks had fought with the Bosnian Serb army in the 'Greek Volunteer Unit', based at Vlasenica, Bosnia.[17] By

September 2001 Greece realised it had backed the wrong man. Four Otpor activists attended a reception at the Greek embassy in Belgrade, after an invitation from Greek foreign minister George Papandreou. Lured outside by Serb police, they were immediately arrested.

The regime cracked first, not in Belgrade, but in the provinces. Through the drab towns of rural Serbia, a cold anger spread. Nowhere more so than Pozarevac, which Marko ran as his personal fiefdom. Unknown faces in town were harassed by state security agents. Marko's mafia allies beat and intimidated Otpor activists at will. 'It was very dangerous here for young people. This is a small place and everyone knows everyone else. There were death threats,' said Slavoljub Matic, a local councillor who took over as mayor after Milosevic was toppled. 'Marko did not have a political position, but he was the son of the president and could do whatever he wanted. He had power, not legal power, but from the shadows, from his family.'[18]

During the NATO bombing Marko had built the Bambiland amusement park on the outskirts of town. Although Serbia was at war, Marko obtained enough building material and manpower to construct an elaborate playground, complete with a large wooden boat painted in day-glo colours. He spent the war strutting around town in uniform, brandishing automatic weapons. Mira Markovic said that her son always carried out his patriotic duty:

Half the money he made in Pozarevac, he gave to the town itself, and to the hospital. He was a volunteer during the war, during the air-strikes. When it was announced that there will be bombing, Marko said he will immediately go to Kosovo. I said to him, why would you go there, you will get killed? Volunteer, but if you have to get killed, then do it here, not in Kosovo. That was his duty, as his father was head of state.'

In fact Marko, said his mother, was always concerned for others' welfare.

My son takes after me in personality. He is vulnerable, romantic. He always has strong feelings for other people. The other day when we spoke over the telephone I asked him, 'Marko, are you clever like your mother or after your father, what kind of intelligence do you have?' He said, 'Mama, I am sorry to say that I have your intelligence, but I would prefer to have my father's.' He didn't want to say that he was stupid because of that, but that he had the kind of intelligence which is difficult for him. He would have liked to have a less complicated intelligence, something more simple. This always creates worries for him.[19]

Marko certainly appears to have had strong feelings about Zoran Milanovic, a young man who worked as bartender at Madona. An indictment issued against Marko in November 2001 claimed that when Milanovic joined Otpor he was beaten by Marko's bodyguards and delivered to Marko. In an interview with an American journalist Milanovic recounted what happened next: 'Marko appeared with the saw. He said, "What's up, you traitor? You scumbag. You will not be the last one or the first one that I have cut up and thrown in the Morava river." Marko put the saw near my head and turned it on. It lasted for several seconds. Then he turned it off and put it on the bar. Marko told his guys to take me away and deal with me promptly. I started crying.'[20]

Mira dismissed these allegations. 'It would be comical if it was not tragic. The charges are that he threatened to cut someone with a chain saw. Our daughter-in-law [Milica Gajic, Marko's wife] wrote in the newspapers that we did not have a carpenter's shop, with saws, because we did not deal with wood. So I could return the charges, and say that someone chased us with a lawnmower. That is all they have discovered and they want to put Marko on trial with these.'[21]

Milosevic had announced that elections would take place on 24 September 2000, even though his mandate did not run out until July 2001. Many saw the date as significant: exactly thirteen years earlier, at the Eighth Session in September 1987, Milosevic had brought down his former friend and mentor Ivan Stambolic. Mira was known to be highly superstitious about this. Slavoljub Djukic notes that she told her JUL colleagues: 'The opposition will not be a problem. We should be concerned about the ghost of the Eighth Session affecting our ranks.'[22] Stambolic had left public life for good. But lately he had been considering a return. The veteran *Times* correspondent Dessa Trevisan had lunched with Stambolic in 1999. 'Stambolic asked me my opinion. I said "No, because you are the one who brought Milosevic into politics."'[23]

According to Dusan Mitevic, American officials wanted Stambolic to stand in the Yugoslav presidential elections. He remained a popular figure, and could have split the Socialist vote. 'Stambolic felt that Milosevic had betrayed him. He had been sidelined for thirteen years and he wanted to become active again. The Americans did not think Stambolic would win, just get ten to twelve per cent. But that would come from Milosevic's vote and so Milosevic would not be able to make a coalition.'[24]

Stambolic travelled to Montenegro at a time when the republic's pro-western leaders were in close contact with the United States. He told Montenegrin television, 'At the end he [Milosevic] must be destroyed, most people are against him and they will get him. He will never go in peace.'[25] On 25 August Milosevic's former *kum* went for his usual jog. While resting on a park bench he was bundled into a white van, according to eye witnesses.

Stambolic was never seen again, and his remains have never been found. No details of the kidnapping have ever leaked out, leading many to believe that the regime, rather than the mafia, was responsible.

An unassuming law lecturer called Vojislav Kostunica presented a more dangerous political threat. Under pressure from the United States, most of Serbia's fractious opposition united around Kostunica as the candidate for the Democratic Opposition of Serbia (DOS). Kostunica had been sacked from Belgrade University for criticising the 1974 constitution that made Kosovo and Voivodina virtual republics. He was a Serbian nationalist, but a moderate, and he was also seen as uncorrupted. He was certainly no fan of Montgomery's Budapest operation. 'I call this affair with the office in Budapest the kiss of death ... It really is counterproductive. Directly, we can get nothing out of forming that office.'[26] Conservative, law-abiding Kostunica did not like Otpor, and the feeling was mutual. But everyone focused on the primary objective: *Gotov je* (He is finished).

By 2.00 a.m. on 25 September, the DOS election monitoring operation announced that Kostunica had won 52 per cent of the vote, while Milosevic took 35 per cent. This was enough to bring Kostunica victory in the first round. He declared: 'Dawn is coming to Serbia.' Milosevic thought otherwise. According to Serbian press reports, he grabbed his fellow indictee Nikola Sainovic by his moustache and demanded that he fix the results.[27] The regime then announced that Milosevic had gained 38.6 per cent of the vote, and Kostunica 48.96 –

enough to stop Kostunica winning on the first round. A second round was planned for 8 October. Milosevic's plan was probably to cancel the second round, blaming outside interference in the election, and move to all-out dictatorship.

In Moscow, Milosevic's defeat sent Russia into a 'state of advanced panic,' according to a senior British diplomat. Not to mention at the Yugoslav embassy where Borislav Milosevic represented his brother's regime. 'The Russians thought that Milosevic would win. Their whole position crashed down around their ears. Russia made a strategic mis-judgement. The Russians had penetrated the Serbian establishment so effectively that they had lost contact with ordinary people. They completely underestimated the effect of the training, and of email. The Serbian opposition said they had never met a Russian diplomat.'[28]

Patriarch Pavle, the nation's spiritual father, helped save the day for DOS. He greeted Kostunica as the president of the country, saying he should take power in a 'dignified manner'. Even the paramilitary leader Vojislav Seselj called for Milosevic to step down. On 2 October Milosevic gave a televised speech to the nation claiming that a DOS victory in the second round would boost crime and poverty. Serbs asked themselves where he had been living over the last decade. Milosevic then met with army chief of staff, General Pavkovic, and intelligence chief, Rade Markovic. They had bad news. Substantial numbers within both the police and the army were moving over to the opposition. Mira became hysterical and had to be given a tranquilliser injection, while Milosevic, according to one report, 'looked like he was going to die'.[29]

The endgame began. A wave of strikes swept through Serbia, demanding Kostunica's victory be recognised. At the Kolubara mine, 7,000 pitmen downed tools. Kolubara supplied the coal that kept Belgrade and north-ern Serbia lit and heated. Schools, shops and businesses locked their doors. The meteorological institute stopped its forecast. Newspapers printed a statement that forecasts would resume when the election result was recognised. As rumours swept through Belgrade that the regime had a death list of opposition figures, Otpor and DOS leaders began to sleep away from home, and wear bullet-proof jackets.

The day and time was set when Serbia would demand that Milosevic step down: 3.00 p.m. on 5 October. But would the response mecha-nisms be blocked? On 4 October Zoran Djindjic met with Milorad

Lukovic (also known as Legija), a commander of Milosevic's feared praetorian guard: the security service's Special Operations Unit (JSO). JSO fighters were trained in low-intensity urban warfare. They were accused of committing atrocities in the Yugoslav wars, and they were the revolution's greatest threat.

Legija had already told Djindjic that his men would not intervene in the first round of the elections. But now? The two men rode around Belgrade in an armoured jeep. The orders he had received were 'extreme', said Legija. 'It's going to be a mess.' Djindjic asked what the opposition should do. 'Don't fire at the police. Don't charge the barracks.' The deal was done. Djindjic said later that the JSO had been his greatest fear: 'When he told me that as far as they were concerned there would not be any intervention it was a load off my mind.'[30]

In the early hours of 5 October Vladimir Ilic led ten thousand people out of Cacak. The convoy of 230 trucks, 52 buses and hundreds of cars was twenty-two kilometres long. 'Revolution or death,' they shouted as they drove the ninety miles north to the capital. Hidden under tarpaulins were the shock troops of DOS, armed with Kalashnikovs, pistols, rocket-propelled grenades and even mortars. A building worker called Ljubislav Djokic drove his bulldozer. At the last moment, he took a passenger in his cab, a seventy-two-year-old baker called Milan Vatic. This unlikely pair would be the heroes of the day.

As the Cacak convoy surged north, four other convoys also trundled towards the capital. Police barricades on the roads were simply barged aside. The police did not resist. The orders of interior minister Vlajko Stojilkovic to use anti-tank grenades and automatic weapons were ignored. The sixth column, the residents of Belgrade, were already in place. Through the morning, a crowd assembled in front of the federal parliament building, cheering and chanting. The first wave attacked at noon, but they moved too soon, and the police beat them back with tear gas and rubber bullets.

The hard men then fell back and regrouped behind an armoured door at a DOS office in downtown Belgrade. Braca Grubacic published his *VIP* newsletter from rooms on the floor above. Gunmen guarded the building's entrance and crowded the staircases. The street fighters used *VIP*'s bathroom to wash off the tear gas. Grubacic recalled:

At the beginning it was touch and go. One of the high-ranking opposition leaders said to me, 'Braca, they dispersed us, it is finished.'

There were people wearing flak jackets and carrying baseball bats. Not gangsters exactly, but people who like to fight. Then someone told me, 'Braca, the decision is taken. We are going until the end.' So they went to the parliament, and then it started.

By 3.30 p.m. hundreds of thousands had gathered in front of the federal parliament. The thin lines of riot police looked nervous. When protesters slapped giant stickers proclaiming '*Gotov je*' on their riot shields, the police stood by. Milosevic had ridden to power on crowds. But this was Canetti's reversal crowd: '—the rebels are always driven to act by the stings they carry within them; and it always takes a long time before they can do so'.[31]

It had taken ten years. Perched in the cabin of the bulldozer, now festooned with Otpor stickers and posters, Djokic the builder and Vatic the septuagenarian baker, vanguard of the revolution, led the charge. 'Fuck those bastards,' shouted Djokic. 'Put your foot down!' yelled Vatic.[32] The bulldozer rumbled forward, crushing the parliament's concrete flower boxes. Djokic raised the great shovel and brought it down on the windows. Glass flew in every direction. The police fired canisters of tear gas and a fusillade of rubber bullets. Protesters began to cough and vomit. Some wore home-made masks of wet cotton and plastic film. They picked up the smoking canisters and hurled them back through the air at the police.

A choking cloud covered downtown Belgrade. Smoke poured from burning police vehicles. Paint blistered and popped. Molotov cocktails rained down on the parliament building, and flames began to spread. Canetti had written: 'if many men find themselves together in a crowd, they may jointly succeed in what was denied them singly; together they can turn on those who, until now, have given them orders'. The sound and fury of revolution: a proud sea of flags; the acrid smell of tear gas and burning rubber; the clarion call of trumpeters blaring out Chetnik marching songs. That magical alchemy had been achieved, when adrenalin overrides fear, when the exhilaration of liberation makes men something more. They clenched their fists, they held hands, they shouted and they charged. A great unstoppable, human tide surged forward. This time, they were going to the end. *Gotov je!*

The police fled, many handing over their gas masks and weapons to the revolutionaries. Milosevic, and the rest of the world, watched his regime go down in flames live on television. As parliament burned, he called the interior minister Stojilkovic and army chief of staff Nebojsa Pavkovic, demanding the uprising be crushed. True to form, he did not bother consulting his ministers. No crisis cabinet was summoned, no urgent conference calls made. Armoured vehicles were sent to Dedinje to protect Milosevic's house but none moved to protect his government. General Pavkovic was a Milosevic loyalist. But he knew many army officers would not follow orders to fire on the people. 'Ultimately even Pavkovic understood that there are certain limits in this kind of scenario. If you have a million people on the streets, all over Belgrade and Serbia, then the army cannot do anything. There is a threshold, a critical mass,' said Braca Grubacic.

In addition, the army and police lacked sufficient available manpower to crush the uprising. This is curious as by this time Milosevic was running a virtual police state. His security services must have known what was being prepared. But government buildings were protected by only a thin line of police, many of whom had been brought in from the provinces. The highly-trained state paramilitary forces remained in their barracks. Dusan Mitevic said: 'Milosevic was betrayed, by the police, by the intelligence services and by the general staff.'[33] Cacak mayor Vladimir Ilic later claimed that senior police officers were feeding him information. 'We saw every order coming from the interior ministry. We knew what they were planning. We saw their faxes.'[34]

As parliament burned, the crowd swarmed through. Boxes of ballot papers were tipped out of the window, fluttering down in the breeze. Bottles of vodka and brandy were passed round. One man helped himself to an armchair. Djokic reversed out, and drove his bulldozer towards Belgrade Television. Back in the street protests of 1991, when the opposition leader Vuk Draskovic had dubbed the station 'TV Bastille' the name had stuck. Like the prison in Paris thrown open in 1789, Belgrade Television was the regime's symbol of power.

It took Djokic four attempts to ram his way into 'TV Bastille'. Bullets and CS gas canisters bounced off his cabin. Two bullets punched holes in the windscreen, narrowly missing him. As he finally crashed through the lobby the police fled. Hundreds poured in behind him, setting light to the building. The remaining police inside reassured the by now terrified journalists that the army was on the way. They were not. Belgrade Television's director Dragoljub Milanovic was severely beaten, as were other male journalists. Women were abused and spat on. The newsreader Ljilja Jovanovic was called 'Milosevic's whore'.

The JSO were ordered to the television station. On the way, their vehicles were hit twenty-nine times by bullets. An elderly man shooting from behind a rubbish container loosed off nine rounds, although no fire was returned.

The JSO pulled up. Behind the bullet-proof window of his armoured vehicle, Legija surveyed the scene.

The crowd held its breath.

Legija gave the order.

His troops gave the Serb three-fingered salute and then drove back to base.

The crowd roared, cheers fuelled by profound relief.

Belgrade police commanders told their men to fall back. '*Gotov je,*' they said.

And he was.

25

SLOBODAN AT THE HAGUE

It's Your Problem

2001–2

His perversion of the truth was simply superb, and we used to say of him that he could make a man believe that Paris was really the capital of England and prove it by statistics.

Reginald Wyon, early twentieth-century British foreign correspondent, on Hilmi Pacha, governor of Macedonia.[1]

Most days Milosevic gets up around 7.00 a.m. He showers and shaves in his cell at the UN detention centre, a short drive from the ICTY at The Hague. If he is feeling spry he greets his fellow inmates with a cheery 'Good morning, comrades!' 'Good morning, Mr President,' the Serbs among them reply. His nine foot by fifteen foot cell boasts cable television, a coffee machine, and a shower. He is reading a lot of Ernest Hemingway and John Updike. In more reflective moments he listens to Celine Dion and Frank Sinatra on a portable CD player. 'My Way' is one of his favourites.[2] Milosevic can use the gym, prepare his own food in a kitchen. He is not beaten, forced to sing nationalist songs, or worse. There is an intimacy room, where husband and wife may enjoy conjugal visits. One prisoner has already conceived a son. Free of the stresses of running a country, sleeping and eating well, no longer downing Viljamovka by the bottle, Milosevic's health has improved since his incarceration.

Mr President enjoys a certain status. He served as the best man at the wedding of Predrag Banovic in mid-May 2002. Banovic is charged with beating prisoners to death at the Bosnian Serb concentration camp of Keraterm, in 1992. Predrag Banovic was arrested with his twin brother Nenad in November 2001 in Belgrade. Nenad was released for lack of evidence. Back in Belgrade he told B92 Television how Milosevic is a rock, on whom distressed prisoners often lean. 'When somebody is shattered, there is the president to give us advice, to help.' He described Milosevic as 'a stable and courageous person'. Milosevic offers advice such as 'Nothing lasts forever', and 'One should stabilise oneself, meaning pull yourself together.'[3] Walking through the prison courtyard Milosevic might get a whiff of the crisp salty air of the Dutch seaside. Perhaps he enjoys a Proustian moment, briefly remembering long-ago family holidays in the old Yugoslavia, driving the family Volkswagen from Belgrade down to the coast at Dubrovnik, with Mira in the front, Marko and Marija in the back.

After Milosevic's fall from power on 5 October 2000, a democratic government took over in Yugoslavia. But virtually the only thing uniting the new regime was its opposition to Milosevic. The DOS coalition immediately split into two camps: conservative nationalists under Yugoslav President Vojislav Kostunica, and pro-western reformers under Serbian Prime Minister Zoran Djindjic. The West, especially the United States, made it clear that future economic aid to Yugoslavia was contingent on Milosevic's extradition. Kostunica was opposed to the very idea of The Hague, let alone extraditing Milosevic. Djindjic took a more pragmatic view.

Kostunica allowed Milosevic, Mira, Milica and baby Marko to continue living in Tito's former residence at Uzicka 15. Marko quickly fled Serbia. His perfumerie 'Scandal', in downtown Belgrade, was completely destroyed and the Madona disco vandalised. Marko fled to Moscow, home to his uncle Borislav. From Moscow he sought sanctuary in Beijing, but despite Mira's admiration for China, he was turned back on 9 October, and returned to Moscow. Mira 'cannot say' where he is now, but he is widely believed to be somewhere in the former Soviet Union. There were reports that Marko intended to set up in Almaty, Kazakhstan, and build a replica Madona disco. However the *de facto* inclusion of Kazakhstan in the US's war against terror, and the protective trade practices of the Kazakh entertainment sector, makes this unlikely.

When Serbia went to the polls in December 2001, Milosevic's Socialists did surprisingly well. The DOS coalition won 64 per cent, but the Socialists took 13 per cent of the votes, making the party the largest opposition grouping with 35 seats. Milosevic retired from public life, but did not disappear. In an interview that month with Palma television, he said his 'conscience is clear and he can sleep well'. He accused Serbs from Croatia and Bosnia of being in the front lines of the October 5 revolution, and blamed them for sanctions and lowering the quality of life in Yugoslavia. The following month, Rade Markovic, head of the Serbian intelligence services, and Milosevic's old ally, Mihalj Kertes, head of the customs service, were both arrested.

The new authorities opened an investigation into Milosevic's abuse of power in Serbia. Serbian police finally moved to arrest Milosevic on 31 March 2001. By then the mordant joke about ever-shrinking Serbia had more or less become true. Milosevic prepared to go out fighting. An impressive arsenal was assembled at the house on Uzicka including: two machine guns; thirty assault rifles, a sniper rifle, a rocket launcher; ten cases of ammunition; twenty-three pistols and two cases of hand grenades. Marija Milosevic alone was packing three pistols: a Beretta, a Walther and a Derringer. Sinisa Vucinic, a political ally of Milosevic's wife Mira, was manning a machine gun.[4]

The police had launched their first charge in the early hours of Saturday morning. Masked plain-clothes commandos smashed their way through the windows and tried to storm the residence. But their attack met heavy resistance, bullets flew across the garden as the defenders opened up. Two police officers were wounded, and a photographer hurt as well. But when Milosevic lost control over his own back garden, as the police commandos there prepared for another raid, even he began to wonder if it was all over. In the early hours of Sunday morning negotiations started. Members of Milosevic's own Socialist Party tried to persuade him and his defenders to lay down their arms. The dawn sunlight brought a new clarity. Milosevic told his lawyer he was ready to surrender.

An investigating judge entered the house and read out the list of charges against him. These included financial misdealings, damaging Serbia's economy and introducing hyperinflation. At the same time a statement was presented, signed by Yugoslav President Kostunica, Serbian Prime Minister Djindjic and Serbian President Milan Milutinovic (also wanted by the ICTY). The statement said that the criminal proceedings against Milosevic were not instituted by The Hague, and guaranteed the safety and property of both Milosevic and his family. The key points were added in two typewritten annexes:

- Slobodan Milosevic will not be handed over to any judicial or other institution outside the country.
- Slobodan Milosevic has guarantees for the daily visits of his family.[5]

The annexes were signed under the authorisation of Serbian President Djindjic, and signed by a DOS official, Cedomir Jovanovic.

Amazingly, despite the bluster and the shooting, and the amount of alcohol and weapons everywhere, no one had died. Slobo's last stand was more Balkan farce than Bonnie and Clyde. But his arrest was real enough. At 4.30 a.m. he walked through his front door for the last time. Mira recalled: 'Our home was full of friends, Marija and I were also there, and people working in the residence, more than fifty people were there . . . They came into the house, and said either we arrest you and take you with us, or we will kill everyone. So what else could he do, just sit in the car? He did not blink an eye, and said of course I will go and he left.'[6]

After taking several of her mother's tranquillisers, and drinking most of a bottle of cognac, a despairing Marija fired five shots into the air as her father was driven off. Bracketed by a convoy of police jeeps, Milosevic was driven to a cell at Belgrade's central prison. Inmate 101980 was housed in the most comfortable wing of the prison, nicknamed 'The Hyatt'. The fourteen-square-metre cells there boasted an *en suite* shower, toilet and sink, and hot running water.

The details of Milosevic's stay in prison were published in a book by the prison governor Dragisa Blanusa, who was promptly sacked. *I Guarded Milosevic* reveals how the former president snored, made fruit tea, ate a lot of beans and smoked Serbian cigarettes. Mira arrived every day at noon, with a packed lunch.[7] She even brought painted eggs at Easter, although neither is religious. Sometimes she lost her temper and harangued prison staff, although she later apologised, blaming 'a surplus of female hormones'. The former ruling couple spent an hour together, holding hands, kissing each other and stroking each other's faces. Milosevic was always polite and correct with prison staff, as he is at The Hague.

It was while Milosevic was incarcerated in cell 1121 that the news broke in Serbia that would speed his extradition. In early summer 2001 a series of mass graves of Kosovo Albanians were discovered. Not in Croatia, Bosnia or even Kosovo, but the heartlands of Serbia itself, including one at Batajnica military base, just outside Belgrade. The corpses had been moved north during the bombing campaign. Yugoslav leaders warned Milosevic that if and when NATO troops entered Kosovo, they would find evidence of massacres. Informed of this Milosevic reportedly told his top brass to 'take care of it.'[8]

They did not do a very good job. Sanitation workers in the southern Kosovo town of Prizren were summoned in the middle of the night and driven to an army rifle range. The workers were ordered to load the corpses into a white refrigerator truck. In April 2000 a fisherman saw a truck from a food processing company in Prizren floating in the Danube. When local police opened the vehicle a human leg fell out. Inside were 86 bodies, which were then taken to Batajnica base. The details of the killings, and the botched attempts to dispose of the bodies were a profound psychological shock for many Serbs. Vital testimony was provided by conscience stricken Serbs who had been ordered to take part in the disposal exercise.

On 28 June 2001 Serb Prime Minister Zoran Djindjic chaired a meeting of the Serbian government. 28 June, St Vitus's Day, or Vidovdan, was the date of the Battle of Kosovo in 1389. Gavrilo Princip assassinated Archduke Franz Ferdinand in Sarajevo on Vidovdan in 1914. The decree authorising Milosevic's extradition was approved by fourteen votes to one, the sole dissenter a member of Vojislav Kostunica's party.

Three hours later Milosevic was told to pack his bag. He asked where he was going, but the answer was obvious. The new government had deceived her husband with a false promise, said Mira. 'They brought a document signed by the Yugoslav president and the Serbian prime minister, and other top officials. He was given this document and we believed it. We believed it. If my husband had signed something, he would not have breached it, as this current president did.'

Milosevic was taken to a police base. Fearful that the army might intervene, Djindjic had ordered an aircraft to land there as a feint, but the military did not move. In what appeared to be a well co-ordinated operation between Belgrade, London and Washington, Milosevic was then taken by helicopter to the US military base at Tuzla in northern Bosnia. From Tuzla Milosevic was flown in an RAF jet to a Dutch military base. At 11.00 p.m. he was led through the gate of the UN detention centre.

★   ★   ★

Milosevic's initial fury against the court appears to have abated. When he first appeared in court before the presiding judge Richard May on 3 July 2000 he refused to enter a plea. He condemned the ICTY as 'a false tribunal' and an 'illegal organ'.[9]

It was an unedifying performance for a former head of state. When Judge Richard May asked if he wanted the indictment read out to him Milosevic replied, 'It's your problem'. Which was incorrect, as it is very much Milosevic's problem. All three indictments against him since have been rolled into one. Milosevic is charged with crimes against humanity in Kosovo, Croatia and Bosnia, as well as genocide in Bosnia.

Milosevic is the first state president to be tried for genocide. His indictment covers three wars, between 1991 and 1998. Milosevic is not personally accused of taking part in massacres and ethnic cleansing. However, in all three indictments he is accused of individual criminal responsibility under article 7 (1) of the ICTY statutes, for having planned or ordered such acts, and of individual criminal responsibility for the acts of his subordinates, under article 7 (3) of the statutes. Had President Tudjman lived he would have almost certainly joined Milosevic in the dock. Both men sat at the apex of power in states that launched sustained campaigns of murder, terror and ethnic cleansing.

Critics charge that the ICTY tribunal is 'victors' justice'. If so, it is tardy. Between 1991 and 1999 Milosevic was treated by the West – and Russia – as a respected international statesman, even though the UN imposed harsh economic sanctions on the Milosevic regime for its role in the Yugoslav wars. Milosevic is charged not just with war crimes in Bosnia, but with genocide. A considerable amount of the evidence on which the prosecution has constructed its case against Milosevic has been supplied, eventually, by western governments. If this is available now, it was certainly known in the mid-1990s. Yet after the war in Bosnia ended, Milosevic was flown to Dayton airbase where his name was spelt out in flashing lights.

In the macabre accounting of the Milosevic era, Kosovo was the least bloody of the regime's wars (excluding Slovenia). Perhaps two thousand people died before the air-strikes began, a mere 1 per cent of Bosnia's losses. But NATO went to war against Serbia for Kosovo, which it would not do for Croatia or Serbia. As one senior British diplomat admitted, 'Of course we all knew Milosevic was the biggest part of the problem right from the outset. But what took longer for us to get was that he could never ever also be part of the solution.'[10]

The indictment for Kosovo is forty-two pages long, plus seventeen pages listing some of the civilians killed. Among the indictment's many details is an account of the final hours of forty-four members of the Berisha family, killed by Serb forces at the Kosovo village of Suva Reka on or about 26 March 2001. The village was surrounded by tanks, and the occupants ordered out. Men were then separated from women and children, and six people immediately killed. Serb forces then herded the survivors and other family members into a coffee shop. In its dry, legalistic language, the indictment notes: 'Forces of the Federal Republic of Yugoslavia and Serbia then walked into the coffee shop and opened fire on the persons inside. Forty civilians were killed and others seriously wounded during this action.'[11] Among the members of the Berisha family killed were Eron and Redon, both aged one year old; Dorentina, aged four and Hanumasha, aged eighty-one. Bodies of the Berisha family members were later dug up at Batajnica military base.

Such accounts of brutality all seem a long way from the ICTY, housed in a former insurance building near the quiet tree-lined streets of Dutch suburbia. Polite, but armed and burly UN policemen scrutinise each visitor's identity documents, before ushering them through two metal detectors. Armed police also control entrance to all office and other areas. After a shaky start in 1993, by September 2001 the ICTY had transformed itself into a major international operation, with an annual budget of $96 million, employing 1,188 staff members from seventy-seven countries. In April 2002, there were forty prisoners held at the ICTY's detention unit. Eight other accused had been provisionally released pending trial, while more than twenty arrest warrants remained outstanding. Cases are also pending, or have been concluded, against Croats, Bosnian Croats and Bosnian Muslims. After sentencing, prisoners are sent to another European country to serve their sentences.

Two television monitors in the foyer announce the days proceedings. The courtroom is open to all. The Milosevic trial is the most popular, and is now a stop on the Hague tourist trail. Visitors walk up a curved staircase and sit in the public seating area. Simultaneous translation is provided in several languages including English and Albanian. Spectators are divided from the courtroom by a plate-glass wall, but otherwise open sessions are held in full public view. There is little sense here of the drama that accompanied the Nuremberg war crimes trials. The most important court case of the new millennium resembles a municipal council meeting. Presiding Judge Richard May sits on a raised dais, between two others. Milosevic sits at one end of the courtroom, usually dressed in one of his double-breasted suits, with a light-coloured shirt offset by a silk tie. He is flanked continuously by two beefy armed policemen.

Milosevic conducts his own defence, aided by one of his Belgrade legal team who sit in the public gallery. His tactics are, broadly, political harangues against the West and NATO for bombing Serbia, which he blames for the mass exodus of Kosovo Albanians, combined with very detailed personal attacks on the character and testimony of witnesses. Many believe that such precise information comes from sympathisers within the new regime. Observers point out that Milosevic's ability to access such information from a prison cell will eventually undercut any defence that he did not know what was happening, for example, at Vukovar, or Srebrenica.

Wary perhaps of being accused of bias, the judges grant Milosevic plenty of leeway. Milosevic's rants provide an intriguing window into his mindset. In a courtroom duel with Kosovo Albanian leader Ibrahim Rugova, on 3 May 2002, Milosevic expounded his favourite conspiracy theory that an 'anti-Serbian policy' was instituted throughout the last decade, 'intended to annul and change the outcome of the First and Second World Wars'.[12] Milosevic then claimed that Germany supported the Kosovo Albanians as a reward for the 'massive participation of Albanian formations on the side of Hitler and Mussolini during the Second World War'.

There are perhaps are two Slobodan Milosevics. One is a charming Balkan rogue – or at least he wants to be seen as one – a confidant of presidents and ambassadors, a deft schmoozer of western diplomats, trying his best to bring his wayward protégés such as Radovan Karadzic to heel. The other is an authoritarian provincial Communist functionary of limited vision and a poor strategic sense.

It is the second Milosevic that is on display at The Hague. His courtroom technique has the effect of intimidating witnesses, often cowed and frightened Albanians who lost their nearest and dearest in the Kosovo war. Milosevic does not show sympathy. Instead he sits back, not exactly sprawled, but certainly comfortable and confident in his chair, before pouncing. He is a commanding presence in the courtroom. Ibrahim Rugova, in contrast, sat hunched and defensive, although it was Milosevic, not he, who was on trial.

Yet like all bullies, Milosevic buckles when he is met with equal force. One of the few courtroom encounters that have left Milosevic flustered was a duel with Lord Ashdown, now the UN High Representative in Bosnia. Ashdown had made repeated visits to Yugoslavia during the Milosevic era. A former soldier in the Special Boat Squadron, Ashdown was calmly confident as he took on Milosevic in mid-March 2002. Ashdown recalled with a certain relish their September 1998 meeting after his visit to Kosovo: 'I warned you that you would end up in this court, and here you are.'

Eventually, when Milosevic steps over the limit, Judge Richard May calls him to order. He often addresses Milosevic in weary familiar tone of old married couples compelled by circumstance to spend lengthy and unwelcome periods of time in a confined space. 'Mis-ter Mi-lo-se-vic,' he sighs, before bringing the defendant back to the matter in hand. Milosevic's wild rhetoric highlights the fact that for a lawyer, his courtroom technique is poor. Less bombast, and more facts would make a more powerful argument. For example, it is now widely believed – and admitted by western diplomats – that German demands in the summer of 1991 for early recognition of Croatian independence, without adequate human rights guarantees for the Serb minority, did accelerate the drive to war. While there was no 'massive' participation of Albanians on the Axis side, several thousand Albanians did join their own dedicated SS division, named after their national hero, Skenderbeg. Albanian SS troops rounded up 281 Kosovo Jews and also aided the German withdrawal from the Balkans.[13]

Milosevic's indictment for Kosovo is comparatively straightforward. About 800,000 Kosovars were forced from their home by Serb and Yugoslav troops while Milosevic, as Yugoslav President and head of state, was commander-in-chief of the Yugoslav military. Croatia and Bosnia are more complicated, as both of these countries had declared independence and so were sovereign states.

Milosevic's indictment for war crimes in Croatia is thirty-two pages long, with a thirty-one-page annex of civilian deaths from Serb forces. Milosevic is accused of 'exercising effective control or substantial influence' over the participants in a 'joint criminal enterprise'. Its aim was 'the forcible removal of the majority of the Croat and other non-Serb population from the approximately one-third of the territory of the Republic of Croatia that he [Milosevic] planned to become part of a new Serb-dominated state,'[14] through murder, terror and ethnic cleansing.

Another fourteen individuals are accused of participating, including Milosevic's political fixer during the early 1990s Borisav Jovic; the leaders of the rebel Krajina Serbs Milan Martic and the former dentist Milan Babic; Milosevic's former intelligence chief Jovica Stanisic, Franko Simatovic, leader of the Special Operations Unit; the ultranationalist paramilitary leader Vojislav Seselj, Zeljko Raznatovic and Radovan Stojicic (a.k.a. Arkan and Badza). Arkan and Badza are dead. Milan Martic, also separately indicted for war crimes, surrendered to the ICTY in May 2002. Borisav Jovic lives in Belgrade where he has reinvented himself as an author and television pundit. Seselj is an MP in the Serbian parliament, representing the Serbian Radical Party, which won twenty-three seats in the December 2001 elections. The others are living freely, probably in Serbia.

Milosevic's indictment for war crimes and genocide in Bosnia is twenty-five pages long with a fifteen-page annex. It is framed in similar terms as a 'joint criminal enterprise', under his effective control. Of the fourteen alleged members of the Bosnian joint criminal enterprise, several are familiar from the Croatia indictment including Borisav Jovic, Seselj and Arkan. Also named are Radovan Karadzic and the architect of the Srebrenica massacre, General Ratko Mladic. Karadzic and Mladic have also been separately indicted.

Uniquely in the Milosevic case, the tribunal decided to list the co-conspirators. All are under investigation for war crimes by the ICTY but have not been indicted. Deputy Prosecutor Graham Blewitt said:

We usually do not do this, as people could sabotage the investigation. Also they may never be charged, so it would not be fair to have this hanging over them for the rest of their lives. But based on their participation in the joint criminal conspiracy, it was obvious who they were. Naming them adds pressure to co-operate. We are confident, and we expect to indict all the co-perpetrators. Some may want to co-operate and do deals.[15]

The human tragedy of the Bosnian war is detailed in court documents such as Schedule E of Milosevic's Bosnia indictment. This details sniping incidents during the siege of Sarajevo. Anisa Pita, aged three, was shot in the right leg while taking off her shoes on the porch of her house on 13 December 1992. Dzenana Sokolovic, aged thirty-one, was walking home with her son Nermin, aged seven, on 18 November 1994. Mother and son had been collecting firewood. The bullet passed through Dzenana's abdomen and into her son's head, killing him. Lejla Bajramovic, aged twenty-four, was sitting in a friend's apartment on 8 December 1994, when she was shot in the head. And so it goes on, rows of names and figures.

Away from the high theatre of the Milosevic trial, less attention is given to the lower profile cases unfolding in the smaller courtrooms. Here the wheels of justice turn quietly and steadily. The Bosnian Serb General Stanislav Galic is accused of war crimes for overseeing the siege of Sarajevo. Galic, a grey man in a grey suit, was commander of the Sarajevo Romanija Corps – formerly the 4th corps of the Second Military District of the Yugoslav army. These were the soldiers who lobbed mortars at civilians queuing for relief aid, and shot down women and children in the street. As Milosevic himself told Bosnian prime minister Haris Silajdzic at Dayton, 'You deserve Sarajevo because you fought for it, and those cowards killed you from the hills.'[16]

Galic's defence is that he was unaware that innocent people were being killed and that fire was directed against military targets. This is hard to believe, when Bosnian Serbs were often just a couple of hundred metres from government-controlled territory. UN military observers who had visited the Serb siege lines also testified at Galic's trial. Jacques Kolp, a Belgian, said, 'The Army of Republika Srpska had good artillerymen . . . they knew exactly what they were hitting.' Major Jeremy Herme noted that, 'Actually where the shells hit, there were no military targets.'[17]

Muhamed Kapetanovic was not a military target. In January 1994, Kapetanovic, then aged nine, was playing with his friends in the winter snow in the Sarajevo suburb of Alipasino Polje when Bosnian Serbs began firing mortars at them. He told the court: 'We were riding sleighs when we heard grenades falling. Then we got scared and started to run . . . Daniel was killed, I was wounded and Admir and Elvir were also wounded.' Six people were killed in the attack, mainly children. Wounded in the head and leg by shrapnel, Muhamed was medically evacuated to Italy. He had seven operations in two years. Italian surgeons managed to save his leg, although it is 2.5 cm shorter than the other. Admir underwent twelve operations before his leg was eventually amputated. Elvir escaped with superficial wounds.[18]

The two most wanted, Radovan Karadzic and General Mladic, remain at large. Mladic was widely reported to be living in Belgrade for some time, but Serbian authorities deny he is still in the country. Karadzic is in Bosnia, where he has so far escaped arrest, despite the presence of a heavily armed NATO force. Both men remain popular among a section of the Serbian population who regard them as national heroes. In spring 2002 supporters of Karadzic staged his new play *Situation* in Belgrade, a drama ridiculing the international community in Bosnia.

These are hard times for the Milosevic family. None of the former statesmen who once courted his views so assiduously have visited Slobodan in prison. Richard Holbrooke and Lord Owen have yet to arrive bearing maps of Bosnia and felt-tip pens to divide it with. Nor has Lord Hurd turned up for a working prison breakfast, although Milosevic certainly could now make good use of his own private telephone network.

Mira visits her husband every month for a few days. She is given a special visa by the Dutch government. Even though he is now in prison, he does not feel betrayed, she said.

Neither East nor West has betrayed him. The only person that can betray him is me. But people have short memories and you have to remind everyone of everything. In the early 1990s my husband was accused by many circles, in Yugoslavia and abroad, that he wanted to keep Yugoslavia alive, even though it was falling apart and the Croats and the Slovenes wanted to leave. That was his big sin. Crazy Serbs and crazy Slobo, they said, they want Yugoslavia. Now in The Hague, they say he broke up Yugoslavia. Let them make their minds up.[19]

Although there are criminal charges outstanding against Marko over the case of Zoran Milanovic, the former Madona waiter who joined Otpor, he could return home to face them. If found guilty, after serving his sentence, Marko could live openly. Neither he, his sister, nor his mother is wanted by the ICTY. However, many in Belgrade believe that fear of retribution from forces outside the law prevents Marko from returning. During the last years of his father's regime, as his business grew rich on the proceeds of crime, Marko rarely left Pozarevac, and always travelled accompanied by several gun-toting bodyguards in an armoured vehicle. Such security would no longer be provided by the state. The family name that once protected him is now the greatest danger to his safety.

Marija lives freely, although she still wrestles with her own inner demons. In December 2001 Marija appeared in court in Belgrade accused of endangering public safety and illegal possession of a handgun, after she had shot in the air five times when her father was arrested. 'I fired into the sky, I emptied my pistol out of despair,' she said. She came to court without her mother, but with her bodyguard. Marija did not go to prison, and there are no more charges outstanding against her.

Marija took the imprisonment of her father very badly. When she visited him in prison in Belgrade she reportedly blamed Slobodan for not resisting arrest. 'If you had resisted arrest none of this would have happened. I want my father by my side. You have already decided to go to The Hague. What am I going to do here?' She screamed at her mother: 'I am not a part of your partisan stories. I don't belong where you are. I am from another story. Everything you do, you do on your own.'[20] Marija aligned herself with Vojislav Seselj, the ultra-nationalist paramilitary leader whom, back in 1994 her mother had described as 'Neither a Serb nor a man'.

Relations between Milosevic's wife and daughter remain poor, which is one reason why Mira has grown closer to Milica, who remains devoted to her mother-in-law, son and husband. Mira said: 'I love our daughter-in-law Milica very much, and we get along very well. This is not only because she is Marko's wife. We have a similar personality, and we are very close. We love little Marko. He is identical to Marko. They are identical, Marko when he was a child between one and three, and little Marko now.'

Mira remains loyal to her daughter: 'Marija does nothing now. She sits at home. She goes to speak with the police, and the ministry of the interior. The only place she has not been called to is the department for prostitution and trafficking in human organs. We think it's not right that only little Marko does not have any charges against him. He is already three years old, and he could have already inspired some genocide.' There are no criminal charges against Mira, although she was briefly embroiled in a scandal over flats being handed out to government cronies under her husband's regime.

Mira, Milica and baby Marko have moved back to Tolstoyeva 33, the house that Slobodan bought in July 1991, as war broke out in Croatia. Rebuilt, and painted baby pink topped with a green metal roof, it is surrounded by a dark metal security fence, reinforced with horizontal bars. There is no name at the entrance gate, and a security camera keeps a wary eye on visitors. Milica often appears on television, but Mira keeps a lower profile, and is accompanied by a bodyguard when she ventures out. A few JUL loyalists drop by, such as the theatre director Ljubisa Ristic, but otherwise Mira has been abandoned by her former cronies.

There are not many places for her to go. Sanctions remain in place on the Milosevics: the European Union visa ban on Slobodan, Mira, Marko, Marija, Milica and Borislav Milosevic is implemented by most western and European countries. Known Milosevic assets in the West have been frozen. New borders make travel impossible, communication difficult. Mira said: 'Slobo has not seen Marko since 6 October 2001. Marko and Marija have not seen each other since then. I have not seen Marko for more than a year. Marko has not seen his son for more than half of a year. That is how the family lives now.'

Like Yugoslavia under his rule, Milosevic's family has been rent asunder.

Afterword

Do we today, in 2003, claim that there were no war crimes? Serbs were killed, but Serbs killed as well. We cannot say that Srebrenica never happened, that Visegrad never happened, that Vukovar never happened. We have the courage to say what happened, as for who is responsible, well, that is for justice to prove.

Dragoljub Micunovic, speaker of the Serbia–Montenegro parliament, April 2003.[1]

Soon after midday on 12 March 2003 Zoran Djindjic, hero of the October revolution and Serbian prime minister, paid the ultimate price for the bargains once struck with the darkest forces of the Milosevic regime. He was shot dead by a sniper as he left his car by the entrance to the Serbian government building in downtown Belgrade. It was the severest blow yet to Serbia's faltering attempts to shake off the debilitating legacy of the Milosevic era and transform into a modern European state.

The killing was blamed on the nexus between one of the country's most powerful organised crime groups, known as the Zemun mob, and Serbian State Security's Special Operations Unit, the JSO. The leader of the Zemun clan was the former JSO commander Milorad Lukovic, aka Legija. It was Legija with whom Djindjic had made a pact in October 2000 not to come to the rescue of Milosevic.

While tributes to the slain leader poured in from world leaders, the Serbian government immediately declared a state of emergency. The Zemun gang was blamed for the murder of the Prime Minister, and the assassination attempt of 21 February; as well as over fifty other murders, dozens of kidnappings, attempting to murder Vuk Draskovic and the kidnapping and murder of former Serbian president Ivan Stambolic, who had disappeared in August 2000 while out jogging in Belgrade. Dusan Mihajlovic, minister of the interior, announced – in language itself somewhat reminiscent of the Milosevic era – 'We will arrest all those who planned this and those who resist we will liquidate.'[2]

Serbia had never recovered from the Milosevic era. Its failure to build institutions powerful enough to fight back against the menacing networks that had not only survived the collapse of the Milosevic regime, but prospered, now threatened the stability of the whole Balkan region. When Djindjic warned that criminals were better equipped than the police and even had their own wiretapping networks, *Identitet*, the newspaper identified with the Zemun mob, was confident enough to publish the transcript of a conversation between the prime minister and one of his closest associates.

Arrest warrants were issued for the Zemun gang's leaders: Legija, Dusan Spasojevic, aka Siptar, and Mile Lukovic, aka Kum (no relation to Legija). The JSO was disbanded and its leaders arrested in a police dragnet that saw thousands taken into custody. Among those detained was Zvezdan Jovanovic, JSO deputy commander, who reportedly confessed to pulling the trigger. His motive, he told an investigating judge, was not money. Rather, Legija had persuaded him that the unit was about to be broken up and its members charged with war crimes.[3]

Also arrested was the turbo-folk singer Svetlana Raznatovic, widow of Arkan, known to her public as 'Ceca', Legija's girlfriend, according to the Belgrade press. Police who raided her luxury villa in the suburb of Dedinje discovered a custom-built, bullet-proof bunker. It held enough weapons to equip a small private army including: 5,000 rounds of ammunition; twenty-one handguns; sniper rifle scopes; laser range-finder binoculars; silencers for sub-machine guns; twenty-one police truncheons and handgun ammunition. Most macabre perhaps were the two licence plates from the Croatian town of Vukovar, which had been levelled by Serb forces in the siege of 1991, and where Arkan's troops had been active.

The Serbian government revealed details of the Zemun gang's lavish lifestyles. Its control of the cocaine and heroin trade across south-eastern Europe brought profits of millions of Euros. Gang leaders lived in luxury villas surrounded by high walls and security cameras, with heated swimming pools. Their restaurant bills for one meal exceeded five years' pension for a retired Serb. Siptar had been arrested by French police in Paris in May 2001 and deported to Belgrade. He and his friends spent over $50,000 a day, according to French intelligence.[4] When not in Paris, the Zemun gang liked to holiday in Monte Carlo, Hong

Kong, Athens, Singapore and Columbia. Legija and Siptar, it seems, had a liking for luxury yachts. But just as Interior Minister Dusan Mihajlovic had predicted, those resisting arrest were indeed 'liquidated'. Siptar and Kum went out shooting and were killed in a gun battle with police. Siptar's luxury villa proved more difficult to deal with. It took several attempts by demolition crews to blow it up.

More significant was the arrest of Jovica Stanisic, State Security (RDB) chief under Milosevic, and Franko Simatovic, another former commander of the JSO. Both men knew where the bodies were buried, literally and metaphorically. Stanisic and Simatovic had been named as co-conspirators in Milosevic's indictments for Croatia and Bosnia. Both men were indicted in May for war crimes and crimes against humanity.

One of the greatest mysteries of the Milosevic era was quickly solved. The remains of Ivan Stambolic were discovered after JSO members confessed to his murder. He had been executed with two shots, and buried in a pit in northern Serbia. Ivan Stambolic, *kum* and patron of Slobodan Milosevic, was finally laid to rest with full state honours at Belgrade's Topcider cemetery on 9 April 2003. Grujica Spasovic, editor of the daily newspaper *Danas* and a member of the committee that had fought to keep pressure on the authorities over Stambolic's disappearance, spoke for many when he said: 'In the previous thousand days we faced brutal truths – mass graves were discovered, freezer trucks have come up from rivers, one prime minister and one president of the state were murdered. All that was the price for a wrong choice made sixteen years ago.'[5] Perhaps the ghosts of the 1987 Eighth Session, when Milosevic and Mira had organised the public crushing of Stambolic that finished his political career, had finally been laid to rest.

Soon after Stambolic's funeral the Serbian police filed charges against Slobodan Milosevic, and Rade Markovic, in connection with Stambolic's murder. Rade Markovic, head of the RDB in the last years of the Milosevic regime, is now serving a seven-year prison sentence for conspiracy to murder Vuk Draskovic in 1999.

Mira Markovic is also wanted for questioning in connection with Stambolic's murder. In February 2003, just before her parliamentary immunity expired, Mira fled Belgrade for Russia. She had been due to go on trial for abuse of office, charged with appropriating state property by giving a luxury Belgrade flat to her grandson's nanny. It seemed a curiously innocuous charge to level against the woman who had stood by Milosevic's side during the destruction of Yugoslavia, yet it was enough to cause her to flee the country. Mira's fate was not yet clear at the time of writing, and Russia could prove reluctant to facilitate her extradition. It does, however, seem certain that it will be a long time before she sees her husband again. Either she will have to join Marko, living on the run as a fugitive, or return home to Belgrade, where she will now face charges far more serious than those of handing out a state-owned flat on the sly.

There was more. The Serbian government announced that the death of Djindjic was to have been the trigger for a coup, and the restoration to power of Milosevic-era loyalists. The plan appeared to be that two groups of conspirators, the first in Serbia and the second based in Republika Srpska in Bosnia, would assassinate not just Djindjic but also other leading politicians. At the same time the JSO, combined with other military and paramilitary formations, would take control of the state. Those behind the aborted coup including criminal gangs, far-right nationalist parties and an obscure grouping dubbed 'The Hague Brotherhood' prepared to fight against further extraditions to the ICTY. In post-Milosevic Serbia, just as in the era of Slobodan, criminals, the military and nationalists all overlapped.

Links were also drawn between Djindjic's assassination and the sudden surrender to The Hague of the ultra-nationalist paramilitary leader Vojislav Seselj. Before leaving for The Hague in February 2003, Seselj had warned of a 'bloody' spring.[6] Seselj had been indicted on fourteen counts of crimes against humanity and war crimes between August 1991 and September 1993. Seselj stands accused of crimes against non-Serbs not just in Croatia and Bosnia, but also in Serbia itself, in the cosmopolitan northern province of Voivodina, home to Croat, Czech, Hungarian and German minorities. Serb authorities plan to send investigators to the ICTY to speak to Seselj about his alleged role in organising the murder of Djindjic. Seselj's party said that the allegations were lies.

As for Milosevic, his trial has moved on from Kosovo to the indictments for war crimes and crimes against humanity in Croatia and Bosnia, as well as genocide in Bosnia. Milosevic's attitude to the trial has altered considerably since he scowled and sneered his way through his first appearances in the dock. He now engages fully with the court, appears quite at home in the dock, and is polite and courteous to the judges. He continues to act as his own defence attorney, although the stream of insider information sent to him from Belgrade supporters about prosecution witnesses has now stopped. The special commission set up by the Yugoslav military to aid his defence has been closed down by the Serbian authorities.

However, despite warnings from doctors that his high blood pressure puts him at risk of a heart attack, Milosevic generally remains as combative as ever. His frequent colds and several bouts of influenza have slowed the trial down. The loss of over two months means that the prosecution case, already cut back, could now last until December. Milosevic will then be granted equal time for his defence. As the trial opened in 2002, his defence could last into late 2005.

The indictments over Croatia and Bosnia are both easier and more difficult for the prosecution. Easier, because the horrific crimes committed in the Croatian and Bosnian wars have been extensively documented. The massacres by Serb forces at Srebrenica, or after the fall of Vukovar, are now matters of public record. But the war in Kosovo took place on Serbian soil, while Milosevic was President of Yugoslavia. The line of command responsibility from the battlefields around Pristina to Belgrade is comparatively straightforward. The wars in Croatia and Bosnia took place in republics that had seceded from Yugoslavia and were internationally recognised sovereign states. During this time, Serbia, as Milosevic repeatedly boasted, 'was not at war', despite the fact that Belgrade was supplying men, weapons, ammunition, funding and political support for armies of Serb-occupied Croatia and Bosnia. The challenge for the prosecution is to prove a connection between Milosevic and ethnic cleansing and the atrocities on the battlefield.

The prosecution's pre-trial brief is full of telephone intercepts which seem extremely damaging to Milosevic's defence, and appear to link him directly with the leaderships of the rebel Serbs in Krajina and Knin. Milosevic's conversations with figures including Bosnian Serb leader Radovan Karadzic, State Security chief Jovica Stanisic and Yugoslav army generals Blagoje Adzic and Nikola Uzelac are extensively documented. For example, point 25 of the brief details the following:

As the Accused explained to Karadzic, '[if Croatia] wants to secede . . . they should be allowed to secede . . . now it's only a question of secession on the line that's suitable to us . . . nothing more.' In another conversation discussing a JNA attack in Eastern Slavonia, the Accused showed he was fully engaged in the Croatian war. He told

Karadzic the JNA attack had gone well, there were many Croatian casualties and '[t]he whole thing is, to carry out a serious operation that we talked about. I think all the steps I have taken up to now have borne fruit.'[7]

Intriguingly, there is also a recording of a telephone conversation between Mira Markovic and JNA General Blagoje Adzic, one of the rare links between Milosevic's wife and the military. In another conversation, Milosevic tells Radovan Karadzic to ask Mira for General Adzic's number.[8]

If nothing else, the hundreds of intercepts reveal that western intelligence agencies, and therefore western governments, were well aware of Milosevic's central role in the Yugoslav wars. It seems almost every telephone call that he made was tapped and taped by a variety of secret services. Which sheds even harsher light on the eagerness of politicians and diplomats such as Lords Hurd and Owen, and the US envoy Richard Holbrooke to flatter and negotiate with him.

His defence is based on a now familiar cocktail of fact, fiction and bluster. This was evident in, for example, his discourse in September 2002 on the Srebrenica massacre. He began by quoting, accurately, from the 3,500 page report into the Srebrenica massacre, compiled by the Netherlands Institute for War Documentation (NIOD), which said there were 'no indications' of political or military liaison between the Bosnian Serb Army and Belgrade. Milosevic then told the court:

Time will show that on the 1st of July, 1995, in the house of a Muslim, the former president of the municipality in Zvornik, where two members of the Muslim government from Sarajevo were present, the representatives of a mercenary military formation within the army of Republika Srpska but not under the command of the army of Republika Srpska but within the French intelligence service, they agreed to have this crime committed, that is to say, to abandon Srebrenica and to carry out this slaughter.[9]

Milosevic's claim that 'a mercenary military formation' within the Bosnian Serb army taking orders from the French secret service had carried out the Srebrenica killings, is both ludicrous and bizarre, although it earned him headline coverage around the world.

Milosevic has scored some points in his courtroom duels, but an

overall picture of his role in the conflicts is steadily emerging. A series
of key witnesses have laid out in detail the web of connections between
Serbia's political leadership, the interior ministry and the paramilitaries
who carried out much of the ethnic cleansing and atrocities, and the
relations between Belgrade and the para-states in Serb-occupied Croatia
and Bosnia.

Some of the most fascinating testimony has come from witnesses
whose identity has been concealed for their own protection. A former
JSO member who appeared under the name of 'K-2' testified in January
2003. K-2 had served in Bosnia. He said that the unit operated under
the direct control of the Milosevic regime, and that wages were paid
by the Serbian Interior Ministry. 'We had full support in the form of
ammunition, uniforms and all other necessities . . . Our unit had to do
whatever it was asked to do. There was no possibility of saying no. The
doors of the president were open to us.' When K-2 was asked which
president he meant, he said: 'As far as I was able to gather, there was
only one president – and that was President Milosevic.'[10]

K-2 was well informed about the darkest episodes in recent Serbian
history. He admitted to Milosevic that he had been involved in the 2001
murder of Arkan. 'That is the main reason why you are no longer in
living in Serbia and are concealing your identity?' he asked. 'Yes,' K-2
replied. Milosevic dismissed K-2 as someone who 'doesn't know what he
is talking about' and claimed that the JSO were 'a regular unit', wearing
red berets also worn by other police and army forces.

Protected witness B-129 also gave important testimony about the links
between the RDB and Arkan, and his Tigers paramilitaries. B-129, who
worked in the Tigers' office, detailed how when Arkan needed help from
Serbian State Security, she picked up the telephone and said the special
password *Pauk*, meaning spider.[11] This would put her straight through
to Franko Simatovic, commander of the JSO. 'Arkan always said that
without orders from the state security, the Tigers never went anywhere.'
The Tigers were deployed on top secret operations during the Bosnian
war, B-129 testified, although they were all instructed to remove their
badges and shoulder flashes in case they were killed or captured.

As Arkan was too recognisable, a JSO commander was put in charge
– Milorad Lukovic, aka Legija. In a small but telling piece of evidence,
B-129 recounted how the Tigers crossed the border from Serbia into
Bosnia bearing special number plates from the Serbian Interior Ministry.
The vehicles were simply waved through the UN checkpoints, she said.

The Tigers were paid in Deutschmarks, at a rate of 1500 a month (about £500). This was a fortune, when most Serbs were paid around five Deutschmarks a month. The money was delivered in sacks, and B-129 counted it into envelopes.

The political links between the rebel Serbs and Milosevic were outlined in December 2002, when protected witness C-61 testified. After several days of testimony, C-61 came out from behind the screen that shielded his face, and also no longer spoke through a voice distorter. But by then most informed observers had worked out that the man engaging in rancorous courtroom exchanges with his ex-boss was the former president of the Serb Republic of Krajina, Milan Babic. Babic, a former dentist from Knin, is also implicated in war crimes. He is named as a co-conspirator in Milosevic's indictment for Croatia, which means he is under investigation and is likely to be indicted himself.

Babic had never forgiven Milosevic for sacking him from the leadership of the Krajina Serbs in 1992. He testified that he had held twenty-five meetings with Milosevic in Belgrade between October 1990 and October 1991. In a dramatic courtroom confrontation he accused Milosevic of leading the Serbs to disaster. 'You dragged the Serb people into war. You brought shame on the Serbs,' he told Milosevic. Milosevic denied his former protégé's claims. He replied that there was no disgrace in Serbia having helped its fellow countrymen. 'Was it a secret that Serbia assisted you? We assisted you in every respect to survive.'[12]

Babic's testimony also detailed how, in 1990 and 1991, the legitimate concerns of the Serb minority living in soon-to-be-independent Croatia were exploited by Belgrade to such a pitch that they felt it necessary to take up arms, and were unwittingly used as dupes in the Milosevic regime's plan for a Greater Serbia. Initially the Serb Democratic Party (SDS) advocated territorial and cultural autonomy for Serbs in Croatia. But under the influence of Belgrade's propaganda, and the parallel para-state set up in Krajina by Serbian State Security, the SDS soon became more extreme and demanded 'self-determination' for the Serbs living in Croatia. The price of self-determination was a war, funded, armed and directed from Belgrade, a war that ended in disaster in the summer of 1995, when the Croatian army swept through Krajina and over 100,000 Serbs fled or were expelled. (See Chapter 18).

Babic himself admitted that he was seduced by Belgrade's line, despite warnings from Stipe Mesic, now president of Croatia, that Milosevic would cheat him and he would lose not just Greater Serbia, but also his dentist's practice. Babic's testimony appeared to have rattled Milosevic, who eventually resorted to abuse. He used the prosecutor's transcript of telephone intercepts of his conversations with Radovan Karadzic, in which Milosevic described Babic as 'an idiot', 'ordinary scum' and 'Tudjman's trump'. Milosevic told the court: 'You see, I said the worst things about Babic'. This may not have been the most useful tactic in the long term for Milosevic's defence, as the prosecution is making liberal use of intelligence intercepts and telephone taps. As the commentator Mirko Klarin points out, 'in this way he confirmed the authenticity of the transcripts and recordings of the intercepted telephone conversations, which he otherwise rejected as a forgery.' [13]

If Milan Babic provided valuable evidence of the political ties between Belgrade and its client state in Knin, the former head of Yugoslav military counter-intelligence service helped fill in the details of the military links. Like Milan Babic, General Aleksander Vasiljevic has his own agenda. He too has been named as a co-conspirator in Milosevic's indictment over Croatia. As a career officer in the Yugoslav army, General Vasiljevic is concerned to try and restore the reputation of the military by blaming the paramilitaries and special forces such as the JSO, under the control of the Interior Ministry, for the atrocities. Nonetheless, General Vasiljevic is one of the best-informed and most important insider witnesses so far.

Testifying in February 2003, General Vasiljevic told the tribunal that Serbian units could only have fought on the battlefield in eastern Croatia with presidential approval. 'I do know that some Serbian TO [territorial defence] units were at the Slavonia battlefield . . . It is my opinion that such a decision would have been under the responsibility of the president of the republic.' [18] Prosecutors also produced a letter from Milan Martic, leader of the Krajina Serbs, written in 1993, which asked Milosevic to pressurise the Yugoslav Army to help the rebel Serbs based in Knin. General Vasiljevic told the court that Martic's letter showed that he believed Milosevic could influence the Yugoslav Army to issue the equipment he wanted.

General Vasiljevic's testimony was also useful for the prosecution in highlighting the complex network of links between the Yugoslav Army and the military forces of the rebel Serb statelets in both Croatia and Bosnia. He said there were 'two armies in two states, and there was the third state – Yugoslavia – which treated these two armies as her own, financed them, armed them and provided commanding officers.'[15] Vasiljevic testified that between 1992 and 1995 up to 13,000 Yugoslav Army officers served in the armies of the Krajina and Bosnian Serbs. Considering that by April 1992 Yugoslavia was reduced to the republics of Serbia and Montenegro, and Serbian President Slobodan Milosevic exerted untrammelled power, this is a potentially devastating piece of evidence, that directly links Belgrade with the wars and ethnic cleansing for which Milosevic has been indicted.

Vasiljevic also testified about the links between the Serbian Interior Ministry and the paramilitary formations that were formed under its tutelage. He told the court that two Serbian State Security officers were assigned to the Eastern Slavonija region of Croatia, in February 1992, after its capture by rebel Serb forces. Eastern Slavonija was the site of some the worst atrocities in the Croatian war. One of the ghastliest mass killings occurred at the village of Lovas on October 15 1991 when about thirty Croatian villagers were forced to walk through a minefield. Twenty-one people were killed, according to Annex One of Milosevic's indictment. Several were relatives. Three members of the Sabljak family lost their lives: Ivan, born in 1960; Marko, born in 1950; and Tomo, born in 1949.[16]

It is impossible to imagine the terror that the villagers must have felt as they were forced to walk to their deaths, wondering when they would hear the click of the mine's trigger, before the explosion that would blow them to pieces, all the while under the mocking laughs of the Serbian paramilitaries. Six days later General Vasiljevic received notice from Yugoslav army security of the massacre, carried out by members of the paramilitary unit Dusan Silni (Dusan the Mighty).[17] As the perpetrators of the massacre were Serbian citizens, Yugoslav Military intelligence informed the Serbian interior and defence ministries, testified General Vasiljevic.

Further insight into the financing of Milosevic's parallel state was provided in July 2002 by the testimony of Rade Markovic, who succeeded Jovica Stanisic as head of Serbian State Security (RDB) in 1998. Markovic related how the RDB's budget was insufficient to meet its needs. The RDB controlled the Special Operations Unit (JSO). When the JSO needed funds, they were obtained from the Federal Customs service, controlled by a long-time Milosevic loyalist, Mihalj Kertes, he told the court. 'In order to get such funds approval was required. This approval for allocating funding for the state security or the army of Yugoslavia or I don't know who else, had to be obtained by Mihalj Kertes from Slobodan Milosevic.'

RDB employees picked up the funds from the customs, and handed it to the Interior Ministry department in charge of finances and pensions. The money was handed over in foreign currency, in cash, detailed Markovic. It was then placed in a bank, from where it was used to pay for goods supplied to the RDB. The bank was Beobanka, a unit of Milosevic's former employer Beogradska Banka. The banker was Borka Vucic, Milosevic's long-term shadow finance minister (see Chapter 17).[18]

Milosevic's successor as Serbian president joined him at the ICTY in January 2003. Milan Milutinovic pleaded not guilty to crimes against humanity in Kosovo. Three months later, a man regarded as a hero by many Bosnian Muslims arrived. Naser Oric, commander of the defenders of Srebrenica, was arrested by UN peacekeepers in the northern Bosnian city of Tuzla. Oric, once one of Milosevic's bodyguards, is accused of war crimes against Serb villagers during the Bosnian war. However, NATO troops were unable to locate or arrest the tribunal's two most wanted, General Ratko Mladic, and Bosnian Serb leader Radovan Karadzic, who remained free at the time of writing.

If one purpose of the ICTY is to promote eventual reconciliation, then the former Bosnian Serb leader Biljana Plavsic made some small amends for the crimes committed by the Bosnian Serb army. Plavsic had initially pleaded not guilty to war crimes, crimes against humanity and genocide. But she later pleaded guilty to one count of persecution, and the other charges were dropped. Shortly before the end of her hearing in December 2002 she made a dramatic courtroom confession, a *mea culpa* that resounded across the former Yugoslavia. 'The knowledge that I am responsible for such human suffering and for soiling the character of my people will always be with me,' she said. Serbs had committed crimes out of 'a blinding fear that led to an obsession, especially among those of us for whom the Second World War was living memory, that Serbs would never again allow themselves to become victims,' she told the court. 'In this obsession of ours to never again become victims, we had allowed ourselves to become victimisers.'[19]

While some dismissed it as empty words, others saw the first glimmerings of the process of a public coming to terms with the bloody events that had torn the country apart. On February 28 she was sentenced to eleven years in prison, which at the age of seventy-two was, in effect, a life sentence. 'This is nothing compared to what misery I have seen in my life,' she said in Belgrade before returning to The Hague for sentencing. 'This is the end of a road which I started a long time ago.'[20]

Yugoslavia too has come to the end of the road. In February 2003 the country officially changed its name to Serbia-Montenegro. Laconic Belgraders have already dubbed the country S&M, or 'Solania', in honour of the EU's foreign policy chief Javier Solana who brokered the deal. One of the first acts of the new parliament was to amend a law to allow more extraditions to the ICTY. But the union of the two republics is unlikely to last long, and it seems likely that both Serbia and Montenegro will within the near future become independent states, the final stage in the process of dissolution that began in 1991.

Historians may debate for decades whether Yugoslavia was a viable entity, but when the forces seeking to break it apart became stronger than those holding it together, it was clear the centre could not hold. War, however, was never inevitable, despite the fact that Serbs – and other nationalities – were spread outside the borders of their home republics. By the end of the twentieth century the craft of statehood was flexible enough to assuage the fears of some Serbs that they were about to be stranded under a unfriendly flag. National autonomy, cultural autonomy, confederation, joint or multiple-citizenship across free and open borders, the list of possible solutions for national and ethnic questions is endless – if the political will is there. Czechoslovakia separated in a smooth and peaceful disassociation, so did – more or less – the Soviet Union, which was potentially far more explosive than Yugoslavia.

Would Yugoslavia have broken apart without Milosevic? Despite his central role, it is too simplistic to blame one man for the destruction of the federation. Perhaps if Ivan Stambolic had triumphed in 1987 at the Eighth Session, Balkan history may have taken a different and more peaceful course. But Milosevic was not a strange aberration in Serbian history. He was part of its continuum and dynamic, a heroic figure around whom a fractious and beleaguered people united, well rooted in Serbian national mythology.

With hindsight it is not surprising that Milosevic should have found such ready support in the late 1980s and early 1990s. These were troubled and frightening times for the Serbs, for all Yugoslavs. The multi-national state in which many Serbs had believed was revealed as a Balkan Potemkin village, with no foundation. It was natural for them to seek a protector. The Slovenes had Milan Kucan, ready to lead the northern republic into a bright new European dawn, no matter what the cost of the chain reaction this would trigger. The Croats were hero-worshipping Franjo Tudjman, a man determined to rehabilitate the symbols of the Ustasha regime. The Bosnian Muslims had Alija Izetbegovic, a former Islamic dissident. In that sense, Milosevic was an obvious leader, especially after he visited Kosovo and declared that Serbs there would be beaten no longer. As Mira Markovic noted, 'It is very simple, if I protect you, you begin to love me.'[21]

The break up of Yugoslavia was not peaceful. War was a deliberate choice, supported by enough of the Serbian military and political elite to ensure that Milosevic remained in power. Slovenia, Croatia and Bosnia also all prepared for conflict. As Mira Markovic argued:

> The most efficient means of ruining a multi-ethnic country was using nationalism and nationalist hatred. The love among Czechs and Slovaks was not so strong, but the love between the peoples of Yugoslavia was very strong, and that is why the disintegration was so painful. I think the Yugoslav nations loved each other very much. Our relations were strong, and that is why our separation was bloody and hard. Yugoslavia died for a long time, and I think it is because we really wanted to be together. Maybe I am wrong, but I think that big loves break up in a difficult manner, while weaker ones are easier to separate.'[22]

The Serbs' love for Milosevic brought them nothing but disaster. Kosovo Serbs are no longer being beaten, because they are no longer there. A few struggle on in isolated enclaves, surrounded by vengeful Albanians and protected by the United Nations, but most have fled, and are unlikely ever to return. Homes, jobs, businesses and land have all been abandoned for a meagre welcome in mother Serbia. There they may struggle to build new lives in competition with their brethren from Croatia and Bosnia. The historic Serb communities of Krajina, brought north by the Habsburgs to protect Europe from Ottoman incursions, have also vanished for ever. As for Bosnia, Republika Srpska is a wasteland, its economy and society as wrecked as the minarets of the mosques blown up by Serb demolition squads.

Yet the ICTY, and the efforts of Serbs themselves are finally shining

a spotlight on the darkest stains on the country's history, such as the
Srebrenica massacre. 'People know as much as they want to,' said
Aleksandar Nenadovic, former editor of *Politika* newspaper.

> Even during the war we had foreign papers on sale in the centre of
> Belgrade, and you could listen to the BBC or watch satellite television.
> But the average man would have only about heard of the ugly things
> being done to the Serbs. The simplest truth is to say that 'We are
> victims, look what they have done to us'. When you believe that,
> it's so easy to get rid of any curiosity to find out more. That the Serbs
> were shooting at Sarajevo for years, shooting at innocent people; that
> some of our writers went there with a machine gun, the average Serb
> doesn't know.'[23]

In Belgrade, across Serbia, there is a stuttering attempt to come to
terms with the legacy of the Milosevic era and its tragic human cost.
But high on the slopes of Sarajevo's Lions Cemetery, where the rows of
grave markers stand in silent vigil, and in the killing fields of Srebrenica,
where shards of bone poke through the earth, there is only silence.

Appendix 1

MILOSEVIC AND TUDJMAN
COURT YUGOSLAVIA'S JEWS

Throughout the Yugoslav wars Belgrade and Zagreb ran public relations campaigns to manipulate Jewish public opinion, both domestic and international. This curious and little-known episode of the Milosevic era began soon after Milosevic's 1987 visit to Kosovo, when Klara Mandic founded the Serbian-Jewish Friendship Society (SJFS). A Belgrade dentist who lost seventy-three members of her family in the Holocaust, Mandic was a charismatic figure, with long red fingernails, who wore two large gold stars of David around her neck. She was well connected among the Serbian intellectuals who were then increasingly comparing the Serbs to the Jews, as two martyred peoples with 'heavenly' missions.

Many prominent Serb thinkers joined the SJFS, including the writer Dobrica Cosic. In an interview in March 1993, Mandic recalled the society's genesis: 'I went straight to Slobodan Milosevic to ask for his support. He agreed, and he stood completely behind me.'[1] Mandic was friends with both the Bosnian Serb leader Radovan Karadzic, and Goran Hadzic, president of the rebel Serb republic in Krajina. Karadzic joined the society and there were rumours that the two were lovers. 'I am an adviser to both presidents, and I am very proud of that,' she boasted. Mandic used her connections to Milosevic to organise 'Serbian Week' in Israel, in May 1990. Serbian Week promoted business and tourism and town-twinning. Belgrade was twinned with Tel Aviv and Novi Sad with Haifa.

Two years later, Mandic went on a speaking tour across the United States, to warn American Jews about Tudjman's new state. Mandic later explained: 'The key issue is that the Orthodox Church did not teach people how to hate, as the Catholic Church did. Jews and Serbs have a common history of genocide. But the difference is that the world knows about Jewish suffering, but we could not speak about Serb suffering. We aim to get the truth out about the Serbs.' This then, was the society's real agenda: to use the claim of a 'common history' to attack Croatia. She continued: 'There is a new fascism spreading through Europe, through Croatia which is an exponent of German and Austrian policies. At the head of this is Tudjman. They wear the same uniforms, use the same symbols and sing the same songs as the Ustasha. Serbs are the first victims of the new fascism. Six million pairs of eyes ask me from the sky, "do you see what is happening – will you try and do something?"'

Mandic claimed: 'Serbia is a country where there has never been anti-Semitism. Not among the laws, nor among the people. The society was founded to further the friendship between Serbs and Jews, that goes back centuries and centuries.' Thus the myth. The historical reality was different. During the nineteenth century several restrictive decrees were passed against the Jewish community and Jews did not enjoy full citizenship until the end of the century. When the Germans invaded in 1941 about seventy thousand Jews were living in Yugoslavia. There were families in Sarajevo who still spoke Ladino, the medieval Judeo-Spanish of their ancestors, expelled from Spain in 1492.

The Serbian puppet regime of General Milan Nedic worked with the Nazis to exterminate most of Serbia's Jews. Concentration camps were set up within Serbia. Jews were gassed in vans – precursors of the gas chamber – that trundled back and forth across the Danube bridges. Others fought as partisans. One, Mose Pijade, had tutored Tito in Marxism in prison, and had risen to be one of Tito's highest advisers.[2] By the late 1980s between five and six thousand Jews lived in Yugoslavia, mainly concentrated in the major cities such as Belgrade, Zagreb and Sarajevo.

Mandic's emotive style may have been in poor taste but the society was initially greeted with enthusiasm – albeit guarded – by many Belgrade Jews. 'What made this society attractive to the Jews was that the greatest Serbian writers, thinkers and philosophers joined and the many calls then to re-establish diplomatic relations with Israel,' said Belgrade community leader Misa Levi. 'But Milosevic tried to take advantage of this. He and the people around him thought that if he has Jews as friends, through this society, he would be able to influence the Jewish lobby in the United States, and make changes in American policy.'[3]

Milosevic himself was open and friendly to Yugoslav Jewish leaders

such as Aca Singer, who knew Milosevic from their banking days. Singer
met with Milosevic to discuss the restoration of Jewish property, and
taking action against the rise in Serbian anti-Semitism. The Milosevic
family home at Tolstoyeva 33 had once been owned by a Jewish publisher
called Geca Kon, killed in the Holocaust, and was later nationalised.
But Singer did not ask for its return, he recalled. 'I said we are both
bankers, let's be rational, let's see how many minutes you have for our
talk. Milosevic said, "For you, time for talking is unlimited. I can talk
with you for ten minutes, half an hour or half a day, so it's up to you."
Milosevic asked me why I spent so much time in the Jewish community,
and said that a banker like me was needed in Serbia.'[4]

Singer had already resisted attempts to recruit him in the era of
pyramid schemes and hyperinflation. 'I told him the Jewish community
had financial problems, and we should get our property back.' Here
Milosevic immediately saw an opportunity. Singer recalled: 'He said,
"Look Aca, let's not deal with this restitution now, but if you have
financial problems, then let's put the Jewish community on the books
of the state budget to support you. We can arrange this."' But Singer,
a survivor of both Auschwitz and Tito's concentration camp at Goli
Otok, was not taken in. 'I said this was not a good idea, either for
the Jewish community nor him. I told him that when I have contacts
with world Jewish leaders, they will say that I am paid by Milosevic.
We agreed to disagree about this and I insisted on the restitution
of communal property. I didn't mention Geca Kon. I didn't want
to sour the conversation. I was not asking for private property to
be returned, but for community property. Milosevic said this would
be OK.'

Singer also wanted a promise of adequate government action against
the anti-Semitism in Serbia that was starting to appear, despite the best
efforts of Klara Mandic. The two men spoke for three hours. 'I had a
positive feeling about Milosevic's attitude towards Jews. I cannot say
that Milosevic was anti-Semitic. Once I just glanced at my watch, I
saw that thirty minutes had passed. He told me, please just continue
with your talk. I said anti-Semitic books are being published and the
judicial system was not doing anything about it.' Milosevic then wrote
a note to himself to call the Serbian Public Prosecutor, who soon called
Singer. The two men met, but with no result, said Singer. 'Two months
went by, nothing happened. We wrote to the Serbian government. We
said we wanted to add documents to our property restitution claim to

Milosevic that he promised to forward to the government. We never had a reply and the issue is still unresolved.'

Mandic's best ally in the war for Jewish public opinion was President Tudjman, who had proclaimed in the 1990 election campaign, 'Thank God my wife is not a Jew or a Serb.'[5] Tudjman decided to abolish the Croatian dinar and replace it with the kuna, the currency of the wartime Ustasha regime. Zagreb's square commemorating the victims of fascism was renamed 'The Square of Great Croatians'. Perhaps the crassest of all was the proposal, supported by Tudjman, to rebury the remains of wartime Ustasha with their victims at Jasenovac. The rationale behind this was a supposed 'reconciliation'.

Tudjman's book, *Wastelands of Historical Reality*, was so littered with anti-Semitism and Holocaust revisionism that foreign journalists in Belgrade were handed a leaflet with translated extracts. Tudjman, for example, suggested that Jews had helped run the Jasenovac concentration camp.[6] Israel refused to exchange ambassadors with Croatia while the book stayed in print. In the summer of 1991 the Zagreb Jewish community centre was severely damaged by a bomb attack. Tudjman ordered that the centre be rebuilt and restored to a new level of luxury and high security. The following year the centre re-opened with a gala party.

Behind the scenes Israel was quietly arranging the evacuation of those Yugoslav Jews who wanted to leave. Channels were opened to Milosevic, Tudjman and Alija Izetbegovic. All saw good relations with their own Jews as an important public relations exercise.[7] As citizens of Yugoslavia and Croatia, Jews were, like everyone else, free to leave whenever they wanted. The problem was Bosnia. Sarajevo in particular, where most of the Jews lived, was besieged and cut off.

Israeli officials based in Budapest directed an international evacuation operation that would happily grace the pages of any thriller, featuring Israeli intelligence, Balkan warlords, dangerous missions across volatile front-lines and high-level international diplomacy. A letter was issued to all Yugoslav Jews, confirming their status. An arrangement was negotiated with the Hungarian government that the letter would be enough to guarantee passage across the border. All expenses would be paid until the person was sent on to Israel. Perhaps not surprisingly, this offer produced a substantial number of what were dubbed 'instant Jews', who suddenly rediscovered their ancestry. As one Jewish leader noted wryly, 'Out of 1,200 Jews in Sarajevo, 3,000 have left.'[8]

Some of Sarajevo's Jews were evacuated on the last Yugoslav planes out of the city, before the war started, with the help of the Yugoslav military. In Belgrade the Jewish community was allowed to run a radio station, with the call-sign 'YU1JOB' (Yugoslavia One Jewish Community of Belgrade) which transmitted messages to Sarajevo Jews twice a week. Not everyone departed, even from Sarajevo. There the city's remaining community earned the respect of all three sides, by running a free soup kitchen, and a pharmacy. The departure of many of Sarajevo's Jews was watched with regret by the Bosnian government. In 1992 it organised a celebration at the shell-scarred Holiday Inn hotel, to commemorate the five hundredth anniversary of the arrival of the Jews from Spain.

The friendship between Klara Mandic and Radovan Karadzic did not prevent Bosnian Serbs soldiers from desecrating Sarajevo's ancient Jewish cemetery. The cemetery, which sits high on a hill overlooking the city, was ringed by mines and turned into a front-line position. Perched on the centuries-old gravestones of long vanished Sephardi dynasties, the Serbs swigged plum brandy and fired down into the city centre.

Tudjman pulled ahead of Milosevic by attending the opening of the Holocaust Memorial Museum in Washington, D.C., on 22 April 1993. He was roundly booed. Just one week earlier, his client army, the Bosnian Croat HVO, had massacred over one hundred Bosnian Muslims at the village of Ahmici. And there was still no invitation to Jerusalem. He decided to make contact with the Israeli government. The man he chose for these sensitive missions was, naturally enough, Hrvoje Sarinic, his secret envoy to Milosevic. Sarinic recalled: 'The Israelis were very against the setting-up of diplomatic relations. They thought Tudjman was a big Ustashe leader. I was in touch with the Israeli foreign ministry, and with some people from their intelligence services. I told them, you can have your opinion as far as Tudjman is concerned, but it is not in your interest to blame all the Croatian people.'[9]

In Jerusalem a growing body of opinion began to think that Sarinic was right. Israel was taking an increasing interest in the Yugoslav wars. Zagreb was a transit point for fighters from Arab and Islamic countries who joined the Bosnian army. The Dutch report into the fall of Srebrenica claimed that in exchange for free passage out for Bosnia's Jews, Israel supplied arms to the Bosnian Serbs.[10]

Even so, Sarinic was told clearly, there would be no progress until Tudjman changed his book. 'This became my personal battle with

Tudjman. I told him, Mr President, if you want to go to Israel, and you want diplomatic relations, with your book as it is now, it is not possible, it is as simple as that. He said to me, "What do you want from me, you discuss my book, and then you say the same thing they do." We worked on it, until he told me one day, "OK you can correct something, but only a little." We pulled out about eighty pages.' Sarinic presented the new version to the Israeli foreign ministry. It was accepted and full diplomatic relations were opened in the autumn of 1997.

As Mandic steered the SJFS further into the orbit of Serbian national-ists, the guarded welcome it had received within the Belgrade Jewish community faded. Mandic was also connected to Dafiment, the pyramid scheme run by Dafina Milanovic. The report of the Serbian Public Revenue Agency describes Mandic as Dafina's 'ambassador'.[11] It became clear that the Society was exploiting a genuine goodwill among Serbs towards the Jews, for suspect political – and business – purposes. There were fears the whole venture could backfire, and trigger anti-Semitism from those disappointed by the 'failure' of the Jews to help the Serbs in their hour of need.

'Klara Mandic's role was positive in the beginning. She did a lot for relations between Serbia and Israel. Why should there not be a society in a country where there was not much anti-Semitism? She liked publicity, she was eloquent,' said community leader Misa Levi.[12] 'She was friendly with Karadzic, but when she realised she could take advantage of her easy access to him and to Milosevic, the problems began for us. But she got involved in politics and businesses with bad results, which were also bad for the Jewish community. At that stage most Jews withdrew. You can suffocate in such an embrace as this.'

Eventually, the SJFS faded away. Any vestigial sympathy most foreign Jews had for the Serb cause faded when news broke of the concentration camps in summer 1992. As for Klara Mandic, she was murdered in her apartment in Belgrade in May 2001.

Appendix 2

TERMS OF SURRENDER

T he letter on the following pages was handed to Slobodan Milosevic
shortly before he finally agreed to surrender in the early morning
of 1 April 2001. The typewritten annexes on the reverse were added
in response to Milosevic's demand for guarantees that he would not
be extradited to the ICTY at The Hague. Cedomir Jovanovic, who
signed Annexes I and II under the authorisation of Zoran Djindjic, later
told the Belgrade press that the guarantee that Milosevic would not be
extradited to the ICTY only applied to the date on the document, i.e.
31 March 2001. A copy of this document was given to the author by
Mira Markovic. The translation was prepared by Vesna Peric-Zimjonic
and the author.

STATEMENT

We, the signatories of this document, as senior officials of the Federal
Republic of Yugoslavia (FRY) and Serbia, being clearly determined to
establish and apply the rule of law, with the aim of preventing further
unnecessary victims, hereby state:

The criminal proceedings before the Belgrade District Court against
Slobodan Milosevic, former President of the Republic of Serbia, FRY,
and President of the Socialist Party of Serbia, were not undertaken in
response to the demand of the International Criminal Tribunal for the
Former Yugoslavia, but because of reasonable suspicion that he has
committed a criminal act as defined in Article 26 of the FRY penal
code, and will therefore be heard before the judicial organs of the FRY.
We guarantee to Mr Slobodan Milosevic that he will have unimpeded
communication with his family during the court proceedings.

   The members of Mr Slobodan Milosevic's family have also been granted
guarantees for their personal safety, and that of their property, as well as the
right to use the residential premises at 11–15 Uzicka Street in Belgrade.

Belgrade
31 March 2001.

PRESIDENT   PRESIDENT
Federal Republic of Yugoslavia   Republic of Serbia
Signature   signature
Dr Vojislav Kostunica   Milan Milutinovic

President
Government of the Republic of Serbia [i.e. Serbian prime minister]
Dr Zoran Djindjic

ИЗЈАВА

Ми долепотписани функционери Савезне Републике Југославије и Републике Србије, јасно определьени да спроводимо закон и успоставимо правну државу а у жельи да спречимо далье непотребне жртве изјављујемо:

Кривични поступак покренут пред Окружним судом у Београду против Слободана Милошевића, бившег председника Републике Србије, Савезне Републике Југославије и председника Социјалистичке партије Србије, није покренут на захтев Међународног кривичног суда за ратне злочине у бившој Југославији, већ због основане сумње да је починио кривично дело из чл. 26 Кривичног закона СРЈ и стога ће бити решаван пред правосудним органима СРЈ.

Ми гарантујемо господину Слободану Милошевићу да ће током судског поступка имати неометану комуникацију са својом породицом.

Породици господина Милошевића се гарантује лична и имовинска сигурност као и могућност коришћења резиденцијалног објекта у Ужичкој 11-15 у Београду.

У Београду
31. марта 2001. године

ПРЕДСЕДНИК   ПРЕДСЕДНИК
Савезне Републике Југославије   Републике Србије

Др. Војислав Коштуница   Милан Милутиновић

                    ПРЕДСЕДНИК
                    Републике Србије

                    Др. Зоран Ђинђић

ANNEX I

Slobodan Milosevic will not be handed over to any judical or other institution outside the country

ANNEX II

Slobodan Milosevic is guaranteed the right of daily visits by members of his family.

Under the authorisation of Dr Zoran Djindjic, the president of the Serbian government, Annexes I and II are signed by

Cedomir Jovanovic
Belgrade, 31 March 2001

ANEKS I

Slobodan Milošević ne'e biti izručen nijednoj
pravosudnoj niti drugoj instituciji izvan zemlje.

ANEKS II

Slobodanu Miloševiću se garantuje svakodnevna
poseta porodice.

Za ANEKS I i ANEKS II po ovlašćenju predsednika
Vlade Republike SRbije dr Zorena Djindjića

Čedomi

Beograd 1. mart 2001 godine

Chronology

May 1989	Milosevic appointed Serbian President
28 June 1989	Milosevic speaks at the six hundredth anniversary of the battle of Kosovo Polje.
January 1990	Last congress of the Yugoslav Communist Party
April 1990	Franjo Tudjman's Croatian Democratic Union wins first multi-party elections.
December 1990	Milosevic's Socialist Party (formerly Communist) wins the first multi-party election in Serbia, Milosevic elected as Serbian President
March 1991	Anti-Milosevic demonstrations in Belgrade broken up by force
	Milosevic meets with Franjo Tudjman at Karadjordjevo to discuss partition of Bosnia
May 1991	Croatian police massacred at Borovo Selo
25 June 1991	Slovenia declares independence, triggers the first Yugoslav war
	Croatia declares independence
Summer 1991	War spread through Croatia
19 October 1991	Kosovo Albanians declare independence (unrecognised)
November 1991	Fall of Vukovar. Croatian POWs massacred by Serb victors
March 1992	Bosnian president Alija Izetbegovic declares the country independent
	War breaks out in Bosnia. Serb and Yugoslav forces begin ethnic cleansing
June 1992	Federal Yugoslavia formed, consisting only of Serbia and Montenegro
Summer 1992	Serb concentration camps set up in northern Bosnia
December 1992	Milosevic and Socialists win Serbian presidential and parliamentary election
April 1993	Bosnian Croats launch offensive against their (intermittent) former Muslim allies
May 1993	Bosnian Serbs reject Vance-Owen peace plan
December 1993	Serbian parliamentary elections, Socialists largest party
March 1995	Mira Markovic launches the Yugoslav United Left party
July 1995	Fall of Srebrenica. Bosnian Serbs massacre over 7,000 Muslim men
August 1995	Croat army recaptures Krajina. NATO bombs Bosnian Serbs
November 1995	US brokers the Dayton Peace Accords to end the war in Bosnia
November 1996	Socialist-led coalition wins Yugoslav federal elections
Winter 1996–1997	Daily anti-Milosevic demonstrations in Belgrade after local election results are annulled.
July 1997	Milosevic appointed President of Yugoslavia
September 1997	Serbian parliamentary and presidential elections, leading to eventual 'Red-Brown' coalition between Socialists and ultra-nationalists
Autumn 1997	First public appearances of the Kosovo Liberation Army
February 1998	Serbs destroy home of Adem Jashari, senior KLA leader
Summer-autumn 1998	Serb ethnic cleansing of Kosovo Albanians

January 1999	Serbs carry out Racak massacre of Kosovo Albanians
March 1999	NATO bombs Serbia, Serb forces launch massive ethnic cleansing of Kosovo Albanians
27 May 1999	Hague tribunal announces that Milosevic is indicted for war crimes
June 1999	Milosevic backs down, NATO forces enter Kosovo. Kosovo Albanians ethnically cleanse Serbs
January 2000	Murder of paramilitary leader Zeljko Raznjatovic 'Arkan'
August 2000	Disappearance of Ivan Stambolic
	Opening of US Office of Yugoslav Affairs in Budapest
September 2000	Milosevic loses elections to Vojislav Kostunica, candidate of the Democratic Opposition
5 October 2000	Popular uprising topples Milosevic. Marko flees Serbia
March 31	Milosevic arrested at home in Belgrade
28 June 2001	Milosevic extradited to the ICTY at The Hague
July 2001	Milosevic appears in court, refuses to recognise jurisdiction
February 2002 to time of writing (April 2003)	Trial of Milosevic at the ICTY
January 2003	Milan Milutinovic, former president of Serbia, surrenders to ICTY, pleads not guilty to crimes against humanity in Kosovo Rade Markovic is sentenced to seven years in prison for conspiracy to murder opposition leader Vuk Draskovic in 1999
February 2003	New constitution for Union of Serbia and Montenegro adopted by Yugoslav parliament
	Biljana Plavsic, former Bosnian Serb leader, sentenced to eleven years in prison for crimes against humanity
	Former paramilitary leader Vojislav Seselj surrenders to ICTY
	Mira Markovic flees to Russia
	Assassination attempt on Serbian Prime Minister Zoran Djindjic
March 2003	Zoran Djindjic murdered by sniper in Belgrade
	Serb authorities arrest thousands in nationwide crackdown on organised crime including Svetlana Raznatovic (aka Ceca), widow of Arkan, Jovica Stanisic and Franko Simatovic. JSO is disbanded
	Vojislav Seselj pleads not guilty to war crimes and crimes against humanity
April 2003	Serbia-Montenegro admitted to Council of Europe
	State funeral of Ivan Stambolic, after his body is discovered in Serbia
	Serbian police issue arrest warrant for Mira Markovic in connection with the murder of Ivan Stambolic, also for Marko Milosevic on charges of assault
	Nasir Oric, leader of Muslim defenders of Srebrenica is arrested and extradited to the ICTY

Notes

Many of the sources of information or quotation in this book are interviews conducted by or on behalf of the author. In each chapter the details of an interview are given at the first instance. Thereafter, when a person's words are quoted, it can be assumed that unless otherwise stated the interview details remain the same.

Chapter 1

1. Seska Stanojlovic, author interview, Belgrade, August 2001.
2. Borislav Milosevic, author telephone interview, April 2002. Many of the hitherto unreported details of the Milosevic family's war years are taken from this interview.
3. Tim Judah, *The Serbs: History, Myth and the Destruction of Yugoslavia*, (New Haven and London: Yale University Press, 2000), p. 130.
4. Draza Markovic, author interview, Belgrade August 2001.
5. These figures, by Vladimir Zerjavec, are quoted in Tim Judah, *The Serbs*, p. 134.
6. Milica Kovac, interview by Vesna Peric-Zimjonic, Pozarevac, March 2002. Milica Kovac is a pseudonym.
7. The country's full name was then the Federal People's Republic of Yugoslavia.
8. Milan Kucan, author interview, Ljubljana, October 2001.
9. Alex Bebler, quoted in Nora Beloff, *Tito's Flawed Legacy: Yugoslavia 1939–1984* (London: Victor Gollancz, 1985), p. 144.
10. Aca Singer, author interview, Belgrade, November 2001.
11. Peter Bacso, *City Lives: Budapest* (television programme), EuroArt Media Ltd, London 2000. Scheduled for broadcast by RTE (Eire) in autumn/winter 2002.

Chapter 2

1. Mira Markovic, author interview, Belgrade, March 2002.
2. Ljubica Markovic, author interview, Belgrade, August 2001.
3. Draza Markovic, author interview, Belgrade, August 2001.
4. Seska Sanojlovic, author interview, Belgrade, August 2001.
5. Dusan Mitevic, author interviews, Budapest, autumn 2001–spring 2002.
6. Nebojsa Popov, interview by Vesna Peric-Zinjonic, Belgrade, April 2002.
7. Zivan Berisavljevic, author interview, Novi Sad, September 2001.
8. Borislav Milosevic, author telephone interview, April 2002.

Chapter 3

1. Nebojsa Popov, interview by Vesna Peric-Zimjonic, Belgrade, April 2002.
2. Tibor Varady, author interview, Budapest, August 2001.
3. Mira Markovic, author interview, Belgrade, March 2002.
4. Aleksandar Nenadovic, author interview, Belgrade, November 2001.
5. Dusan Mitevic, author interviews, Budapest, autumn 2001–spring 2002.
6. Milica Kovac, interview by Vesna Peric-Zimjonic, Pozarevac, March 2002.
7. Ljubica Markovic, author interview, Belgrade, August 2001.

Chapter 4

1. Mihailo Crnobrnja, author interview, Belgrade, March 2002.
2. Milos Vasic, author interview, Belgrade, August 2001.
3. Mira Markovic, author interview, Belgrade, March 2002.
4. Aca Singer, author interview, Belgrade, November 2001.
5. Dusan Mitevic, author interviews, Budapest, autumn 2001–spring 2002.
6. Zivorad Kovacevic, author interview, Belgrade, November 2001.
7. William Montgomery, author interview, Belgrade, November 2001.

Chapter 5

1. Reginald Wyon, *The Balkans From Within* (London: James Finch & Co., 1904), p. 38.
2. Dusan Mitevic, author interviews, Budapest, autumn 2001–spring 2002.
3. Zivorad Kovacevic, author interview; Belgrade, November 2001.
4. In 1977 the magazine *Komunist* attacked Cosic for claiming that Serbs were being 'exploited and denigrated by other Yugoslav nationalities'. See Judah, *The Serbs*, p. 157.
5. Mira Markovic, author interview, Belgrade, March 2002.
6. Nora Beloff, *Tito's Flawed Legacy: Yugoslavia 1939–1984* (London: Victor Gollancz, 1985), p. 136.
7. Mihailo Crnobrnja, author interview, Belgrade, March 2002.
8. Draza Markovic, author interview, Belgrade, August 2001.
9. Milos Vasic, author interview, Belgrade, August 2001.
10. Dessa Trevisan, author interview, London, September 2001.
11. Slobodan Milosevic, *Years of Clarification* (Belgrade: Belgrade Publishing House) 1989.
12. Seska Sanojlovic, author interview, Belgrade, August 2001.

Chapter 6

1. Braca Grubacic, author interview, November 2001.
2. Ljubica Markovic, author interview, Belgrade, August 2001.

3. Tahir Hasanovic, author interview, Belgrade, November 2001.

4. Dusan Mitevic, author interviews, Budapest, autumn 2001–spring 2002.

5. Zivorad Kovacevic, author interview, Belgrade, November 2001.

6. Mira Markovic, author interview, Belgrade, March 2002.

7. Janet Garvey, author interview, Budapest, October 2001.

8. Mihailo Crnobrnja, author interview, Belgrade, March 2002.

9. Seska Stanojlovic, author interview, Belgrade, August 2001.

10. Aleksa Djilas, 'A Profile of Slobodan Milosevic', *Foreign Affairs*, summer 1993.

11. General Nikola Ljubicic in Stavoljvb Djvkic, *Milosevic and Markovic: A Lust for Power* (Montreal: McGill Queen's University Press, 2001), p.15.

12. Draza Markovic, author interview, Belgrade, August 2001.

13. Ivan Stambolic, *Mladina* magazine, Ljubljana, 6 August 1996.

Chapter 7

1. Slobodan Milosevic in Robert Thomas, *Serbia under Milosevic* (London: Hurst and Co., 2000), p. 44.

2. Mihailo Crnobrnja, author interview, Belgrade, March 2002.

3. 'The Memorandum' in Tim Judah, *Kosovo: War and Revenge* (New Haven and London: Yale University Press, 2000), p.49.

4. Between 1971 and 1981 the Albanian population of Kosovo increased from 916,168 to 1,226,736, i.e. from 73.7 per cent of the population to 77.4 per cent. In these years the Serb population dropped from 228,264 to 209,498, i.e. from 18.4 per cent to 13.2 per cent. Figures based on Federal Institute for Statistics. Judah, op. cit.

5. It was not altogether surprising that SANU members had exhibited a maudlin ethno-centrism when they demanded a defence of 'Serbian interests'. For those brought up on western European traditions of inquiring scepticism, the role of the intellectual is to question established truths. In other words, dissent. In a state reasonably confident of its own identity, and with a long enough history, these truths to be deconstructed are those previously accepted as self-evident: the founding myths of nationhood, for example. In eastern Europe the role of the intellectual has in the past been very different. Until 1989 most of the region was for centuries ruled by foreign powers, whether Ottoman, Habsburg or Soviet. Yugoslav nationalist intellectuals, such as Cosic or his counterparts in Zagreb, could agree that Tito's creation was a 'prison of nations'. Prevented from fulfilling their manifest destiny by foreign occupation, such countries have historically charged their writers – seen as the standard bearers of the national soul – with keeping the patriotic spirit alive. Their job was not to deconstruct national myths but to forge them. The very notion of national identity was fused literature and language. Across eastern Europe in the nineteenth century lexicographers such as Serbia's Vuk Karadzic classified and codified the dialects of their native tongue into a unified language. To write in the national tongue, to bring it alive and create a corpus of literature was to legitimise it and, by

extension, the nation itself. The Hungarian poet Sandor Petofi even started a revolution by reading one of his works on the steps of the National Museum in 1848.

6. Study commissioned by the Forum for Human Rights, 1990. This study of rape allegations in Kosovo concluded that inter-ethnic rape was relatively rare and heavily over-represented in the media. Cited in *Conflict in the Former Yugoslavia*. ed. John B. Allcock, Marko Milivojevic, and John J. Horton (Denver and Oxford: ABC-CLIO, 1998), p. 234.

7. Exchange between Milosevic and demonstrators as included in 'Enter Nationalism', episode one of *The Death of Yugoslavia*, the six-part television series by Brook Lapping Associates, first broadcast on BBC1 in autumn and winter 1995.

8. Dusan Mitevic, author interviews, Budapest, autumn 2001–spring 2002.

9. Mira Markovic and Slobodan Milosevic in *The Death of Yugoslavia*.

10. Miroslav Solevic in *The Death of Yugoslavia*.

11. Azem Vllasi in Lenard J. Cohen, *Serpent in the Bosom: The Rise and Fall of Slobodan Milosevic* (Colorado: Westview Press, 2001), p. 63.

12. Miroslav Solevic in *The Death of Yugoslavia*.

13. Elias Canetti, *Crowds and Power* (London: Phoenix Press, 1998 edition), pp. 58 & 73.

14. *The Death of Yugoslavia*, episode one.

15. Lenard J. Cohen, op. cit., pp.64–5.

16. Ivan Stambolic in *The Death of Yugoslavia*.

17. Mira Markovic, author interview, Belgrade, March 2002.

18. Poem quoted in Dusko Doder and Louise Branson, *Milosevic: Portrait of a Tyrant* (New York: The Free Press, 1999), p. 44.

19. Zivorad Kovacevic, author interview, Belgrade, November 2001.

20. Milan Kucan, author interview, Ljubljana, October 2001.

21. Tahir Hasanovic, author interview, Belgrade, November 2001.

22. Slobodan Milosevic in Tim Judah, *The Serbs: History, Myth and the Destruction of Yugoslavia* (New Haven and London: Yale University Press, 2000), p. 160.

23. Milos Vasic, author interview, Belgrade, August 2001.

24. Bosko Krunic, author interview, Novi Sad, August 2001.

25. Dusko Doder and Louise Branson, op. cit., pp.46–7

26. Dragisa Pavlovic, in Lenard J. Cohen, op. cit., p. 68

Chapter 8

1. Ivan Stambolic in Laura Silber and Allan Little, *The Death of Yugoslavia* (London: Penguin/BBC, 1995), p. 45.

2. Dusan Mitevic, author interviews, Budapest, autumn 2001–spring 2002.

3. Borisav Jovic in *The Death of Yugoslavia*, episode one. All quotes by Borisav Jovic are taken from this series only.

4. Milosevic learnt this early on which has bedevilled investigators from the Hague tribunal trying to establish a paper trail to connect him to war crimes.
5. Milosevic in Silber and Little, op. cit., p. 44.
6. Mihailo Crnobrnja, author interview, Belgrade, March 2002.
7. Account and film footage of the Eighth Session of Serbian Communist Party as included in *The Death of Yugoslavia*, episode one.
8. Ljubinka Trgovcevic in Silber and Little, op. cit., p. 46.
9. Azem Vllasi, ibid., p. 46.
10. Zivorad Kovacevic, author interview, Belgrade, November 2001.
11. Mira Markovic, author interview, Belgrade, March 2002.
12. Tahir Hasanovic, author interview, Belgrade, November 2001.
13. Dobrica Cosic in Lenard J. Cohen, *Serpent in the Bosom: The Rise and Fall of Slobodan Milosevic*, (Colorado: Westview Press 2001), p. 73.

Chapter 9

1. Reginald Wyon, *The Balkans from Within* (London: James Finch & Co., 1904), p. 46.
2. Slobodan Milosevic in Laura Silber and Allan Little, *The Death of Yugoslavia* (London: Penguin/BBC, 1995), p. 6.
3. Mira Markovic, author interview, Belgrade, March 2002.
4. Braca Grubacic, author interview, Belgrade, November 2001.
5. Zivorad Kovacevic, author interview, Belgrade, November 2001.
6. Milovan Djilas, *The New Class* (New York: Harcourt, Brace, Jovanovic, 1983), p. 60.
7. Bosko Krunic, author interview, Novi Sad, August 2001.
8. The source of this nickname is uncertain, but he was caricatured on Croatian television in a waiter's uniform.
9. Zivan Berisavljevic, author interview, Novi Sad, August 2001.
10. Silber and Little, op. cit., p. 66.
11. Miroslav Solevic in *The Death of Yugoslavia*.
12. Dessa Trevisan, author interview, London, September 2001.
13. Zivorad Kovacevic, author interview, Belgrade, November 2001.

Chapter 10

1. Slobodan Milosevic, speech at Kosovo Polje, 1989.
2. Dessa Trevisan, author interview, London, September 2001.
3. Mihailo Crnobrnja, author interview, Belgrade, March 2002.
4. Mira Markovic, author interview, Belgrade, March 2002.
5. Louis Sell, *Slobodan Milosevic and the Destruction of Yugoslavia* (Durham, NC: Duke University Press, 2002), pp. 25–26
6. Mira Markovic, author interview, Belgrade, March 2002.
7. Mira Markovic, *Answer*, (Kingston, Ontario, Quarry Press, 1995) p. 33.

8. Milan Kucan, *The Death of Yugoslavia*, episode three.
9. Milan Kucan, *The Death of Yugoslavia*, episode one.
10. Milan Kucan, speech at Cankarjev dom, 27 February 1989. Translation supplied by the Slovenian president's office.
11. For a fuller discussion of the role of the Serbian Jewish Friendship Society and the rivalry between Milosevic and Tudjman to recruit Jewish supporters, see Appendix 1 p. 331.
12. Serb television, quoted in *The Death of Yugoslavia*, episode one.
13. Elias Canetti, *Crowds and Power* (London: Phoenix Press, 1998 edition), p. 49.
14. Borisav Jovic in Laura Silber and Allan Little, *The Death of Yugoslavia* (London: Penguin/BBC, 1995), p. 70.
15. John Reed, *War in Eastern Europe* (London: Phoenix, 1994 ed.), p.22.
16. Slobodan Milosevic, speech in Robert Thomas, *Serbia under Milosevic* (London: Hurst and Company, 2000), p. 50.
17. Mira Markovic, author interview, Belgrade, March 2002.
18. Warren Zimmerman, *Origins of Catastrophe* (New York: Random House, 1996), pp. 22–3.
19. Zivorad Kovacevic, author interview, Belgrade, November 2001.
20. Draza Markovic, author interview, Belgrade August 2001.
21. Reginald Wyon, *The Balkans from Within* (London: James Finch & Co., 1904), p. ix.
22. Mihailo Crnobrnja, author interview, Belgrade, March 2002.

Chapter 11

1. *The Death of Yugoslavia*, episode one.
2. Sandor Marai, *Embers* (New York: Alfred A. Knopf and London: Viking Penguin, 2002), p. 43.
3. This exchange between Milan Kucan and Borisav Jovic is transcribed from *The Death of Yugoslavia*, episode one.
4. Ljubica Markovic, author interview, Belgrade, August 2001.
5. Milan Kucan, author interview, Ljubljana, October 2001.
6. Slobodan Milosevic in *The Death of Yugoslavia*, episode one.
7. Ivica Racan, author interview.
8. Momir Bulatovic in *The Death of Yugoslavia*, episode one.
9. Communique of 23 January 1991. Translation supplied by the Slovenian president's office.
10. Borisav Jovic in *The Death of Yugoslavia*, episode three.
11. Vaso Predojevic, author interview, Ljubljana, October 2002.

Chapter 12

1. Reginald Wyon, *The Balkans from Within* (London: James Finch & Co., 1904), p. 13.

2. Borisav Jovic in *The Last Days of Yugoslavia* (Belgrade: Prisma, 1996 Serbian ed.), p. 108.
3. Borisav Jovic in Tim Judah, *The Serbs* (London: Yale University Press, 2000), p. 169.
4. Also alleged to be members of the 'joint criminal enterprise', as detailed in the ICTY indictment, are: Borisav Jovic, Branko Kostic, General Veljko Kadijevic, General Blagoje Adzic, Milan Babic, Milan Martic, Goran Hadzic, Jovica Stanisic, Franko Simatovic, Tomislav Simovic, Vojislav Serselj, Momir Bulatovic, General Aleksandar Vasiljevic, Radovan Stojicic and Zeljko Raznjatovic, a.k.a. Arkan. Mihajl Kertes is not mentioned.
5. Milan Kucan, author interview, Ljubljana, October 2001.
6. Misha Glenny, *The Fall of Yugoslavia* (London: Penguin, 1992 ed.), p. 27.
7. Although no copy of the RAM plan has yet been produced as evidence, its existence was reported by senior Yugoslav figures such as then federal prime minister Ante Markovic (see Chapter 14). Whether or not RAM actually existed as a single document, the ideas attributed to it certainly represented a sustained current of both nationalist thought and early Milosevic-era policy. The US writer Louis Sell, a former diplomat in Yugoslavia, notes: 'While I was serving in the US Embassy in Belgrade from 1987–1991, I cannot recall ever hearing of the Vojna Linija or the RAM plan, although the actions of the Serb authorities in providing military and other forms of support to Serbs in Croatia and Bosnia were well known. At some point during my last year in the embassy, I was shown a covertly obtained document that revealed contingency plans by the military to rapidly carve out a zone of control over an area marked on a map that roughly approximated the areas of the Serb agitation that later became the so-called Krajina. This may have been the RAM plan or something similar.' Louis Sell, *Slobodan Milosevic and the Destruction of Yugoslavia* (Durham, NC: Duke University Press, 2002), p. 374.
8. ibid., pp. 110–11.
9. Testimony of Jerko Doko, Prosecutor v. Tadic, case IT-94-1-T, 6 June 1996, pp. 1359–61.
10. Former Serbian intelligence officer, author interview, 2001.
11. Marcus Tanner, *Croatia: A Nation Forged in War* (London: Yale University Press, 1997), p. 228.
12. ibid., p. 223.
13. The power of such symbolism as a manifestation of patriotic defiance should not be underestimated. During the winter of 1991, when Croatia was under severe attack, the author dined one night in Zagreb. A salad was served which contained a radish. Into the red skin of the radish, the chef had cut a tiny but precise *sahovnica* pattern.
14. Mira Markovic, author interview, Belgrade, March 2002.
15. Mihailo Crnobrnja, author interview, Belgrade, March 2002.
16. Borislav Milosevic, author telephone interview, April 2002.

17. Conversation recorded on 15 March 1997, published in *Globus* magazine, Zagreb, February 2002.

18. David Austin, author interview, Zagreb, September 2001.

19. Stipe Mesic, author interview, Zagreb, September 2001.

20. Milan Babic and Petar Gracanin, *The Death of Yugoslavia*, episode two.

21. Radmilo Bogdanovic in Laura Silber and Allan Little, *The Death of Yugoslavia* (London: Penguin/BBC, 1995), p. 155.

22. Adam LeBor, 'A Survivor's Guide to the Osijek Underground', *Independent* (London, December 31, 1991).

Chapter 13

1. Dusan Mitevic, author interviews, Budapest, autumn 2001 – spring 2002.

2. Tahir Hasanovic, author interview, Belgrade, November 2001.

3. Belgrade Television in Eric D. Gordy, *The Culture of Power in Serbia: Nationalism and the Destruction of Alternatives* (University Park, Pa.: Pennsylvania State University Press, 1996), p. 33.

4. Braca Grubacic, author interview, Belgrade, November 2001.

5. Eric D. Gordy, op. cit., p. 33.

6. Slobodan Milosevic in Laura Silber and Allan Little, *The Death of Yugoslavia* (London: Penguin/BBC, 1995), p. 132.

7. Vuk Draskovic, author interview, Belgrade, November 2001.

8. General Adzic, *The Death of Yugoslavia*, episode two.

9. Slobodan Milosevic in Silber and Little, op. cit., p. 134.

10. Vasil Tuporkovsky (and Borisav Jovic), *The Death of Yugoslavia*, episode two.

11. Vuk Draskovic, author interview, Belgrade, November 2001.

12. Slobodan Milosevic in Silber and Little, op. cit., p. 139.

13. ibid., p. 141.

14. ibid., p. 142.

Chapter 14

1. Stipe Mesic, author interview, Zagreb, September 2001.

2. ibid.

3. Milan Kucan, author interview, Ljubljana, October 2001.

4. Adam LeBor, 'Vukovar Veteran Bitter over Tudjman "Betrayal"', *Independent* (1 January 1992). Marcus Tanner quotes an interview with General Anton Tus, commander in chief of Croat forces, opposing this. General Tus argued that diverting military supplies to Vukovar at this time would have left other frontlines over-exposed. Tanner wrote: 'Vukovar's fall formed no part of a strategy of recognition; on the contrary General Tus believed the fall of Vukovar would lead to a massive assault on the rest of Slavonia which could be countered only by years of sustained guerrilla warfare.' Marcus Tanner, *Croatia: A Nation Forged In War* (New Haven and London: Yale University Press, 1997), p. 266.

5. Milos Vasic, author interview, Belgrade, August 2001.

6. Hrvoje Sarinic, author interview, Samobor, Croatia, September 2001. Some details taken from Sarinic's book, *All My Secret Talks with Slobodan Milosevic: Between War and Diplomacy 1993–1995* (Zagreb: Globus International, 1999 Croatian Edition).

7. According to the 1991 Yugoslav census.

8. Milosevic at this time promoted a Muslim businessman called Adil Zulfikarpasic, who had split with Alija Izetbegovic to form his own party, the Muslim Bosnjak Party. The party was given substantial airtime on Belgrade Television, often the best weathervane of Milosevic's thinking, as means of showing that Bosnian Muslims really wanted to stay in Yugoslavia. But Zulfikarpasic lacked any real base of support and the initiative faded away.

9. Laura Silber and Allan Little, *The Death of Yugoslavia* (London: Penguin/BBC, 1995), p. 141.

10. ibid. p. 233.

11. Tim Judah, *The Serbs*, (New Haven and London: Yale University Press, 2000), p. 199.

12. It was a curious feature of the Yugoslav wars that so many Serb warlords were medically trained. The leader of the Krajina Serbs was Milan Babic, a dentist. His predecessor Jovan Raskovic was a psychiatrist. The Yugoslav system that demanded quotas from every republic for prestigious jobs was one factor in bringing such personalities into the healing professions.

13. Dusko Doder and Louise Branson, *Milosevic: Portrait of a Tyrant* (New York: Free Press, 1999), p. 115.

14. Tim Judah, op. cit., p. 191.

15. ibid.

16. *The Death of Yugoslavia*, episode four.

17. Final Report of the United Nations Commission of Experts established pursuant to Security Council resolution 780 (1992). Prepared by M. Cherif Bassiouni, Chairman and Rapporteur on the Gathering and Analysis of the Facts, Commission of Experts. Annex IV: The Policy of Ethnic Cleansing. 28 December 1994.

18. *The Death of Yugoslavia*, episode four.

19. Tim Judah, op. cit., p. 236.

20. Mark Danner, 'America and the Bosnia Genocide', *New York Review of Books* (4 December 1997).

21. Adam LeBor, 'Forgotten Victims of Balkan Nationalism Take Refuge in Serbia', *The Times* (London, 3 March 1993).

22. David Austin, author interview, Zagreb, September 2001.

Chapter 15

1. Vojislav Seselj, *The Death of Yugoslavia*, episode four.

2. Dusan Mitevic, author interviews, Budapest, autumn 2001–spring 2002.

3. Slobodan Milosevic, quoted in Robert Thomas, *Serbia Under Milosevic* (London: Hurst and Company, 2000) page 50.

4. Mira Markovic, *Night and Day*, (Kingston, Ont.: Quarry Press, 1996), pp. 92–3.

5. ibid., p. 111.

6. Slobodan Milosevic in *The Death of Yugoslavia*, episode four.

7. Mira Markovic, author interview, Belgrade, March 2002.

8. Dusko Doder and Louise Branson, *Milosevic: Portrait of a Tyrant* (New York: Free Press, 1999), p. 140.

9. David Owen, *Balkan Odyssey* (London: Indigo, 1996), p. 292.

10. Genocide in Bosnia-Hercegovina. A Hearing before the Commission on Security and Cooperation in Europe, Washington, D.C., 4 April 1995. http://www.fas.org/irp/congress 1995 hr/index.html.

11. Final report of the United Nations Commission of Experts. December 1994. Annex. III.a, Special Forces.

12. Arkan, in Ivan Colovic, 'Football, Hooligans and War', *The Road to War in Serbia: Trauma and Catharsis* (Budapest: CEU Press, 1996), p. 388.

13. ibid.

14. Final Report of the United Nations Commission of Experts, op. cit.

15. Milosevic – Initial indictment for war crimes in Croatia. The International Criminal Tribunal for the Former Yugoslavia. Case No. IT – 02 – 54. Kosovo, Croatia, Bosnia and Herzegovina. October 2001. Annex One paragraph 53.

16. Interview with Radmilo Bogdanovic by Nenad Stefanovic. *Duga*, 7–20 January 1995, p. 22. Quoted in Paul Williams and Norman Cigar, *A Prima Facie Case for the Indictment of Slobodan Milosevic* (London: Alliance to Defend Bosnia-Herzegovina, 1996), p. 35.

17. Interview with General Tomislav Simovic, *Srpska Rec*, 25 November 1991. Quoted in Paul Williams and Norman Cigar, op. cit.

18. ibid., p. 21.

19. Milosevic also sidestepped opposition within the Yugoslav airforce to the use of the paramilitaries. Squadron 252, based at Batajnica air base, was deployed without the knowledge of the General Staff to provide military helicopters. The squadron became known as the 'First Serbian' because of its close links with the paramilitary leaders, including Arkan and Vojislav Seselj. Dr James Gow, 'Belgrade and Bosnia – An Assessment of the Yugoslav Military, *Janes Intelligence Review*, 1 June 1993.

20. Dragan Vuksic, author interview, Belgrade November 2001.

21. Warren Zimmerman, *Origins of a Catastrophe* (New York: Random House, 1996), p. 39.

22. Mira Markovic, op. cit., p. 242.

23. Tim Judah, *The Serbs* (New Haven and London: Yale University Press, 2000), p. 188.

24. Detailed information about the attack on Zvornik taken from Annex IV, Part

III. Report on ethnic cleansing operations in the north-east city of Zvornik. The Policy of Ethnic Cleansing, Final Report of the United Nations Commission of Experts, 28 December 1994.

25. Final Report of the United Nations Commission of Experts.
26. Jose Maria Mendiluce in Laura Silber and Allan Little, *The Death of Yugoslavia* (London: Penguin/BBC, 1995), p. 246.
27. ibid.
28. Vojislav Seselj in Silber and Little, op. cit., p. 247.
29. The author is grateful to Peter Maass, who generously provided a transcript of his interview with Milosevic. The interview took place in Belgrade in April 1993.
30. Markovic, ibid., pp. 63–64.
31. Hrvoje Sarinic, *All My Secret Talks with Slobodan Milosevic: Between War and Diplomacy 1993–1995* (Zagreb: Globus International, 1999 Croatian Edition), p. 46.

Chapter 16

1. Milan Panic, Laura Silber and Allan Little, *The Death of Yugoslavia* (London: Penguin/BBC, 1995), p. 287.
2. Dusan Mitevic, author interviews, Budapest, autumn 2001–spring 2002.
3. Warren Zimmerman, *Origins of Catastrophe*, p. 198.
4. The term 'concept deficit' was first used in the mid-1990s to describe the inability of Swiss bankers to understand the seriousness of the charges against them in the scandal over Holocaust-era bank accounts.
5. Warren Zimmerman, op. cit., p. 198.
6. Dusan Mitevic, author interviews, Budapest, autumn 2001–spring 2002.
7. Tibor Varady, author interview, Budapest, August 2001.
8. Silber and Little, op. cit., p. 175.
9. Silber and Little, op. cit., p. 215.
10. Mihailo Crnobrnja, author interview, Belgrade, March 2002.
11. Some years later Professor Varady met Edit on a train between Budapest and Novi Sad. He told her about Milosevic's great interest in her well-being and career. Edit was 'taken aback'.
12. Silber and Little, op. cit., p. 287.

Chapter 17

1. *See You in the Obituaries*, a television documentary about Belgrade gangsters, B-92, 1995.
2. Ljubica Markovic, author interview, Belgrade, August 2001.
3. Financial details of the Milosevic house purchase at Tolstoyeva 33 as detailed in *The Seven Biggest Swindles of the Milosevic Regime*, pp. 37–8. This highly detailed fifty-two page report on the financial mismanagement and institutionalised corruption of the Milosevic era was compiled by the Investigating Commission

of Economic and Financial Abuses of the Milosevic Regime (ICEFA). A copy
was made available to the author in November 2001.

4. Diplomatic source, author interview, Belgrade, November 2001.

5. Ian Traynor, *Search for the Missing Millions*, *Guardian* (29 March 2001).

6. Stefan Wagstyl, Irena Guzelova and Kerin Hope, *Milosevic's Murky Fortune*,
Financial Times, (6 April 2001).

7. Serbian inflation figures as reported in Eric D. Gordy, *The Culture of Power
in Serbia: Nationalism and the Destruction of Alternatives* (University Park, Pa.:
Pennsylvania State University Press, 1996), pp. 170–1.

8. Aleksandar Radovic, author interview, Belgrade, November 2001.

9. Aca Singer, author interview, Belgrade, November 2001.

10. The Boss eventually returned to Belgrade, in December 2001.

11. Borisav Jovic, in Eric D. Gordy, op. cit., p. 172.

12. Dusan Mitevic, author interviews, Budapest, autumn 2001–spring 2002.

13. Ian Traynor, *Guardian*, op. cit. Traynor quotes 'Yugoslav government sources
and western diplomats in Belgrade'.

14. Budomir Babovic, author interview, Belgrade, 2001.

15. Under this system students unable to attend classes – for example because of
illness – are allowed to take examinations when they are ready. Marko was not
ill but just did not want to go to school.

16. *Vreme* magazine, Belgrade, 25 January 1993. *Vreme* printed a transcript of an
interview Marko gave to the Pozarevac radio station Bum 93.

17. Mira Markovic, *Night and Day*, p. 239.

18. Zoran Kusovac, 'Crime and Culpability in Milosevic's Serbia', *Jane's Intelligence
Review*, 1 February 2000.

19. Quoted in *See You in the Obituaries*.

20. ibid.

21. ibid. The gangsters interviewed who survived were later angered by the fact that
the programme was watched by western embassies, who subsequently refused to
issue them visas.

22. ibid.

23. Conversation recorded by the Croatian secret service and printed in *Globus*
magazine, Zagreb, 1 February 2002.

Chapter 18

1. Hrvoje Sarinic, *All My Secret Talks with Slobodan Milosevic: Between War and
Diplomacy 1993–1995* (Zagreb: Globus International, 1999). p. 255.

2. Hrvoje Sarinic, author interview, Samobor, Croatia, September 2001. All
quotes by Sarinic in this chapter are taken from this interview, unless otherwise
indicated.

3. Hrvoje Sarinic, op. cit., pp. 187–189.

4. Milosevic – Initial indictment for war crimes in Croatia. The International
Criminal Tribunal for the Former Yugoslavia. Case No. IT – 02 – 54.

Kosovo, Croatia, Bosnia and Herzegovina. October 2001. Annex One paragraph 53.

5. Hrvoje Sarinic, op. cit., p. 202.

6. Mira Markovic, *Night and Day*, (Kingston, Ont.: Quarry Press, 1996) p. 244,

7. Lord Owen disputes Hrvoje Sarinic's statement that he made these comments, describing them as not correct. In an email to the author Lord Owen wrote: 'I always believed the Croatians could win back at the negotiating table land lost to the Serbs in Croatia.'

8. As recounted in Bosnia Report April-July 1999. The Bosnia Report is published by the Bosnia Institute, a London-based charity dedicated to information and education about Bosnia. www.bosnia.org.uk. *Further adventures of Hrvoje Sarinic in the land of the Serb aggressor.* This three part series was based on Sarinic's book. Lord Owen disputes Hrvoje Sarinic's comments about Mira Markovic's book, describing them as incorrect. In the same email he wrote to the author: 'I never knew about Mrs Milosevic's book, let alone made any suggestions.'

9. Tibor Varady, author interview, Budapest, August 2001.

10. Lord Owen disputes Tibor Varady's account of this occasion. In an email to the author he wrote: 'In August 1992 I had not met Milosevic. I was only appointed the EU's envoy in late August and only visited Belgrade in September, so Tibor Varady's recollection is incorrect that I had lunched with him.'

11. Mira Markovic, author interview, Belgrade, March 2002.

12. Lord Owen actually described Mira Markovic as 'a Marxist theorist, as is obvious from her words'. He noted: 'It is not possible to anticipate where Milosevic will lead his country without also analysing the views of his wife. Fortunately he does not take much note of her economic views and shows every sign of wanting his country to have a market economy.' David Owen, *Balkan Odyssey* (London: Indigo, 1996), pp. 291–2.

13. Yves Goulet, 'MPRI: Washington's Freelance Advisors', *Jane's Intelligence Review*, 1 July 1998.

14. ibid.

15. Atif Dedakovic has entered legend.

16. Mira Markovic in Tim Judah, *The Serbs* (New Haven and London: Yale University Press, 2000), p. 296.

17. Stipe Mesic, author interview, Zagreb, September 2001.

18. The largest wave of ethnic cleansing was the expulsion of the Kosovo Albanians in the spring of 1999 when hundreds of thousands fled from Serb forces.

Chapter 19

1. Radovan Karadzic, 'Pax Americana', *Death of Yugoslavia*, episode six.

2. The Surrealist Hit Parade radio show was hugely popular all over Yugoslavia, and tapes of the programmes were even circulated through refugees in western Europe, wrote Chuck Sudetic in the *New York Times* in July 1993. The Surrealist Hit Parade mocked everything from Serbian ethnic cleansing techniques to

rising Muslim nationalism. A Serbian commander details his plans for dealing with the US Navy: 'First we sign a ceasefire. Then we surround them and give them forty-eight hours to hand over their weapons. When they refuse, we burn their houses and kill the cattle. Then we march in and declare it the Serbian Autonomous Sixth Fleet.' A Muslim nationalist discusses his newborn baby with his Serbian wife. 'I'm a liberal. We don't have to call it Mehmet or Alija. We'll name him Mehmet-Alija.'

3. Hrvoje Sarinic, *All My Secret Talks with Slobodan Milosevic: Between War and Diplomacy, 1993–1995* (Zagreb: Globus International, 1999) p. 201.

4. Slobodan Milosevic, letter to the Bosnian Serbs. Dusko Doder and Louise Branson, *Milosevic: Portrait of a Tyrant* (New York: The Free Press, 1999), p. 181.

5. Doder and Branson, op. cit., p. 182.

6. Risto Djogo died in September 1994 in Zvornik, Bosnia, in mysterious circumstances, the night that Ceca, the singer married to Arkan, gave a concert.

7. Doder and Branson, op. cit., p. 187.

8. Laura Silber and Alan Little, *The Death of Yugoslavia* (London: Penguin/BBC, 1995) p. 374.

9. ibid., p. 380.

10. ibid., p. 381.

11. ibid.

12. In April 2002 the Dutch government resigned after the publication of a 3,500-page report on the fall of Srebrenica, *Srebrenica, A 'Safe' Area* (Amsterdam: Netherlands Institute for War Documentation (NIOD), 2002). Point two in the epilogue highlighted the vagueness of the term 'Safe Area': 'Nothing was clear about it except that the dominant light option ruled out a mandate for a genuine military defence of the area or its population. The presence of UN troops was intended rather to be a warning by the international community not to attack ("to deter by presence"). The proclamation of the zone as a safe area created an illusion of security for the population.'

13. The report's epilogue also argued that the Bosnian Serb onslaught was partly ad hoc in nature: 'With hindsight there are no indications that the increased activity of the VRS [the Bosnian Serb army] in east Bosnia at the beginning of July 1995 was aimed at anything more than a reduction of the safe area Srebrenica and an interception of the main road to Zepa. The plan of campaign was drawn up on 2 July. The attack commenced on 6 July. It was so successful and so little resistance was offered that it was decided late in the evening of 9 July to press on and to see whether it was possible to take over the entire enclave.'

Therefore the author would argue that if General Mladic was responding to changing circumstances, a military response by the international community early in the attack on Srebrenica might have deterred him from going as far as he did.

14. The fall of Srebrenica did not hinder the career of one of the most senior

UN officials in charge of peacekeeping operations at this time. Kofi Annan, now Secretary General of the UN, served as Assistant Secretary-General for Peacekeeping Operations (March 1993–February 1994) and then as Under Secretary-General (February 1994–October 1995; April 1996–December 1996). 'His tenure as Under Secretary-General coincided with unprecedented growth in the size and scope of United Nations peacekeeping operations, with a total deployment, at its peak in 1995, of almost 70,000 military and civilian personnel from 77 countries,' notes his biography on the UN website. www.un.org/overview/sg. The UN later published a self-critical report on Srebrenica.

15. Sandy Vershbow, in 'Pax Americana', *The Death of Yugoslavia*, episode six.

16. Senior US official, author interview, November 2001.

17. David Owen, *Balkan Odyssey* (London: Indigo, 1996) p. 143.

18. Dr James Gow. 'Belgrade and Bosnia: An Assessment of the Yugoslav Military', *Jane's Intelligence Review*, 1 June 1993.

19. Slobodan Milosevic, in Louis Sell, *Slobodan Milosevic and the Death of Yugoslavia* (Durham, NC: Duke University Press, 2002), p. 230.

20. Point ten of the conclusion of the epilogue of the NIOD Srebrenica report argues: 'There are a number of indications that it [the massacre] was a central command from the General Staff of the VRS. There are none pointing to political or military liaison with Belgrade. The involvement of the then president Karadzic (Republika Srpska) is unclear. In any case, the main responsibility for the mass slaughter lay with the military. Mladic's central role was unmistakable and beyond doubt. He was a dominant presence during these days and was clearly in command. That does not alter the responsibility of others in leading positions in the VRS, the Drina Corps and in the special troops and security services.'

21. Sell, op. cit., p. 233.

22. ibid.

23. ibid.

24. Slobodan Milosevic, in Laura Silber, 'Milosevic Family Values', *New Republic*, 30 August 1999.

25. Charles Lane and Tom Shanker, 'Bosnia: What the CIA didn't tell Us', *New York Review of Books*, 9 May 1996.

26. Roy Gutman, 'Big Atrocity; Serb militia chief said to have role', *Newsday*, 8 August 1995.

27. Richard Holbrooke, in 'Pax Americana', *The Death of Yugoslavia*, episode six.

28. Haris Siladzic, in 'Pax Americana', *The Death of Yugoslavia*, episode six.

29. David Austin, author interview, Zagreb, September 2001.

30. Momir Bulatovic, Slobodan Milosevic and Patriarch Pavle, in 'Pax Americana', *The Death of Yugoslavia*, episode six.

31. Louis Sell notes, 'The contents and tone of Mladic's message raised serious questions in the mind of those who read it about the Bosnian Serb commander's grip on reality'. Sell, op. cit., p. 248.

32. Richard Holbrooke, in 'Pax Americana', *The Death of Yugoslavia*, episode six.

33. Momir Bulatovic, in 'Pax Americana', *The Death of Yugoslavia*, episode six.
34. Hrvoje Sarinic, author interview, Samobor, Croatia, September 2001.
35. Richard Holbrooke, *To End A War* (New York: Random House, The Modern Library, 1999), p. 160. Interestingly, Holbrooke admits he later had doubts as to the wisdom of this decision. On pp. 166–7 he writes: 'But I am no longer certain we were right to oppose an attack on Banja Luka. Had we known that the Bosnian Serbs would have been able to defy or ignore so many of the key political provisions of the peace agreement in 1996 and 1997, the negotiating team might not have opposed such an attack.'
36. Richard Holbrooke, in 'Pax Americana', *The Death of Yugoslavia*, episode six.

Chapter 20

1. Haris Siladzic quoting Slobodan Milosevic, in 'Pax Americana', *The Death of Yugoslavia*, episode six.
2. Slobodan Milosevic, in 'Pax Americana', *The Death of Yugoslavia*, episode six.
3. Richard Holbrooke, *To End A War* (New York: Random House, The Modern Library, 1999). The author has drawn on Holbrooke's account for many of the details of the Dayton conference.
4. ibid., p. 244.
5. ibid., p. 245.
6. Haris Silajdzic, in 'Pax Americana', *The Death of Yugoslavia*, episode six.
7. Richard Holbrooke, in 'Pax Americana', *The Death of Yugoslavia*, episode six.
8. Holbrooke, op. cit., p. 285.
9. Senior US official, author interview, November 2001
10. David Austin, author interview, Zagreb, September 2001.
11. Holbrooke, op. cit., p. 288.
12. Richard Holbrooke, in 'Pax Americana', *The Death of Yugoslavia*, episode six.
13. Haris Silajdzic quoting Slobodan Milosevic, in 'Pax Americana', *The Death of Yugoslavia*, episode six.
14. US official, author interview, November 2001.
15. Mira Markovic, author interview, Belgrade, March 2002.
16. Graham Blewitt, deputy prosecutor at the ICTY in The Hague, May 2002.

Chapter 21

1. William Shakespeare, *Macbeth*, Act 1, scene 5, ll. 72–4.
2. Richard Holbrooke, *To End a War* (New York: Random House, The Modern Library, 1999) p. 322. Holbrooke adds that President Clinton was 'cool and slightly distant'.
3. Transcript of conversation on 13 January 1996, as recorded by the Croatian Secret Service, printed in *Globus* magazine 1 February 2002.
4. ibid.

5. Serbs who make a pilgrimage to the holy sites of the Orthodox church in the Middle East preface their name with 'Hadzi', just as Muslims who travel to Mecca add the word 'Hajji' to their name.

6. *Globus* magazine, 1 February 2002.

7. Dayton guaranteed free passage all over the country, but for some time UN troops guarded the crossings between the Croat-Muslim Federation and Republika Srpska. The border was known as the 'Inter-ethnic boundary line'.

8. The ICTY was established by UN Security Council resolution 827 in May 1993. Its authority is to prosecute four clusters of offences committed on the territory of the former Yugoslavia (i.e. the six federal republics) since 1991: 1) Grave breaches of the Geneva Conventions; 2) Violations of the laws or customs of war; 3) Genocide; 4) Crimes against humanity.

9. See the essay on Todorovic at the excellent website *Free Serbia: Other voices from Serbia* (www.xs4all.nl). The name Kundak comes from a description Todorovic gave of a barnstorming political speech to which he had listened. He described the peroration as a *kundacenje*, beating someone with a rifle butt.

10. Mihailo Markovic, in Robert Thomas, *Serbia under Milosevic* (London Hurst and Company, 2000), p. 246.

11. Slavoljub Djukic, *Milosevic and Markovic: A Lust for Power* (Montreal and London: McGill-Queen's University Press, 2001), p. 110.

12. Thomas, op. cit., p. 231.

13. Serbian Public Revenue Agency, *The Seven Biggest Robberies of the Milosevic Regime*, p. 29.

14. See, for example, Francis Wheen, 'How our politicians helped keep the butcher of the Balkans in power', *Bosnia Report*, New Series No. 19/20, October 2000 or Noel Malcolm, *Daily Mail*, 6 November 1996.

15. ibid., p. 46.

16. David Leigh and Ed Vulliamy, *Sleaze: The Corruption of Parliament* (London: Fourth Estate, 1997), p. 110. This book has a detailed account of the work of the Serb lobby in Britain, and its links to the Conservative Party.

17. David Owen, in 'A Safe Area', *The Death of Yugoslavia*, episode five.

18. Simms, op. cit., p. 176. Simms quotes from Gen. Sir Michael Rose's memoirs, *Fighting for Peace: Bosnia 1994* (London: The Harvill Press, 1998), p. 18.

19. See Ian Traynor, 'Serbs question Hurd's role in helping regime', *Guardian*, 2 July 2001.

20. Braca Grubacic, author interview, Belgrade, March 2002.

21. Thomas, op. cit., p. 287.

22. High level source, author interview, March 2002.

23. ibid.

24. Laura Silber, 'Milosevic Family Values', *New Republic*, 30 August 1999.

25. Thomas, op. cit. p. 305.

26. ibid., p. 308.

Chapter 22

1. William Shakespeare, *Macbeth*, Act 1, scene 2, l. 36.
2. See Michael Dobbs, 'The Crash of Yugoslavia's Money Man', *Washington Post*, 29 November 2000.
3. *Globus* magazine, 1 February 2002.
4. ibid.
5. Free Serbia, *All the President's Dead Men*, 'Radovan Stojicic Badza 1951–1997', www.xs4all.nl/freeserb/feuilleton/e-index.html
6. Former regime sinder, author interview, 2001. See also the report on the hearings of the Federal Yugoslav Parliament committee, chaired by Vojislav Seselj, investigating the 2002 killing of the former federal defence minister Pavle Bulatovic. Transcripts of the hearings were published in book form by the Serbian Radical Party in Belgrade, January 2002. The book includes some of the testimony of former intelligence chief Rade Markovic, in which he talks about Radovan Stojicic and the tobacco trade.
7. Investigating Commission of Economic and Financial Abuses of the Milosevic Regime (ICEFA), *The Seven Biggest Robberies of the Milosevic Regime*, p. 28.
8. Slavoljub Djukic, *Milosevic and Markovic: A Lust for Power* (Montreal and London: McGill-Queen's University Press, 2001), p. 98.
9. Douglas Hurd, letter to *The Times*, 6 February 1997.
10. *Globus* magazine, 15 February 2002.
11. Dusan Mitevic, author interviews, Budapest, autumn 2001–spring 2002.
12. *Globus* magazine, 1 February 2002.
13. Free Serbia, op. cit., www.xs4all.nl/freeserb/feuilleton/e-index.html
14. Federation of American Scientists, *Intelligence Resource Programme*, www.fas.org/irp/world/serbia/cfs.htm
15. Many believed that the real reason Arkan set up shop in Pristina was to take his cut of the smuggling rackets. None the less, the fear his men inspired was real enough.
16. The KLA was not the only armed faction, but it was the main one. Nor was it a cohesive, organised force, especially in the early days.
17. The praise was for backing the supposedly 'moderate' faction of the Bosnian Serb leadership, led by Biljana Plavsic, against Radovan Karadzic. Just how moderate Plavsic is will be examined at her trial for war crimes and genocide at the ICTY.
18. Tim Judah, *The Serbs* (New Haven and London: Yale University Press, 2000), p. 138.
19. Mira Markovic, *Night and Day* (Kingston, Ont.: Quarry Press, 1996), p. 242.
20. General Klaus Naumann, author interview, Budapest, March 2002.
21. Boris Yeltsin, in Louis Sell, *Slobodan Milosevic and the Death of Yugoslavia* (Durham, NC: Duke University Press, 2002), p. 286.
22. Tim Judah, op. cit., p. 166.
23. Louis Sell, op. cit., p. 289

24. General Wesley K. Clark, *Waging Modern War*, (New York: Public Affairs, 2001) p. 150.
25. ibid.
26. ibid., pp. 153–54
27. General Klaus Naumann, author interview, Budapest, March 2002.
28. Milosevic indictments. IT-02-54.
29. General Klaus Naumann, author interview, Budapest, March 2002.
30. Slavoljub Djukic, op. cit., p. 113.

Chapter 23

1. Vasko Popa, 'The Warriors of the Blackbird's Fields' (London: Anvil Press, 1996).
2. Investigating Commission of Economic and Financial Abuses of the Milosevic Regime (ICEFA), *The Seven Biggest Swindles of the Milosevic Regime*, p. 37.
3. General Klaus Naumann, author interview, Budapest, March 2002.
4. Tim Judah, *Kosovo: War and Revenge* (New Haven and London: Yale University Press, 2000), p. 158.
5. Louis Sell, *Slobodan Milosevic and the Death of Yugoslavia* (Durham, NC: Duke University Press, 2002), p. 297.
6. ibid, p. 300.
7. Mira Markovic, *Hard Talk*, BBC Television, 3 September 2001.
8. Tim Judah, op. cit., p. 227.
9. Jane Perlez, 'Purges Hint at the Beginning of the End for Milosevic', *New York Times*, 29 November 1998.
10. Slobodan Milosevic indictments. IT-02-04. 'Kosovo', Count One, deportation, paragraph 63.
11. Tim Judah, op. cit., p. 241
12. Michael Montgomery and Stephen Smith, transcripts of their interviews for *All Things Considered*, broadcast on US National Public Radio on 25 October 1999, are available at www.americanradioworks.org/features/kosovo/more1.htm.
13. Senior British diplomat, author interview, 2001.
14. Louis Sell, op. cit., p. 312.
15. Mira Markovic (to come).
16. Robert Block, 'Milosevic's Cronies Struggle for Removal from Blacklist', *Wall Street Journal*, 1 October 1999.
17. ICEFA, op. cit., p. 39.
18. Robert Block, op. cit.
19. Jelena Grujic, 'Milosevic wields Psychic Weapon', Institute for War and Peace Reporting, 1999.
20. Blaine Harden, 'The Milosevic Generation', *New York Times Magazine*, 29 August 1999.
21. Graham Blewitt, author interview, The Hague, May 2002.
22. Senior British diplomat, author interview, November 2001.

Chapter 24

1. Leon Trotsky, in Gordon G. Chang, *The Coming Collapse of China* (London: Century, 2001).

2. Douglas Waller, 'Tearing Down Milosevic', *Time Magazine*, 12 July 1999.

3. Adam LeBor, 'Blair tells Serbians to Overthrow Milosevic's "corrupt dictatorship"', *Independent*, 5 May 1999.

4. Senior British diplomat, author interview, November 2001.

5. Senior US official, author interview, May 2002.

6. Braca Grubacic, author interview, Belgrade, March 2002. Launched in 1993, the *VIP* newsletter – full name *VIP Daily News Report* – is an authoritative daily English-language press digest of the Serbian media, published by Braca Grubacic. Both *VIP* and Grubacic are well-regarded by journalists and academics alike.

7. Louis Sell, *Slobodan Milosevic and the Death of Yugoslavia* (Durham, NC: Duke University Press, 2002), p. 331.

8. High-level Serbian source, author interview, March 2002.

9. High-level Serbian source, author interview, March 2002.

10. Graham Blewitt, author interview, The Hague, April/May 2002.

11. 'Milosevic Faces A New Challenge', Associated Press, 3 March 2000.

12. Roger Cohen, 'Who Really Brought Down Milosevic', *New York Times*, 26 November 2000.

13. Gene Sharp, *From Dictatorship to Democracy*, (Boston, MA: Albert Einstein Institution, 1993).

14. British diplomat, author interview, Belgrade, November 2001.

15. Senior US official; author interview, May 2002.

16. High-level Serbian source, author interview, March 2002.

17. Takis Michas, *Unholy Alliance: Greece and Milosevic's Serbia during the Nineties*, (College Station, Texas: A&M University Press, 2002). See also review by Tim Judah: www.tol.cz

18. Matic Slovoljub, author interview, Pozarevac, August 2001.

19. Mira Markovic, author interview, Belgrade, March 2002.

20. Blane Harden, 'The Unrepentant', *New York Times* Sunday magazine, 20 January 2002.

21. Mira Markovic, author interview, Belgrade, March 2002.

22. Slavoljub Djukic, *Milosevic and Markovic: A Lust for Power* (Montreal and London: McGill-Queen's University Press, 2001), page 146.

23. Dessa Trevisan, author interview, London, December 2001.

24. Dusan Mitevic, author interviews; Budapest, autumn 2001–spring 2002.

25. Ivan Stambolic, in Louis Sell, *Slobodan Milosevic and the Death of Yugoslavia* (Durham, NC: Duke University Press, 2002), p. 337.

26. Paul Watson, 'US Aid to Milosevic's Foes is Criticised as "Kiss of Death"', *Los Angeles Times*, 28 August 2000.

27. Louis Sell, ibid., p. 342.

28. Senior British diplomat, author interview, March 2002.

29. Dusan Stojanovic, 'Milosevic's Final Days: From Arrogance to Panic to Disgrace', Associated Press (Belgrade Bureau), 7 October 2000.
30. Dragan Bujosevic and Ivan Radovanovic, *October 5: A 24-Hour Coup* (Belgrade: Belgrade Media Centre, 2001), p. 52. The author has drawn on this fine account for many details of the fateful day.
31. Elias Canetti, *Crowds and Power* (London: Phoenix Press, 1998 edition), p. 59.
32. Dragan Bujosevic and Ivan Radovanovic, op. cit., p. 143.
33. Dusan Mitevic, author interviews, Budapest, summer 2001–spring 2002.
34. Steven Erlanger and Roger Cohen, 'From a Summons to a Slap: How the Fight in Yugoslavia was won', *New York Times*, 15 October 2000.

Chapter 25

1. Reginald Wyon, *The Balkans from Within* (London: James Finch & Co., 1904), p. 38.
2. Paul Gallagher, Reuters, The Hague, 8 February 2002.
3. Dragan Stojkovic, 'Like A Freak Show', *Transitions Online* (www.tol.cz), 24, May 24 2002.
4. Details of arms found in Milosevic household as reported by Carlotta Gall and Steven Erlanger, in the *New York Times*, 2 April 2001.
5. See Appendix: 2.
6. Mira Markovic, author interview, Belgrade, March 2002.
7. Zorka Milin, 'Slobodan Snores!', IWPR Tribunal Update, July 16–21, part one, 2001, www.iwpr.net.
8. Roy Gutman and Rod Nordland, 'Body of Evidence', *Newsweek*, 23 July 2001.
9. Milosevic Court Appearance, Associated Press, 3 July 2000.
10. Senior British diplomat, author interview, November 2001.
11. Slobodan Milosevic indictments. IT-02-54. 'Kosovo'. www.un.org/icty
12. Mirko Klarin, 'Rugova Recounts "Cordial" Milosevic Meeting', Tribunal bulletin, 29 April–4 May 2002, www.iwpr.net
13. Noel Malcolm, *Kosovo: A Short History* (London: Macmillan, 1998) pp. 309–10. Though it should be pointed out that most of the Jewish community in Albania proper was hidden and saved from the Nazis.
14. Slobodan Milosevic indictments. IT-02-54. 'Croatia'.
15. Graham Blewitt, author interview, The Hague, April/May 2002.
16. 'Pax Americana', *The Death of Yugoslavia*, episode six.
17. Vjera Bogati, IWPR Tribunal Update, No. 265, 6–11 May 2002, www.iwpr.net.
18. Mira Markovic, author interview, Belgrade, March 2002.
19. Blane Harden, 'The Unrepentant', *New York Times* Sunday magazine, 20 January 2002.

Afterword

1. Beta news agency report, Belgrade, 15 April 2003.
2. Alex Todorovic, 'Two Hundred Arrested as Serbs Hunt Assassins', *Daily Telegraph*, 15 March 2003. Mihajlovic's menacing statement was perhaps an unintended reminder that his New Democracy party had joined the Milosevic regime in a coalition in the latter years of his rule, and had helped keep the former Serbian leader in power.
3. Stevan Zivanovic, 'Serb PM Killed to Avoid War Crimes Charges', UPI Belgrade Bureau, 9 April 2003.
4. Serbian government website, 'Zemun Gang Made Millions from Drug Sales', 23 March 2003. www.serbia.sr.gov.yu/news/2003-03/23/328326.html
5. B-92 news, Belgrade, 9 April 2003.
6. Reuters report, Belgrade, 14 April 2003.
7. ICTY Case No. IT-02-54-T, Slobodan Milosevic. Prosecution's Second Pre-Trial Brief (Croatia and Bosnia Indictments), p. 9. Filed on 31 May 2002.
8. Mirko Klarin, 'Analysis: New Phase in Milosevic Trial', *IWPR Tribunal Update* 281, 27 September 2002.
9. ICTY Milosevic case transcript, pp. 10309–10310. 27 September 2002.
10. Guardian staff and agencies, 'Milosevic Returns to the Dock', the *Guardian*, 9 January 2003.
11. Chris Stephen, 'Courtside: Serbia's Dirty War', *IWPR Tribunal Update* 309, 14 April 2003.
12. Ambrose Evans-Pritchard, 'Milosevic Accused of "Pulling Strings" in Croatia's Serb Uprising', *Daily Telegraph*, 7 December 2002.
13. Mirko Klarin, 'Milosevic Trial: Protected Witness Goes Public', *IWPR Tribunal Update* 292, 2 December 2002.
14. BBC News, 6 February 2003. news.bbc.co.uk/2/hi/europe/2733575.stm
15. Mirko Klarin, 'Milosevic Trial Enters Second Year', *IWPR Tribunal Update* 299, 7 February 2003.
16. ICTY Case No. IT-02-54, Slobodan Milosevic. Croatia indictment, Annex 1 – Victims, Lovas Minefield, paragraph 52.
17. Mirko Klarin, 'Milosevic Insider Details Serbian Crimes', *IWPR Tribunal Update* 300, 15 February 2003.
18. ICTY Milosevic case transcript, pp. 8685–8694. 25 July 2002.
19. Adam LeBor, 'Former Serb leader "haunted by role in ethnic cleansing"', *The Times*, 18 December 2002.
20. Adam LeBor, 'War Crimes Tribunal Jails the "Iron Lady" of the Balkans', *The Times*, 28 February 2003.
21. Author interview, Belgrade. March 2002.
22. Author interview, Belgrade. March 2002.
23. Author interview, Belgrade. November 2001.

Appendix 1

1. Klara Mandic, author interview, Belgrade, March 1993. See also 'The Jewish Question', Adam LeBor, *The Times* Magazine, May 8 1993. All Mandic quotes from this interview.

2. The Yad Vashem Holocaust Memorial Museum in Jerusalem records 213 Yugoslavs, of all nationalities, as 'Righteous Among the Nations', who risked their lives to save Jews in the Second World War. By comparison, for example, there are 336 Germans, 5,373 Poles and the comparatively high number of 56 Albanians, even though there were only a handful of Jews in Albania.

3. Misa Levi, author interview, Belgrade, November 2001.

4. Aca Singer, author interview, Belgrade, November 2001. All Singer quotes from this interview.

5. Marcus Tanner, *Croatia: A Nation Forged In War* (New Haven and London: Yale University Press, 1997), p. 228.

6. Franjo Tudjman, *Wastelands of Historical Reality* (Zagreb: Matice Hrvatske, 1990), p. 319.

7. On one level, the Serb propaganda worked. The American photographer Mark Milstein was based in Sarajevo for lengthy periods of time during the Bosnian war. He would pass effortlessly through Serb checkpoints, by merely saying the word 'Yevrei', meaning 'Jewish'.

8. As told to the author, Belgrade, March 1993.

9. Hrvoje Sarinic, author interview, Samobor, Croatia, September 2001. All Sarinic quotes taken from this interview.

10. Netherlands Institute for War Documentation, *Srebrenica, A 'Safe Area'* (Amsterdam: Boom, April 2002). Supplement, *Intelligence and the War in Bosnia 1992–1995*, pp. 215–16. Jezdimir Vasiljevic, head of the Jugoskandik pyramid scheme, is named as the go-between of Belgrade and Israel.

11. Serbian Public Revenue Agency, *The Seven Biggest Swindles of the Milosevic Regime*, p. 16.

12. Misa Levi, author interview, Belgrade, November 2001.

Bibliography

Books

Aarons, Mark and Loftus, John, *Unholy Trinity: The Vatican, the Nazis and the Swiss Banks*. New York: St Martins Griffin, 1998.

Allcock, John B., Milivojevic, Marko and Horton, John J., eds, *Conflict in the Former Yugoslavia: An Encyclopaedia*. Denver, Santa Barbara, Oxford: ABC–CLIO, 1998.

Almond, Mark, *Europe's Backyard War: The War in the Balkans*. London: Mandarin, 1994.

Andric, Ivo, *The Bridge on the Drina*. Chicago: University of Chicago Press, 1997.

Arendt, Hannah, *Eichmann in Jerusalem: A Report on the Banality of Evil*. London: Penguin, 1994.

Avramov, Dr Smilja, *Genocide in Yugoslavia*. Belgrade: BIGZ, 1995.

Beloff, Nora, *Tito's Flawed Legacy: Yugoslavia and the West: 1939 to 1984*. London: Victor Gollancz, 1985.

Bennett, Christopher, *Yugoslavia's Bloody Collapse: Causes, Course and Consequences*. London: C. Hurst and Company, 1995.

Boyes, Roger, *The Hard Road to Market*. London: Secker and Warburg, 1990.

Bujosevic, Dragan and Radovanovic, Ivan, *October 5: A 24-Hour Coup*, Belgrade: Media Centre Belgrade, 2001.

Canetti, Elias, *Crowds and Power*. London: Phoenix Press, 2000.

Clark, General Wesley K., *Waging Modern War*. Oxford: Public Affairs, 2001.

Cohen, Lenard, J., *Serpent in the Bosom: The Rise and Fall of Slobodan Milosevic*. Boulder, Colorado: Westview Press, 2001.

Collin, Matthew, *This is Serbia Calling: Rock 'n' roll Radio and Belgrade's Underground Resistance*. London: Serpent's Tail, 2001.

De Jonge, Alex, *Stalin and the Shaping of the Soviet Union*. London: Fontana, 1987.

Djilas, Milovan, *The New Class: An Analysis of the Communist System*, San Diego, New York and London: Harcourt, Brace, Jovanovich, 1985.

Djukic, Slavoljub, *Milosevic and Markovic: A Lust for Power*. Montreal and London: McGill-Queen's University Press, 2001.

Doder, Dusko and Branson, Louise, *Milosevic: Portrait of a Tyrant*. New York: The Free Press, 1999.

Draskovic, Vuk, *Knife*. New York: The Serbian Classics Press, 2000.

Glenny, Misha, *The Balkans 1804 – 1999: Nationalism, War and the Great Powers*. London: Granta, 2000.

Glenny, Misha, *The Fall of Yugoslavia*. London: Penguin, 1992.

Goodwin, Jason, *Lords of the Horizons: A History of the Ottoman Empire*. London: Vintage 1999.

Gordy, Eric D., *The Culture of Power in Serbia: Nationalism and the Destruction of Alternatives*. University Park, Pa: The Pennsylvania State University Press, 1999.

Hall, Brian, *The Impossible Country: A Journey Through the Last Days of Yugoslavia*. London: Secker and Warburg, 1994.

Halpern, Joel M., and Kideckel, David A., *Neighbours at War: Anthropological Perspectives on Yugoslav Ethnicity, Culture and History*. University Park, Pa: The Pennsylvania State University Press, 2000.

Holbrooke, Richard, *To End A War*. New York: The Modern Library, 1999.

Jovic, Borisav, *The Last Days of Yugoslavia* (Serbian language edition). Kragujevac: Prisma, 1996.

Judah, Tim, *The Serbs*. New Haven and London: Yale University Press, 2000.

Judah, Tim, *Kosovo: War and Revenge*. New Haven and London: Yale University Press, 2000.

LeBor, Adam, *A Heart Turned East: Among the Muslims of Europe and America*. London: Little, Brown, 1997.

LeBor, Adam and Boyes, Roger, *Surviving Hitler: Choice, Corruption and Compromise in the Third Reich*. London: Simon and Schuster, 2000,

Leigh, David and Vulliamy, Ed. *Sleaze: The Corruption of Parliament*. London: Fourth Estate, 1997.

Lewis, Bernard, *Islam and the West*. Oxford University Press, Oxford, 1993.

Maass, Peter, *Love Thy Neighbour: A Story of War*. New York: Knopf, 1996.

Magas, Branka, *The Destruction of Yugoslavia: Tracking the Break-Up 1980-92,* London and New York: Verso, 1993.

Malcolm, Noel, *Bosnia: A Short History.* London: Papermac, 1994.

Malcolm, Noel, *Kosovo: A Short History.* London: Macmillan, 1998.

Marai, Sandor, *Embers.* London: Viking, 2001.

Markovic, Mira, *Night and Day: A Diary.* Ontario: Quarry Press, 1996.

Markovic, Mira, *Answer.* Ontario: Quarry Press, 1996.

Neuffer, Elizabeth, *The Key to My Neighbour's House: Seeking Justice in Bosnia and Rwanda.* London: Bloomsbury, 2002.

Norris, H.T., *Islam in the Balkans.* London: C. Hurst and Company, 1993.

Owen, David, *Balkan Odyssey.* London: Victor Gollancz, 1995.

Paris, Erna, *Long Shadows: Truth, Lies and History.* London: Bloomsbury 2000.

Pavlowitch, Stevan K., *Tito: Yugoslavia's Great Dictator, A Reassessment.* London: C. Hurst and Company, 1992.

Popa, Vasko, *Collected Poems.* London: Anvil Press, 1997.

Popov, Nebojsa, *Football, Hooligans and War, The Road to War in Serbia: Trauma and Catharsis.* Budapest, CEU Press, 1996.

Popov, Nebojsa, ed., *The Road to War in Serbia: Trauma and Catharsis.* Budapest, Central European University Press, 2000.

Ramet, Sabrina Petra, *Balkan Babel: The Disintegration of Yugoslavia from the Death of Tito to the War for Kosovo.* Boulder, Westview Press, 1999.

Reed, John, *War in Eastern Europe: Travels Through the Balkans in 1915.* London: Pheonix, 1994.

Sell, Louis, *Slobodan Milosevic and the Destruction of Yugoslavia,* Durham and London: Duke University Press, 2002.

Shawcross, William, *Deliver Us From Evil: Warlords and Peacekeepers in a World of Endless Conflict.* London: Bloomsbury, 2000.

Silber, Laura, and Little, Allan, *The Death of Yugoslavia.* London: Penguin and BBC Books, 1995.

Simms, Brendan, *Unfinest Hour: Britain and the Destruction of Bosnia.* London: Allen Lane, 2001.

Tanner, Marcus, *Croatia: A Nation Forged In War.* New Haven and London: Yale University Press, 1997.

Thomas, Robert, *Serbia under Milosevic: Politics in the 1990s.* London: Hurst and Company, 1999.

Thompson, Mark, *A Paper House: The Ending of Yugoslavia*. London: Vintage, 1992.

Thompson, Mark, *Forging War: The Media in Serbia, Croatia, Bosnia and Herzegovina*. Luton: University of Luton and Article 19, 1999.

Tudjman, Franjo, *Wastelands of Historical Reality* (Croatian language edition). Matice Hrvatske, Zagreb, 1990.

Wyon, Reginald, *The Balkans From Within*. London: James Finch and Co., 1904.

Zimmerman, Warren, *Origins of a Catastrophe: Yugoslavia and its Destroyers – America's Last Ambassador Tells What Happened and Why*. New York: Random House, 1996.

Articles

Associated Press, 'Milosevic Faces New Challenge', 3 March 2000.

Barnett, Neil, 'The Criminal Threat to Stability in the Balkans', *Jane's Intelligence Review*, 21 March 2002.

Beta news agency report, Belgrade, 15 April 2003.

B-92 news, Belgrade, 9 April 2003.

Block, Robert, 'Milosevic's Cronies Struggle For Removal From Blacklist', *Wall Street Journal*, October 1 1999.

Bogati, Vjera, 'Courtside: Sarajevo Trial', *IWPR Tribunal Update*, nos. 265, 266, May 2002. (www.iwpr.net.)

Cohen, Roger, 'Who Really Brought Down Milosevic?', *New York Times*, 26 November 2000.

Colovic, Ivan in Popov, Nebojsa, *Football, Hooligans and War, The Road to War in Serbia: Trauma and Catharsis,* Budapest, CEU Press, 1996.

Danner, Mark, 'America and the Bosnia Genocide', *New York Review of Books*, 4 December 1997.

Djilas, Aleksa, 'A Profile of Slobodan Milosevic', *Foreign Affairs*, vol. 72, no. 3, Summer 1993.

Dobbs, Michael, 'Crash of Yugoslavia's Money Man', *Washington Post*, November 29 2000.

Erlanger, Steve and Cohen, Roger, 'From a Summons to a Slap: How the Fight in Yugoslavia was won', *New York Times*, 15 October 2000.

Evans-Pritchard, Ambrose, 'Milosevic Accused of "Pulling Strings" in Croatia's Serb Uprising', *Daily Telegraph*, 7 December 2002.

Foreign Staff, 'Ashdown and Milosevic Clash in Court', *Scotsman*, 16 March 2002.

Gall, Carlotta and Erlanger, Steven, 'The Milosevic Surrender: The Overview; Milosevic Arrest Came With Pledge for a Fair Trial', *New York Times*, 2 April 2002.

Gallagher, Paul, 'Sinatra's "My Way" Soothes Milosevic Behind Bars', Reuters, The Hague, 8 February 2002.

Goulet, Yves, 'MPRI: Washington's Freelance Advisors', *Jane's Intelligence Review*, 1 July 1998. (http://jir.janes.com)

Gow, Dr James, 'Belgrade and Bosnia – An assessment of the Yugoslav Military', *Janes Intelligence Review*, 1 June1993. (http://jir.janes.com)

Grujic, Jelena, 'Milosevic wields Psychic Weapon', *IWPR*, 1999.

Guardian staff and agencies, 'Milosevic Returns to the Dock', the *Guardian*, 9 January 2003.

Gutman, Roy, 'Big Atrocity; Serb militia chief said to have role', *Newsday*, 8 August 1995.

Gutman, Roy and Nordland, Rod, 'Body of Evidence', *Newsweek*, 23 July 2001.

Harden, Blaine, 'The Milosevic Generation', *New York Times* Magazine, 29 August 1999.

Harden, Blaine, 'The Unrepentant', *New York Times* Sunday Magazine, 20 January 20 2002.

Klarin, Mirko, 'Analysis: New Phase in Milosevic Trial', *IWPR Tribunal Update* 281, 27 September 2002.

Klarin, Mirko, 'Milosevic Insider Details Serbian Crimes', *IWPR Tribunal Update* 300, 15 February 2003.

Klarin, Mirko, 'Milosevic Trial: Protected Witness Goes Public', *IWPR Tribunal Update* 292, 2 December 2002.

Klarin, Mirko, 'Milosevic Trial Enters Second Year', *IWPR Tribunal Update* 299, 7 February 2003.

Klarin, Mirko, 'Rugova Recounts "Cordial" Milosevic Meeting', *Tribunal bulletin* 264, 29 April 29– 4 May 2002. (www.iwpr.net)

Kusovac, Zoran, 'Crime and Culpability in Milosevic's Serbia', *Jane's Intelligence Review*, 1 February 2000. (http://jir.janes.com)

Lane, Charles, and Shanker, Tom, 'Bosnia: What the CIA Didn't Tell Us', *New York Review of Books*, 9 May 1996.

LeBor, Adam, 'A Survivor's Guide to the Osijek Underground', *Independent*, 31 December 1991.

LeBor, Adam, 'Vukovar Veteran Bitter Over Tudjman "Betrayal"', *Independent*, 2 January 1992.

LeBor, Adam, 'The Jewish Question', *The Times* magazine, 8 May 1993.

LeBor, Adam, 'Blair tells Serbians to overthrow Milosevic's "corrupt dictatorship"', *Independent*, 5 May 1999.

LeBor, Adam, 'Former Serb Leader "haunted by role in ethnic cleansing"', *The Times*, 18 December 2002.

LeBor, Adam, 'War Crimes Tribunal Jails the "Iron Lady" of the Balkans', *The Times*, 28 February, 2003.

Milin, Zorka, 'Slobodan Snores!', *IWPR Tribunal Update*. 16–21 July, part one, 2001. (www.iwpr.net.)

New York Times, 'Milosevic Brings Air of Scorn to Tribunal', 4 July 2001.

Perlez, Jane, 'Purges Hint at the Beginning of the End for Milosevic', *New York Times*. November 29 1998.

Reuters report, Belgrade, 14 April 2003.

Silber, Laura, 'Milosevic Family Values', *New Republic*, 30 August 1999.

Stephen, Chris, 'Courtside: Serbia's Dirty War', *IWPR Tribunal Update* 309, 14 April 2003.

Sudetic, Chuck, 'In Bosnia, Wit is an Escape from Tears', *International Herald Tribune*, 8 July 1993.

Stojanovic, Dusan, 'Milosevic's Final Days: From Arrogance to Panic to Disgrace', Associated Press, 7 October 2000.

Stojkovic, Dragan, 'Like a Freak Show', *Transitions Online* (www.tol.cz) 24 May 2002.

Todorovic, Alex, 'Two Hundred Arrested as Serbs Hunt Assassins', *Daily Telegraph*, 15 March 2003.

Traynor, Ian, 'Search for the Missing Millions', *Guardian*, 29 March 2001.

Traynor, Ian, 'Serbs question Hurd's role in helping regime', *Guardian*, 2 July 2001.

Wagstyl, Stefan, Guzelova, Irena and Hope, Kerin, 'Milosevic's Murky Fortune', *Financial Times*, 4 April 2001.

Waller, Douglas, 'Tearing Down Milosevic', *Time Magazine*, 12 July 1999.

Watson, Paul, 'US Aid to Milosevic's Foes is Criticised as "Kiss of Death"', *Los Angeles Times*, August 28 2000.

Zivanovic, Stevan, 'Serb PM Killed to Avoid War Crimes Charges' UPI Belgrade Bureau, 9 April 2003.

Transcript of Marko Milosevic interview with Radio Bum 93, published in *Vreme* magazine, Belgrade, 25 January 1993.

Transcripts of tapped Milosevic conversations published in *Globus* magazine, Zagreb, 1, 8 and 15 February 2002.

Reports

Srebrenica, A 'Safe' Area, Netherlands Institute for War Documentation, NIOD, Amsterdam, 2002.

Anastasijevic, Dejan, ed., with Borden, Anthony. *Out of Time: Draskovic, Djindjic and Serbian Opposition Against Milosevic.* Beta News Agency and Institute for War and Peace Reporting, Belgrade and London: 2000.

[Bosnia] *Final Report of the United Nations Commission of Experts established pursuant to Security Council resolution 780, (1992).* Prepared by M. Cherif Bassiouni Chairman and Rapporteur on the Gathering and Analysis of the Facts, Commission of Experts.

The Seven Biggest Swindles of the Milosevic Regime, Serbian Public Revenue Agency, Belgrade, 2001.

The New Serbia Forum: A programme for the reconstruction of Yugoslavia, British Association for Central and Eastern Europe. London: December 2000.

A Prima Facie Case for the Indictment of Slobodan Milosevic. Prepared by Paul Williams and Norman Cigar. Alliance to Defend Bosnia-Herzegovina. London: 1996.

Television

Andras Der, *City Lives: Budapest,* EuroArt Media (for RTE and others). London: 2000.

Norma Percy, Angus Macqueen, Paul Mitchell, producers, *The Death of Yugoslavia,* Brook Lapping Associates for BBC. London: 1995. Six episodes:
1. Enter Nationalism
2. The Road to War
3. Wars of Independence
4. The Gates of Hell
5. A Safe Area
6. Pax Americana

See You in the Obituaries, B-92 productions for B-92, Belgrade 1995.

Websites

http://www.bosnia.org.uk (Bosnia Institute)

http://www.fas.org/irp/world/serbia (Federation of American Scientists – Serbia Intelligence and Security Agencies)

http://www.oorlogsdoc.knaw.nl (Netherlands Institute for War Documentation, publishers of the Srebrenica report)

http://www.un.org (United Nations)

http://www.un.org/icty (ICTY at The Hague)

http://www.un.org/icty/latest/index.htm (Milosevic case update)

http://www.srebrenica.nl (NIOD Srebrenica report)

http://www.tol.cz (Transitions online)

http://www.xs4all.nl/freeserb/feuilleton (Free Serbia: Other voices from Serbia)

http://www.iwpr.net (Institute for War and Peace Reporting)

http://www.iwpr.net/index.pl/tribunal–index.html (ICTY Tribunal Update)

http://www.iwpr.net/index.pl/balkans–index.html (Balkan Crisis Report)

http://jir.janes.com (*Janes Intelligence Review*)

http://europe.cnn.com/2000/WORLD/europe/09/25/ milosevic.chronology.reut/ (CNN chronology)

http://www.newyorktimes.com (*New York Times*)

http://www.washingtonpost.com (*Washington Post*)

http://www.guardian.co.uk (*Guardian*)

http://www.independent.co.uk (*Independent*)

http://news.scotsman.com (*Scotsman*)

http://www.fas.org/irp/congress/1995 *Genocide in Bosnia-Herzegovina. A Hearing before the Commission on Security and Cooperation in Europe, Washington DC. April 4 1995.*

http://www.bbc.co.uk/worldservice/index.shtml (BBC World Service)

http://www.serbia.sr.gov.yu/news/2003–03/23/328326.html

http://news.bbc.co.uk/2/hi/europe/2733575.stm

Other

Transcript of Peter Maass' interview with Slobodan Milosevic in Belgrade, April 1993.

Transcript of Tim Sebastian interview with Mira Markovic on BBC *Hard Talk*, 3 September 2001.

ICTY Case No. IT-02-54-T, Slobodan Milosevic. Prosecution's Second Pre-Trial Brief (Croatia and Bosnia Indictments). Filed on 31 May, 2002.

Index

Garvey, Janet, 67–8

Gazda Jezda *see* Vasiljevic, Jezdimir

Gazimestan, 120–1, 124, 153–4, 163, 183

Gdansk, 54

Gelbard, Robert, 278

Genscher, Hans-Dietrich, 196

German, Patriarch, 123

Germany: in Yugoslavia in World War II, 3–4; recognises Croatia and Slovenia, 168, 196, 321; in plans to remove SM, 301

glasnost, 60

Glenny, Misha, 142

Glina, Serbia, 4

Globus (magazine), 288

Goli Otok (island), 12

Gorazde, 238, 247–8, 250

Gorbachev, Mikhail: reforms, 34, 59, 84; political career, 59–60, 108; visits Belgrade, 100

Gotovina, Major General Ante, 229–30

Gow, James, 236

Gracanin, General Peter, 94, 150

Grbavica, 251

Greece: supports Serbia, 209, 233; refuses to recognise Macedonia, 291; supports plans to remove SM, 304–5

Greer, Ian, Associates, 262

Grizelj, Jug, 102

Grody, Eric D., 159

Grozny, Chechnya, 293

Grubacic, Braca, 70–1, 101–2, 158, 263, 300, 309, 311

Habsburg, Otto, 196

Hadzic, Goran, 331

Hague, The: Doko testifies about RAM plan at, 143; Martic indicted in, 228; SM indicted in, 253, 318; and Jovic's published diary, 258; SM's life in, 313–14, 316; other war crimes trials, 323; *see also* International Criminal Tribunal for the Former Yugoslavia

Hammer, Armand, 50

Harvard University, 44

Hasanovic, Tahir: relations with Marija

Milosevic, 64–5, 147; on SM's family life, 65; undergoes military service, 65, 96; early faith in SM as reformer, 67; disenchanted with Mira's teaching, 68; on SM's view of Serb nationalism as dangerous, 84; dismissed for advocating democratic reform, 154–5; and Marko's shooting, 215

Havel, Vaclav, 124

Herceg-Bosna, 180–1, 224–5, 252

Herme, Major Jeremy, 323

Herzegovina: Croatia seeks to annex, 180–1, 224–5; *see also* Bosnia-Herzegovina

Hill, Chris, 288

Hitler, Adolf, 3, 85, 97–8

Holbrooke, Richard: relations with SM, 43, 111, 241–2, 249, 296; on response to Sarajevo shelling, 238; saves Banja Luka, 241; at Dayton conference, 245–6, 248–51; intervenes over war in Kosovo, 281–2, 285, 288; dispute with Madeleine Albright, 298; non-visit to SM in prison, 324; *To End a War*, 242

Honecker, Erich, 34

Hoxha, Enver, 33

Hungary: annexes Voivodina (1941), 4; revolution (1956), 33, 97; under Kadar, 96; character, 125–6; arms smuggled from, 168

Hurd, Douglas (*later* Baron), 261–2, 272–3, 291, 296, 324

Husrev Beg, Ghazi, 172

ICEFA *see* Investigating Commission of Economic and Financial Abuses of the Milosevic Regime

ICFY *see* International Conference on the Former Yugoslavia

ICTY *see* International Criminal Tribunal for the Former Yugoslavia

Ilic, Vladimir, 301, 309, 311

Investigating Commission of Economic and Financial Abuses of the Milosevic Regime (ICEFA), 210

plan for protection of Serbs, 176–7;
and paramilitary units, 189; in attacks
on Bosnian Muslims, 192; desertions
and protests in, 196–7, 220; SM
withholds from helping Krajina
Serbs, 228
Yugoslav National Bank, 209
Yugoslav United Left (JUL): formed
from LC-MY, 259–61; SM
supports, 263–4; increases profile,
274; election victory (1998), 275;
in coalition government (1998–9),
279; members promoted to power,
283–4; undermines Socialist
Party, 300
Yugoslavia: formed (1918), 3–4; as
monarchy, 3–4; in World War
II, 3; World War II atrocities and
genocide, 5, 7; Communist regime
established, 7–8, 14; character and
diversity, 9–10, 38–9, 56, 136; under
Tito, 9–11, 35; western support
and aid for, 12, 67–8; renamed,
29–30; relaxed temperament, 34–5;
emigrant guest workers abroad, 35;
open borders, 35;

tourism in, 36; new constitution
(1974) and organisation, 37–9, 53;
mixed marriages in, 38; economic
management, 41, 49; foreign debt
and inflation, 53, 214; as one-party
state, 81; economic reforms in, 100,
131; federal structure weakened,
121; economic difficulties (1987–9),
129–31; and break-up of republics,
136, 138, 139–40, 144, 164, 328;
Federal Republic formed (1992),
195; not under SM's control, 201;
intelligence service, 264; democratic
government following SM's fall, 314

Z4 plan, 228
Zadar, 31, 151, 221, 224
Zagreb: character, 10; unrest in, 32; in
war with Serbs, 168
Zajedno (coalition), 265–8, 272, 275,
279, 303
Zepa, 238
Zimmerman, Warren, 123–4, 190,
197–8, 213, 280
Zvornik, 191–2, 197

A NOTE ON THE AUTHOR

Born in London, Adam LeBor extensively covered the Yugoslav wars for the *Independent* and *The Times*. He worked for several national British newspapers before becoming a foreign correspondent in 1991. He is the author of *Hitler's Secret Bankers: How Switzerland Profited from Nazi Genocide* (shortlisted for the 1997 George Orwell Prize); *Surviving Hitler: Choice, Corruption and Compromise in the Third Reich* (with Roger Boyes); and *A Heart Turned East: Among the Muslims of Europe and America*. Currently Central Europe Correspondent for *The Times*, he also contributes to *Literary Review*, the *Jerusalem Report*, *Condé Nast Traveller* and the *Budapest Sun*. His books have been published in ten languages.

A NOTE ON THE TYPE

The text of this book is set in Bembo. The original types for which were cut by Francesco Griffo for the Venetian printer Aldus Manutius, and were first used in 1495 for Cardinal Bembo's *De Aetna*. Claude Garamond (1480–1561) used Bembo as a model, and so it became the frontrunner of standard European type for the following two centuries. Its modern form was designed, following the original, for Monotype in 1929 and is widely in use today.